Ruby

An Ordinary Woman

Ruby

An Ordinary Woman

edited by
Bonnie Thompson Glaser
&
Ann Martin Worster

Faber & Faber
Boston · London

Copyright © 1995
by Bonnie Thompson Glaser
and Ann Martin Worster

Cataloging-in-Publication Data for this book
is available from the Library of Congress

ISBN 0 571 19858 9

Jacket design by David Shultz
Jacket photograph of Ruby Side Thompson
from the collection of Bonnie Thompson Glaser

Printed in the United States of America

for
David
and William

ACKNOWLEDGMENTS

Pulling this book together has been a challenging and exciting project. Many of our friends, family, and neighbors have been encouraging and helpful and we thank you most appreciatively. From those ranks we especially wish to thank Barbara Addicott, Jan Andres, Lori Arnold, Jessica A. Bolker, Joan Bolker, Rhea Cohen, David W. Concepción, Pat deJong, Gay Fawcett, Aathi Gurnani, Kay Hartshorn, Elizabeth Leavitt, Leslie Mayns, Jesse S. Miller, Jerri Ricca, Bob and Louise Schreiner, John and Ruth Thompson, Sket (Cuthie) and Reta Thompson, James Thompson, Margaret Ann Vickers, Judith Wallerstein, the women of the book club, and the late Lucille M. Worster. These are the people who were excited for us when our energies flagged, humorous when our perspective narrowed, knowledgeable where we were ignorant, and resourceful when we became blocked. Thank you again.

PREFACE

In the attic of the house where I was born, in Tenafly, New Jersey, and where my grandmother Ruby and her family once lived, was her battered steamer trunk. I still remember the rush of moth-balled air each time we opened it. I was intrigued by that strange and special smell. I thought it was *her* smell. Those memories, which were once my link to Ruby, have been eclipsed by her journals. Ruby longed for "some woman of my blood who might be able to find in my journals the explanation of her own cursed self." She wished a "granddaughter could come to understand and love" her. Both her wishes have now been fulfilled.

My grandmother's journals are made up of forty-two hand-written books spanning the sixty years from 1909 to 1969. Although she had seven sons, while she was alive she gave half of her journals to my mother, her favorite daughter-in-law. The rest came after Ruby's death. My mother read them, shared them with women in the family, but kept them from my father for fifteen years. When he was finally allowed to read them he said: "They embarrass me but they fascinate me. I love them. Everybody should read them."

During a visit with my parents in southern California in early 1992, I asked for a chance to read one of the journals. Although my parents responded with apparent enthusiasm, I soon realized they had changed the topic. I found myself listening to my mother telling me about her family, about her own mother. I left Ojai empty-handed.

Much to my surprise, a volume of Ruby's journals arrived in the mail a few days later. My mother wrote, "I forgot to get a journal for you when you asked. If you like it, there are plenty more."

The journal my mother sent me put Ruby at about my own age. It was World War II. She and Ted, my grandfather, were living just east of London. They were close enough to hear Big Ben strike the hour, close enough to be within the target area of German raids. Ruby spoke with naked honesty. In that journal she recounted her bowel-emptying terror during those air attacks. She painfully described her husband's admonishments for letting her feelings interfere with her reason. She told how during those air raids he went out to church or to tend to the neighbors, leaving her alone. She spoke of her fury at men for making war and at the pope for not speaking out against the fascists. She talked of endless household chores and the trap of being without her own money. She talked of her pleasure and desire in Ted's touch and her pain in being ignored. As I read I squirmed at Ted's criticisms, loathed him for his smugness, his coolness, his self-righteousness, but I got most angry when Ruby melted under his smiles. She longed to feel less vulnerable.

Ruby's journal provoked a rush of discovery within me, about my grandmother, my father, and ultimately, myself. As I read it I began to feel at one with her. Her perceptions challenged long-standing family myths, touched me, altered my angle of vision. I discovered I was that woman of her blood whom she longed for.

After reading my first Ruby journal, I lent it to Ann Martin Worster, a public historian and friend. When she returned it the next day, for a moment I thought she hadn't liked it, couldn't be bothered to read handwriting. But as soon as we began talking we realized that we had found something exciting and agreed to collaborate on editing the journals for publication.

We have been fascinated not only by what Ruby has to tell us about herself and her world but also by why this *unimportant, unfamous,* and *unglamorous* woman is so riveting. She is an able writer who deals with basic topics ranging from abortion and suicide to adultery and sexuality. She is interested in people: her husband and children, her friends and neighbors. She is an addicted reader and she tells us of her *specials,* including Virginia Woolf, D. H. Lawrence, Mary Baker Eddy, and the Bible. Her writing offers us an intimate portrait of a woman with well thought out, frequently controversial, rarely simplistic opinions on all these topics. Ruby's most heroic passages consist of her struggles to achieve an honorable balance in that tension-filled zone between external accommodation and internal integrity. While she attempted to live a life of family harmony, her journal became the refuge where she sought to know herself, to report and honestly examine thoughts and feelings whether fair or ugly. In doing this she frequently states, or challenges, private, unvoiced thoughts and feelings that I have experienced, that are universal. She reports periods of boredom with her closest friends, resentment of her in-laws, and even doubts of her suitability as a mother. She regrets never having taken a lover. As a young mother, screeching at her rambunctious children, she is startled to realize that she sounds just like her own mother. There is very little nostalgia here. The beauty of Ruby lies in her honest confrontation of pain and rage.

Ultimately, Ruby is interesting because she is an ordinary woman, because she speaks for all of us, struggling with situations we confront every day. Her failure of nerve at crucial moments, her escape into literature, her serene exterior force us to identify with her rather than permit us the comfort of admiring her. She is also a sobering reminder of how hard it is to escape from a woman's place. She is both unsettling and reassuring.

In editing these journals, we have kept her writing as she wrote it with the exception of modernizing her punctuation and Americanizing some of her spelling. In this volume we meet Ruby when she starts her journal in 1909 and follow her until 1938 and the heating up of World War II. We were unable to include her entire diary and had to omit many reports of small happinesses like the pleasure in a birthday celebrated, or the ease of an escapist afternoon in a movie house or an art museum, or the satisfaction of a great haircut. We also left out most of the comments she made about current events. They have been amply covered elsewhere.

We were sad to take out Ruby's first trip to the Bronx Zoo with her two sons. She was amused that her boys were more intrigued by the legs of the giraffes than by their necks. We left out the many times when Ruby's women house guests were bedded with her and she reported their all-night talk sessions. We were also sad to omit Ruby's reading lists, the thousands of books she read and commented on. We did all at this at the risk of making Ruby sound much more interested in her internal life than in the external world, when in reality she lived a quite balanced life. We did this in order to cover as much of what she thought about as possible.

It is fascinating to watch Ruby evolve from a young bride to a mature and complex woman. Throughout this volume we identify with her as her mood lightens with a compliment; we understand her depressive response as she tries to handle each rejection; we witness her vocabulary become childlike when she recalls incidents from her distant past; we rejoice when her low moods transform from depression into anger and then into action. Ruby has expressed herself in such a way that we feel compassion for her and understanding for ourselves. Because of her remarkable candor, perhaps we come to know Ruby better than she knew herself. Ruby is an ordinary woman who has expressed herself in an extraordinary way.

Bonnie Thompson Glaser
Berkeley, California
August 1994

INTRODUCTION

Ruby Alice Side was born in England in 1884, the oldest of the six children of Eliza Alice Searle and Charles Henry Side, an employee with the London Metropolitan Railway. The family home was in Hammersmith, a solidly middle-class section of London. As a child, Ruby attended a private girl's school until she was fifteen and then, after a year in a business school, she began work in the telegraph section of the London General Post Office.

The London of Ruby's young adulthood was a city of ferment, with a restlessness about the constrictions imposed upon women. Education was beginning to be encouraged for both upper- and middle-class women, and women were striving for new ideals of equality and opportunity. Urban poverty was widespread and reform movements were being led by women concerned about the welfare of children and single women. By 1891 much of England's population was concentrated in urban centers and nearly half of the women were single and working. Although most men believed that equality for women was a threat to the social order, women continued to develop confidence in their rights, abilities, and goals. They wanted opportunity, the vote, birth control information, and decent working conditions for all.

During the late 1890s Ruby explored the radical political, social, and religious ideas of London with her father and with her friends. She met, among others, William Morris, George Bernard Shaw, and William Butler Yeats. She became a Fabian because that organization promoted the ideas of equality for women, a "national standard of civilized life," universal education, and international disarmament. Along with Shaw and Yeats, Annie Besant and Olive Schreiner were active Fabians.

It was through a Fabian weekly, the *Clarion*, that Ruby met the man who was to become her husband. Edward (Ted) Thompson, an Englishman working for an insurance company in New York City, read a letter-to-the-editor from Ruby extolling the special abilities of the women working at the post office. Ted thought her "full of life" and, on a trip to London in 1904, made arrangements to meet Ruby on the steps of the General Post Office building. She, nervous and cautious, hid behind a pillar to observe him before making herself known. She liked what she saw, introduced herself, and a romance blossomed between the two young idealists. They spoke of going to a socialist colony in Paraguay, of religion, of America. Ted was an atheist, Ruby an agnostic.

After several months of courtship, and although her parents disapproved of the match, Ted and Ruby became engaged just before he returned to New York. Six months later, on her twenty-first birthday, she booked passage, set sail for New York, and married Ted upon her arrival. They settled in Bayonne, New Jersey.

In 1905, the year Ruby arrived in New Jersey, America too was in the grip of a reform movement. Business was booming but at a terrible cost to working class families, both native born and immigrant. Labor, consumer protection, and woman and child protection laws were being passed in Congress as a series of exposés was being written by muckrakers such as Upton Sinclair, Ida Tarbell, and Frank Norris. Theodore Roosevelt and the Progressives were fighting to control monopolies that had an economic stranglehold on the country. In literature, Edith Wharton, Ellen Glasgow, and Willa Cather were writing about the country's social ills.

Like their English sisters, American women were organizing to improve the status of women in an increasingly urban society. At the turn of the century 50 percent of urban single women suffered from venereal diseases. Information about birth control was difficult to obtain and abortion illegal and dangerous. The diaphragm was available only to the wealthy, and infanticide was the poor woman's abortion. A double standard of sexual behavior for men and women was universally accepted.

In response to an awareness of these conditions, American women began to organize for reform of marriage and divorce laws, employment conditions, prenatal and maternity care, and equality of opportunity in education. They began women's clubs, the W. C. T. U., settlement houses, and the Y. W. C. A. These activities captured Ruby's attention.

Ted and Ruby began their family and within the next three years they had two sons, Edward and Harold. Then, in 1908, Ruby took her sons to London to visit her family. While she was gone, Ted converted to Catholicism. This was a surprise to Ruby, but in the flush of homecoming, and wanting to stay aligned with her husband, she also joined the Catholic Church. In 1907, at the age of twenty-one, Ted's younger brother Arthur joined the family in Bayonne in order to take advantage of American business opportunities. Two years later, Ted's twenty-five-year-old sister Grace moved in with the family on a stopover visit on her way to New Zealand. She was going to be married to a man she had known in London. As the journal begins, Ted is working as a credit man in New York. Both Arthur and Grace are part of the household and Ruby is pregnant with her third child.

Ann Martin Worster
Berkeley, California
August 1994

1909

554 Avenue E
Bayonne, New Jersey
U. S. A.

TUESDAY, DECEMBER 28TH.

This is my twentieth beginning of a journal. All the other beginnings are in limbo. Most possibly this will reach there too but, for a while at least, I must write again. I need to make a friend out of something even if it is only paper. I must talk, really talk, and speak the truth to someone sometimes. This journal shall be my confidential friend. I write the truth to friends occasionally, but the best and longest of letters are unsatisfactory things. A journal, perhaps, will be not quite so unsatisfactory.

WEDNESDAY, DECEMBER 29TH.

I am twenty five and the trivial, everyday annoyances are worrying me to death. I do not smile at them, but weep. I become enraged and miserable over "trifles." There is such a multitude of them. However, I feel less angry now that I have opened this book. Perhaps if I can be faithful to a diary it will be faithful to me and friendlily help me over the rough places.

It is the domestic worries that drive me mad. It is not the actual household ones as much as the perpetual presence in the house of Arthur and Grace, my brother-in-law and sister-in-law. I hate it. And I hate it more and more. I want the home to myself, just the children and Ted and me. Surely it ought to be that way. But I cannot get it so and so I grieve. I grow vixenish. Every trifle annoys me and I *cannot* help it.

Is there any other young woman anywhere, in love with her husband, away from all her own friends, with two small children to care for, and big with a third, who could endure a grown man and woman added to her household without finding it an intrusion and a burden? My God, I know there is not.

I do not know what I am going to do. If I insist that they go away Ted will not like it. If they stay, I will eat my heart out with the weariness of keeping silent. Perhaps if I were not so physically weary with this pregnancy, I could endure better, but life is such a burden just now. It is so hard to tombstone down one's feelings and live instead by pure reason.

I have written this by my bedroom window. Grace is ironing in the kitchen, Edward is playing in the dining room with his Christmas toys, and

Harold is asleep in the next room. I am now going down to the cellar to stoke the furnace, but I already feel far less angry and agitated than when I sat down to write. I have let off steam. A diary is a safe friend.

FRIDAY, DECEMBER 31ST.

Shall I ever see anything of my writing? This summer I did write two chapters of one of the books I have in mind but destroyed them a week afterwards. Today I am telling myself I will take up my writing again this new year. Shall I be able to? What time for my own self have I now, with two children? How much less will there be when the third child is here? And then, Grace in the house all the time. I haven't a minute to call my own. I can hardly find time once a week to write a letter to Mother. George Sand wrote when she had two children, but she had efficient servants and no relatives-in-law. Mrs. [Margaret] Oliphant, and also Mrs. Trollope, Anthony's mother, wrote and looked after a family. They were driven by the necessity of bread-winning. I am not. It would be only to amuse myself. Is that a strong enough propeller? Ted would laugh and say I have nothing to say that needs to be heard. But I just want to express. Can I? Shall I? I have believed so long in the books I could write but I will wait. I do not give them up but I must wait until I am freer, till my children are older, till I am forty. For fifteen years I have been planning my books; when another fifteen are gone I can begin to write then.

When Grace came she was supposed to be on a two-month visit on her way to New Zealand. I thought it was a funny way round to New Zealand. She has been here three months now and is talking of next summer *here.* If she had stayed her proposed two months, and then gone on again, it would have been a pleasant visit. But I resent this indefinite staying on, settling down. Why should I keep house for the Thompson family? Arthur has been with us two years now. He does have his business, which keeps him out all day, but a woman, eternally in the place, Lord deliver me. What am I going to do in 1910?

Three-thirty P.M. I have just heard from Mrs. Terhune that she will not take my case so I must hustle around for a nurse. I had wanted her to come at once and act as a housekeeper until I was confined and then nurse me. Now I must look for somebody else. The time is getting too close to have nobody engaged. I wish it was all over. I am deathly afraid this time.

1910

WEDNESDAY, JANUARY 5TH.

Grace went off to Brooklyn yesterday afternoon to go to a dance and Arthur says she intends to stay there till Thursday. So I get the whole day to myself. It is heavenly. It is as it should be.

Ted has had the boys out sledding through the holidays. Young Edward hates the cold weather but Harold revels in it as he does in everything.

WEDNESDAY, JANUARY 12TH.

I have been reading Hans Andersen to Eddie until my throat is sore. Grace now has the two children out with her shopping.

Mrs. Whitaker "blew" in yesterday morning for half an hour. That is the exact expression for her arrivals. I wish she would come in and see me oftener for she blows the cobwebs away.

Now I want a new solid book friend. I have tired of the Brontës and George Eliot. I have lost companionship with them but I want something in their place. I think it is Montaigne I want.

Ted has a new craze: skating. He came in with a new pair of skates, spent half an hour trying them on shoes, and then went out on the pond, skating till eleven. He intends to go every night, I suppose, until there is a thaw.

Poor Mother has had another unfortunate Christmas. Joanie was in the hospital with diphtheria and Dad was in bed with a badly bruised thigh. Mother's troubles never end and they always intensify at Christmas time.

I am going to sew. I want some pretty work to occupy my fingers. I am going to make some new baby clothes, dainty enough for a girl, if only this might be one. I want a daughter.

Joan is Ruby's youngest sister. At this time she is about six years old and referred to in the diminutive. The youngest of Ruby's siblings is Eric, born several months after Ruby's own first child, Eddie, was born.

THURSDAY, JANUARY 13TH.

I have settled with Nurse McAllister. She is very Scotch and has only been in the country since last June. She talks very broad Scotch and gives an impression of capability and cheerfulness. I am glad that business is settled. I have only six or seven weeks to wait and I can wait in quietness now. I worry that I could die in this confinement. I will never endure another pregnancy, never. The misery and the burden of it! I am so awfully tired. I find motherhood so hard.

THURSDAY, JANUARY 27TH.

I think my time is drawing near quicker than I expected. I cannot rest anymore at night but keep waking with a pain in my waist. My breasts, too, are full and very tender. I hope Ted will be home when the time does come. I have everything in readiness except myself. I am not going to be a good soldier this time. I am too afraid. The thought of the pain does not put spirit into me but fear and shrinking. I feel too weak and tired to fight at all. God help me. I dread it. I shall be so thankful when everything is safely over.

MONDAY, FEBRUARY 7TH.

I declare it is impossible to find good American servants and the Irish variety is a positive torment. The latest specimen in my kitchen is a terror. She is drab and a most awful bell-clapper. I would like to run a mile from her voice. I never heard one so raucous: it splits my ears. She will talk of nothing and not even continuous silence from her unwilling hearers will stop her. She distresses Eddie too. She antagonizes him, which is worse. I hope my nurse will come to his rescue whilst I am in bed. Poor youngsters, they will miss me when I am laid away in bed.

It is frightfully cold. All the windows, on the inside, are coated with a thin sheet of ice, but still there is a glorious bright sunshine.

SATURDAY, FEBRUARY 12TH.

As soon as Grace Thompson comes into this house I am a different woman. I feel thoroughly miserable and bad. She came in with Arthur last night just before seven and by eight o'clock I was swearing at her! How *can* I live in the house with this woman and be the woman I ought to be? I hate her with a fierce hatred. I cannot control it. I try but I cannot. I am miserable now and it is hard to keep the tears back. It is a bad, bad state of affairs. I feel dreadful about myself. And now I put down that if I die in this confinement I absolutely forbid Ted to let Grace look after the children. She has not enough love for the children. All she is looking for is a good time for herself.

WEDNESDAY, FEBRUARY 16TH.

Today is Mother's birthday.

This book is a good thing. It gets all my grouches and then downstairs I can be good-tempered. Grace is machining for me. A kindness. Yesterday she made up a flannel petticoat for me. I am grateful to her for the work. I had expected to have it all to do when I got up again; instead, I will be sufficiently stocked with underwear.

Harold has been very sick with a very bad cold. I had to call the doctor in to him on Sunday, and he was afraid of pneumonia. That would have been awful. Yesterday the fever broke, his cough has loosened, and he was much better. Today he is almost quite well. Children recover so quickly. Edward also has a bad cold.

I am, well, middling. These last two days the child is much lower. The birth must be getting very near. I can hardly move for stiffness and being in my own way. The nights seem so awfully long.

WEDNESDAY, APRIL 6TH.

My baby was born at a quarter to seven, a Monday morning, February twenty-first. Another boy, so now I have three sons. He was baptized his first Sunday when he was six days old; named John Henry. The other two boys were also re-baptized there the same time. So now they are three Catholics.

FRIDAY, APRIL 8TH.

I wanted to write the other day but the babe interrupted my plan. I shall have less time than ever now. If I haven't time to be melancholy that will be a good thing for me. These last two weeks I have been quite gay and this very night we were all laughing and joking

I am not as strong as I would like to be; not so strong this time as after the other confinements. I long for my mother. I would like to lay my head on her shoulder (fancy! Mother! and me!) and quietly go to sleep. I long for her understanding, her rock-strength. I would like to give her the love and sympathy, and the *signs* of love, that I know she has asked for all these years and never received. I wrote to her today, but the letters are family letters for all the youngsters to see so what good are they? I told her months ago I wouldn't write at all if she couldn't have my letters to herself. She promised that she would keep them herself alone but now again her last letter says that that is going to cause jealousies and rows. Dad has been demanding my letters and, when she wouldn't produce them, he raked up the old row about me and says she drove me away. I have promised to write Dad letters for himself but haven't sent one yet. My days are so full.

SATURDAY, APRIL 23RD.

The whole of yesterday I spent in New York and took Nurse and baby with me. Ted met us at Macy's and took us to lunch. I got very tired, of course. I weighed myself at Macy's and was greatly surprised to find I weigh 170 pounds. That is twelve stone two. I thought I might have been 150 pounds, but 170 is most disagreeably surprising. Good job I am good and tall. I bought some good reducing corsets. It is alright being an anti-corsetite when you are thin and flat, but 170 pounds positively needs a little supporting and repression. Disguising. I don't like being so much of a Juno.

THURSDAY, APRIL 28TH.

Grace and I had a wonderful day together. Yesterday, just after breakfast (which was the first breakfast I had downstairs since my confinement), we were seized with the idea of pulling up the parlor carpet. We made a good job of it and the room looks comfortable at last. Ted and I had this evening to ourselves, for once. We have been talking money matters. I hate that. Ted hugs his usual idea that this household can be fed on rice. We have decided on the vegetarian tack again, for Ted thinks it is cheaper than a meat diet. I don't agree, but I shall give him his delightful rice.

I was sewing this afternoon. I have a Wilcox machine on trial and would like Ted to buy it for me in place of the old treadmill one I have. I am afraid he won't, for he thinks them too expensive, considering we should later have to pay freight to get it to England, or else sell it at half price. So I suppose I shan't get one. I am not asking for a jewel but for a good tool. It is when I cannot supply these wants that I feel my dependence so hard. When I took a salary I could spend, *waste*, my money as I pleased. Now as a married woman I have to beg for every little thing. Why should I not ask for a personal allowance? Surely my household services are worth at least a dollar a week? I certainly do not perform them for pleasure.

After a conversation like this evening's, I feel sick with sadness, for where is the romance of five years ago? Now, it is continual criticism. I am looked upon as the ordinary fool of a woman.

I am tired and cold so will go to sleep. John Henry is stirring, and I am glad, for I love the little live thing on my arm, at my breast. I love this last baby intensely; more than the others. He is so friendly.

TUESDAY, MAY 3RD.

This is the anniversary of our wedding; we have been married for five years today. Five minutes ago I was telling Grace that though every woman ought to marry to complete and satisfy her womanhood, yet it was a foolish woman who married twice. This is a confession that matrimony leaves something to be desired. Deplorable. I, who had determined that my marriage should not be like the others, making us both blasé, forbearing. Why could I not keep the glamour?

When am I going to write my dream book?

When am I going to stop having children?

WEDNESDAY, MAY 4TH.

Tomorrow is Ascension Day. Ted told me this at supper tonight and asked me at the same time the question I have been expecting for weeks: when am I going to church again? I must go to Communion before Trinity Sunday or else I shall be excommunicated.

I had not the courage to say right out I was not going to church anymore. It will be hard to tell Ted I have decided to leave the Church, not because it is hard to leave, but because Ted will feel grieved about it. He does not suspect such a thing.

Ted joined the Church whilst I was home sometime last January twelvemonth, and I joined it just before Easter last year, a few weeks after my return to Bayonne. I joined it hastily then because he said he would wait for me to make his first Communion so that we could be together. My chiefest impulse was the pull of love which I had for him. I did it principally to please him.

Also, I did believe the Roman Church was the right one for all, and as Ted's intellect and reason had been convinced, satisfied, I was ready to rest on his judgment. Also, I had seen at home (as I thought) the distress and unhappiness of a home without a religion and so was willing to give my own children a religion.

Now, however, I think it is not the lack of a religion which makes Angel Road so unhappy, but more, the insufficiency and lackadaisicalness and irritability of its head, and the perpetual hatred and discord between parents. Happy, upright, and united parents could have a happy and good home without any kind of religion at all. Well, I also joined the Church because, as a mother and wife, I wished to agree with my husband and act with him.

It was a mistake I made in the flush of the homecoming, and the enthu siasm of the joining at the same time as Ted, which covered my doubts. The set morning and evening prayers are not prayers for me. I cannot pray by rote. I cannot believe so much. I hate to tell this to Ted. He will be so hurt.

TUESDAY, MAY 12TH.

This afternoon I took John Henry out in the go-cart for the first time.

Ted and Art have bought a plot in the woods in Somerville. As soon as some kind of shed or bungalow can be built, we are all going up there camping for the summer. It will be lovely for the kiddies and I think I'll enjoy it too. There will be no house and no visitors to look after.

TUESDAY, MAY 17TH.

The talk came last night. Ted asked me if I had made up my mind what I intended to do about the Church. I said I was not going. The reason? I did not believe. Why not? I did not know. You must not: or else you had been dishonest when you joined. Then fruitless words. I cannot explain, whilst he insists on having an explanation. When, he questions, did you begin to doubt: two weeks after? I don't know. Two months after? I don't know. Six months after? I don't know. You must know. And so we go. First I refuse to answer questions, but he insists and I give in. I shall not record the talk. There were ugly words not easily forgotten. I let it go but I feel hopeless. How can we speak of it now: he believing so deeply and me believing not at all?

TUESDAY, MAY 24TH.

Ted and Art begin bungalow building next Saturday. They will have a jolly holiday over the weekend, I think.

Last Sunday was Trinity and I did not go to church. So I have excommunicated myself. Ted has not mentioned the subject since last week. He will probably tackle it again in a month or so.

I am so weary of things as they are, these domestic things. It was a mistake ever to have admitted anyone into our home. It has been no home ever since. Nor has it been the same husband and it certainly hasn't been the same lover. If the outsiders were to go tomorrow, could Ted and I go back to where we were before? I ought to have husband and home to myself and he ought to have wife and home to himself. It is not like a home at all but like a mere old boarding house, a family hotel.

MONDAY, JUNE 20TH.

Ted is in Somerville. Yesterday Blanche Sivell came for a long visit. I like her very much. Grace took Eddie to New York to see Teddy Roosevelt in a parade. They viewed him from Ted's windows on Fifth Avenue. Last week I went out myself, with the baby, to Brooklyn to visit the Seales and stayed for a dinner along with several other people. I had a very pleasant time. It took me so out of my rut that I think I shall give a party myself.

SUNDAY, JUNE 26TH.

Twelve-fifteen in the morning. It is really Saturday bedtime. Ted and I and Grace and Blanche have been playing whist since nine o'clock. There is great excitement in the household, for Brooklyn has awakened me. I am going to give a card party: a progressive whist. It will be next Wednesday and two dozen people have already accepted. There is lots of bustle. I hope it will be a great success, which means to stay up late and have dancing after cards.

I am making a green silk princess gown for Wednesday.

SATURDAY, JULY 2ND.

I have been thoroughly tired for a week, first of all getting ready for the party, and then getting over it. However, it was a great success and we all feel pleased. Mrs. Bellamy, Alice, and Blanche stayed all night and Blanche stayed till five o'clock helping me with the dishes. We had thirty people. Lots of fun. Nellie, Gertie's sister, helped me finish my dress and it was a most becoming one.

Ted and Art have gone out to Somerville again. They think they can finish up the bungalow. If so, we shall all soon be departing. Bayonne is frightfully hot.

It has been four months since I wrote here and, of course, much has happened in this time, but I do not start now to record the happenings but just to note today.

Today Ted was confirmed. I had not known this was to be till last night. My heart ached when he left this afternoon: he is making such a definite parting of the ways. Now I am hurt again for he returned about ten minutes ago and said Hewetson had asked him to tea. So he has gone. This day, which means so much to him, he chooses not to share with me. I feel thrust aside, entirely alone, passed by.

1911

TUESDAY, JANUARY 3RD.

It is a misty morning and I feel blue. Here I am again, by my bedroom window, with you, old book.

I am thankful 1910 is out. There were spots of pleasure in it but the old family trouble has abided all the time and the religious trouble has been added. The family trouble looks to be solving now but the religious is very far from solution.

After various decisions, Grace is making actual steps towards departure for New Zealand! That disposes of one of my burdens. As for Arthur, he is paying very marked attentions to Beatrice Hewetson. Maybe it is only a fancy, but we do think he is serious this time. I shall hope for a speedy marriage. One thing I *do* know: should I become pregnant again this year, which is one of the new year's things to fear, I myself shall immediately tell Art and ask him to make arrangements to live elsewhere. I will not have another child whilst so burdened.

When I think of myself, only twenty-six years old, yet tied down with the household cares of a woman of fifty, I get angry, I rebel. I certainly did not give up my girlhood and my independence for this. Yes, I am a discontented woman. I long for the freedom and brightness of my girlhood and when I was a girl I wished for the freedom of a new country, of matrimony. Shall I ever be satisfied? I do not wish for my girlhood back but I do wish for its liberty, its carelessness. Marriage has given me so much I would not lose. But if only I had my man and my children all to myself I would not murmer here. I have had to learn silence. If only I can say nothing I keep better off. So my New Year's motto is: be quiet. My mother says a woman's refuge and consolation is Duty. If she can find comfort in doing her duty, then so can I.

I had strange news from Gladys last week. She writes that she has definitely joined the Student Volunteer Missionary Union. She speaks of her interest in Christianity and her proud spirit to be overcome. I shall write to her today. Sometimes I think it will be forever impossible for either of us to be Christians. If only we could. We have been bred-up so anti-christianly, denial and negation and doubt and scoffing have become part of our selves. How, when we *do* see the reality and comfort and strength of religion to the believers, how can we help wishing to believe? Our pride is the stumbling block.

Yet, if Christianity is all a mistake, what a glorious mistake at that. Surely it could be better to live with that mistake than to live without it? Oh, God, give me a contrite heart. Give me faith. Cast out from me all uncharitableness. Give me patience.

Gladys is twenty years old and is at London University, in England, studying astronomy and mathematics. She is the sibling closest to Ruby in age.

WEDNESDAY, JANUARY 4TH.

I should like to begin my book on *Hamlet House* this year but don't know whether I shall be able to manage it. I intend to dig into Thackeray for this year's reading. Except for the beloved *Vanity Fair*, I have never got on very far with him. However, I intend to study him now. For pleasure I shall go back to my dear old Anthony Trollope, old Sobersides.

I have read Arnold Bennett's *The Old Wives Tale* this week. I liked it because it was strong but gloomy, pessimistic. It was Arnold Bennett who read my very first manuscript eight or nine years ago. Shall I *ever* begin another book?

Hamlet House is the name Ruby has chosen for the novel she is thinking of writing. It is to be set in 1880s London and will be the fictionalized story of her mother's family.

SUNDAY, JANUARY 15TH.

Arthur announced his engagement to Beatrice.

FRIDAY, FEBRUARY 3RD.

Much has been happening this past week. It is as though everything has swung round to the other side. It doesn't seem to me that Grace is starting off gladly to New Zealand. From all one can gather, the man doesn't seem good enough for her. If she goes to New Zealand, it's almost sure we shall never, any of us, see her again. I told Ted I had talked with her and begged her to stay here, which, of course, from me, surprised Ted. I'm not bad at heart about Grace, and though I shall always detest this living together, I have come to know her very well, and to be fond of her. I shall miss her when she does go. I would not for worlds have Grace chance an unsatisfactory marriage so that I might be free. She is welcome to stay here, unless she goes elsewhere gladly and with prospects of happiness and content.

Of course, I can sympathize with her position. Who should know better than I the doubts and fears of a girl who is leaving not only friends, but also country, for a man? So Ted spoke with Grace on Wednesday night while I was out with Mrs. Hewetson. When I came in I could see that she had been crying, though nothing was said until we went to bed. Then Ted said that Grace has decided to put off her departure for a little while and think things over a bit more. I was glad and said so. Marriage is so vastly important, a woman needs to be sure she is doing the right thing, choosing the right man.

The strangest thing of all is that Grace thinks of joining the Church. Lately, as we have grown more intimate and so come to speak of religion together, she has spoken several times of her attraction to the Roman Church. She has even jested that if she became a Catholic she could not marry till after Easter. Seriously, she says, if she was away off in New Zealand, lonely, perhaps not entirely happy, maybe disappointed, she thinks Catholicism would be a comfort and a strength to her. She sees, as I do, the absolute reality of religion to the Catholics.

So, she is going to join the Church and is to write to New Zealand, delaying her departure for this reason, and, of course, giving the man the opportunity to break the engagement. She imagines he is very prejudiced against the Catholics. That is not strange: we have all been prejudiced against them, I think. The very fact of being English is enough for that.

As for me, I have decided to go back to the Church. I do so want to believe. I must believe.

SUNDAY, FEBRUARY 5TH.

Ted and Grace and I have had a day out together without the children. We went to New York to mass at St. Patrick's Cathedral, then luncheon, and from there walked through Central Park to the Museum of Art to see the pictures. A thoroughly enjoyable day. I am very happy.

MONDAY, FEBRUARY 6TH.

In talking to Father Reilly, I told him about Grace's skeptical remark about praying to the saints. She liked the idea to a certain extent but she would "just as soon pray to Grandpa as do that." He said, "Well, why not?" Anyone who dies in a state of grace, Catholic or no, is a saint in heaven. He impressed me with the fact that we do not die at death. That beyond the grave we are still existing. It is reasonable to ask the help of our friends just as we would if they

were alive. He also said that the list of saints was not complete, only sugges-
tive, and if we wished to invoke our good departed friends, it was reasonable
to do so. There are millions of saints.

For so very long death has been in my thoughts. I have never seen a dead
person and I am afraid to meet the experience. So often when I think of Ted
and how deeply I love him, I hope that I may die first. I could not bear life
without him. This new thought of religion has a comfort, for it makes me believe that the grave will not utterly divide us.

WEDNESDAY, MARCH 22ND.

Measles in the house. Edward started with them two weeks ago, then Harold
took them, and now yesterday, the baby. I have had a very bad day with the
baby, poor little chap. I think his case is going to be the worst of the three. The
Board of Health has affixed a great white sign on the house, placarded:
MEASLES WITHIN. How thankful I am the winter is breaking up. It has seemed
interminable this year.

I got weighed on Sunday and, I'm glad to say, I have lost ten pounds in a
month. My weight now is 150 pounds. I would like to lose another twenty
pounds and then I'd be satisfied.

Surprising note: last week I actually began the book I have in mind concerning *Hamlet House*. I wrote two sheets. I must systematize my time. I do
waste time in the course of the day, I know. Much of it is wasted in lazy socia-
bleness with Grace: dallying, chatting. Am I going to *determine* to write this
book? I have been brooding on it a long time. I wish I could write it out.

SATURDAY, APRIL 22ND.

I am in a fiendish temper this morning, irritated by Grace's lie-abedness. Silly,
I know, but there you are. I have just been letting out on Eddie with the strap
and it doesn't do a bit of good. It simply teaches him to be hasty too, and then
to let out on Harold. I loathe myself when I lose my temper with the children,
especially Eddie. Oh, how thankful I shall be to have them to myself. Grace
plans now to go the end of May. I shall hate the wrench of parting but how
happy I shall be afterwards. I chafe continually because I have to live with
Grace, but then I should chafe if I had to live with an archangel. I long for
home and husband to myself. I ache for it.

And now I dread fresh trouble before me. Last Monday Arthur came
home at noon, having had a hemorrhage at the office. Then he had another in
the night. We have all been very worried. He ought to throw up business for a
while and go away, but he says he cannot afford to drop business. I think he
cannot afford to drop his health: neglect menaces tuberculosis. What is the
use of working another three months only to pay the undertaker? If it is con-

sumption coming along, I am not going to be a nurse. I have three children to think of.

> *At the turn of the century,* **tuberculosis** *was so common it was called the "white plague." It is highly contagious and, before antibiotics, impossible to cure. The standard treatment was bed rest. This was to both allow the lungs to repair and to isolate the infectious patient.*

WEDNESDAY, MAY 3RD.

Our wedding anniversary. Six years today, yet completely forgotten until late tonight. How enthusiastic we are!

Six years ago I first left home for America. We shall be settled at home again before we have time to blink at this rate. Ted is positively sure of being ready to retire in five years from last January and he thinks it may be sooner. One day, I am afraid, I shall wake up a grandmother.

THURSDAY, MAY 4TH.

Three weeks today, Grace starts off.

FRIDAY, MAY 19TH.

I am sick with excitement. Ted told me last night that Arthur is going off to Canada next Sunday! Grace leaves next Wednesday. I am all impatience. It is an effort to wait quietly. I feel I want to shoo them off like chickens, at once, and then come in and lock all the doors.

Grace is packing this morning, in tears. Arthur has just gone off looking very ill. He saw a specialist yesterday and has been ordered to go away immediately and rest for six months. He is not even waiting for Grace's departure, but is going three days ahead of her. Everyone but me is gloomy and sad at the partings. I am wild, wild with joy. I have to remember to walk and not dance about. Oh, I am so thankful. It is a millstone off me. Yet I am afraid even now something will prevent it all, after all. I think I should go crazy if that happened. I positively feel faint with gladness at the thought of release. I am so glad.

Ten P.M. Ted has just told us that Arthur is not going on Sunday after all. He made a new decision this afternoon. I am sick with disappointment.

SATURDAY, MAY 20TH.

Grace's trunks all went off today. This time next week she will be nearly to San Francisco. Arthur is now supposed to go to Canada next Tuesday or next Sunday. Grace leaves on Wednesday. After all these years, to be free, I cannot believe it!

MONDAY, MAY 22ND.

Another surprise. A horrible one for me. At three o'clock this morning the telephone rang furiously. Ted went down to it. It was transmitting a cable message for Grace from New Zealand. The message was, "Wait."

So she is not going Wednesday after all. I am overwhelmed. It is incredible. She is not going after all! Now what am I going to do? I am stunned with disappointment. My brain will not take it in. She isn't going. I see she is glad about it and relieved.

She feels reprieved. I feel condemned.

I am fond of Grace. I do think, and have done for months, that she would be making a mistake to marry Syd Prentice. I am glad she is going to break the engagement but I am very sorry she must still stay here. I must be alone with Ted.

WEDNESDAY, MAY 24TH.

This is the day Grace should have started, but that seems a myth now. I shall never be rid of Ted's family. I shall be shut up with these damned people forever. These are the things that make marriage a failure. The greater part of my married life has been burdened and shackled by his relations. I am worn out. I long for sleep and to wake up and find them all gone. Impossible. This is how a woman must feel when she goes to the whiskey bottle. My head hurts and it is a frightful effort to think.

WEDNESDAY, MAY 31ST.

I had a very happy day with Ted today. Just the two of us. Ted behaved like a lover all day and I thoroughly appreciated that. It was delightful to be out alone with him again.

Nine P.M. Arthur has actually departed. He left this evening for Toronto and he intends to stay in Canada until Christmas. And so, thank God, that is the end of one of them.

FRIDAY, AUGUST 25TH.

I have not written since the end of May when Arthur went to Canada. The heat has been frightful this summer. I have never known it to be so hot. Even in the woods at Somerville it was unbearable. People in the streets were dropping dead by the scores and horses by the hundreds. This was the year of the seventeen-year locust too. Oh, the millions of them, horrible things!

The children want me now. Ed is in bed today. He is chilly, feverish; a cold, I suppose. Really, they are all very well. They hardly noticed the heat, playing all through it as hard as possible. Ed's health steadily improves and so does his temper. He is much happier than he used to be. The baby walks now, of course, though he does not yet attempt to talk. He is like a sunny Eddie, so beaming and roguish. Eddie has always been like a little shadow.

SATURDAY, AUGUST 26TH.

I have been rereading Mrs. Oliphant's *Autobiography* this week. It is a book that fascinates me, but so sad, so deeply pathetic. It makes me cry. I suppose a quiet grief is always the most touching. A frenzy can be allayed. It gives something for friends to do, to sympathize, to soothe. A quiet sorrow shuts all friends outside and that is why we feel it more, because we cannot help.

TUESDAY, SEPTEMBER 5TH.

School began today and Eddie is delighted to start again. He will remain in the kindergarten until February. Then I think I shall send Harold, for he will be four by that time. Two boys at school will be something indeed.

MONDAY, SEPTEMBER 11TH.

I took the train to town and was shopping all morning. I bought flannelette, laces, and some oddments and I can see the sewing I now have before me. Is it any wonder with my housework, my cooking, my children, and my sewing that I do not find the time to write the books I am always dreaming about?

Ted met me in Macy's for lunch and then I went to see the new New York Public Library. It is a magnificent building, very stately and dignified for an American building. One expects almost to meet Julius Caesar crossing its vast halls or descending its austere staircases. But like most American libraries, it seems to me, its books are few. I remember once being shown a new house in East Orange. When we came to the "library," the furnishings of which were shown with great pride, I didn't see a single book in it.

A tiring but an enjoyable day.

FRIDAY, SEPTEMBER 29TH.

Grace has altered her mind again, deciding, finally, to return to England after all. She is to sail October 7th. And I really do think she will go this time.

SATURDAY, SEPTEMBER 30TH.

The strangest thing has happened. Although considering it is me, only the inevitable thing after all. I have been to confession tonight. Last night we were sitting around, talking about religion, and about Arthur, who has decided to join the Church. I was very cantankerous and irreligious. Behold, religion has pursued me every moment since. After talking the most emphatic denials I am immediately flooded with belief again. So I went down to the church tonight whilst the spirit moved me. I told Father Reilly that I am afraid of these sudden drawings and that the disbelief is sure to surge up again. He says to pray, persevere, the Lord will help me. I think he understands my wretched doubting mind and he does encourage me. I know if only I could continue in belief, how much happier I should be. The worst of it is that when I disbelieve, I don't care. I don't *want* any religion then.

SATURDAY, OCTOBER 7TH.

Grace left on the *Majestic* for Southampton.

THURSDAY, OCTOBER 12TH.

I have come upstairs to rest for five minutes.

I cannot realize Grace has really gone, but keep expecting her to come to the door, returned from Brooklyn, or somewhere. By this time, she is more than halfway across the ocean. It is a week of beautiful weather so she should be having a good trip.

MONDAY, OCTOBER 16TH.

Arthur and Beatrice are talking of marrying, very possibly before Lent. He is to begin business again next month. He says he's quite recovered but I don't know. I think for him it is a good thing to get married right away, but for Beatrice I think it a very risky thing to do. If I were Mrs. Hewetson I should insist on a delay till it could be seen that Arthur was capable of staying in business. It would be a great misfortune if his health broke down again after six months or so of matrimony.

SATURDAY, OCTOBER 21ST.

Friday, my friend Mrs. Harvey surprised me by walking in at twelve o'clock. She does not look a day older than when I first saw her more than six years ago. I guess *I* look the full six years older, alright. Indeed, I know I do, for I am no longer the bride of twenty-one, but the matron of twenty-seven with three children to my count and a fourth on the road. I have lost my color, and I begin to see little lines creeping into my face. Thursday, when I was expecting visitors, I put on corsets when I got up, but yesterday I did not and Mrs. Harvey spotted my condition directly as she came in the room. Now I suppose everybody will know it. I am more than five months gone and nobody has seen it yet. This will make four children before I am twenty-eight. We are not extinguishing the race in this house, that is sure.

Shall I get my little girl this time? Oh, how much I hope so. I do so very greatly want a little daughter. I ache for one. I am taking pleasure in the baby-work I am doing: making the little clothes as dainty and pretty as I can, *in case* I get a girl, I tell myself.

SATURDAY, NOVEMBER 4TH.

I have just got back from a trip to the library with the three children and am absolutely tired out, for it is such hard work to get them along, particularly Johnny. I never missed the baby carriage so much as I have this fall. I don't suppose we shall get another until number four has arrived. I have the children in Ted's room now to play, and I am going downstairs to get a cup of tea and a rest before I begin their bathing operations.

The clock has just struck six and I have just got the last child into bed. Now I have to go downstairs, clear away the remnants of their supper, and get supper ready for Ted. I am too tired to move and am trembling with fatigue. I'd rather go to bed myself. This pregnancy must have taken another leap forward. I feel so weary.

MONDAY, NOVEMBER 27TH.

I telephoned to the Registry Office for a girl this morning, for I have come to the end of my tether and cannot work alone here any longer. Mrs. Appleton, the Registry woman, says help is scarce now so I may still have to wait a week or two before I can get a girl, especially as I have barred Irish girls. No more Irish girls for me. They are incorrigibly dirty and slack. I have asked for a Pole or a Swede, varieties I have never tried and which are said to make particularly good servants. I have been shy of them before because of the language difficulty. Now I'd rather have a Pole who couldn't talk than an Irish tongue to drive me out of my own kitchen. But some sort of help I have got to have, and pretty soon now. I am feeling so tired and everything is becoming an effort.

FRIDAY, DECEMBER 1ST.

After all my emphatic refusals I have accepted an Irish girl. There was nothing else, and this girl impressed me favorably, so I took her. Her name is Katie O'Brien. Of course she is Catholic. I like her and I think she is going to suit.

Yesterday was Thanksgiving. In the afternoon we had some fun at the Opera House. Ted took us all, including Katie and the baby, to vaudeville. It was great fun to watch the boys' enjoyment. Eddie particularly liked the jugglers and the tumblers. Harold liked them too, I think.

1912

SUNDAY, JANUARY 13TH.

I am thoroughly miserable. All the children are sick with very heavy colds, and Eddie and John are cutting teeth into the bargain. Eddie has also had an earache for a week. They take days, turn and turn about, in bed, and one or the other of them is crying after me all day long. They wake me up five or six times a night, so altogether I am very, very tired and worn out. Added to this I had Gertie here for two solid weeks. I was glad to give her a holiday, but her silly chatter spins my head off.

Then I have had bad news from home which rather worries me. Gladys's Christmas letter said Mother was expecting another child pretty soon and that she was threatening to leave Dad directly after she was through her confinement. I hate to think about it all. Oh, that disastrous home and the misery it inflicts on us children. It is a shame. I am worrying most about Aileen now. I think I shall have her come to me if Mother and Dad do part. Mother would take the younger children with her, I suspect. Gladys would have to finish college so Aileen would be the stranded one, poor child.

I am very uncomfortable physically just now. I am very large and heavy, have a bad varicose ankle, cannot rest at night for cramps, and feel irritable and tired all the time. I suppose I shall be alright again when the child is born, but it is hard work going around every day fighting this miserable, disheartened feeling that will possess me.

I hope I get a daughter for I never want to go through this suffering again. I am so tired of bearing children. It is such a perpetual weariness. I am dispirited. I can't read, I can't write, I can't sew, I can't think, and as for religion, I haven't a shred of feeling left. Religion is no comfort to me now as it has been before. I wish I could feel that comfort again. I wish a hundred things. I wish it was bedtime, I wish it was summer, I wish the baby was born.

Aileen *is one of Ruby's younger sisters. She is seventeen.*

THURSDAY, JANUARY 25TH.

I try to imagine what a quiet house would be like. The children din in the nursery all day and Katie chants an interminable Irish doggerel about "Come back to Connemara, I am lonely, dear," wherever she goes. I think of Mother, who would complain sometimes that she could not hear herself think, for that is true for me too. What would I not give for a solid day of quietness! Old Schopenhauer himself could not have suffered more from noise and tongues than I do.

SATURDAY, FEBRUARY 10TH.

Still on my feet. I have had to get a different nurse. Mrs. McAllister has not yet gone to the case she has before mine. We are running too close for comfort, for mine might even come first. I surely cannot have much longer to wait. I am feeling very well and I am sure it is another boy. My daughter is not to be.

I have been reading Thackeray's *Paris Sketch Book*, tiresome nowadays and too horribly British. I've also dipped into *Heretics* by G. K. Chesterton, thunderous but amusing and most of it *right*, and *A Woman Hater* by Charles Reade.

A Woman Hater is an excellent novel and far ahead of the novels turned out today. I think I shall read all Reade's books now. I remember reading *Foul Play* years ago with Dad. It was a Robinson Crusoe story and I found it very interesting. Whether it is so I do not know, for I am sure I was only fifteen or so when I read it, and every mortal thing and every blessed book was interesting then. Dumas too, I mean to try, and Besant. I have tried them both before but could not manage much of them. I am not in such a desperate hurry for reading nowadays. In fact, the reverse is true, for when I do find something readable now I take it slowly, to spin it out, to have something left. Moreover, sad thing, I am growing older, more sedate, conventional, and so I find the old books have more appeal for me than the new ones. I am growing tired of psychology, realism. What does all that matter? My mind is not so curious nor so cruel as it used to be.

In fact, the sedate matron is content with a plain story. If it is pungent, good. If it is prosaic, good. She is tired of insides and Henry James-ism. Yes, give me less thinking, which is most of it wrong thinking, and more action.

I have also tried to re-read *Adam Bede* but gave it up in weariness. George Eliot's work strikes me now as no cleverer than Mrs. Oliphant's, or Mrs. Henry Wood's, or the rest of the ladies'. All those women did good work as craftswomen and made no pretensions. But I am turning to the prosy middle-aged men: Reade, Besant, Trollope (although he always was a favorite of mine), Dumas, and even Wilkie Collins!

FRIDAY, FEBRUARY 16TH.

This is Mother's birthday. I wonder where she is spending it, in bed or out. I am feeling very shaky and very weary. I wish everything was over. Beatrice brought my newly trimmed baby basket in today. It is all gay and dainty with blue under white and a little pink silk crib coverlet in it too. These preparations are running to "pretties" *in case* there is a little girl, but I am afraid not.

MONDAY, FEBRUARY 26TH.

Nine o'clock in the morning. I have heard from Gladys that it isn't a child with Mother after all. She is in St. George's Hospital for a rupture operation. They are all so thankful it isn't a child and so am I. Poor Mother is too old for any more babies.

My baby hasn't come yet. I do wish it would hurry. I am so dreadfully sick and weary with this one. I have been looking for it every night and day for two solid weeks now. I even begin to get a little nervous and think there

may be something wrong this time, a misplacement or something. I suppose
I am having what the books call "false pains" but they are pretty real enough,
all the same.

Harold was four years old yesterday. John was two last Wednesday.

I am horribly restless. Oh, this waiting, waiting! It makes me miserable.

WEDNESDAY, FEBRUARY 28TH.

Today I got four new books: *Lorna Doone, Woman in White, Hard Cash,* and *It
Is Never Too Late to Mend.* I want to begin them *all* at once but am refraining,
for I intend to read them in bed if I ever get there. Ted says this baby is waiting
for the Fourth of July and I almost think so too.

This is leap year. Tomorrow is the twenty-ninth of February. I wonder if
this inconvenient infant will choose that odd day to be born on. I shouldn't
wonder.

TUESDAY, MARCH 5TH.

I am still up and feeling more miserably than ever. I am beginning to long for
the baby itself now. I dream of it every night. I want the tiny mite in my arms
to love.

THURSDAY, OCTOBER 3RD.

Ten A.M. A new chapter.

First, for history. My baby was born on the eighth of March, about six in
the morning, another boy, of course. Ted has called him Stephen Gerard.

The second week in June we took all the children and Katie up to the
bungalow for the summer. While there, all the children except Eddie took ill
with the whooping cough. They did not have it very badly but we had to stop
all visitors, nevertheless. The new baby, Stephen, got chicken pox too. Poor little mite was beginning teething also. However, it was a very cool summer and
they all might have been much worse. Katie objected to the loneliness of the
place but stuck it out bravely.

I made the acquaintance of Miss Terry this year. She is a single
Englishwoman of forty-eight. She is a dressmaker and a bright and loyal little
woman whom I like very much. She made me a gorgeous new gown. It is the
best frock I have had since I was married: a symphony in brown and green. I
got it to wear to Arthur's wedding. After their honeymoon, Arthur and
Beatrice moved to Lancaster, Pennsylvania. Arthur had already taken a house
and bought some furniture, so they have begun straight away at housekeeping. He is coughing and looking very thin.

Now, here is the present portion for me. I have four small children, an
eight-room house (a husband, of course!), and no maid. I have undertaken to

run the whole concern, barring Ted's expenses, on a hundred dollars a month. I am going to do it, too. I feel particularly well and particularly ambitious. I am full of plans to run the house. I keenly realize that housekeeping is my profession now and I am going to attend to it. Katie was the best girl I have ever had, but she gave me notice: not enough meat in the house for her. We eat plainer foods now, mostly vegetarian. Also, Katie wanted to go to New York. I am glad of it. So now this place is my own with no domestics in it. It is a big economy besides. On wages alone it will save us twenty dollars a month. I can manage here alone as long as I keep well and there are no more babies en route.

FRIDAY, DECEMBER 13TH.

Yes, decidedly life is a great torment. I thought everything was going so swimmingly, everything perfect, and then I came right up against a horrible fact. Last month Dr. Davey told me I had a malignant cancer which must be cut out at once. Fortunately it was in a very accessible spot and in a good place, if anything about a cancer could be good. It arose on my old birthmark on my scalp. It had annoyed me all summer but what I thought was the actual thing was only an exudation of it. The cancer lay below the scabby place I had been treating on the surface and the doctor had to cut right down to the skull and dig it out. It was a three-hour operation and raging pain for a couple of hours afterwards. He did it here at home as it was not in a sensitive spot and he could do it with cocaine only. Mrs. Seale came over to look after the house and children for me. Since then I have been going around as usual except for a cap, and the doctor comes every day to dress the wound. Unlike a clean cut, where two edges of flesh could quickly heal together, this place is a hole which has to slowly fill itself in. Dr. Davey is very sanguine about it, although he won't assure me that it will not grow again. What makes me worry is the idea of the thing. Having had one, may not the germ of cancer be in my blood? If one grew again in the same place, might it not, instead of eating out to the surface, eat through the skull to the brain and make a lunatic of me? Dr. Davey assures me it couldn't eat through the skull, but nevertheless I know the fear will dog me. Cancer, of all the loathsome, dreadful, fearful things.

I write today because I want to begin to write regularly again. I shall grow incoherent if I do not practice writing of some sort. I will not drop my dream of literary work which I have preserved so dearly until now. I must write and someday I shall. When shall I begin? Here is another year ended and still nothing done, nothing begun. I did make twenty five dollars this year on a little magazine article, but it was only a silly domestic thing. I must practice writing. I resolve it once more.

Mrs. Jellyby, Dad called me, years ago. I wish I were, for then I might do something. She neglected everything for the pen, whereas I neglect the pen for everything. The literary temperament is something of a curse, and my life may eventually be as futile as Dad's. I do wonder if *he* ever dreamed of writing. Indolence is his hold-back and mine too, I'm afraid. We are alive with appreciations, glowing with ideas, but too lazy to get to work and actually write them down. There is always the tempting thing to read instead. Yes, reading is our mania. I think that neither Dad nor I could live without books. I must begin to write.

> *Cocaine was used as an anesthetic and was especially effective for surgeries of the eyes, throat, or nose. It was used here because it was an excellent local anesthetic and was probably administered in the form of a spray.*
>
> *Dr. Davey was the family practitioner and, as was the custom of the time, made house calls and provided most of the medical care required in the household.*
>
> *Mrs. Jellyby was a character from Charles Dickens's* Bleak House *with whom Ruby identified. Mrs. Jellyby was an enthusiastic but unproductive type of person who neglected everything for writing.*

1913

THURSDAY, JANUARY 2ND.

Vi Charleton sent me a book of Austin Dobson's verses for Christmas, but I am so little interested that I have not finished cutting the leaves yet. I never, or hardly ever, read poetry now-adays and I ought to if only for the sake of its educative vocabulary. My attention wanders so quickly now when reading verse. It seems I cannot concentrate on it and I don't try very hard. I shall make myself read poetry again as a literary exercise.

Dr. Davey was in last Monday to look at my head for the last time. He says it has now all healed and is well again. In about a week's time, when the skin is strong, I may safely wash my head. I am so thankful it is all over with.

Last night, on New Year's evening, Mrs. Hewetson and Bay came in to play bridge. We did play for a little while but I wasn't feeling a bit like cards. We gave up about ten and had tea and cake, nuts, raisins, and tangerines, and played the zither. John fell out of bed about eleven-thirty, which broke up the party, so the Hewetsons went home and the Thompsons went to bed.

> *The pages of a book are made, sixteen to a sheet, on large sheets of paper which are then folded into folios. In those days, and up through the 1950s, the pages of many books were left with these sheets uncut. They had to be hand-sliced by the purchaser of the book.*
>
> *Vi Charlton was Ruby's friend from her days of working at the General Post Office in London. Ruby believed her to be a lesbian.*

SATURDAY, FEBRUARY 15TH.

Three P.M. I have just baked five loaves, an apple pie, a plum cake, and a jam tart. I am foot-sore weary but now I have to go and bathe all four children, give them their supper, and put them all to bed. Ted calls me the Old Woman Who Lived in the Shoe. And so I am. So many children! So much to do! I am so tired of babies and baby minding. It is an incessant wear on the nerves; no rest, night or day. I wish I were too old to have children. I would rather be fifty and be free than thirty with this tribe. I suppose all women have to go through it, and time does pass.

WEDNESDAY, MARCH 12TH.

Just now, when I came home from church, Ted gave me a setback which has made me sick. He suddenly said we had better get his sister, Emily, out here. She has been too sick to work for three months past.

All my reason emphatically says "no" to it. I know how awfully hard it is for me to live with other people. That is something Ted cannot understand and never will. My idea of happiness is to live alone, not even husband or children do I want. The older I get, the more do I see a resemblance to Dad. He should never have married, nor should I. We are not fitted for it. I don't know if Dad ever realized it, but I have. God knows how hard it is for me to fulfill the duties I have undertaken; to make pleasure and happiness in what is really not pleasure to me at all. I shall never be a happy domestic family woman, though I may appear it. Never.

Now Ted wants to put Emily on my shoulders too. I have told him to wait whilst I think it over. If I refuse it will bulk large against me in Ted's estimation. He will never forget it and he will never understand. He thinks it would be nice for me. Emily is a nice woman, I know, and I like her, but I do not want her as a perpetual inmate of the household. I do not.

It is a quandary. Can I purchase his good opinion and affection by deferring utterly to all his whims and ideas, or can I keep his good opinion and affection by asserting some of my own ideas, my own individuality, my right to what I consider freedom? How far am I bound to him and his ideas? *Do* I belong to him? He certainly believes so, whereas I think not. I belong to myself. Then what shall I give him? What is the use of thinking and thinking? It is striking twelve, I must attend to the children.

124½ Lexington Avenue
Jersey City, New Jersey

WEDNESDAY, MAY 21ST.

Another change. We had known for nearly a year that we would eventually come to Jersey City to live because Ted's company, Griffen, meant to build a factory here. Ted intended to transfer his office here so he could cut out all train traveling and save a couple of hours a day. We had been watching, on and off through the winter, for a likely house and a month ago we saw this place by a fluke and we took it.

Ted is still commuting, but the factory is rapidly building and when it is finished he will be able to walk to his work and to come home to a midday meal. That is, if we stay here. Just last week I discovered the charming fact that I am again pregnant. It has made me furious and despairing. I am so tired of babies and so tired myself. I did so much want a rest from them. I must have conceived before I weaned Stephen, and knew nothing about it, for I thought I was clear and was taking precautions to keep so. I have been raging about it but am calm now, succumbing as usual to the inevitable.

This will mean another removal. This house is too small for such a family. It has only three bedrooms and no room for a maid. It is a dear little house, new and pretty and convenient, with all the modern improvements: white tiling, electricity, etc. It is also close to work, cars, stores, park, church, and school. We have only just barely got settled and now I have to house-hunt again.

On Friday I phoned Dr. Davey to come and he simply confirmed my suspicions. I needn't have bothered to call him for each morning I have been nauseatingly sick with that unmistakable sickness. When Mrs. Fleming was in on Monday I told her. It is a relief to tell somebody. Ted cannot be sympathetic. He sees no drawback to it because the child can be provided for. He doesn't think of the suffering for me.

Upon my word, what does a modern woman who has been economically free get out of marriage? Matrimony meant liberty to our mothers. To us it means slavery. What a reversal. Honestly, when I straight-face my marriage, I regret it. What a plague I must be to Ted.

The precaution Ruby was referring to was probably a postcoital douche.
Although these have never been considered particularly effective, they were
used in those days when dissemination of birth control information was still
illegal.

MONDAY, MAY 26TH.

Yesterday we spent with the Flemings. We had a jolly day and the children were very good. Chester Biggs had his automobile there in the afternoon and took us all for a ride so we had a good sight of old Bayonne. Yet we didn't feel as if we belonged anymore. I felt like a visitor only.

I have written this on my new desk, which arrived on Friday. I am delighted with it but Ted is not enthusiastic. It is a combination bookcase and secretary and Ted says he doesn't like com-binations. I don't mind it at all, in fact I rather like it. I am so glad to get a real desk to write at and keep papers on. I have wanted one ever since I was a young girl.

WEDNESDAY, JUNE 18TH.

Another surprise. Ted has actually decided to take a holiday and is going home for it. He sails in the *Majestic* next Saturday and will not be back again until July seventeenth. Don't think I shall be a very merry widow. The time will seem like three months to me, but I am so glad he eventually decided to go, for he certainly needed a holiday and he certainly deserved one too. Such a complete change and rest will do him a world of good. I shall stay quietly here with the children.

THURSDAY, JUNE 26TH.

I do detest the American summer. The children are all ailing more or less and I am suffering from violent indigestion again. It is nothing but the weather. I never get right again until the cool weather comes. The poor little baby is having a hard time. I think it is his stomach teeth that won't come through. He is very white and weak and listless. I have not called the doctor in, though I have thought of doing it several times. I don't know what he could do or say more than I know already. It is the teething and this summer weather the poor child has to fight. I don't suppose he will be properly well either until fall. Detestable New York summers; I wonder the whole population doesn't die off.

Ted got safely off on Saturday and must be well past mid-ocean now. Here it is Thursday, one week nearly gone. The time is not going as slowly as I anticipated it might. The children keep me so occupied I can't watch the clock. Blanche was here when Ted left and I should have been awfully mopey all day if she hadn't been with me. It was hard work not to cry in the morning. I do hate all partings, even mere holiday ones.

TUESDAY, JULY 12TH.

I have just read an article by Dr. Marcus Pembrey, an English biologist who is opposed to educating women. I think he is right. It is our education which has made modern women so discontented. For three or four years now I have

26   *RUBY*

thought popular education a mistake and particularly the education of women. Every educated woman of my age or younger whom I know suffers, positively suffers, with an underlying discontent. But our mothers? No. Generally it is a struggle to get the education which then warps our nerves and our tempers. For all the aspirations we generate, our achievements are nothing. Then when we marry and our academic acquirements grow rusty, we resent that. Think of all the terms I put in at French. Could I read a French book now? No. Where is mathematics when it comes to a poultice? Where is the connection between book psychology and a real living child?

We all think we are so clever when we are not at all. Even when we are up to our highest standard (*for women*) we are still only mediocre. Our education finally finishes us off with such an extraordinary conceit that is bound to be continually pricked and smarting when we enter into real life, which for us, of course, is matrimony and maternity.

Yes, occasional women geniuses there may be and they can look after themselves, but for the mass of women higher education is a mistake.

Elementary education was made compulsory in England in 1880. Until she was fifteen, Ruby attended the Flora Gardens School, a private girl's school in Hammersmith. Much of her education came from her father, who enjoyed her company at lectures, concerts, and plays. He shared his love of books with her and introduced her to the classics and popular books of the turn of the century.

WEDNESDAY, JULY 23RD.

Ted has been home a week. He looks splendid: tanned, fatter, and ten years younger.

FRIDAY, JULY 25TH.

Last night Ted and I had one of our periodic differences about money and about diet. He wound up the evening's dispute by saying that I hadn't said a single sensible thing and I was a perfect fool about the whole thing. Consequently I went to bed to cry and to feel hurt. I still feel hurt and I have shed a few tears about it this morning. I do try hard and think hard about the whole domestic problem, and I can't help feeling deeply hurt when he says he thinks me such an idiot about it.

Last night I showed Ted the monthly bills and asked him to look after them. He won't, Or rather, he said he would settle them another time and that I ought to try, even if it was hard, to manage on my monthly hundred dollars. How can I? If there were any luxuries, I could cut them out but there are none. The children must be fed sufficiently and this is where Ted provokes me so. His solution is to cut out meat. I say that is no economy because the articles which take its place, eggs, milk, cheese, and butter, are more expensive than meat is. Twenty-five cents' worth of eggs won't go as far as twenty-five cents' worth of meat, as any housewife knows. Ted maintains that meat does not require any substitute, which is nonsense. Protein has to be supplied in the diet some-where. No. His plan is to live on all that monotonous, insipid, unappetizing stuff: rice, prunes, cornmeal, porridge, and macaroni. I don't see why we should. We are not peasants, used and compelled to live on pulse and grains. I detest this vegetarianism idea of his.

What makes me so furious is that he attributes my misfortunes about my head and my feet to my wrong feeding. Such nonsense makes me speechless. My cancer was no more explainable than anybody else's cancer and as for my feet, it is ceaseless childbearing and child tending that wears them out. When I haven't the weight of a child within to carry, I have one on my arm. I feel I have no sympathy at all for all the pain and the labor. Here is the fifth child stirring within me and because I have not the energy of an athletic girl of twenty, Ted is sure there is something wrong with my diet, with my manner of living.

Ted also accuses me of buying unnecessary things and mentions the two dollars' worth of books I bought whilst he was away. That is what galls me so and has all my married life. It is so humiliating to feel I have never any money of my own. No money for books, flowers, fallals, sweetmeats, or any of the pleasurable things of life. If I should indulge in chocolates, I feel I am wasting his money. If I spend half a dollar for a book, I feel ashamed of myself, almost a criminal. Why should I feel so? I am surely entitled to something. I can't bear it. Whenever I do spend money for such things I *always* feel guilty.

If only I had some money of my own which I could throw down the sewer if I wanted to. Ted is certainly one of the best of men and I know he loves me, but he is also one of the most unsympathetic and uncomfortable. See how he makes me grumble. I am so heartsore today. I am always conscientiously trying to do my best and then I am told I am always wrong; a fool. That hurts.

Four-thirty P.M. I have to smile. I have just received this telegram:

> JUST ARRIVED PHILA BUSINESS IF NOT HOME TONIGHT
> DONT WORRY   GROUCHO

"Groucho" is right, though.

TUESDAY, AUGUST 5TH.

I spent the greater part of the day in Bayonne house-hunting. Colville took me over to Avenue A and showed me something very promising. A ten-room house, newly painted, with entirely new plumbing, and it is to be redecorated throughout. It is up for sale for $4,200 or with additional new floors and steam heat, $4,500.

This is the best thing offered so far. Both house and garden are very large.

I should think the drawing room was *at least* thirty feet long. Comparing the price with the prices asked for only small houses on the Avenue E side of town, it seems a bargain. Of course, it is four long blocks from the station, but Ted is talking of getting a motor, too, and this particular place is large enough to put a garage in the garden. The garden looked to me immense for a city garden. We could easily keep chickens in it and grow all of the green stuff we needed. I do wish Ted would take it. He liked my description of it but seems chary of buying.

Ted is going to look at this new place on Saturday and I hope the big garden and the big rooms will appeal to him as strongly as they did to me. I wish we had never begun to talk about buying because I am afraid I shall be disappointed now if we don't do it. How I should love to own a place! Imagine the pleasure of it.

MONDAY, AUGUST 25TH.

The unlikeliest things are really happening. Ted bought an automobile about three weeks ago and now there is a great likelihood that he will buy a house also.

We have had some fine rides in the car. Yesterday we went up to Nyack on the Hudson and the previous Saturday we went out to Somerville. Next Saturday we are to go to Philadelphia.

I have been reading *Anna Karenina* for weeks. I finished it about a week ago and feel lost without it to peruse. This is my third reading of it. It has always fascinated me. Not Anna herself so much but Levin and Kitty.

In the early years of the century Henry Ford introduced the assembly line to manufacturing. The production of the Model T beginning in 1909 made the automobile affordable to many Americans. Although Ted was secretive about his money, the family was solidly middle class. They were able to enjoy a summer cottage in rural New Jersey, vacation trips, and now, a car and a house.

SATURDAY, SEPTEMBER 6TH.

Three-thirty P.M. This time last week we were all riding down to Philadelphia to visit the Grays. At dusk, only about a mile out of Trenton, we got a blowout which took till ten o'clock to fix. Such a lovely experience! When the car was fixed there was nothing else to do but turn around and go back to Trenton for the night. We reached the Grays for breakfast the next morning and I enjoyed the visit immensely. Old Mrs. Gray is one of the sweetest and dearest old ladies it is possible to meet anywhere. Sunday afternoon we rode out to Willow Grove to hear Sousa's band and the evening we spent in confabulation. We came back home via Princeton, which I was very interested in seeing.

It is the most dignified, restful, and English-looking place I have yet to see over here.

I cannot pay proper attention to anybody or anything, for the perpetual under-thought in my mind is "houses," and will be until the matter gets settled. Nothing is settled yet and we have to be out of here by the end of this month. The Avenue A house fascinates us but we make no decisions. I went down to Bayonne yesterday morning just to take another look at it. I examined the place minutely for all its defects and then made a list of them. It certainly would make a lovely home and it is the place where we would prefer to live, but the great query is, Could we dispose of it again? The very reasons for which we like it, its bigness and its old style, are just the reasons why it would be hard to sell.

John Philip Sousa (1854–1932) was the composer of stirring marches such as "The Stars and Stripes Forever."

FRIDAY, SEPTEMBER 19TH.

Still nothing settled! We want the Avenue A house if we can get the price right. Ted has been dickering about it for weeks and something *may* be settled today. I am impatient for tonight to come to hear, and yet I shall be afraid to ask. If the project falls through now I *shall* be disappointed. If we have not bought the Avenue A house by the end of this month then we shall have to rent. It is impossible to remain here longer than that. I expect to be confined towards the end of December. This arrangement only leaves me two months in which to settle the house and prepare for the sickness. And such a two months! The heaviest and weariest of all the time. There is nothing to do but wait and be patient.

THURSDAY, OCTOBER 16TH.

I am in the throes of moving and I hope that I never have to move again. The work, the worry, the dirt, the chaos, the dead-tiredness; no more! Ted bought the Avenue A house after all and took up title yesterday. We move tomorrow. I can't express how glad and delighted I am about it. It seems too good to be true. I actually cannot take the fact in yet. Perhaps I shall tomorrow when the moving vans drive up.

758 Avenue A
Bayonne, New Jersey

SATURDAY, NOVEMBER 1ST.

We had been here just two weeks when last night our friends gave us a surprise party for Halloween and a housewarming. It was the greatest, greatest fun and I enjoyed it immensely. It was a regular surprise and we had the jolliest midnight supper. They brought everything, even coffee and cream. Homer Fleming brought a batch of the funniest cartoons. The first one they pinned up was of me on a stepladder hanging up a picture of Woodrow Wilson whilst Ted, with a fearfully disgusted face, was taking down a picture of King George. Awfully, awfully funny. There was another silly one of Art and Bee about Art's new hat and another on the subject of Ted's whiskers. I don't think I ever enjoyed an evening so much before.

I love this house already!

MONDAY, DECEMBER 15TH.

Here am I, still up. On my last legs, though, and very weary and cranky. The children get on my nerves dreadfully. I get so tired of them and lose all patience. It looks almost a surety now that I shall have to spend Christmas in bed, which is aggravating. I can only await events, and maybe since things have delayed so long already, they may delay a little longer still and wait till Christmas is past. It won't be a proper Christmas for any of us if I have to spend it in bed.

I have a very capable girl in the kitchen which is one great, good thing. The first girl I got proved too stupid so I got rid of her. This present one is efficient and reliable and I don't have to bother myself about anything. She is a thorough good cook, also, and that is a treat for me. I never have to go near the kitchen. Her name is Bertha and I devoutly hope she will stay with me.

Our house is going along in great style but last week we got a horrible setback. The National Bank, where Ted had started an account when we came back to Bayonne, closed down. The excitement in town has been continued all week but no statements have been made and the bank is still closed. Half the population is sanguine that all accounts will be paid out in full. The other half is doubtful about collecting even thirty percent. It is a calamity for the town, particularly at this time of year. It is horribly awkward for us because Ted's insurances have to be paid in January. Ted says not to worry, and all I can do is to cut down as much as I can on kitchen bills. I have changed my grocer and I'll have to change my butcher. Credit accounts are too expensive to pay for when the same goods can be bought elsewhere cheaper for cash.

1914

WEDNESDAY, JANUARY 7TH.

And still up! When will this child be born? I am so weary of it, this awful burden and pressure, this perpetual weariness. Every night I think it must be born but it doesn't come and so I hope for the next night and so on and so on.

The children try me dreadfully. Fortunately, Eddie and Harold started back to school this week, but neither John nor Jimmie, which is what we call Stephen, will leave me for two minutes. They even follow me into the bathroom. Jimmie is standing on the back of my chair now and clutching around at my cheek, trying to make me turn round to him. Now he is bawling because I have smacked his fingers for scratching me. Oh, how tired I am of little children.

THURSDAY, JANUARY 8TH.

Yesterday I began Cross's *Life of George Eliot*. I could only skim the first hundred pages. They were the record of a very priggish, stilted miss, very evangelical and striking me at least as very insincere. After the year 1849, a natural woman appears, that is when she is thirty. So I think the rest of the book will be interesting, after all.

In Christmas week I had news of Grandma Side's death. This gave me the first live hope I have had that my child will be a girl. Absurd. Irrational. The crazy imaginative soul in me insists that Grandma cannot be wasted, that she must be coming to me because I understood her and because I loved her so.

When I was only ten years old, Grandma Searle died a few months before Aileen was born. I was sure that was why she died, so that she could begin again. For years, I privately looked upon Aileen as Grandma as a little girl. Even now I never entirely dissociate Aileen and Grandma Searle. To think of one is to think of the other. Yet the only resemblance I could ever find between the two was that they both had the same kind of hair. Now dear Grandma Side is gone and when I heard it, the old foolish, childish thought came rushing back to me with a certainty and a confidence against all sense and reason.

I cannot argue it down. I cannot be reasonable. I expect a girl now and if I don't get her, I know I shall be more deeply disappointed than ever before. So foolish, so silly, but I can't help it.

MONDAY, JANUARY 12TH.

I finished the *Life of George Eliot* this morning and have found it very much more interesting than I expected to do when I began it. How discouraging to a woman with my ambition. I am abashed. It seems presumption to even dream of writing, let alone trying.

TUESDAY, JANUARY 13TH.

My resolutions to write are very promptly nipped in the bud. Yesterday I wanted particularly to say what I thought of the George Eliot book but the children simply wouldn't let me. Johnnie and Jimmie are here with me all day long and as soon as I sit down to write, Jimmie mounts the back of my chair and plays "getty-up-car" or gets on the stool beside me and rummages all the pigeonholes. Here he comes now for that very purpose, so I shall promptly close up again.

WEDNESDAY, MARCH 11TH.

Trouble. The bank remains closed down and, into the bargain, last Sunday night Ted informed me that Griffen wants to reduce his salary ten dollars a week and that we have about two hundred dollars' worth of unpaid bills on hand. Ted says he will refuse the reduction so that probably he will soon be out of a job altogether. Income: nil.

Query: How can we reduce expenses? One thing I foresee, I shall very shortly be managing without a maid. That is the only way to reduce kitchen expenses and it is in the kitchen where most little leaks are. It will be hard, but debts would be harder.

This last baby, another boy, of course, was born January 14th. We have called him Charles Hilary. Charles after my father; Hilary because he was born on St. Hilary's day.

Ted changed jobs frequently and advanced in his career by moving from one company to another. He reasoned that an employee always looked better to a competitor than to his boss. Changing employers was unusual as most Englishmen stayed with the same company for their entire lives.

TUESDAY, MARCH 17TH. ST. PATRICK'S DAY.

I cannot get a minute and a good job too, for I should only record how miserable I am. Here it is, the middle of March, and the town is still covered with snow. We have had two very severe blizzards this month and intense cold. I think the weather is responsible for everybody's bad temper, for everybody is cross.

I'm tired of everyone and I don't doubt everyone is tired of me. The Woodwards took Johnnie for nearly six weeks when the baby was born and then I asked Gertie to stay a couple of weeks, which she did. I got so tired of her I nearly went crazy. Such black ingratitude. I am tired of all my friends and don't want to bother with any of them. I'm tired of my servant, tired of my children, tired of my husband, tired of myself.

Here is Jimmie now, sweetly bawling at my elbow. How lovely to be a young mother. I wish anybody else had my job. I must stop and pacify this little angel.

MONDAY, APRIL 27TH.

Wash day; so exciting.

Spring at last, but still late and cold. However, the sun is shining at last in a blue sky. Soon I can hope for a little geniality. A week ago I was thirty. Thirty years old and five sons. What a record! I am getting the spring-y ambition fever. I feel ready and able to do anything.

Last Saturday I joined the Bayonne Suffrage Club. Ted is mightily amused.

Suffrage proponents were, for the most part, middle-class women whose goal, beyond securing the vote, was political power. Individual reform issues were not part of their agenda. Unlike their sisters in England, most American suffragettes were conservative. Their organizations evolved from women's culture clubs, which existed in towns and cities throughout the country, and they rarely practiced civil disobedience. Although Ruby, a British citizen, could not vote in America, she supported the goals of the suffragettes.

American women gained the vote in 1920 after the ratification of the Nineteenth Amendment to the Constitution.

SUNDAY, JUNE 21ST.

This is my vacation day and it has come just now at dusk to absolute peace. I have laid the baby asleep in his crib. Jimmie is asleep in his room. Lena, the new maid, is out. Ted and the other boys are in Brooklyn fetching John, who has been with Gertie for a week. So my little John is coming home tonight and I'm so glad, torment though he is.

Too dark to see anymore. I want to say I have been dreaming about *Hamlet House* all week and trying to write a chapter about it.

SUNDAY, JULY 5TH.

This is another vacation day for me. Last Friday afternoon I took Eddie, Harold, and John up to Ted in the city to be taken away for the Fourth of July. I don't know where he has taken them except it is a beach somewhere on Long Island. These have been peaceful days for me and I appreciate the rest as much as the children do the holiday. It is dusk again now and I am going to sit out on the porch.

TUESDAY, JULY 7TH.

The longer I live the farther away floats my dream of authorship. I have stumbled upon Henry Kingsley now, and it strikes me that his style of work would be mine. I suspect it is a very bad style, but it carries over the illusion of reality to the reader very well. It is colloquial, anecdotal, and avowedly omniscient about its characters. It is scrappy, spiky, but it tells.

I read *Ravenshoe* two or three weeks ago. Now I am reading *Silcote of Silcotes*. I like them very much. Particularly, I like his children. They are not book children but real ones. He writes about the mid-Victorian era. I want to take up the story from 1880 on. Oh, if I could only do it. My darling, darling dream.

TUESDAY MORNING. JULY 14TH.

I am in a fiendish temper this morning, raving and roaring at the children in just the way Mother used to do to us. Like a fishwife. Everything seems vexatious and unbearable. It is nerves and the weather plus the need of a little sleep.

I have completed one chapter about the story of *Hamlet House*. I am most firmly resolved to persevere with it. I will write the story out even if I have to stay up to two or three o'clock in the morning to do so. I am determined to find out what I can and cannot do. There is no sense in forever brooding and dreaming and wishing about the matter. If I can write, as I am so fond of imagining I can, well then I can write and am going to do so. I know I have got the ideas for making good books. Let us see if I have the grit and the persevering industry to actually produce them.

I shall never have peace of mind until I have found out if my books are good or bad. I must know. If bad, well then it is proved a fool ambition and can be effectually stopped, buried, and tombstoned.

I am going right along with *Hamlet House*. In imagination I have it complete. Can I get it satisfactorily onto paper?

SATURDAY, JULY 25TH.

Ted has just closed the door and gone off to confession. I hope it will do him good. He was home early this afternoon and so critical and disagreeable to me that he effectually spoiled my temper all the rest of the day. I feel fiendish. I can't stand his cross-questioning, bullying manner, his superior air, and his sarcastic tongue. I hate him when he is like this. Let's hope he'll get a penance which will put a little kindliness and courtesy back in him.

MONDAY, JULY 27TH.

Eight-thirty A.M. Glorious wash day.

Ted remains out of humor, consequently so do I. I wonder how many wives are the patient butts for their husband's sense of humor? Is the weather upsetting my man so that he cannot utter one civil remark? He cuts me to the quick and delights to do it.

When I was a girl, I used to hear my mother say, "I wish to God I could hold my tongue." I must have wished that a hundred times or more by now. A most innocent and inoffensive comment, the merest conversational remark, will fillip his sarcastic tongue. I do not know what to say, for whatever I say is sure to be wrong. The only safe topic to converse on is the sayings and antics of the children. When we can mutually admire them we can agree, otherwise we cannot agree at all. Really, in all our married life, Ted has never sympathized with me about anything, and as for giving me a word of encouragement—. Brutally, the only thing I am good for is to satisfy his lust. I have determined a thousand times to live my own interior life regardless of him, but every time he is a little genial again, I so foolishly forget and open to him only to be hurt all over again.

He must be as disappointed in me as I in him or he wouldn't say out what he does. But as everything material is successful and we both are doing our duty the best way we know how, the fact that we do not understand one another should not be a grievance. All the same, I am heartsick.

TUESDAY, JULY 28TH.

There it is! Ted comes home and shines out a little and all my clouds dissolve away. A little tangible loving and I love him back more than ever.

TUESDAY, AUGUST 4TH.

Pandemonium! I have just come from tubbing and head washing four of 'em. Heaven deliver me from grandchildren, for I shall fairly hate all children by that time.

A European war has started. The pretext is a quarrel betwixt Austria and Serbia over the assassination of an archduke a few weeks ago. Why on those grounds does Germany assault France? Of course the newspapers are startling, but this does look like a very serious thing. It makes me sick to think about it.

MONDAY, OCTOBER 19TH.

Today I am in real trouble. Edward has diphtheria. I had been treating him for tonsillitis, but this morning I called in Dr. Davey, who gave him antitoxin at once. He is coming to see him again this evening.

Yesterday was one of the most senselessly miserable days of a lifetime. I was literally consumed with a raging anger for nothing. I was just like my own mother. I remember her raging days and how I first hated and then despised her for a vixen. Poor Mother, was it dead tiredness with her and nerves from the effort to run and soothe an entire household? Or is it just plain vice? I have got to watch.

Diphtheria was once a serious disease of childhood with a 10 percent mortality rate. Immunization for diphtheria did not become available until 1920.

SUNDAY, NOVEMBER 8TH.

Troubles never come singly. Just as Edward was recovering from his diphtheria, I took it. Dr. Davey gave me antitoxin and installed a nurse from the hospital. Ted at the same time was sick with tonsillitis. Last Friday Dr. Davey declared us all well, dismissed the nurse, and had the rooms fumigated. Yesterday morning down goes little Jim with the diphtheria. Fortunately, his is proving only a mild attack.

Lena, my Russian servant girl, is behaving like a second mother to my little baby, Charlie. I have had to wean him. I daren't go near him. Lena bathes him, feeds him, plays with him, and puts him to bed. That ignorant peasant girl is a thousand times more of a friend to me than that fine lady, Mrs. Arthur Thompson, who refused to take Harold and John while we were all sick.

FRIDAY, NOVEMBER 27TH.

Yesterday was Thanksgiving Day. We did not observe it with the turkey rite. We only went the length of a small steak, a small mince pie, and no company. We need a thousand dollars between now and February first. It is years since we met such a tight fit for money; not since we were waiting for the birth of Harold. I wish I could make a little money. If I could hand in a hundred of my own now, what a happy woman I'd be.

The book *is* progressing. Will its ultimate worth be a cash value? I am very happy about my *Hamlet House* story. It is a pleasure working it out, however, I am afraid my grammar will have to be furbished up. How easy to rust when I cannot even get five minutes. Charles is crying for me to pick him up, the furnace needs attention now for it is growing dusk, the little boys need their supper very soon, and then they must be put to bed. Then it is supper-time for me and Ted. The days go so quickly. One week simply tumbles after another.

1915

MONDAY, JANUARY 18TH.

I went down to lunch with Alice Taft and she showed me an old diary of her mother's. It covered only about three months and was written in 1867. What an illumination it is about young mothers. There she was, just as much harassed by babies as we are today. Children's cries and fretfulness and the mother's unending tiredness ran all through the little record. This motherhood game must have always been the same, and I suppose always will be.

I think I would just as soon die and be done with it as have another child.

I am so tired of babies. To have grown sons may be lovely but to mind, bear, and rear up small children is a mighty hard task.

I have just returned from the most charming break. Young Jim, who is nearly three years old, filled his pants. I had to stop, strip him to the skin, bathe him, and dress him up in clean clothes again. Such a sweet task. No wonder the maids don't want to stay here. I wouldn't stay here myself if I didn't have to.

I was going to say that I used to look forward to being forty and being free to be myself once more. Fifty, I think, will come nearer. Another twenty years to wait, good Lord! To think I dare dream of writing books! I have been reading some novels of late: whimsical; gay; pathetic; droll; so pretty. Thank God for books. If I couldn't lose myself in a book I know I should go insane.

SUNDAY, JANUARY 24TH.

Ten-thirty A.M. As long as I can remember I have hated Sundays. Today is one of the choicest of them. Things started wrong today over the ashes. Ashes! Ted is absolutely no good as a houseman. Whenever there is a little household task for him to do, he is horrid. He is incompetent about such things and doesn't like them. Then he gets that deliberate patient streak of his which drives me crazy. He takes the tone of a martyr, his sweet little voice so low and distinct. What an irritation.

Now he has gone off to mass. He has taken Eddie, Harold, and John with him, and I am going to begin to cook the dinner. Oh, I do hate Sundays.

FRIDAY, JANUARY 29TH.

Bad news last night. Ted has had a letter from Art saying he has been very sick. He has been ordered away to a sanitarium again. Poor fellow. Their baby was two weeks old this past week and I wonder if Beatrice is up yet. I am not surprised at the news. All last year the poor boy looked sick and was coughing incessantly when I saw him. I am awfully sorry for him.

THURSDAY, FEBRUARY 4TH.

There was a regular blizzard on so I thought I had better go down to the bank before the roads were impassable. I kept Eddie home from school after lunch to mind the little ones and called in on Alice for a half an hour after the errands. It did me good. I let out a good growl and felt better for it. Alice told me to go home and pray to St. Anthony for my lost sense of humor.

Ted is to go to Arthur's to help them pack up ready for storage. Arthur is to go to a sanitarium and Beatrice is to go to her mother's. Ted says Bee is getting very fat. Thank heaven I'm getting thinner.

I am re-reading Balzac's *Cousin Bette*. He is a marvel. I admire him more than any other writer. Some of his stories are preposterous but, ye gods, how he knows people.

FRIDAY, FEBRUARY 5TH.

I had a good long talk with Ted last night. It is so seldom we come to explanations. I wish we could do so oftener, for it does put things straight. So many grievances evaporate when spoken of. The thing is that Ted gets harassed with business and I get harassed with babies and then we are mutually irritable, and then I don't think he loves me anymore and life doesn't seem worth living. Last night we cleared the air and now I guess we can stay happy awhile. Only, oh dear, Lent is coming. Ted will starve himself and we shall spark and spark along to Easter.

MONDAY, FEBRUARY 8TH.

Ted and I had a very cozy evening alone together. A beautiful fire in the parlor and the two of us in the Morris chair like years and years ago. How glad I am that *he* keeps well. He brings such a bad report of Arthur. Ted thinks he will have to be away at least a year to get well. The boy is desperately ill.

MONDAY, FEBRUARY 22ND. WASHINGTON'S BIRTHDAY.

I have a sad record to enter. Poor Arthur died last Monday and we buried him in the Staten Island Moravian Cemetery last Wednesday. Ted had spent the afternoon with him and the next morning Mrs. Hewetson found poor Art dead in his bed. He had died in the night alone.

My poor Ted is heartbroken and so is poor, bewildered Beatrice. Arthur fought until the last. He never told us he was suffering. That's a hero. He must have known how sick he was and yet he went on working. Poor boy.

WEDNESDAY, MAY 5TH.

Over two months have passed since I last wrote. It is unfair to judge lives from diaries, for we record more often something that wounds than something that pleases. I was so unhappy two months ago; yet I had forgotten all about it.

Bertha Hludensky came back to service here in April. I am glad to have her in the house again. She is so capable and faithful. Of course she has her oddities but then, we all have. Today she has been clearing up the garden and it looks wonderfully nice tonight.

We have chickens now.

FRIDAY, JUNE 4TH.

Dreadful things are happening in the world. I do not write about them for history will be recorded elsewhere. But this last atrocity has stunned me. The

Germans have sunk the *Lusitania*. She was torpedoed without warning and practically all on board perished. Many of the passengers were American women and children. President Wilson is exchanging diplomatic letters with the Germans, but it looks as if America may soon be in the war.

Last night Ted and I went to dinner at the Tafts'. I received a very great surprise there. Ted gave me something across the dinner table. It was a gorgeous dinner ring: twenty-one diamonds set in platinum in a very pretty scroll and floral design. I was so surprised. It was only back at Easter that he surprised me with a pearl and diamond pendant. He gave me a gold chain for it on my birthday. Then I think what a grumbler I am.

There was a downturn in the U.S. economy on the eve of World War I that was followed by a war boom fed by Allied orders for war materiel and sustained by America's eventual participation in the war. At this time the country, and Ted in particular, are enjoying the effects of prosperity.

FRIDAY, JULY 2ND.

When I can only find time to make an entry here once a month, so much seems to have happened.

I was ill the whole of June. I had been feeling poorly for two or three weeks and, on the tenth of June, I collapsed with a miscarriage. It was a dreadful mess and I really thought I was dying. It was far worse than any of the births except the awful first one. I have been around for a couple of weeks now but feel anything but strong. What is there in marriage for a woman besides children, children, and perpetual suffering? Five births and a miscarriage in ten years is too much for me.

With all this to suffer still Ted will not sleep with me. He does not give me that intimacy and companionship of the night. That one sexual act of love is not the whole of loving. I hate it when he only comes to my room for a casual hour or a casual night and then leaves me alone for weeks. It is a torment to me and it hurts my pride. I think he does not care for me but only for that. I have begged him so often to sleep regularly with me but he won't. He says he cannot sleep properly unless he sleeps alone. Why do I write all these things that I shouldn't write? Yet whom can I speak to except this blank page?

We are having a siege of chicken pox. Harold took it whilst I was in bed. Then as he got well, John developed it and now, just as John gets clothed again, Jim and Eddie have it. This house is nothing but a hospital. It is one thing after another.

I did some reading and a little scribbling whilst laid up. My *Hamlet House* story is nearly finished. Shall I offer it to Lazarus as a serial for the *Bayonne Times*? The subject, a story of London in 1880, isn't likely to interest Bayonnites, but a mysterious, anonymous story by an unknown resident of

Bayonne might draw if properly advertised. Everyone could suspect his neighbor and Lazarus might strengthen the paper's wobbly circulation. Still, the story isn't finished yet. As my John says, "Don't count your chickens until you see their tails."

I have been reading several of Mrs. Oliphant's books and a couple by Kathleen Norris. The latter is a new American author, very popular and having large sales. There is not much to her books but she writes of lifelike people and the real problems of normal life. For that, praise be to her.

MONDAY, JULY 26TH.

Every year about this time I am freshly bitten with the economy bug. This morning I have been ruling out a new blank book for household accounts and am getting ready to systematize. I am turning over the idea of doing without a maid again. Bertha has become so bossy she is getting on our nerves.

I sent Gertie home last Friday. Three weeks of her! She is so unalterably foolish she gets on my nerves. In the future, shorter visits from Gertie.

The whole of last week Ted was away with the three eldest boys holidaying. They went to Woodbourne, New York, and seem to have had a very jolly holiday. I am so glad Ted took the time. They all look splendid. Harold is brown as a berry.

The Standard Oil workers were out on strike all last week and there was much rioting and loss of life in Bayonne. Many fires were started, ambulances were destroyed, and there were threats of dynamiting and murder. There are about six thousand men out in Bayonne. They may go back to work today but it is doubtful.

Gertie was a friend to Ruby for years. She was always considered "good-hearted" but not intellectually challenging. Of the boys, Gertie favored John.

FRIDAY, AUGUST 6TH.

I owe so many letters. Gladys's birthday is this month and I haven't written her a word. Of course any letter now would be too late for her birthday, but I must write. Poor old girl, staunching it out there in India. It must be so lonesome. When I was in bed I got a letter from her with a beautiful piece of real lace inside. About three yards, I think. A recent letter I had from Mother said both the Frippard boys were lost. One had been killed fighting at Ypres and the other, after engaging in a skirmish at the Dardenelles, was missing. He may be a prisoner or he may be dead. I don't know which of the men was Gladys's lover, but she cared very much for the whole family.

Oh, these awful times. The war has been raging a year now. There is talk of conscription for England in October.

Gladys went to India to become the headmistress of a school. She stayed for five years teaching the children of British civil servants.

TUESDAY, AUGUST 10TH.

I have been in a fiendish temper for a couple of days. I am now recovering, though I am hardly normal yet, I am afraid. These fits help me excuse Mother. This temper has been positive suffering to me, and I could not help it. Mother's rages must have been just the same. I think it is our nerves that torment us.

Bertha, too, is in a wax. She wants to be boss of the household. Ted, in fun, calls her "my wife." When he receives an invitation he will say, "I don't know. I must ask Bertha." A very capable woman but too bossy: She must go. Besides, I am happier with something to do. It is true. When I am busy in the house I am not moody. As long as there is not a small baby in my arms, or one on the way, I can manage alone. I don't think there are going to be any more babies for me. Dr. Davey doesn't think so either.

SUNDAY, AUGUST 15TH.

I discovered today why I was so unreasonably cross last week. I came sick this morning. There, you see how helplessly a woman is at the mercy of her sex. I have moods of anger and irritation before the climax. It is disgusting.

I have given Bertha four weeks' notice today. She was taken aback. She thought she was here for life and could do as she liked. I told her I was going to do my own work, which is the simple truth.

"Came sick." Ruby is referring to menstruation. Menstruation and childbirth were typically referred to as sicknesses.

FRIDAY, AUGUST 20TH.

I went to town to shop. I got weighed and am at 168 pounds. It is only ten pounds heavier than I ought to be for my height. Ted talks as though I was Barnum's fat woman.

SATURDAY, SEPTEMBER 4TH.

Nine A.M. This is Bertha's last day here. If only I can manage without a servant. I know at first I shall be dead tired and overwhelmed and irritable too, but I am resolved to go slowly and steadily until I get hardened up and used to working again. I am also resolved to keep my temper. I must keep sweet and smiling and not grow into an angry crank. I pray for patience.

I have promised to take the boys to the movies this afternoon to see Charlie Chaplin. This is a good windup for their summer holiday. School starts again next week.

SUNDAY, SEPTEMBER 12TH.

A new chapter: It has been a solid week now without a maid. I have managed ever since and hope I can keep it up indefinitely. I spent today jellying the grapes. It has proved a whole-day job but now I have forty-one jars of jelly and two baskets of leftover fruit to give away. I am so glad this job is done.

I got a letter from Mother yesterday. They have all managed to get a holiday this summer in spite of the war and increased prices. They can't be suffering too much. There is an alarming article in the *Herald* today about a zeppelin raid over London, particularly Trafalgar Square. It breaks my heart.

TUESDAY, SEPTEMBER 21ST.

My housework is going finely. The house is in good order and looks it. Better, there is peace in the kitchen whenever I don't have a maid in our home. Why wasn't Eddie a girl? He is nearly ten years old now and what a darling companion and help a girl of nearly ten would be. Eddie is helpful but he is unmistakably boy and wants to be out. Even if I had a girl next year, it would be another ten years to wait before she could catch up to where he is now.

My mind is turning over the adopting plan again. How I do return and return to that. I am so lonely for an intimate of my own sex. Could I bring up a young girl to give me the sympathy and companionship I hunger for? That is a big query. I hate to take the risk and yet I can't stop thinking and hankering about it.

Last night I wrote to Gertie. After packing her off summarily in the summer, I have written to invite her here for next week. Ted is going away again this Saturday and Gertie can be my companion.

MONDAY, SEPTEMBER 27TH.

Gertie left this morning after breakfast and I say thank goodness. Her talk leaves me speechless sometimes. I don't know what to think about her. Certainly she is man-mad. It wouldn't surprise me if she turned out to be a victim of self-abuse, horrible as it is to suspect it. Poor girl, she is nearly twenty-eight. I suppose her sex torments her intolerably. And the life she leads, the drudge of a poor household, no refinements, everlasting dishes, and everlasting naggings, the old maid sister of despicable younger women. What hope is there for her?

WEDNESDAY. SEPTEMBER 29TH.

I wonder if there will ever come a time when I don't have to do a baby wash five days out of seven. I have been doing that for ten years now.

I was very Mrs. Jellybyish all last week. I did far too much reading. This week I am trying to be systematic. It is so hard not to take out a book at breakfast and that is the mischief that spoils my day. I must work hard all morning, and every morning, and leave the books for the afternoons. I want to write in the afternoons. My *Hamlet House* story is so nearly finished, but it has been at a standstill so long. I'll stop reading when I take this batch of books back to the library and I won't take out any others. I'll try thinking about my own stories and try to get them onto paper.

THURSDAY, SEPTEMBER 30TH.

Ted brought home a big box of windfall apples. I have been in the kitchen all day making jelly of them: fourteen jars. But my hands are black as ink from the juice and scalded tender from pressing the jelly bag. And my feet! They are burning and pricking from standing all day long. I don't want to do any more preserving this year. I also baked two more fruit pies.

WEDNESDAY, OCTOBER 6TH.

It is a month today since I've been without Bertha The house is in good order and so am I. I am sketching out an article on birth control for the *Pictorial Review*.

WEDNESDAY, NOVEMBER 3RD.

Yesterday was Election Day. Women's suffrage was defeated in New York, Massachusetts, and Pennsylvania. It lost in New Jersey last week. For me, time to start my housecleaning.

MONDAY, NOVEMBER 15TH.

I am just going to write to Aileen. Last week I had three delightful letters, a knitted doily, and a book on Hammersmith from her. I also had a letter from Gladys with a snapshot in which she looks old, haggard, and ill. She looks forty-six instead of her twenty-six. I am sure the Indian climate must be bad for her. I must write to her, too, if the letter is to reach her in time for Christmas.

WEDNESDAY, DECEMBER 8TH.

The house was in an awful state this morning. A big packing crate arrived yesterday containing thirty-four pictures and a couple of vases. Ted unpacked it last night. This morning, with all last night's dishes unwashed, excelsior all over the house, and such a headache I couldn't see straight, I just sat down and wept. However, I buckled to and now the floors are swept, the dishes washed, lunch over, ashes out, the kitchen scrubbed, and myself dressed and in an amiable frame of mind at last.

I have been going to Rosary two or three times a week of late. It is a struggle to get out but worthwhile. The church rests me. I find there the half hour's quiet for meditation that I can never find at home. At home now I so often think of Mother's old phrase: "I can't hear myself think."

I received a letter from Gertie announcing her engagement. Incredible. But she will make a fine wife and she certainly deserves happiness.

FRIDAY, DECEMBER 31ST.

We had a delightful Christmas. It was the best one yet for the children.

I am now excited over a plan of adoption that is maturing. As usual at Christmastime, the *New York Times* published a list of New York's hundred neediest cases and solicited aid for them. Among them was the case of a destitute Roman Catholic girl of fourteen for whom a Catholic home was sought. Ted made further inquiries to the charity organization but learned that the child had already been provided for. He was asked if any other child would be desirable and was given an application to fill out. Last Monday a Miss Spalding came out here to interview me and make an investigation. If everything is found satisfactory to the society, arrangements are to be made for us to look over some likely little girls with the view of choosing one for adoption.

Is it possible this is going to come to pass? The ideal would be to find an affectionate and normal child and rear her to become a daughterly companion for me. What will the actual be? Now that it is coming so very near and so very likely, I am getting frightened. Shall I draw out or am I so far committed that I must go through with it? Do I really want to? I dream of the satisfaction of feminine companionship in the house but do I want the trouble and the responsibilities of bringing up a strange child? I certainly said I do, and set the train in motion, but I wish I didn't feel so sick and unsure about it now.

We are going to the Jenningses' tonight for a party to see in the New Year.

1916

SATURDAY, JANUARY 1ST.

It was an exceptionally jolly evening last night. The Jenningses hosted a champagne supper with dancing, singing, hand-walking, and generally foolish stunts. We kept it up till after two this morning.

TUESDAY, JANUARY 18TH.

The orphan girl affair has gone through. We have been investigated all around and passed upon. We have chosen a little girl merely from a photograph. Her name is Loretta Kelly and she has been in the institute since 1910. She was born August 15, 1904. So she is Irish and eleven and a half years old. All the preliminaries now being finished on both sides, the child is to be handed over to Ted today.

I am so eager to see her and yet frightened too. The poor child. I suppose after five years in an orphanage she must, in a way, have been at home there. Now she is to be given over to a strange man, brought to a strange town, a strange house, and a strange woman. The poor little frightened thing. How shall I greet her?

God give me the grace to have a real affection for her and to treat her lovingly and faithfully all her life.

MONDAY, FEBRUARY 7TH.

The orphan girl affair is a grand fiasco. I have returned the child to the Charities Association agent this afternoon. I have had a frightfully trying three weeks with her. Had I kept her much longer I should have hated her.

There has been a series of mistakes all through. The night she arrived she wasn't even the child we had picked out. The Charities people had mixed their photographs and, though the girl answered to Loretta Kelly, she wasn't the girl in the photo labeled so. There was a further mistake about her age and a worse one about her relatives, of whom it appeared there was a whole tribe, including a live mother.

Ted will take it hard that I should send the child back again but I cannot do anything else. I don't like her and I simply can't keep her. I don't want any other girl either. I am through with that dream.

John reports remembering the Loretta Kelly experiment. He says that he and his brothers' form of welcome was to spontaneously close ranks. They teamed up and tormented Loretta unmercifully and relentlessly. It is not clear that Ruby was aware of their behavior, or that she consulted Ted before returning Loretta to the orphanage.

TUESDAY, MARCH 14TH.

My old maid, Katie O'Brien, now Mrs. Carmody, came out from New York to see me. She is just the same old Katie, a nice woman. She is bringing out a young niece from Ireland and will place her with me if I agree to it. I would like a nice Irish girl in the house. If she is only half as nice and good as Katie, she'd do.

TUESDAY, APRIL 4TH.

Last night Ted and I had a very serious talk. Things have been fermenting between us for months or years, maybe. Last night we talked them out until past two o'clock. My, what a talk, but thank God I was able to. I was getting more and more unhappy. Marriage seemed less satisfactory every day. I have been so desperate I have been ready to run away. Writhing under Ted's scathing tongue, I have felt that I hated him.

So we talked and talked and at last Ted got my point of view. He was surprised, and hurt too, I think. He actually does not know how cruelly sarcastic he is, or how bitterly malicious is his tongue.

Now we have cleared the air, chased the shadows, and struggled down to a clear understanding of one another again. I hope we will be better comrades for it. It is so hard to get these serious, intimate talks. If only we could talk more freely to each other about what really matters, we would get along so much easier. Marriage is awfully hard.

MONDAY, APRIL 24TH. EASTER MONDAY.

Another turn of the wheel! Scarlet fever now. Jim, Charlie, and Harold have it. It developed a week ago and we have them all isolated on the third floor with a trained nurse in charge. I gave her her first week's check tonight for thirty dollars.

Harold has the worst case but there is no need for anxiety about any of them now. Edward and John show no signs of the disease yet so we are hoping those two will escape it altogether.

It is very hard work downstairs for me, for the laundry will take no more washing. We are absolutely quarantined and no woman will come here to work. I have to do all the washing myself. There is a heavy load of it each day from the top floor, which has to be boiled, doubly rinsed, and hung out. Fortunately, the winter has broken.

Scarlet fever was a dangerous childhood illness. Until the contagion period was known, forty days was a standard quarantine. Because the skin of scarlet fever patients often peels after the rash subsides, these patients looked as if they might be contagious for many weeks.

With the quarantine restrictions of scarlet fever, the laundry had to be done by Ruby herself. This involved boiling or soaking, followed by washboard scrubbing, and then rinsing and hanging out to dry of each piece of wash. Clorine bleach was not available for household use until 1916. When the weather was inclement, the wash was hung to dry in the kitchen.

WEDNESDAY, MAY 3RD.

This morning Dr. Davey said the boys were out of danger and that he will come every other day now. It will be four weeks more before they can come out of quarantine because of the skinning. Today is our eleventh wedding anniversary. Ted and I had dinner at Lucca's in New York and then went to see

John Barrymore in *Justice*. Next week we plan to see Sir Herbert Tree play Shylock at the Amsterdam Theater.

FRIDAY, MAY 19TH.

This afternoon I took Edward and John to the Hippodrome to see their first circus. It was mine too. We all enjoyed it thoroughly. Afterwards, we took the elevated down to Macy's, where I went to their delicatessen to get our supper to carry home. We met Ted at Saks, where he is now employed, and all traveled home together. All tired.

TUESDAY, MAY 23RD.

I finished my *Hamlet House* story at last, but feel forlorn about it. However, I intend to begin another pretty soon.

SUNDAY, JUNE 4TH.

The doctor removed the ban today. He will send the Board of Health man here tomorrow to fumigate. In the morning the nurse will give the children disinfectant baths and hand them over to me. The seventh week will, at last, be completed tomorrow.

FRIDAY, JUNE 9TH.

Alice Taft was here for lunch. She made pancakes and strawberry shortcake especially for Eddie. He was to have gone to a pancake feast at her house for his birthday but, of course, the scarlet fever stopped that. Then we invited her Ted [Taft] to come for supper, which he did, and we grown-ups had a jolly evening. They are our first guests since the quarantine was raised.

TUESDAY, JUNE 13TH.

I have a Julia now. She is a stout black-haired Pole about twenty. Mary, the maid next door, brought her over. I think she will suit and I think she will stay after a week's trial. From Mary's report, she chose this place from five others because she hears there is enough to eat here and I am not bossy. "Girls are not afraid of hard work if they only have the right sort of mistress," says Mary. Evidently, in spite of my numerous babies, as a mistress I must have a good mark in their secret records. I hope she will stay awhile. Domestic servants are diminishing since the war. No new immigrants come in and the old girls are getting husbands. Wages are up to thirty and thirty-five dollars a week now.

Well, she got up at five o'clock this morning and went to the washtubs, so that is a good sign.

WEDNESDAY, JUNE 14TH.

Last night Ted and I met for dinner in New York and I was surprised and very pleased to find that the Utards joined us. We had a truly pleasant dinner at Murray's and, at parting, Mrs. Utard invited us both to their country house in Connecticut this summer.

After parting, Ted and I went into the Allied Bazaar. It was a wonderful sight, full of enthusiasm. The resulting funds are for the wounded allies. Last week the bazaar made a million dollars. That is good.

SUNDAY, JUNE 18TH.

I went to five-thirty mass with Ted again this morning. After mass, Ted played tennis all morning. In the afternoon, he sent a message to me that there was a lady at the tennis courts who would like to meet me. I took the babies and met Mr. and Mrs. Thomlinson, an English couple, and their babies. They came back here to supper with us and we had a pleasant evening with music and talk. They have two little babies, and being girl-babies, fascinating to me. I imagine Mrs. Thomlinson is about twenty-eight. She is a pretty brunette and, as an Englishwoman alone in New York with two babies on her hands, I can sympathize with her. I hope she will like me. I would so appreciate an understanding English friend.

WEDNESDAY, JUNE 21ST.

I finished reading the life of Harriet Beecher Stowe. If I were a New Englander, or old enough to remember the abolition of slavery, I might find it more interesting. I'll extract a piece that did interest me. "Since I began this note, I have been called off at least a dozen times: once for the fish-man, to buy a cod fish; once to see a man who had brought me some barrels of apples; once to see a book agent; then to Mrs. Upham's to see about a drawing I promised to make for her; then to nurse the baby; then into the kitchen to make a chowder for dinner; and now I am at it again, for nothing but deadly determination enables me to write, it is rowing against wind and tide." Ruby Side, note the deadly determination.

In the same year she wrote this to her husband, who was in Cincinnati: "When I have a headache, and feel sick, as I do today, there is actually not a place in the house where I can lie down and take a nap without being disturbed. Overhead is the schoolroom; next door is the dining room, and the girls practice their two hours a day on the piano. If I lock my door and lie down, some one is sure to be rattling the latch before two minutes have passed." How realistic, just what every mother goes through.

What a life of drudgery and anxiety she must have had. But all the same she wrote some good stuff and made a name for herself. The deadly determination propelled her, I suppose, and lots of talent.

SUNDAY, JUNE 25TH.

The whole family, little Chili and all, went to mass to see Harold and Edward make their first Communion.

The Thomlinsons and their darling little baby girls came for the afternoon. In the evening the Hewetsons and the Tafts joined us and we had a good old roaring sing-song evening.

SUNDAY, JULY 30TH.

I received a call on the telephone from Cousin Jack Hedges this afternoon. His boat got into port yesterday and he suggested coming to call. I haven't seen Jack since he was a baby of five. Now he is twenty-five and looks like a Searle to me. Ted thinks he looks like Gladys.

We filled the evening with war talk. There was a frightful explosion last night about two o'clock. Train-loads and boat-loads of dynamite and munitions, waiting in Jersey City to be transferred to ships, were blown up. There were reports of almost universal window shattering in the area of New York, Newark, Jersey City, the Oranges, and Montclair. All were shaken in their beds. Reports expect about fifty killed in the direct explosion. It is supposed that it is another German spy trick.

Documents revealing German sabotage activity in the U.S. were obtained by the U.S. Secret Service in 1915. Various German and Austrian-Hungarian diplomats were recalled as a result. In 1916 several munitions and railroad explosions in New Jersey were attributed to German sabotage, including one on Black Tom Island resulting in property loss of $22 million.

FRIDAY, AUGUST 4TH.

I went out at six this morning with Ted to try to play tennis. I have never played before.

MONDAY, AUGUST 14TH.

I have been having an orgy among the newer novelists lately. They are all so thoroughly alive and up-to-the-minute, full of all the new words and the new ideas of the day. I think of the tame little narratives of the past that I write and I despair.

I am Dad all over again. I have got brains; I have got an education; I have got keen appreciation for the best in the arts; I have aspirations; but I have not got stick-at-it-ness. I am physically and mentally lazy. Knowing it, I still don't conquer it. That is the maddening point. I am drugged with too much reading and, like all drug fiends, I can't stop. I think I am so much cleverer than all around me yet I never do a thing to prove it, either to them or to me. When I was at Flora Gardens School, Mrs. Currie used to say to me, "The sooner you come down off your pedestal, the better for you." She saw the trouble with me then when I couldn't have been fourteen and now, at thirty-two, I am still on that pedestal. Is anything going to smash it up? When you know your own failings and impotencies, and don't try to overcome them, what is going to help? Anything?

Ted leaves on Saturday for a week's vacation.

TUESDAY, AUGUST 22ND.

I have been down to Jersey City to find a bookbinder. Mrs. Peters at the library gave me the address of one on Third Street. I found him easily and spent quite a jolly morning talking to him. He comes from Glasgow but he looks a duplicate of that old bookbinder in Hammersmith. He has the same old white-whiskered serenity, and the same pleasant smile. I must have talked to him for an hour. I took three books to rebind. I also had the audacity to take along my manuscript of *Hamlet House* to be bound. It might as well be bound as lie in a bundle in the drawer. I was looking through it again this morning. Parts of it are not so bad, and it can make a volume for my bookcase.

SUNDAY, AUGUST 27TH.

It has been a very long day. Lots of socializing and company. Ted is home again and we all had a jolly meal with lots of laughter. Ted looks well and I'm glad he is home again.

MONDAY, SEPTEMBER 12TH.

I have been out paying calls with Gertie. She and Leslie Chandler were married on September second and they are spending their honeymoon with us. Leslie goes to work every day so Gertie and I are gadding about.

There has been a case of infant paralysis on either side of my usual butcher. Both children have died. Today I went down to Kamman's to get my meat. The children's schools have not opened yet on account of the infant paralysis.

Infantile paralysis, or poliomyelitis, is a viral infection and no effective treatment was known at this time. It seemed to strike young, well nourished children and was not particularly a disease of immigrants.

SATURDAY, SEPTEMBER 23RD.

Such mortification! Just now, after lunch, I was standing at the back door, shouting and bawling at the boys to get out of the house. In a little silence I heard a voice from Bryce's cellar saying, "It sounds like it, doesn't it?" Presumably a remark on my awful noise. Oh, dear. This horrible shouting that I do indulge in, when am I going to stop it? I want to conquer these miserable fits of exasperation. I need patience.

MONDAY, SEPTEMBER 25TH.

I have just finished reading *The Early History of Jacob Stahl* by J. D. Beresford. It is a stupendous work. It is realism, and so, of course, happens to appeal to my especial idiosyncracy in taste and goes home to me with a conviction like the truth of my own history. As I read, my mind involuntarily exclaims, yes, this is the truth: Jacob is me. In Jacob I see my own futilities: my self depreca- tion; my mental laziness; my irradicable dreaming; my hatred of continued effort; my overwhelming desire to be loved, coupled with the conviction that nobody could ever really love me; my fundamental lack of religion; my ques- tioning of authority; my fits of temper; my carelessness; the whole basic anar- chy of my character. Above all, I am like Jacob in the regular recurrence of my good resolutions and intentions to start again. I always wish to obliterate the muddles of the past and make one grand new beginning. Then there are my backslidings. However, it is an actual gratification to my spirit to know that there *is* a real live person like Beresford who can understand and sympathize with people like me whose interior and secret lives are such hideous and dev- astating whirlpools. I salute you, J. D. Beresford, whoever you are.

The three boys started back to school today, thank heaven. Mrs. Norval was in for tea today. I think she is rather enjoying her widowhood.

THURSDAY, SEPTEMBER 28TH.

Ted put on a mustache last week and this week he is starting a beard. I have been fighting him about it ever since Sunday, but he won't give it up, so I must reconcile myself to a hairy face and be pleasant about it, I suppose.

MONDAY, OCTOBER 2ND.

The great thing for me yesterday was a visit from my cousin, Mabel Jackson. She arrived with a Yorkshireman, a Mr. Barnsbee, and we invited the Thomlinsons to join us for supper. It was a jolly, jolly evening.

At first I couldn't recognize Mabel a bit, but later in the evening I began to get glimpses of the child I used to know. I don't remember seeing her after she was eight or nine years old, but she says she remembers seeing me after I was in the Civil Service. She said the last time she saw me was in Angel Road, in 1902, and that I was upstairs, busy writing a book! I have absolutely no recollection at all of that meeting. Evidently I was Jellybying even then. When she remarked about the writing, Ted exclaimed, "Oh, she's still at it and always has been."

How queer it is that after busying myself with the *Hamlet House* story, which is really the story of my mother and her sisters, much embroidered upon and arranged and fictionalized from memories of Mother's tales, that children of two of the sisters have turned up so close to each other. My mother was Alice Searle. Jack Hedges, who showed up here in August, is the son of

Nell [Ellen] Searle, and Mabel is the eldest daughter of Belle [Isabel] Searle. We only need one of Uncle Will's girls to come here to complete our specimens. I think I will give my *Hamlet House* story to Mabel to read and see if she can discover any family history in it. In fact, my story is mostly the story of *her* mother's girlhood.

Four-thirty P.M. Eddie is practicing the piano in great style below me. Alice Taft came in this morning for an hour. I was so glad to see her. But what I want to make a note about is my steady deterioration of manners. It has been doubly brought home to me; first by Mrs. Utard's exquisite good manners, and now by Gertie's excruciatingly bad ones. In one woman I see the lady I might be, in the other the vulgarian I shudder at, and yet approach. When I came back from the visit to the Utards I brought a resolution to elevate our standard of living. Alas, it was a resolution that quickly wilted. Now again, this month of Gertie's grating mannerisms and speech and absolute lack of fine feeling, modesty, and reticence have strengthened in me that same resolution. I simply must pull up.

TUESDAY, OCTOBER 3RD.

I have spent the morning creating a sancta sanctorum for myself. I have tried to arrange the alcove in my room as a practical and comfortable writing room. I have brought down from the attic a long rectangular table. I have hung up red curtains at the arch and made a red slipcover for the chair. The floor has a good reddish rug and a biggish wastepaper basket. I have my pet pictures in the alcove: my Rosetti of course, my Eve, and a few photographs. Now all I have to do is wash the window, hang up a white curtain, and invite the muse.

This evening I found this in Julia Ward Howe's *Reminiscences.* "He had some fanciful theories about the traits of character usually found in conjunction with red hair. As he and I were both distinguished by this feature, I was much pleased to learn from him that the highest effort of nature is to produce a *rosso*." Well, I, too, am a rosso, alright. I couldn't count the fits of despair my red head has given me ever since I can recall. Occasionally it has been a pleasure to me, but far oftener, a mortification. The keenest pleasure I have got out of my hair was through a remark of a doctor at St. George's hospital. I had to have surgery on my scalp when I was about fifteen years old. As I was struggling out of the chloroform, I heard the doctors talking. "Jove, what hair!" said one. "She won't thank you, old man, for mussing it up." "No, it is too bad to hide it. It is simply the most gorgeous hair I have ever seen in all my life. What a color!" That was the first time I remember the color being referred to in tones of admiration. It was balm to me.

The color, and the quantity, is diminishing now that I am in my thirties, but it still receives comment. Funnily, I do privately hold it responsible for some of my annoying and eccentric ways. Sometimes when Ted is aggravated by my whims and passions, I have the audacity to say, "Oh well, you know, you should never have married a redheaded woman." Now that I think of it, Eddie is redheaded too and a terrible crank. He is the most difficult one amongst the children. I wonder if he will ever curse his color as I have mine.

I also found reference in Julia Howe's book to my dear Charles Voysey. She mentions going to one of his Sunday morning services where the lesson for the day was taken from the writings of Theodore Parker. I can imagine it all. That dear old Theistic Church did more for me spiritually than anything else in my life. I will write more about this later.

Julia Ward Howe (1819–1910) was an author and social reformer. She was a strong abolitionist and women's suffrage proponent. Howe wrote "The Battle Hymn of the Republic."

Charles Voysey was the minister of the Theist Church in London that Ruby attended as a young woman. He was Ruby's pastor as well as theologian. She describes him as a kind man and she holds him in affection and respect. His good example and his theistic teachings stay with Ruby throughout her life.

Theodore Parker (1810–1860) was an American theologian and minister who was a leading light in the Unitarian movement in Boston.

Theism and Unitarianism share the belief in the existence of one personal God who is viewed as the creative source of man and nature. Both have their roots in the Transcendentalism of Emerson and both reject the idea of the divinity of Christ.

WEDNESDAY, OCTOBER 4TH.

I looked up my old motto from Goethe today. Here it is.

> "Lose this day loitering 'twill be the same story
> Tomorrow and the next more dilatory;
> Then indecision brings its own delays,
> And days are lost lamenting o'er lost days.
> Are you in earnest? Seize this very minute.
> What you can do, or dream you can, begin it.
> Boldness has genius, power, and magic in it.
> Only engage, and then the mind grows heated—
> Begin it, and the work will be completed!"
>
> from *Faust.*

I see by the flyleaf I got that book in 1901, and these lines have been at the back of my mind ever since. I know I copied them on a piece of scrap paper and carried them in my old brown packet, back and forth on the

Underground, for years. I shall copy them out and stick them up in front of me again.

I have put all my bookcases to rights after Gertie's visit. I do hate to have my books un-understandingly interfered with. I am too touchy about my books, but I can't help it.

At supper tonight Ted said he had seen Mr. Barnsbee in New York, who reported that Mabel had got a job and was to start work tomorrow.

MONDAY, OCTOBER 9TH.

After having lunch with Beatrice, she showed me a new diamond solitaire ring and told me she was engaged to Mr. Milton Berry. He is a friend that she and Arthur made when they lived in East Orange. She wants the engagement kept secret in Bayonne because she says she will lose her music pupils if they knew. She wants to keep them all winter as she does not intend to marry again until next summer.

Julie is getting married too. I am glad for her, but sorry to lose a nice maid. New old problem again: Shall I hunt for another or shall I run the house this winter unassisted?

FRIDAY, OCTOBER 13TH.

Mabel has been sewing for me. She has made two fine overcoats for the two babies out of one of Ted's old overcoats. Jim gets the top of it and Charlie, the bottom. Very clever, and I couldn't have done such work in a thousand years.

The new kitchen table I ordered from Macy's arrived about noon, just as Julie came in for her money and clothes. She wants me to take all the children to her wedding and reception, so we will go.

THURSDAY, OCTOBER 19TH.

I finished the Julia Ward Howe biography over breakfast. I have enjoyed it immensely and one day shall buy a copy. This second volume, the record of her as an old woman, has frequently reminded me of my darling Grandma Side. Grandma was always my heroine and Mrs. Howe approximates her.

Grandma kept a diary for years as a young woman. When in my twenties I screwed up my courage to ask her to give me the old books, she confessed that she had only recently destroyed them. That was a blow to me. I should have treasured them. Grandpa and Grandma always supported Disraeli. He was always her hero. She was the first woman known to climb Mt. Snowden. She did not marry until she was twenty-eight, which was hopelessly, scandalously late in her day. Grandma was always my darling.

Mrs. Howe reminds me of her in her abounding interest in life, her keen, vital mind, and in the adoration she drew from all who knew her. There is a record in Mrs. Howe's book of a Dickens party in Boston which she attended at the age of eighty, going as Mrs. Jellyby, "a character she professed to resemble." Righto for Ruby!

Mrs. Howe's book, with its frequent allusions to Unitarianism, takes my mind back to theism and the little church in Swallow Street. I must have attended that church about four years and the service was always a comfort and inspiration to me. The other day, I hunted out the prayer book Mr. Voysey gave me. If Mr. Voysey were alive I would write to him again. I will read his books again anyhow. I suppose I will keep going to mass for the family's sake. I will not go to confession again. I have got Balfour's book *Theism and Humanism* to read. Ted is laughing at it, of course.

It was about a year ago that the Passionate Fathers moved me so deeply that I thought I was converted, at last, to the Catholic Church. I wasn't. I was wobbly in belief and knew before going that they would "convert" me because they are trained to convince and because they would raise a body of hysteria in the church. Yet they preached so well that I really thought they had me for good. But no, religion with me has always been like the tides of the sea. It will roll in and overwhelm and swamp me and then it flows out again, leaving me high and dry.

What I can't escape is Dad's long years of agnostic and atheistic training. Disbelief was bred into my bones. I haven't the faculty of faith and yet religion remains a torment to my mind. Believing or disbelieving, it is the same old torment. Now I care less about disbelief than I ever have.

Benjamin Disraeli (1804–1881) was British prime minister during the reign of Queen Victoria. He championed social reform at home as well as the expansion of the Empire abroad.

Mt. Snowden is the highest mountain in Wales at 3,560 feet.

Arthur Balfour (1848–1930) was the British foreign minister in 1916. He was interested in the problems of modern religion and wrote Theism and Humanism *in 1915 and* Theism and Thought *in 1923.*

TUESDAY, OCTOBER 24TH.

I am sick with anger this morning. Ted received a letter from his sister Emily yesterday, and as he left it open on the dining room table, I thought he meant me to read it. Evidently not. In it she thanks Ted for making Grace and her the beneficiaries of two of his insurances. It is a fine brotherly thing, no doubt, to provide for his sisters at his death, but at whose expense? Ever since we have been married he has been towing some member of his family along. What hurts so is that he should do this without telling me. It makes me feel that his family is far more to him than I am and I simply can't stand it. I've always been jealous of Emily because Ted thinks she is such a paragon.

I could throw up the whole game. Ted is a good provider and a good home man but this lack of confidence in me drives me mad. Of course I shall get over my anger. That annoying placability will soon overlook the slight, but I feel devilish and heartbroken. I know matrimonial love won't stand too many of these wrenches. When I feel Ted has no regard for my sensibilities then I am disgusted that he should touch me. I hate marriage. The woman has the worst end of it. Be a sister to a man. That is evidently the better part.

Three P.M. I have had my cry out and my temper is exhausted. But I shall not tear out what I wrote this morning. Angry or not, every word of it is still true. I have been lonely, I can stay lonely. But the religion game is up. I have tried to be a good Catholic for Ted, but now I am determined to live my life to myself. That's all.

FRIDAY, OCTOBER 27TH.

Ted came home at quarter to one after his Credit Men's dinner in New York and came to my bed. I am feeling very cheerful this morning and thinking how much I really do love him. I have been thinking over the insurances business and have decided to say nothing about it. He has done a good thing and I was despicable about it and I will try to dismiss it from my mind and be more amiable.

As for the religion, that must stand. Harriet Martineau describes herself as a philosophical atheist and that is getting rather near to a definition of me. I am not philosophical nor yet quite an atheist. All the same, I am not so definitely the theist I was in 1903 and positively not a Catholic anymore.

*John reports that it was Ted's idea to start the **Credit Men's dinner**. Men in credit departments of stores in the area met monthly to discuss professional ideas of common interest.*

*   **Harriet Martineau** (1802–1876) was an English writer and social scientist who traveled extensively in the United States. In her book* Society in America *she discusses the similarity of the positions of slaves and women. She was a radical Unitarian.*

SUNDAY, OCTOBER 29TH.

I have just come up to bed while Ted has gone off to call on the Tafts. This has been as hateful a Sunday as any Sunday, and at last I have fathomed why Sunday is the unpleasantest day of the week. It is because it is the husband's holiday but the wife's drudgery cookery day. First I got breakfast, then to mass with John and Jim, then straight back to the kitchen to get dinner. Dinner was at noon but it took me until after two-thirty to get rid of the debris. Ted, of course, took to his bed until four o'clock. Then he went visiting until after six and returned for supper and left again. It was quarter to eight before I finished with that lot of dishes. It is too much, for it leaves me bank-rupt of leisure and energy.

But I got a good idea for a story while in church today. I will brood on it and try to shape the plot more definitely. Now I shall sleep on it.

Goodnight, old book.

TUESDAY, OCTOBER 31ST.

The boys were out Halloweening until ten o'clock, when Ted had to go out and find them. Then both Charlie and Jim woke up with the croup. I have dosed them with olive oil and sugar and plastered them with wool, camphor-ated oil, and turpentine. Ted has Charlie with him and I have Jim, the worser of the two, in my bed. I am afraid I am in for a bad night.

TUESDAY, NOVEMBER 21ST.

I was surprised in reading Lacordaire to find encouragement for birth con-trol in an old book published in 1870. The book was a record of French Catholic conferences which took place before the Franco-Prussian War. In effect, this account states that the population of the world increases too quickly and that France cannot take care of so many children. Wise men should restrict the size of their families through chastity and continence. The surprise is that such counsel should come from a Catholic priest to Frenchmen!

For the past ten or twelve years the question of birth control has been continuously before the public; in novels, in magazines, in club discussions, and in public lectures. The advocates have never let the subject drop and the adversaries have never stopped declaiming against it.

Today, one of the frequently met statements of the Catholic Church is that the Church has always been against birth control and that birth control is a mortal sin. Yet here, before 1870, a French priest was scolding his country-men for presumptuous paternity. It sounds incredible but there it is.

Jean Baptiste Henri Lacordaire (1802–1861). An ultra-liberal French Roman Catholic priest who preached in Notre Dame in Paris. He advocated com-plete separation of church and state.

WEDNESDAY, NOVEMBER 22ND.

Katie O'Brien, now Mrs. Carmody, brought her baby to see me. A very nice baby girl. Katie is now bucking up against her husband's relatives. She told me she used to feel sorry for me because I was in this country all alone. She now thinks I should be glad that I have no relatives, mine or Ted's, to bother me. I'm best off alone.

TUESDAY, NOVEMBER 28TH.

I was so sick Sunday I had to spend the day in bed. I think it is influenza. Ted was nice with the children. They had to get all their meals themselves for I am still maid-less. Yesterday I was better, but kept Eddie from school all day to mind the little ones. I had a killing headache and could only sit by the kitchen fire.

SATURDAY, DECEMBER 2ND.

Today, coming out of the library, I met Father O'Donnell, who stopped me to ask if I had ever heard of a "laying out." Then he told me of an old Irish Paddy who had a pipe put with his corpse when he was laid out because he didn't look natural without one. Father O'Donnell said I reminded him of that story because it wouldn't be natural to see me without a book or two in my arms. Then we talked a little of English versus American reading and of London. I had to tell him how homesick I am, so foolish.

SUNDAY, DECEMBER 3RD.

Cousin Mabel came out yesterday and stayed until this morning. She is going to be married to Alec Barnsbee, the man who first brought her here in his automobile. The ceremony will be at the Little Church Around the Corner in New York. She has asked Ted to give her away and, marvel, he says he will.

MONDAY, DECEMBER 4TH.

An old darkie called on me to ask if I would like a colored maid as she knows a good one who wants a place. I said I didn't know, as I had never had colored help before. She is to ring me up tomorrow for an answer. I talked it over with Ted this evening and he thinks I had better take her. I haven't been able to get white help for two months, so I will give the colored girl a trial. She might be alright.

THURSDAY, DECEMBER 7TH.

A colored girl called this afternoon. She won't do for me. It wasn't me trying to engage the maid, it was Miss Ethel Washington considering whether I would do as a mistress. She won't wash, she won't attend fires or ashes, she won't cook, she wants to sleep out, she wants every Sunday off, and breakfast is too early for her and dinner too late. She will think it over and let me know! Let me know, indeed! I'll not be beholden to any servant, white or colored. I offer wages for work and there is no condescension either for mistress or maid.

SUNDAY, DECEMBER 17TH.

We all went to the High Mass together. I noticed Harold up at the altar. He has a real little angel face. It is a pity, for beauty's sake, that he isn't a girl. He would have made a perfectly lovely blonde.

MONDAY, DECEMBER 18TH.

I met Ted in town for lunch at the Collingwood and then we went to the toy department at Macy's. We bought a magic set for Eddie among other things that specially delighted Ted's heart. Then we went off to Gimbel's for more. Then Ted returned to Saks, and I finished shopping alone. We have got a splendid lot of toys and a new suit for each boy. For Ted there are special pearl cuff links. I bought port, sherry, gin, and figs, nuts, and ginger at Macy's. I called for Ted at six and we traveled home together. We called in at Loft's and Ted bought seven pounds of candy. I've got the Christmas feeling today, alright.

SUNDAY, DECEMBER 25TH. CHRISTMAS DAY.

We all got up at four o'clock this morning and Mabel came to five o'clock Mass with Ted, me, and the three eldest boys. Barnsbee also got up and when we returned from church he had a nice breakfast ready for us: cereal, grapefruit, kidneys and bacon, tea, coffee, hot milk, and toast. It was good. He has been very helpful all day in the kitchen. He sharpened my knives whilst I stuffed the turkey and washed up all the dinner dishes including the pots and pans! On the whole, we have had a very jolly and happy day.

1917

WEDNESDAY, JANUARY 3RD.

A set of chessmen came out from the city today. Ted showed me how to play tonight and I beat him.

THURSDAY, JANUARY 4TH.

This is Billie Thompson's wedding day. He is to be married in Bromptom Church in London and the breakfast is to be served at the Paddington Hotel. His bride is named Dorothy. All the Thompson boys are married now.

Billie is Ted's youngest brother. He is twenty-six.

THURSDAY, JANUARY 11TH.

Ted was happy and jocular tonight. He has had another raise.

We have been hearing awful explosions today. Detonating began at three o'clock this afternoon and it is still continuing, at midnight, with shocks felt every minute. I can see a big conflagration across Newark Bay and every window in Bayonne must be shaking from the explosions. It is supposed that it is German spy work again at the ammunition works near Newark.

WEDNESDAY, JANUARY 24TH.

Jim and Charlie were invited to Bobbie Jennings's birthday party today. Nettie had a very nice party for them with ice cream, candies, and a birthday cake. Souvenirs for all the children were laid out on the table. There were Indian dolls for the little girls and horns for the little boys.

My poor John feels sadly treated over parties. Harold and Edward got invitations to Francis's party and Charlie and Jimmie were invited to Bobbie's. Poor John got left out on both; too young for the first and too old for the second. Alice Taft, in her nice way, has volunteered to give him a day's outing and a soda as compensation.

I am writing this in the in-between hour. Charlie and Jim are taking crackers and milk in the kitchen, getting ready for bed. Eddie is at the piano and Harold is attending to the parlor fire.

MONDAY, JANUARY 29TH.

I prepared a supper of "Nuttose" and I wouldn't even taste it. The look of it was enough for me. Ted made a meal of it even though it smelled like peanuts and putty. Dr. Davey has put Ted on a no meat diet for gastritis, so I bought about five dollars' worth of the Kellogg's prepared vegetable meat substitutes. They are all horrible. I got Nuttose, Protose, Meltose, Vegeton, Granola, Nut Soup, Vege-table Gelatin, and Malted Nuts. Muck, all muck. If anything would make me a voracious carnivore, Kellogg's health food surely would.

After our mucky meal (I took tea and toast), we went off to the Republican Club to hear a Christian Science lecture. I think it was alright. Christian Science is a definite optimistic belief calculated to appeal to serious people who have no religion and no religious upbringing: not free thinkers but people who have simply missed religion. The hall was so hot and I so tired that I began to go to sleep as soon as the speaker became oratorically flowery.

Nuttose. In the 1870s Dr. John Kellogg of Battle Creek, Michigan, developed vegetarian preparations that became popular as meat substitutes and breakfast foods. Among other products, he developed peanut butter, granola, and, with his brother, corn flakes. The popularity of these products occurred through a vast advertising campaign complete with pretty girls on billboards and well designed, factory-filled packages.

SATURDAY, FEBRUARY 3RD.

President Wilson has broken off diplomatic relations with Germany. Germany has altered her submarine policy without warning, and will sink every vessel, including neutrals, found in the war zone.

THURSDAY, FEBRUARY 8TH.

All of us narrowly escaped asphyxiation today. The gas sprang a leak at the meter last night whilst we were all sleeping. We were all half suffocated before Blanche, who is staying with us, woke up and gave the alarm. It was a dreadful time. The children were all unconscious and everybody was vomiting and suffering palpitations. We had to send for the doctor. Every window and door, from cellar to attic, remained open until this afternoon to clear all the gas out. Fortunately, Blanche was sleeping in the back room, or we should have awakened too late to save the children.

TUESDAY, FEBRUARY 13TH.

We've had to endure another perfectly horrible day. The water froze during the night and the plumber was here all afternoon, thawing the cellar pipes. Just after breafast the oilstove in the dining room smoked abominably. There was a thick fog of smoke, and I had to open the windows and the door to the porch. Consequently, the temperature there promptly dropped to freezing. I cleaned the room the best I could without water. Then callers began to arrive! Some confusion.

TUESDAY, FEBRUARY 20TH.

Bertha Hludensky called this morning, looking for work, but only daily work as she is a married woman now. So I have settled with her to come one day a week to clean house and two days a week to do the washing when the weather improves a little.

I met Ted in town for luncheon and then went to Macy's. I intended to buy some sugar and ended up spending nearly twenty dollars in groceries. Prices are going up daily. It is ominous. There was a street riot yesterday. Bands of women raided City Hall and demanded bread. Some were arrested, and they got nothing. It will soon be starving America as well as starving Europe. This is ridiculous in a land of plenty.

During World War I the Food Administration, headed by Herbert Hoover, was given the task of increasing the production and decreasing the consumption of food so that the Allies would be adequately supplied. There was a systematic campaign to persuade Americans to cut down food waste and reduce consumption. Wheatless Mondays, Meatless Tuesdays, and some higher

prices became an accepted part of the national regimen with surprisingly few
complaints.

THURSDAY, FEBRUARY 22ND.
GEORGE WASHINGTON'S BIRTHDAY.

This is a holiday for Ted. Edward has been unwell and I had put it down to his
fasting for Ash Wednesday, but last night he had a rash which this morning
was worse. I called the doctor in and he says *scarlatina* and another six weeks
of isolation. My luck!

FRIDAY, MARCH 2ND.

I was looking around the house today at how much secondhand stuff I have.
Ted lavishes his money and his attentions on the drawing room, his music,
and his paintings. The rest of the house I have to contrive for as best I can. I
have been pretty easily satisfied, but all my married life I have longed for a
nice bedroom with good furniture and pretty things. Sometimes I feel sore
about it. Surely a mother is entitled to a comfortable bedroom. If I were a lady
of money and leisure I might appreciate a drawing room, but what do I care
about the drawing room now when my time is divided between my bedroom
and kitchen only?

My idea of something really jolly would be to burn out the whole house
and then refurnish entirely with everything brand new and of my choosing.
But how impossible.

TUESDAY, MARCH 6TH.

My quiet evening with Ted ended in bitter tears under the bed clothes. The
combination of long winter weather, a cold house, Lenten fare, constant visitors, and bills is too much for us. Every Lent I feel that Ted hates me and that I
hate him. It makes me grind my teeth.

If every wife could remain a young maiden, love would last forever.
However, it seems to me that no man has any use for a conscientious matron.
A mother is simply regarded as a commonplace household mechanism, and
a faulty, worn-out one at that. It is hateful to be a modern woman married to
a man with mid-Victorian ideas about sex, marriage, the "place" of woman
and her "duties," of course. Those old ideas make me seethe. Whoever could
have dreamed that Ted would have turned out so frightfully old-fashioned
and conventional. Upon my word, the longer I live with him, the more revo-
lutionary and atheistic I become.

WEDNESDAY, MARCH 7TH.

This winter is a tight financial squeeze for us again. Prices are prohibitive. There have been food riots in New York, for the poor simply cannot live at all. I hope the poor women will continue to riot, and the middle-class women will continue to boycott the high priced foods until the producers and middle-men are forced to bring down prices or else have their stores go bad and themselves go bankrupt.

This week, one hundred and sixty coal merchants have been charged with deliberately planning to boost fuel prices. They have netted a surplus profit of thirty-four million dollars, and many of them have been sentenced to prison. A jolly good job, and I hope they'll get hard labor.

SUNDAY, APRIL 1ST.

Billy Sunday is to begin a revival in New York. I am afraid he has chosen a bad time. War is so imminent and so much in the minds of everybody, the ordinary crowd will have no interest in his howling religion. This ought to be our last Sunday of seclusion, for Eddie completes his sixth week of scarlatina next Thursday and we ought to get relieved by the Board of Health before next Sunday comes around. Thank goodness the laundry can go out again!

Billy Sunday (1862–1935) was a popular and entertaining evangelist who made appearances all over the United States.

MONDAY, APRIL 2ND.

I have been to town for spring shopping and spent eighty-five dollars on the children. Except for new shoes, that should keep them well clothed for six months. But I see that my Easter bonnet has gone to pot. Thank goodness styles don't bother me or I should be in the dumps now. As it is, my last year's spring clothes will do very well for awhile.

FRIDAY, APRIL 6TH. GOOD FRIDAY.

The United States *has* declared war against Germany. At last!

MONDAY, APRIL 9TH.

Eleven-fifteen A.M. I was up at six-thirty this morning to six inches of new snow. Now I am waiting for some cakes to bake. I expect a procession of callers this week so I need plenty of cake on hand for afternoon teas. All the boys except John are outside playing in the snow. John is playing chess with himself in the kitchen and grunting away quite orchestrally.

Mrs. Beatrice Forbes-Robertson Hale is to lecture at the high school tonight on the *Awaking of Women*. I want to hear her and have asked Ted to come with me but he won't. He says women are not awakening. Their "awaking" is only their discontent and their discontent is only part of the general world discontent, as witnessed in the strikes, the war, the Russian Revolution, the Socialists, the heretics, and so on. That idea had not occurred to me before. However, I will go to hear Mrs. Beatrice-and-so-on tonight if I can.

WEDNESDAY, APRIL 11TH.

I have been ill ever since Monday night. I don't know whether it is la grippe or temper. Mrs. Thomlinson and I went to the lecture on Monday night. It was a very good lecture and also amusing. We were sorry the men didn't come to hear it. Afterwards, we went to the Thomlinsons' and Ted came to fetch me at their new apartment. Then we talked suffrage and the discussion got heated, of course. Ted kept it up after we got home and I was exasperated again to passion and tears. I cried during the night and as a result got up with a shocking, sick headache.

I have had aching bones all through me and fever, chills, and vomiting. It is an overwhelming nuisance to be sick when you are the mother of a large household. I stayed in bed until five o'clock alternately reading and sleeping. I had no dinner to get for Ted as he is at one of the Credit Men's dinners tonight. I have been re-reading the few Voysey books I have left and I am finding them more illuminating than ever before.

FRIDAY, APRIL 13TH.

I have just noted the date and it is a diabolical date indeed. That is, for me. I am in an absolutely fiendish mood today.

I am trying to write some of my temper out and see if I can get rid of it that way. I am remembering poor Mother and her recurrent days of inexplicable and diabolical rages and have come to the conclusion that they were caused through physical reasons. I have been behaving just as Mother used to behave: nagging, shouting, scolding, whipping. It is awful. I am all hot and seething inside and every trifle has the power to enrage me. I know I am wrong and foolish but I *can't* calm down.

Mabel Barnsbee is coming this afternoon to visit for the weekend and I want to be alone, absolutely alone. It is too much of a nuisance to talk to anybody, to get meals for anybody, to be amiable to anybody. Also, Beatrice sent a postal about starting Edward's music lessons again and that made me mad. I'm mad at Bertha because she hasn't cleaned up the cellar and because she hasn't shown up this morning and she said she would. I am mad because the noise of the children annoys me. Jimmie is giving his piercing scream in the backyard, and with pleasure I could wring his neck! I am mad because I am mad.

I want to sit and cry. I want to go to sleep. I want to run away. Instead, I have to go and make beds, clean Ted's room, prepare lunch, think of dinner, quiet the boys, listen to Mabel, think of bills, and biggest of all, I have to take myself sternly in hand and coerce my fiendish soul into amiability for the next twelve hours.

It is sex, I suppose. I am suffering an extra severe menstrual flow this week. The curse of women! The fact of the matter is that I am exhausted. It is simply hateful to be a woman and be at the mercy of one's womanhood.

WEDNESDAY, APRIL 18TH.

I am thirty-three years old today. I feel more like forty-nine.

I finished reading the *Autobiography of John Stuart Mill* tonight and have been discussing it a little with Ted. It is extremely interesting to me. I have also been re-reading my Voysey books with deep attention and I think I find religious truth in them. I am afraid to say, even to myself, that I am a theist again. It is certain I am not a Catholic any longer. I do not believe the Christian scheme of salvation. I try to persuade myself that I am a Christian, that I believe the Church and the gospel, but I cannot.

I doubt I can talk to Ted about this matter. If he makes a point of it, I will consent to attend Mass on Sundays, for the sake of appearances before the children. As for the children's religion, being only their mother, I can do nothing but acquiesce in Ted's designs for them. They will have to continue at the Catholic school and be brought up in all things as Catholics. I only hope they will be able to think for themselves in these matters when they become men. I will say nothing to disturb their faith. I will only speak if any of them wish to become priests. I should loathe that. Then I should speak. After all, they are equally my children as his and I should have to speak.

John Stuart Mill (1806–1873) was an English philosopher and economist. His doctrine of Utilitarianism identified happiness as the base of morality. With his collaborator, Harriet Taylor, he wrote essays on marriage and divorce. His essay "The Subjection of Women" was one of the major suffrage documents of the nineteenth century.

FRIDAY, MAY 11TH.

I was bitterly humiliated last night. In talk it came out that Ted has found and read my *Hamlet House* story. I thought it was safely hidden in my drawer but he says he found it and read it the night Blanche and I went to the theater. That was all that was said. I am cut to the quick. I am disturbed that he should search my drawers; disturbed that he should keep his marauding secret so long; disturbed by the cynical look in his eye. I know it is a silly book, but it is my little ewe-lamb and it was never meant for his eyes. I am hurt.

Although Ruby does not admit to herself that Ted is a powerfully negative and controlling force in her life, his belittling of her Hamlet House *caused her to join his opinion of it and to destroy it.*

MONDAY, MAY 14TH.

I made bread and did the laundry today.

This writing of mine is only a so-far record. I never dare write all I think and do and feel. I wouldn't dare write down all I am seething with tonight. I'd have to tear it out in the morning. It would be too hateful to face in visible words.

I am suffering a real physical pain from heartsickness. I wonder if there is any woman anywhere more often and more bitterly humiliated than I. I have bolted my door tonight. I have never done that before, though I have wished to. I feel I never want to see Ted again, never speak to him again. There *is* nothing to say. I am in the wrong forever. I try and try, but I can never suit him. My face, my figure, my voice, my words, my ways, everything that is me offends him. I can't help being myself and I can't make him like my kind of a being. What are we going to do?

It is twelve o'clock now and there is no sleep in me. I can't read or write either, nor think. If only I could stop crying and think!

TUESDAY, MAY 15TH.

Ted kissed me good-bye this morning with laughter. He simply does not know how he hurts me. I suppose it would be impossible to find two people more diverse than Ted and I are. We have not only the natural differences of sex to combat, but also the extreme differences of mind and temperament. Tonight he has gone off to see Billy Sunday.

TUESDAY, JUNE 5TH.

There were huge parades everywhere for Conscription Day. It makes me downhearted. Who cares for such an endless river of human atoms? Motes. They are just tools for governments.

Conscription Days were held periodically to register all men between the ages of twenty-one and thirty for military service as mandated by the Selective Service Act. When the registration offices closed on June 5, 1917, over nine million men had registered and there had been no opposition or disorder.

SATURDAY, JUNE 9TH.

Johnnie made his first confession today. He told me that there are ten sins he can commit and he has committed four of them. He was seven last February. Such a sinner! I hate it but I can't stop it.

Tonight at supper John made another funny remark. We were having clam chowder and, in the midst of a silence, he threw in this remark. "Hey, Captain. How do you spell clam chowder? With one clam or two?"

Eleven P.M. Something big is brewing. Ted is keen to go off to the war. When it first started, he wanted to go. He said then that if only he could leave twenty-five dollars a week to feed the family, he would go. Now since America got into the war, and specially since Conscription Day, he is chafing to go. So I said if I could get a job at twenty-five a week, I would let him go. He was delighted.

Well, I wrote off to the Western Union Telegraph Company, stated my experience at Central Telegraph Office, and asked for work. Tuesday I got a reply advising me to see the employing supervisor. I went, but found out American Morse code is twelve letters different from English Morse and I would have to learn a new code, which would take me six months in school. When qualified, I would only be paid fifty dollars a month. However, I was given introductions to other heads of different departments with the conse- quence that I have spent the past three days having interviews. I could have taken several jobs, only they do not pay enough. It looks certain that I could never make one hundred dollars a month, but I think I might get seventy-five or eighty.

This afternoon I had an interview with Mr. Sarnoff, commercial manager at Marconi's, because they use Continental Code. Marconi is training six thousand men so there is nothing for a woman. That is the answer in so many places for this kind of work: "Do not employ women." However, Mr. Sarnoff said there might be something obtainable at the Commericial Cable Company, which is an English company, and uses only Continental Code. He phoned them for me, got the same answer, no women, but obtained the con- cession that I might send in a written application to Superintendent Mr. Austin, mentioning the application as advice of Mr. Gerard, and giving Mr. Sarnoff's name. I have sent off the letter tonight and this is my last hope. Bed now, I am dog tired.

Ten-forty P.M. I am dead tired but want to write up my record. I am a busi- nesswoman now and have been since June 20th. I obtained my interview with Mr. Austin of the Commercial Cable Company and got a job. He offered me a position at a salary of sixty dollars a month with speedy advancement if I prove capable. I went into their school for a couple of weeks to pick up wire work again and have been on the real wires now for a week. Then this week they have given me an appointment to take charge of the school for two months from July 16th. I think I shall like that and I will install some of the old

Moorgate Street methods if they give me a free hand. I don't know if this means more money already. Moreover, I am expecting to hear something advantageous about wireless work at Hunter College.

The business end is coming out alright, but the home end bothers me. I am having great difficulties finding a housekeeper. If I can't get the right help at home, I shall have to give up business and Ted's idea of going to war.

THURSDAY, JULY 26TH.

I grow misanthropic. I watch the city crowds. I look and listen to the hundreds that pour on and off the ferries night and morning. I look at my train companions, my office companions, the pupils in my school. I look and I have miserable and callous thoughts about them all. I think of the old Greek myth, of the gods assembling on Olympus amusing themselves with the woes of mortals. Is there a god who cares for all these midges on an anthill? After all, there is something in that ancient idea of amused and mocking and tantalizing and uncaring deities.

SATURDAY, JULY 28TH.

We have had bad news from England. Emily Thompson has been operated on for cancer and has had her left breast entirely removed.

This may decide our plans for us. If Ted throws up his work to go soldiering, it is certain that the income I can make would be insufficient to help Emily. I should say there is no question of Ted's duty now. Poor Ted! I think he is fonder of Emily than any other living creature. In his eyes she is the perfect woman. She and he were the two especial chums in their family. I think this will end his idea of enlisting.

WEDNESDAY, AUGUST 15TH.

I am making up my mind to quit the Cable Company at the end of the month. I do not relish being a businesswoman again and the housekeeper problem is insoluble. I *must* mother my children and run my house. Nobody else is willing to do it for me.

Ruby has had a variety of women come to help her while she was going to New York to work. What she discovers is that she needs what we would call today an executive housekeeper to oversee the overall running of the household, including the marketing, caring for the children, housecleaning, laundry, cooking, canning, sewing, and so forth. She cannot find anyone who can manage this job and her house is becoming chaotic.

MONDAY, AUGUST 20TH.

Ted is starting a holiday today. He took all the boys up to Bronx Park and then met me with them after my work. He did not come home with us for he was off to Cleveland to a Credit Men's convention for the week.

Today I had an interview with Mr. Wenman and gave in my resignation. He was surprised and sorry to lose me. I have promised to work until the end of the month to oblige the company. They are very short staffed just now. They gave me the job as a favor, yet I have proven of value to them so I do them a favor by working on.

To be a professional married woman is a very different thing from being a professional single woman. As soon as you have a family, you no longer have a free mind. I like the money and I like the work. I like the importance and the responsibility, but I am thirty-three years old and sometimes I like to be kimonoed and lazy around the house. Perhaps this experience will do me good in teaching me to appreciate the house life. After a steady dose of New York business life, I have come to the conclusion that housework and running a home is a cinch. I am dead tired now.

WEDNESDAY, SEPTEMBER 26TH.

Charlie is still poorly due to his vaccination of Monday. I had all the boys in bed before Ted came home so we had a quiet supper together alone. He told me that there was something doing about a new job again. He says it is a large Detroit dry goods business that wants a New York credit man. I hope he will get the job. It would mean selling this house and making a new home in Detroit. I should rather like that. I must try not to dream about Detroit or I shall surely be disappointed.

FRIDAY, OCTOBER 12TH.

This is Columbus Day and a holiday for the boys. I sent them to the movies to celebrate whilst I wrote letters.

I wonder if I am ever going to write anything worthwhile. I have done absolutely nothing this year. I think I must write in this old diary more often, too, for I am losing fluency. I don't get enough practice. I have been thinking a lot about Grandma Side of late. I think I will try to write a sketch of her. She was a noteworthy woman and it might interest some of my children or grandchildren. I am really writing this diary for my grandchildren. Diaries seem awful nonsense when you look back through those you write. You appear such a conceited fool in them, but still, to grandchildren they may present a curious fossilized tableau of our times. What I would not give for Grandma Side's old diaries! She was writing from 1840 to 1870. Why did she destroy them? What treasures they would have been to me! I hope I won't get a fit of disgust at mine and destroy them pell-mell twenty years hence.

I have a dream favorite granddaughter and these scribbles are for her. Doubtless, she'll read me a disagreeable crank of a fool woman between the lines, but I hope she will love the old woman I'll be then. I hope she will love me well enough to be lenient in her judging of this woman who is writing now.

FRIDAY, OCTOBER 15TH.

Eleven-thirty A.M. I have been miserably unhappy these last two days. I have cried a whole bucket of tears and hated marriage. I realize our romance is about ended and that our lives continuously diverge wider and wider apart. It seems to me Ted is a sensualist in religion. The passion Ted once gave me is now given to his crucifix, his scapulars, his prayers, and his rosary. I'll try not to let his religion kill all religion in me. I won't let his attitude fret me and spoil me. I'll stop looking to him for happiness and find my happiness in my children, my books, and my silly scribbling

Goodnight, old book. You are the only friend I can give a confidence to.

TUESDAY, OCTOBER 16TH.

Ironing took my entire morning. What work!

This afternoon I went to New York to shop and found a secondhand bookstore on Fourth Avenue. I had good luck and came home laden with *Tom Brown's Schooldays* for Harold, a biography of Mozart for Eddie, *Jack and Jill* by Louisa May Alcott for John, and four books for myself. My, but it was an arm-acher lot.

Ironing. Though the electric iron was patented in 1882, most women smoothed and pressed the family's clothes and linens with flatirons heated on the stove, be it wood, coal, or oil burning. The clothing first had to be damp-ened with water and then ironed soon afterwards to avoid mildew. Starch was used generously on men's shirts and women's blouses or "waists." The pleats, smocking, and voluminous sleeves and nightdresses made ironing dif-ficult and tedious. Often the ironing board was the kitchen table or a board supported on wooden chair backs.

WEDNESDAY, OCTOBER 24TH.

Liberty Loan Day and it is a half-holiday for schools, banks, and business houses that will follow the proclamation of President Wilson. There is to be a huge parade in New York today.

This past week has been devoted to the purchase of a new coat. Winter coats are very expensive this year. The stores are asking anything from seventy to one hundred and seventy dollars. The fashion this year is for a loose, belted coat with fur trim, cuffs, and collar. There is a cheap imitation of the mode at about thirty dollars. I finally decided on a coat at Saks. It is a material called velour cloth, taupe in color, with black jet buttons and a collar of black Hudson Bay seal. There is no fur anywhere else but that piece is genuine. It is one of the very long and loose models but with a shaped back to the waist, which is a good style for me. It is lined throughout with silk and interlined with lamb's wool. The price: fifty dollars. I never paid so much for a coat in my life.

Liberty Loan drives sold bonds to the public and the money raised provided loans to the Allies for the purchase of food and war supplies. The Liberty Loan Day held in November of 1917 raised over three billion dollars.

SATURDAY, OCTOBER 27TH.

Vera, the new washerwoman, is without exception the most wildly superstitious, religious-mad person I have ever encountered. She gives me tales of the devil and of the devil visiting girls at night who thereupon conceive devil-children, etc., etc., etc. However, policy makes me keep quiet, for in spite of the endless talk, Vera is an excellent workwoman, and it is essential that I keep her interested enough in "the family." She knows all about us and the wonderful story of our "conversions" so that she is willing to continue to work for me. Help is scarcer and scarcer and it is best to overlook oddities in a good worker.

WEDNESDAY, OCTOBER 31ST.

There was ice in the gutters this morning. This afternoon, Edward and Harold and I began struggling with the double windows. We got them up from the cellar to the roof safely, but it is a very plague to screw them up. There is not a workman or odd jobber to be found and it is no use waiting for Ted to do this job. The boys and I have got to make a grand attempt at it. We managed to fit two of the three and then had to quit, for it was dusk and our hands were numbed with cold. I was getting dizzy. The difficulty is that, even on a ladder, Eddie is hardly tall enough to get enough power into his screwdriver and I don't dare get up on the ladder or the roof. We hope to finish tomorrow.

MONDAY, NOVEMBER 12TH.

There is something again doing about Detroit. Ted phoned me to take in his new suit and clean shirt and collar and handkerchiefs to the Hotel McAlpin. Someone from Detroit was here in New York and wanted to see him and he wanted to spruce up. I packed up a bag in a hurry, left a note on the back door for the boys to go to Thomlisons', and reached the hotel around noon. Ted and I lunched together.

When I returned to pick up the boys at the Thomlinsons', they were having a very good time. I had to persuade them to come home. Charlie wanted to stay all night.

Ted rang up at supper to say he would not be home and would stay at the McAlpin. He reports that he has had a satisfactory interview with the Detroit man and is to have another meeting with him tomorrow. Nothing is settled, but a fair outlook. This is exciting! I wonder if we are going to get to Detroit after all. I hope so.

TUESDAY, NOVEMBER 13TH.

The Detroit affair is not yet settled. The job is for a supervisor for four credit men at the Hudson Store. Mr. Clark, the comptroller who was interviewing Ted, told Ted that he is going to Boston to see another man. That's fair telling, but I hope the Boston man won't be younger and cheaper than Ted and so get the job. I would like so much to leave Bayonne.

WEDNESDAY, NOVEMBER 14TH.

Mrs. Norval and I went into New York to the Strand Theater. We heard a symphony concert and then saw a movie with Mary Pickford, the tiresome. After the show we went down to Macy's for tea. We found it was a Wheatless Day and we could get neither cake nor pie. We had to content ourselves with an omelet and French fried potatoes.

FRIDAY, NOVEMBER 23RD.

Mrs. Thomlinson and I went to town to buy groceries. Prices are soaring higher than ever. Many articles are becoming scarce and some are altogether unobtainable. In Macy's, we could buy no flour, no salt, no matches, and no condensed milk. Only two pounds of sugar were allowed to each customer. Soap that used to cost two cents a cake now costs seven cents. We each bought one hundred bars of Sunlight but the clerk had to investigate if it was on the premises before she could take the orders.

TUESDAY, NOVEMBER 27TH.

I went into town with Edna Thomlinson and Sadie Andrews to meet the men for Christmas shopping. We ran into the Sivells and Smiths and all went to the Hotel McAlpin for supper. After wining and dining we watched the dancing until one o'clock, then home. When we got out of the tube in Bayonne we found snow falling. We all bundled up in the Thomlinsons' car and spun along the boulevard at a great rate, all singing all the way.

We got home after two and found Edward and Harold wide awake in the dining room with a good fire in the kitchen stove. I made cocoa whilst the kids examined my bag of purchases. We bought mostly toys, to be ready for Santa Claus and the stockings, and they all have to be hidden for a few more weeks. Harold and Eddie have outgrown Santa Claus so it didn't hurt for them to take a look over. All to bed at three o'clock.

MONDAY, DECEMBER 3RD.

I had an accident on Saturday. On my way to the library, I fell flat on the as-
phalt, crumpling my left arm under me. I picked myself up and proceeded on
my way, but by the time I got home it was numb and then it began to swell. I
tried to bathe it in hot water but had to stop as I was on the verge of fainting.
The pain was excruciating. When Ted came in he called the doctor, who diag-
nosed severe sprain of the wrist and thumb. He bound it up and put my arm
in a sling.

I have had a hard time sleeping but last night was much better. Ted and
the boys were good about helping themselves and me. Ted had to dress me,
Eddie brushed my hair, and Harold cut up my dinner. Luckily, there were leftovers from Thanksgiving in the icebox. I went into the kitchen to give direc-
tions. Edward shaved up cabbage and got it in the pot. Harold did the potatoes.
When all was cooked, Ted came in to do the straining. We got along fine.

In the evening the Thomlinsons called and I was such a sketch. There I
was in an old flannel dressing sacque, my hair just scragged back, and a great
dab of cotton wool at the back of my neck to keep the sling knot from hurting.
I am wondering how in the world I am going to pin up my hair. It is hanging
in two braids now and looks a sight.

This morning the pain is almost gone. The doctor says the hand will be
absolutely useless for at least a month. I do hope he is wrong as Christmas is
only three weeks away. It is a good job that it was my left hand that was injured.
If it had been the right, I would be even more helpless. I can at least write all the
letters I owe.

TUESDAY, DECEMBER 4TH.

Mrs. Norval, having heard of my sprain, came over this morning to get the
boys' lunch. Wasn't that nice of her?

THURSDAY, DECEMBER 6TH.

It was a day of surprises. At noon, as I was rustling the boys back to school,
Gertie appeared with her baby. I was so glad to see them. Gertie has a dear little baby girl named Dorothy. She looks so little to me. She is only six months
old and has the brightest and most intelligent baby eyes that I have ever seen.
I wish I had a little baby girl.

SATURDAY, DECEMBER 8TH.

Eight-forty-five P.M. The doctor has been in to re-bandage my wrist. He tells
me that three hundred soldiers were brought into Bayonne early this morning
and stationed at the Hook. The authorities are anticipating trouble there.
Yesterday's war declaration makes all Austrians aliens and many of them at

the Hook will be thrown out of work and be compelled to leave the city. Naturally, they won't understand and will be angry. If they can do any ugly action they will, hence the soldiers. Bayonne would be wiped out of existence if the oil tanks were set ablaze.

War between the United States and Austria-Hungary was declared on December 7, 1917. The United States had already declared war on Germany on April 6, 1917.

TUESDAY, DECEMBER 11TH.

The cold is piercing. Every window in the house is sheeted over with ice.

This morning's *Times* reports the capture of Jerusalem and the great care that was taken to avoid damage to its sacred places. What a pity! Since Europe has to be obliterated, I think it would be a good thing for the next generation if the Holy Land was obliterated too. It is positive this war has shown the uselessness of Christianity. Comte's religion of humanity is better than that old, dead Christianity. It is the human spirit that is sympathizing with all the world suffering and working for its alleviation. I am trying to take hold of God the Father, but it is hard to find him.

MONDAY, DECEMBER 17TH.

Today, just before four o'clock, we heard a thunderous row. The parlor ceiling had fallen down. Not the whole of it, but it might just as well have been all for the damage done. I am disheartened. There are no words for this mess.

I have come to the conclusion that the cold affects Ted even more than it does me. He would deny that it affected him at all but I begin to see the same old winter's story for us. Every winter we get on each other's nerves dreadfully. We jangle and jangle from the first blizzard to the last spring thaw. It's nothing but the cold, and we have to fight that so hard that we begin to fight everything, and so we get mutually annoyed. Ted's spiritual thermometer dropped this week, as well as the weather one. Now I know what the trouble is and I am going to watch it. I hate to grow cross and ugly, but how in the world am I going to keep sweet all through the winter?

SATURDAY, DECEMBER 29TH.

We had a quiet Christmas, which is unusual for us. I received a letter from Mother Christmas morning, but it was full of bad news. She writes that Eric has put out both his shoulders, Sonnie is awaiting an operation for a rupture, and little Joan is very frightened of the German air raids and has developed heart trouble. Mother also writes of increasing food scarcity in London.

I am writing this note while waiting for the kettle to boil. When the water is boiling, I have to go down to the cellar and pour it over the service pipe to the gas meter. This is the fourth winter running that we have had the gas freeze in this house. The weather is most intensely cold, and it is horrid. The laundry, of course, has frozen solid and I have been spending the morning thawing it out over the kitchen fire, and it looks as though the job will continue till midnight. How I hate winter washing!

The *boys* had a good day.

Sonnie is Ruby's twenty-six-year-old brother. He is between Gladys and Aileen.

1918

WEDNESDAY, JANUARY 2ND.

The temperature remained below zero all day. The schools, which should have opened today, are to stay closed all week because of the shortage of coal.

MONDAY, JANUARY 3RD.

We had difficulty getting to the Jennings' tonight as all the streets are in darkness. The city has only seventy-two hours' supply of electricity and must conserve, hence no streetlights.

Ted did not get home until after eight-thirty. He said he had to wait at Liberty Street for an hour in a train with neither heat nor light. He said you couldn't see your train-seat neighbor for there were not even candles in the train. He added that to break the monotony and the strain, he commenced to sing loudly, "Pack up your troubles in your old kit bag," and that all the other men caught it up and, presently, the whole train was singing with a good swing. He said it sounded great. I bet it did.

We had a pleasant evening at the Jennings' with cards and wine and later a rarebit and tea. We made it home by moonlight. It was too cold even for Ted, who joined me in the back bedroom for sleeping.

THURSDAY, JANUARY 4TH.

Oh, the cold!

We had a hot little discussion this evening. Mrs. Whitaker and I, in the morning, had a rather seditious conversation about war and religion and I was telling Ted about it just to make conversation. Ted jumped on me in his usual way and called me a boob. My contention was that war was *not* Christian, since it is entirely opposite to the teachings of Jesus. Ted maintained that any man who wouldn't fight couldn't be a good Christian. The conversation was a fine sample of how professing Christians try to fool themselves that they are following their religion. Ted didn't see what I was driving at. I was only showing that war could never be reconciled with the teachings of Jesus and that I was impatient with the religious people who try to maintain the impossible argument.

The world has never followed the teachings of Jesus about passive resistance, forgiving your enemies, and loving them, and all the rest of that branch of the teachings of Jesus. This is a war about political honor. To call it a Christian war is nonsense, for there never could be a Christian war. To call it a religious war is a blasphemy against God. God allows it, as I see it. But to say that He ordained it, as so many say now, saying that the world had become so wicked, this war is the suffering for sin, that is the worst blasphemy. When I hear that argument, my blood boils.

SUNDAY, JANUARY 6TH.

Nettie Jennings invited Alice Taft, Mrs. MacNeill, and me to a lecture at the Metropolitan Museum for today. She called for me in her big car and Bob dropped us off at the train station. It was a pleasant lecture, a pleasant crowd, and a pleasant saunter around the galleries by ourselves afterwards. We left at dusk because the museum was closing then in order to conserve both light and coal. We rode down to the Plaza Hotel for tea, which was Frank MacNeill's treat. Then home.

I got in at seven o'clock and found Charlie and Jim still up. Old Mr. Russell was in the parlor, taking a nip with Ted. Ted had managed to get the parlor warm again. Later, the Kimpells came over and we had our usual chatty evening, not breaking up until after midnight. They only left then because they could see I was so tired I couldn't keep my eyes open.

MONDAY, JANUARY 7TH.

Two-thirty P.M. The children all came in to lunch wet legged through to the skin. Hooray! A good, big thaw!

I have sent off for a new vegetarian cookbook written by the chief dietitian of the Battle Creek Sanitarium. Ever since America went into the War the government has been asking people to conserve and economize food. Nearly every shop window carries a large sign with these words:

FOOD: SAVE IT. EAT LESS MEAT AND WHEAT.
EAT MORE CORN, OAT MEAL & VEGETABLES.
FOOD WILL WIN THE WAR. USE IT WITH CARE.
EAT FRUGALLY.

It seems to me the entire city is placarded with these signs.

I think now with the New Year we will try to do without meat altogether. Ted can do without meat forever, I know, but I doubt my own powers of abstinence. After two or three weeks of doing without I get very hungry for meat. The children, of course, will eat anything. Milk went up again at the first of the year. It is now fifteen cents a quart. Butter is sixty cents a pound. Eggs, seventy-five cents a dozen. Even vegetarianism is not cheap.

THURSDAY, JANUARY 10TH.

The House of Representatives is to vote today upon the women's suffrage amendment. I hope it gets settled definitely and finally one way or the other. On principle I am for the vote, of course, but I got out of the suffrage club in this town a few years ago because I couldn't stand the suffragettes. If the ladies get the vote now, I am sure I don't know what the advocates in this town will do in the future to amuse themselves and to keep in the public eye.

I have just put all the washing in to soak, rubbed well with Sunlight soap. I really do not know what to do about the washing. I hate to send the clothes to the laundry again, and I hate to have them washed at home. I have soaked the lot in soap today so that they need not be boiled tomorrow, and so that will save some of the steaming up of the whole house, and then maybe we will have no more collapsing ceilings.

FRIDAY, JANUARY 11TH.

The House voted for suffrage today!

Mrs. Whitaker rang me up and asked me to go with her to a food demonstration. I was delighted to accept. We went by trolley to Mrs. Benny's house. She had patriotically opened her house to the public as all the halls are closed because of the coal shortage. Miss Ware, a graduate of an agriculture college, was sent from Washington to lecture to housewives about conservation of food. Today her talk was about the newest and fullest use of cereals and took place in Mrs. Benny's kitchen. Five different recipes were made, cooked, and tasted. They were good once you got accustomed to them. I will try them on my family, though truly I think it will be starvation that will induce them to eat a mixture of barley and prunes.

Ted was particularly nice tonight, not spoony, but thoughtful and courteous. He said the explosions we heard last night were here in Bayonne, where the Texaco Company was dynamiting the ice, trying to get boats out into the bay. The ice is fourteen inches thick all along the shore. Hardly anybody can remember a winter so severe as this.

THURSDAY, JANUARY 17TH.

Today's news is startling. Washington has ordered the shut-down of all factories for five days, beginning tomorrow; and also ten weekly idle days, Mondays, beginning January 28th and continuing up through March 25th.

The reason is shortage of fuel. There is much consternation. I went to town today and heard mutterings all around me. The poor clerks in the stores are afraid it means loss of a day's pay for them. This is arbitrary government, indeed. What next?

SUNDAY, JANUARY 20TH.

A surprise today. Ted went off to town this afternoon, a Sunday, in response to a telegram to meet a Mr. Kaufman from Pittsburgh about a job. He did not seem very eager about it, but came home in better feather, with the prospect of a bigger job in sight. We chatted and speculated about it all evening. He is to think it over tonight and talk with Mr. Kaufman tomorrow.

MONDAY, JANUARY 21ST.

This was a very queer day; the first of the government compelled holidays. Blanche is staying with us, Ted is at home, but the children are at school. The schools were exempted from the fuel saving order. It has seemed neither like a Sunday nor a holiday, but a kind of prolonged Saturday afternoon. Ted took Jim and Charlie out sledding but brought them home in about an hour, both crying with the cold.

TUESDAY, JANUARY 22ND.

Ted saw Mr. Kaufman again this morning and has accepted his offer to go to Pittsburgh. This means more than another hundred dollars a month for us. I don't know that I am keen on Pittsburgh. Detroit rather attracted me. Pittsburgh doesn't.

WEDNESDAY, JANUARY 23RD.

Pittsburgh is in doubt. Saks is anxious to keep Ted with them and will give him the same figure that Kaufman offers. It's good luck if we can get the extra money without the nuisance of going to Pittsburgh. Ted and Tomlinson have gone to the Astor tonight to hear a lecture on the war.

FRIDAY, FEBRUARY 1ST.

Oh, this horrible, interminable winter. When will it end?

At noon, Jim came home much excited because he was promoted from the kindergarten to the first grade and had to go back to school this afternoon. This means an all-day session for him now.

Having only Charlie on my hands, I took him shopping in the city. I bought some patterns and white goods and then made a call at the Commercial Cable Company. I went to the school room and saw some of the girls and boys. I went home again on the same old train that I caught all last summer. Jolly glad I was returning home as a matron and not as a business-woman. Charlie was good all the time and great company.

SATURDAY, FEBRUARY 2ND.

I think it is definitely settled that Ted is to remain in New York, but all the same I would like to leave Bayonne. I would prefer to live in a prettier and more countrified suburb. I am going to do my best to get rid of this house this year, and I am going to work every idea I get to the purpose. It is impossible to leave Bayonne unless we sell the house, and sell it for a fair figure. I am going to do my darndest to get it sold.

SUNDAY, FEBRUARY 3RD.

Mrs. Whitaker rang up and asked if I would go with her to a socialist meeting to hear Rose Pastor Stokes. I agreed, and in the face of a miserable snowfall, too. Ted was derisive and also hurt. He is scornful of Rose Pastor Stokes, and dead nuts on all socialists generally. He said I ought to be ashamed of myself to even think of going and that only regard for a higher principle, that of the freedom of the individual, prevented him from forbidding me. He asked me why exactly I wanted to go, and I told him that I wanted to please Mrs. Whitaker. He told me I was stupid and that if I had a real regard for her I wouldn't go with her to such an affair. I only laughed and went off. Mrs. Whitaker and I tried both the Opera Hall and the Odd Fellows Hall and found no sign of a meeting. We decided to return to her house, where Mr. Whitaker also met us with sarcasm and derision. He said we looked like Cox's Army. We took some tea and found she had misread the paper. The meeting is next Sunday. I have agreed to go with her then, if possible.

Rose Pastor Stokes was a Russian born socialist who grew up in London. She was imprisoned in the United States for violating the Espionage Act of 1917. This law imposed a $10,000 fine or a twenty-year prison sentence on anyone found guilty of interfering with the draft or encouraging disloyalty.

MONDAY, FEBRUARY 25TH.

Today is Harold's tenth birthday. Ted says, "Gee, he's getting old, isn't he?" I say, so are we. I feel it too. I have the blues. There is still no letter from home. No word since the letter of bad news which I got on Christmas morning. I am fidgeting for news, like a young girl for a love-letter. The war news is sickening.

I have caught a bad cold and am feeling rather seedy. Charlie too has a very bad cold with a cough. I have camphorated oil and turpentine on him, and some syrup of eucalyptus inside him. Myself, I am now heating milk, to which I am going to add a big dash of whiskey, which I shall drink as I ready for bed.

The rigors of Lent are on. Ted is being particularly disagreeable in talk and manner. One night this week he accused me of laziness and indifference. I did not defend myself because that is partly just. I haven't done much work since Christmas because I am too restless to settle to anything. I am still fretting at the lack of news from home. Indifference is an unjust accusation, but I let it pass.

Tonight I am awfully sore. Ted was reading some Yorkshire papers, with advertisements of houses and of land prices. Then he said that if it hadn't been for me, we would have had the price for an English house long ago. I made no answer. Later in the dining room, he continued by saying that there was no use speculating about these houses because I'd never consent to live in the country, because I had to have the city and precious *society*. I protested. I have never objected to living in the country, but I have objected to doing without modern conveniences. I should hate to have to pump my water from a well, and to throw it all away by bucketful, and I should detest having to fill oil lamps every day.

Good God, but I am mad and bitter. He is preposterous. Look at the situation. We have an income that is equivalent to about one hundred pounds a month and I haven't even one general servant. The only help I have, and this is a large house, is a charwoman three days in a fortnight. I provide the children with three meals a day, and keep the house in order. The boys haven't had a new suit in a year and every pair of shoes goes to the cobbler's at least twice before it is discarded. I did buy myself an expensive coat this year, but all the money I made last summer was turned over to Ted as I earned it. I am so mad! Love is nothing but a poet's dream.

Jim's sixth birthday.

I have had a serious but friendly chat with Ted this morning. I was raving last night, but I was deeply hurt. I suppose I am often the same thorn to his flesh that he is to mine. The fact is that we are now having our old spring song as of yore. Physically we are both tired out from fighting the hard winter, and Ted himself is half-starving from the severity of his usual Lenten fasting, and consequently, we are knocking into each other's raw edges. He tells me plainly I am a fool and an incompetent and my pride can't take it. I am homesick and fretty and want to be petted and Ted never pets me. There you are: Love means only one thing to a man, but to a woman it means a thousand things and on nine hundred and ninety-nine of them she forever goes unsatisfied. How often I have longed to be one of those *little* women from whom nothing is expected, to whom everything is given, and for whom everything is done.

SUNDAY, MARCH 10TH.

I have been having another long and serious chat with Ted about our different ideas of managing the children. I say that he never seems to remember that I have five *boys* to handle. I told him that what a woman resents so much is the continuous masculine assumption, inferred or expressed, that a man is a born oracle of wisdom but a woman is a born fool. Ted gave some of his academic theories as to why I am unhappy. But the poor blind bat, he never sees that what I need is a little steady petting and fussing, a few visible and tangible daily endearments. A woman cannot slake her thirst for happiness on some lofty and proved axiom that she is loved. She wants the little, petty, daily tellings and showings.

THURSDAY, MARCH 14TH.

The play is played out. Love and the marriage is finished. Ted had some horrid things to say last night. He called them out to me from his bed whilst I stood in the passage. This morning he came to my room to say a few more. The upshot is, and this is his own definite and positive telling, that I am a worthless woman and he has absolutely no respect nor regard for me anymore. He cannot treat me with friendship because he has no friendly feelings for me. He would not even employ an office boy who had my character and philosophy. Even if I changed, he could not trust me or believe in a permanent change of heart. He is disappointed and sorry. He'll try to be kind and courteous and do his duty and that's all. Oh yes, he'll do his part and pay the bills.

I am driven back to an old thought that Ted never did really love me but only married me as Petruchio married Katharina, to tame me and make me over to his liking. He hasn't been able to change me sufficiently to his liking and now that my youth, and what beauty I had, is gone, he has no further use for me. At times I think he hates me. I know I have many faults, but I had believed and boasted that I was loved, not for my virtues but in spite of my faults. Now it seems I am not loved at all.

I am going to stop writing and go out for a walk. It is silly and foolish to write all this down but somehow it helps me bear it. And if I didn't write it down here, I should go to some woman and utter it all, and that would be very much more foolish, for the spoken word can never be called back. I see I must beware of my friends. I must shut my mouth. I will not pour out my troubles to anyone. Moreover, I must evade friends, and gradually drop them all, else, in spite of myself, they will see that I am unhappy. When I must speak, I will write in here.

The church is calling me again, and again I am afraid to surrender. Now, in this agony of trouble, I must turn to something.

TUESDAY, MARCH 19TH.

Ten-thirty A.M. I have just read through my last entry and have been hesitating whether or not to tear it out. I think I will let it remain. I meant every word when I wrote them. I wrote them in a tempest and now I am at peace. I think I will let the remainder of the storm stay because it may remind me sometime that all storms exhaust themselves and pass away.

I have made peace with Ted and I am happy again. Friday night I went to church and when I came back, I did not speak to Ted but went into the kitchen to make some tea and read the newspaper. Very shortly Ted came in and asked why I didn't come into the dining room. I answered because I thought he didn't want me. That led to remonstrances and explanations. We talked until half past two in the morning and got most of our difficulties untangled. I can't bear to live unhappily with Ted. It is intolerable. What a weight has been lifted from me since last Friday. I simply cannot tell it.

Jim is in bed with a broken arm. This happened last Friday also. Jim is the most unfortunate child of them all. Before he was out of long dresses his troubles began. He is calling me now to read to him.

Three P.M. Bertha has just been in to see me, bringing her pretty little baby boy. I had several times wondered what had become of Bertha, and had intended to go and hunt her up as soon as the weather was mild. She looks very well and tells me that when her husband works full time, he receives thirty-five dollars every two weeks. That must be poverty. She says she would like to go out to daily work but with the baby, of course, that is impossible.

I am wondering what is going to happen to us financially if Ted is compelled to go to the war after all. I think the governmental allowance I would receive would be exactly forty-five dollars per month. I cannot think they would take a man who has five children to support, but the war is getting worse and worse and the need for men greater and greater, and they may take any man who can hold a gun, regardless of his responsibilities. If they do take him, it will be grinding poverty for us indeed.

THURSDAY, MARCH 28TH.

I had the fire department here this morning. In clearing up the yard, the boys started a bonfire which got out of their control and rushed over the entire ground. Then the fire attacked the fence, spread all over the Winslows' yard, attacked the next fence, and burnt up a tree before the firemen got here. They had to play the hose all around for about a half an hour before it was all out.

Sergeant Smart was here for dinner tonight. The Thomlinsons came also to meet him. The result was that Ted left the house with Smart after dinner and went to police headquarters, where he filled in, but has not yet signed, some preliminary enlistment form.

Also, Charlie is very sick, in bed, with the measles.

GOOD FRIDAY, MARCH 29TH.

I have had an anxious day. I went to police headquarters twice to try and find Sergeant Smart to give him the enlistment papers which Ted had signed after filling in some qualifications. He signified that he was not signing for actual enlistment, but for registration only, and to agree to appear before the medical examiners. I finally got hold of the sergeant but he would not accept the papers with Ted's emendations. Meanwhile, Ted has been to British Headquarters in New York today, on his own, and has not signed as a volunteer, but has decided, in consideration to me, to wait for conscription.

If conscription must be, and the government inevitably decrees it, I will endure it with a shut mouth and what spirit I can muster; but to voluntarily suffer it, no. I tried last year to go to work, and I know how the children and this house went to pieces. I am thankful to Ted for considering me. I hadn't trusted him. I know he would like to enlist and that he feels badly that he hasn't. Thank God he hasn't, and now I'll try and stop my worrying. But the war news is simply awful, with the Germans making all the gains.

THURSDAY, APRIL 18TH.

I am thirty-four years old today. Ted has given me a diamond and pearl crescent brooch. A quiet day but a happy one. It seems almost out of memory how unhappy I was such a short time ago.

WEDNESDAY, APRIL 24TH.

I went to the Women's Club meeting at the Y.M.C.A. Lady Aberdeen spoke and asked for money for the war effort. I was introduced to her ladyship twice over. Mrs. Nighman made the first introduction and Mrs. Agnew the second. I tried to explain that I already had been introduced but it was no use. Both ladies seemed so excited at being able to produce a real live Englishwoman, so I succumbed, and went through the second introduction.

The principal treat for me in the whole affair was in beholding once more a quietly and inconspicuously dressed gentlewoman, and hearing again the soft and slightly muffled English feminine accent. Lady Aberdeen was a striking model on how to speak and how to dress to set before American women. However, I doubt if any other woman there was aware of the example, or, if so, would ever follow it.

TUESDAY, APRIL 30TH.

We went to town tonight to hear Harry Lauder at the Metropolitan Opera House. The Redmans and their little boy went with us, though none of ours went along. There were several speeches for the Liberty Loan sprinkled through the performances, and a lot of money was subscribed. It was an enjoyable evening.

*Harry Lauder (1870–1950) was a popular Scottish singer, performer, and
recording artist.*

SUNDAY, MAY 5TH.

A very nice Sunday, for once in a lifetime, and even Ted remarked about it. For
one thing, I did no cooking today. It is the Sunday cooking that tires a woman
so much. I roasted a fresh ham last night and cooked enough vegetables and
gravy to have leftovers today.

We went to the Hippodrome tonight for the Canadian Patriotic Rally
and Benefit.

WEDNESDAY, MAY 15TH.

I am feeling only so-so and am loafing.

This evening Ted and I went to see the art exhibition at the library. Ted
lent four of his pictures for view and his landscape was given the place of
honor. It was the best picture there.

From the library we went visiting and then home. Little John had washed
up all the supper dishes and made the morning's porridge. Good for Johnnie.

*Ted did not paint pictures himself, but had a large collection of oils that he
greatly valued.*

SUNDAY, MAY 19TH.

Ted has been reading all the advertisements about country houses and farms.
Oh, how much I wish he would sell this place and we could make a change!

I have been feeling seedy and bilious again today.

MONDAY, MAY 27TH.

We spent a long day in the country yesterday. Mr. Redman met us at the station in Englewood and drove us to Tenafly, where we had an engagement with
a real estate man. We saw an old stone colonial house with thirteen acres, for
only fifty dollars a month. Both Ted and I rather liked it, and we are to think it
over. It is picturesque and comfortable and the grounds would be heavenly for
our boys. Moreover, it is very accessible to New York, with good train service,
and it would give us a good testing-out experience with country life.

The complication is this Bayonne house and the difficulty in selling it.
We seem chained here. I have been seeing that house and grounds all day.
The more I think about it, the more I want to go there, but I am afraid it is
impossible. I have felt very tired all day. I think it is because Charlie was sitting on my knee so much.

TUESDAY, JUNE 4TH.

This past week has been a particularly trying one. The war news has been awful, the weather has been abominable, and I have a fresh trouble now. Each day last week my leg felt worse and worse, so that I could hardly stand. By Friday it was so fevered, swollen, and ugly that I asked Mrs. Terhune to go to the doctor's with me. I had an examination of both legs and the result is that I have to wear two elastic stockings. I am suffering agonies with the right leg. It is a hideous looking mess, enlarged and enflamed, and so painful I can hardly bear the stocking to touch it. It is very hard to rest at night because I can't bear the pressure of the leg on the bed. It makes me think of poor Mother and what she must have suffered all these years with varicose veins.

MONDAY, JUNE 24TH.

Yesterday was a very lively and jolly day. I showed the house to Mr. Gordon, a neighbor, and he was ready to talk business right away. Since the Thomlinsons, Mrs. Andrews, and Mrs. Oliver were here, we decided to postpone the talk until Wednesday. I hope the house and price will suit him and that he will buy it.

When Mr. Gordon left I discovered two French sailors in the parlor. Ted and Edgar Thomlinson had seen them walking near the park and asked them if they would like a drive. Of course they said yes, so they got in the car and Thomlinson drove them around town and then brought them here to visit and to get a feed. We had great fun trying to understand each other. They had no English and we had only schoolbook French. We invited Martha Hoagland in because we thought she spoke French, but she only knew German. Then we thought of Miss Russell and though she didn't know as much as Ted, she had more nerve about dashing in. However, after lots of work and laughter, we did find out something about each other.

It appears they are gunners off an oil boat that is in the harbour at Constable Hook, and that they are part of the convoy to take it back again to France. They had both been torpedoed by submarines, and been exposed for hours in the water, but not on this trip. One boy told of one of his boats that was sunk and that the Germans cut the throats of the captain and first mate. They were both twenty and from Marseilles. This was their first trip to America and they knew nothing of the French Bayonne. We told them that General Joffre had visited here and that interested them.

We all sat down to supper, and an uproarious meal it was. Everybody seemed to have the idea that if we only shouted somehow they would understand us. Then different ones would suddenly think of a word but couldn't remember a phrase. Edgar began to recite his old French verbs but one can't converse in conjugations. It was funny! Then we thought of songs and began to sing the "Marseillaise," which went home. We had a jolly evening and it was quite apparent the sailors were enjoying themselves. Edna Thomlinson played checkers with one. Sadie Andrews played ragtime to the other. The Thomlinsons stayed for a good-night drink after everyone had left, and then Ted and I sat by the fire for awhile chatting. It was a very nice day.

FRIDAY, JUNE 28TH.

I have heard nothing further from Mr. Gordon and I'm disappointed.

There are rumours tonight that ex-Czar Nicholas of Russia has been murdered, that the czarevitch has been dead a couple of weeks, that Moscow has fallen to the Germans, and that the Bolsheviks are overthrown. Perhaps this is only like the report of Hindenburg's death, only talk. I wonder how these reports get started. I suppose since so many incredible things have happened, one cannot be thoroughly incredulous about anything anymore.

SATURDAY, JUNE 29TH.

I have been canning this week. Miss Cold of Jersey City gave a demonstration at the local school and enthused the housewife in some of us. Yesterday I put up peaches, cherries, and raspberries. Today I have been doing rhubarb. I have forty jars all told. I am so tired.

FRIDAY, JULY 5TH.

I took all the boys, except Eddie, who is not well, to town to get shoes and stockings. Ted met us for lunch at Macy's. We had fun with the children. Ted took charge of John and gave him some office boy's work to do. I kept the other three. Vera had supper early for us and the boys did the dishes for me whilst I sat on the porch with Ted.

SATURDAY, JULY 6TH.

I saw my first aeroplanes in flight today. I heard their noise and, going outside, saw two come over the house tops and go over Newark Bay. These were quite low and distinguishable.

In 1917 the army began the war with fifty-five airplanes. Civilian planes were oddities at this time. At war's end there were sixteen thousand planes in service.

FRIDAY, JULY 12TH.

We had two British naval officers in for supper. We met them down at the Russells' a few days ago. I am not sure of their rank, for my ignorance of the insignias is complete. I shall leave it to my boys to find out, for when they see them, the boys are bound to ask what all the stripes and things mean. I served a real English supper of cold roast beef, pickles, pineapple pie, and pekoe tea, and how we talked! They told us so much about England and the war. The one most impressive thing is that conditions are much worse than we can conceive. I note behind all the tellings the imperishable, indomitable, uncomplaining English endurance. I am glad I am an Englishwoman.

SATURDAY, JULY 13TH.

I've been talking with Ted about farming all the afternoon and evening. He would like to farm.

SUNDAY, JULY 14TH

A crowded day. The Thomlinsons, Sadie Andrews, and the Kimpells have been here all day. We have had a very argumentative night discussing suffrage, love, business, families, and so on. We broke up at one in the morning. Luckily, the Thomlinsons are automobilists and can get home any hour they please.

FRIDAY, JULY 19TH.

I am packing up tonight for Ted, Harold, and John to go away tomorrow. They are invited to the Utards' in Connecticut. I was invited, but declined. I am going to take a vacation loafing at home.

SATURDAY, AUGUST 3RD.

The war is drawing ominously near to us. A notice to Britishers was published in all newspapers soliciting their enlistment in the British or Canadian Army. They are appealing to all men up to the age of forty-five to enlist by September. If they do not do so, they will be subject to the draft of the American Army.

Ted went to the British Recruiting Headquarters and learned that if he enlisted in the Canadian Army I would be given a total allowance of seventy-nine dollars a month. The American allowance would be much less than that. Ted said that they seemed to consider his responsibilities, his five children, no obstacle at all. They told him that he had better enlist whilst he could because they would get him in the draft anyhow.

Why threaten him? They'll get him anyhow. We know we tried to make a way for him to enlist last year and it proved not possible. I could work then and pull up the income. We couldn't find a housekeeper and I had to give up the work and come home. This year I cannot work. I am pregnant again. There will be a new child here by the New Year. Now what are we going to do?

MONDAY, AUGUST 12TH.

I am going through a hard time of late. Ted and I are pulling a very bad stroke again. Ted thinks it is his duty to England to enlist in the army. I cannot see it that way. There is more than one duty in life. Moreover, I should say that as far as duty to country lies, Ted's duty is to America. He only lived in England eighteen years, but he has lived here, and established himself here, for twenty-one. He says I have no ideals. Perhaps I haven't. If he goes to war it will mean hardships and grinding poverty for his children. He says I am selfish and mercenary. So be it; it is for the sake of his young sons. If the American government decides for us that it is his duty to go and fight, very well, I must suffer it, but his voluntary enlistment I shall certainly oppose. There is no doubt about that.

TUESDAY, AUGUST 13TH.

We have had a letter from Billie Thompson telling of the sudden death of Emily Thompson from stroke on the twenty-fourth of July. This was a big shock. Ted is very hard hit, for Emily was especially dear to him. It is a hard day for Ted, who can neither eat nor speak. I am awfully sorry for him.

MONDAY, AUGUST 19TH.

Ted is taking another holiday this week and wants to take trips around looking at farms and country houses. We shall only make daily trips, but I want to cook up as much stuff as I can today, so as to have something ready-to-eat when we get home in the evenings.

TUESDAY, AUGUST 27TH.

Loafing. Ted went swimming in the bay with the boys whilst I spent the morning canning tomatoes. We thought about taking the boys to the beach but by the time lunch was over, it was too late. Instead, the boys made kites this afternoon. They have been flying them from supper time until dark.

WEDNESDAY, AUGUST 28TH.

I am without any household help again. Vera has got herself a job in a factory.

Ted says he has made arrangements, at the French Hospital in New York, for his double hernia operation for next week. He says it will take at least three weeks for a safe recovery, and perhaps a little longer. At home, I can take things quietly. I can excuse myself from all visitors and visiting because of frequent visits to Ted. The children will all be back at school and dinner can be taken at midday. I am very tired.

TUESDAY, SEPTEMBER 3RD.

School opened. "Thank goodness," exclaim all the mothers in town. Summer vacation is always too long for the mothers.

Ted came home wearing spectacles, which make him look very strange.

WEDNESDAY, SEPTEMBER 4TH.

This new baby is going to be a very expensive one. I gave away all my baby clothes to Beatrice, so there is nothing whatsoever left for this coming one. I have to get an entire new outfit just as though this was number one instead of number six. I am going to begin right now to do the sewing. I am going to cut out everything and get all the machining done as quickly as I can. Then I can do all the trimming and finishing at my leisure when I am no longer able to work the machine. I am anticipating this work with great pleasure.

TUESDAY, SEPTEMBER 10TH.

I have been to town to see Ted. Poor boy, he is in agony. I saw the doctor who performed the operation and he assured me everything is going as it should. Nevertheless, I am very worried and grieving for poor Ted and all the pain he is suffering.

The registration day for all males in the United States between the ages of eighteen and forty-five is set for Thursday. I went to the district board to find out the particulars for Ted. They gave me a card for Ted and the doctor to sign. Ted was so exhausted that he could barely manage to write his name. He is a very ill man. God help him to bear this night.

MONDAY, SEPTEMBER 16TH.

I have been in to see Ted every day. He is very, very ill and has suffered a set-back of an infected wound. This seems to me carelessness somewhere. Last Thursday I thought he was dying. Yesterday I found him better, but saw fever and exhaustion, from the Sunday noise in the hospital, develop in him before I left. Three men from Saks came in whilst I was there, but Ted was too tired to speak to any of them. I am hoping I will find him better this afternoon.

SUNDAY, SEPTEMBER 22ND.

I have been to see Ted every day, and wouldn't miss it for anything, though it fatigues me to the extreme. He began to mend early in the week and is continuing to do so. On Thursday he asked to see the boys, so I have been taking one child with me each day. Today Ted told me that the doctor said he might sit up in bed tomorrow. On one side he has had the stitches removed but the other side is still open and has to be dressed every day. The pain and the gas have ceased and Ted is beginning to look very well in the face. How glad I shall be when he is home again!

I heard from Gladys during the week. Her letter was dated in May, and she speaks of just receiving the book I sent, I thought, in time for Christmas. She says she will be unable to leave India this October because all furloughs have been stopped on account of the war. She writes more cheerfully and contentedly than usual. I only hope she has continued in that frame of mind. On the whole, she has been most unhappy since she went to India, though it is likely she would have been just as unhappy anywhere else. It is our cursed temperament.

WEDNESDAY, SEPTEMBER 25TH.

Yesterday I found Ted shifted into a different room at the hospital. I was scared for a moment, thinking he must be worse. However, it appears that the hospital is very crowded with French sailors who have come into port suffering with Spanish influenza. This is a new kind of influenza, which is becoming epidemic. It is very serious, generally changing into pneumonia and terminating in death. Deaths from it are being reported daily and several camps have been quarantined for it. It is very infectious, so the hospital has been making isolation quarters for the sufferers. Ted says there must have been about fifty sailors brought in suffering from the illness.

Ted is beginning to look well. Practically all pain has ceased, and one side has healed completely. I have kept Edward home from school these last two days with a very severe cold with cough and fever. I don't want him to contract the Spanish influenza. We've had raw, damp, and foggy weather this past week; just the kind of weather for the grippe.

I asked Mrs. Terhune if she could take care of me for a month around New Year's and she said she could. Now the nurse question is settled. The next thing is to find somebody to help in the house for December and January.

MONDAY, OCTOBER 14TH.

I have been very ill with the Spanish influenza. This is an epidemic that is killing thousands. I am lucky to have recovered, as it is fatal nearly every time when it strikes pregnant women. I had to get a nurse, of course, but she left last week. I am very weak and exhausted. Yesterday I went in terror all day. I was so afraid I was going to miscarry or have a premature birth. All is well so far.

Ted is home from the hospital. I think he returned about two weeks ago, but I have rather lost track of time. He still has an open wound on one side, which has to be dressed. Otherwise he is quite well.

I heard news from Mother that Aileen was married to William Mears on September eighteenth last.

WEDNESDAY, OCTOBER 16TH.

I have been sewing all day. I hemmed two dozen diapers and did all the machine work on five nightgowns. I feel stiff and tired now. The work just piles around me.

Now I suppose I am bearing another incomprehensible male being. A being whom I shall never understand and who will never understand me. If I ever had a daughter she might never think as I do, but at least she would feel as I do and comprehend me. But there are no daughters for me; only these baffling men folks.

Mrs. Pritchard came over to do some sewing. She began right away to make me a maternity skirt, finished it, and I wore it to supper. She also fitted a maternity gown contrived from my brown serge dress and brown checked skirt. This she has taken home to finish. Now I shall be able to look respectable until Christmas.

I am tired to exhaustion. I was remembering Mother today and her fits of irritability and scolding. I now think I know what she was suffering from. Poor Mother, she must have been always carrying, nursing, or mourning a child. No wonder she shouted and scolded at us so often. She must have been racked to nearly the breaking point. This evening I felt I couldn't endure the house or the boys another minute. I must have been shouting and scolding at the children to hurry up for supper when Ted came in. He said it sounded like Billingsgate, and he wouldn't eat any supper, and then up to his bed. Oh, dear. If instead he only had tried to soothe me down or been pleasant or sympathetic—but he shows simply icy superiority and disdain. What I want, what I *need*, is a course of steady petting and visible loving. I am just about as likely to get it as I am to get a diamond tiara.

Ruby's mother had ten children, six surviving to adulthood, and many miscarriages. **Billingsgate** *was the name given to the fish market in London. The name has become synonymous with the abusive and loud language heard there.*

I have been trying to talk future plans with Ted, but of course we are unable to reach any agreement. Last week we showed another party through the house and now Ted says we have to make up our minds about what we would do if we sold the house, and whether or not we really want to sell. Ted's idea is to buy a farm, whilst I am against that. My idea is to sell here, bank the money, move into smaller rented quarters until the end of the war, and then go home. Although Ted is keener on living in England and educating the boys there than I am, he doesn't want to work there. He has a fixed idea that he could make a success of farming here in the States if only he dared try it. So deadlock.

TUESDAY, OCTOBER 31ST.

This is Halloween, and I was surprised the great fuss the children made of it. They begged to duck for apples, so after supper, they got a pan of water in the kitchen, threw in apples and pennies, and amused themselves hugely ducking for them. They did it by lantern light, too. Mrs. Slocum presented them with four paper lanterns and candles, so these were fixed up and lit whilst the gas was put out for the fun.

I expect there are not many parties in Bayonne tonight. The war finished parties long ago. It is five years ago tonight that the Flemings gave us a surprise Halloween party here for a housewarming. I wonder if even the Flemings can get up the party spirit now.

WEDNESDAY, NOVEMBER 6TH.

I had to take Ted's enlistment questionnaire to the local board today. Then I went to see Beatrice and her new baby boy. When I got home, I heard Charlie singing loudly and over and over, "Hip! Hip! The kaiser's got the grip!" He explained that he didn't mean the kaiser had influenza, but that he was gripped by American soldier boys. Austria surrendered yesterday.

THURSDAY, NOVEMBER 7TH.

The children have just gone back to school and all the whistles and sirens in town have begun to blow like mad. Germany has surrendered!

MONDAY, NOVEMBER 11TH.

Germany had not surrendered but she has today. The news of last Thursday was that Germany had asked for an armistice and passage through the lines for a delegation to speak with General Foch. America rushed to the conclusion that Germany had definitely surrendered right then and there and went joy mad and began to celebrate the peace. It was a premature celebration. Today the armistice actually is signed. The war is over as far as the fighting goes.

In the depths of the night all the whistles and sirens in town began to blow again. It was the hour the news of the signing of the armistice was received and they have been blowing without cessation ever since. It is now noon. The noise is awful, most excruciating on the nerves, but as America has few church bells to ring, I suppose she must vent through her factory whistles. The children were all sent home from school, and ever since, they have been playing "war" in the back garden!

THURSDAY, NOVEMBER 21ST.

We have sold the house! Mrs. Nagengast called last night to make an offer herself, bringing contracts ready for signing and a check for a hundred-dollar deposit. Her offer was six hundred dollars less than we were asking, but four hundred dollars more than what we paid for the house. She offered us the privilege of remaining here at a nominal rental until the first of May. That was a very acceptable offer in present circumstances.

This sale gives us plenty of time to arrange future plans. Since the armistice, Ted and I have talked of the possibility of going home to England. I cannot think or dream of anything else. I am so tired of a big house and the incessant work of taking care of it. Give me next a little six-room cottage.

TUESDAY, NOVEMBER 26TH.

Miserable and full of trouble. Things happen, words are said, and I will not record them here, because I think they were not meant, or will be forgotten. Ted wounds me deeply. I despair. I suppose part of the trouble is that I am essentially a modern woman, whilst Ted becomes more of an old-fashioned man every day.

Last Sunday the argument began with Mrs. Thomlinson halting him when he made some expression about the husband being the head of the house. She wouldn't allow it, insisting that marriage was an equal partnership and that neither party should be the head over the other. Neither yielded and somehow the discussion passed on to religion. I kept quiet.

Last night Ted began by saying how well Mrs. Thomlinson argued "for a woman," but of course she was wrong, though she tried to be logical. Then he went on to say that I agreed with her. He could tell by the look I had had on my face and that my bad disposition and philosophy was stamped on my countenance and made me look disagreeable and ugly, and what a disagreeable person I am, and how everybody knows it. I didn't answer. I made no defense. Then he scolded me for a long time about religion and belief and how foolish and bad I was, and so on. I looked down at my hideous figure, my swollen ankles and I broke up. There isn't a characteristic I possess, either physical, mental, moral, spiritual, or social, that suits him. There isn't a thing I can do or be that he will approve. He seems to have made up his mind that he has a thoroughly bad bargain, but he is going to be sensible and abide it. As a Catholic, he cannot think of divorce. He must keep his wife in respectable condition and decent order, the same as the rest of his worldly belongings.

The wife must be obedient. She must succumb to the bodily possession whenever lust sweeps him. That is what galls. That is the degradation. He will score me up like this, tear me to pieces like an old circular, breaking my heart, and not care at all. But any night he wishes, he may walk into my room without a knock or a by-your-leave and work his will with my body. That is what I *hate*. It is humiliating. It hurts.

THURSDAY, NOVEMBER 28TH. THANKSGIVING DAY.

I was surprised that Ted did not go to Mass today. He has never been on a Thanksgiving Day before, but I had thought he might go to celebrate the peace this year. Edward was to church twice, once with the school boys and then for High Mass, as he is an altar boy. Our goose turned out to be a tough old bird. In the dusk, the Thomlinsons came over for tea, and we all had a pleasant evening together. A good day.

SUNDAY, DECEMBER 1ST.

It is quite cold, for winter has come at last. Ted has been pleasant and chatty, and we've been sketching plans about what to do in the spring. I say that if we ever intend to break up here and go to England, that we should do it when our lease is up in May. We were discussing possible ways and means.

MONDAY, DECEMBER 2ND.

I am a wretch. I don't wonder there are times when Ted hates me. It is not Ted I have been upsetting this time, but the boys. I have been raving and nagging at them ever since I got up this morning. They don't know it is nerves and pregnancy, they just think I am a detestable mother. I am waiting for them to come in from school to see if they've forgotten, to see if I can make it up to them. They *are* good boys. It is disgraceful that I go off in an ungovernable rage. I must control myself. It is only a little while now to wait for body ease.

TUESDAY, DECEMBER 10TH.

I woke up crying in the middle of the night over a dream. I was dreaming that two other women and I were being simultaneously delivered of child and a nurse told me that mine was the boy. I answered that I knew it would be and immediately began to sob, and sobbing, I woke up. Why was I so distressed in my dream? I am neither wishing nor praying, nor thinking for a girl this time. I have taken it for granted it is to be another boy. Why should I fret about a boy in my dream?

WEDNESDAY, DECEMBER 11TH.

I was startled tonight by the reflection of my face as I lit the gas by my bedroom mirror. The poor light and the shadows dulled the colors and obscured my hair, but the white face that looked out at me was exactly Mother's as I remember it in my girlhood. For the first second I actually thought it was Mother facing me and I wanted to call out to her. Oh, that I could see her!

SATURDAY, DECEMBER 14TH.

I felt very ill during the night and thought something was going to happen but nothing has. All the same, I got busy preparing the back bedroom for instant occupation. I intend to have my party there as it is the warmest room in the house. I shall let Jimmie stay in it until things happen and then he can go into my room. In the afternoon I re-covered some pillows and made a small feather bed for the infant.

SUNDAY, DECEMBER 15TH.

I have been talking "farm" again with Ted this evening or, rather, he was advocating "farm" whilst I was protesting against it. He has such theories! He says that with an hour's work a day from the boys we ought to be able to make all our living off a farm, and by selling produce and eggs, we could make twenty-five dollars a week. All I should have to do would be to give orders and see that they were carried out. Meanwhile, he would continue going to business and, out of his salary, we could save five thousand dollars a year. Talk about get-rich-quick schemes! He thinks the boys are a positive source of labor and wealth. Mind you, by next spring John will attain to the age of nine, Harold to eleven, and Edward to thirteen. Ted is certain his theories will work and he gets very irritated with me because I contest them.

I will set my face against this farm-dream. To try it would be madness. I am not a wonderful success now as a town dweller and housekeeper. As a farmeress I *know* I'd be a dead failure, and I'm not going to try it. Neither Ted nor I ever lived on a farm in our life. To think that we could learn farming now, and make a success of it, and teach the boys, and utilize their labor while they are schoolboys is crazy.

He is cross. He says it is only my disinclination that is against it. I am the only obstacle and am following my selfish way of refusing to do anything I don't personally like. Poor Ted, what a disappointing time he does have with me!

TUESDAY, DECEMBER 17TH.

I could hardly hoist myself out of bed this morning, I am so stiff and swollen. Then I found I was unable to reach my feet and had to call Ted to put on my shoes and stockings for me. I started crying like a child. Then I endured an agony to walk downstairs. I have varicose veins at the mouth of the vagina and to walk at all is excruciating. So is sitting. What a curse a woman's body is. Perhaps I should be glad all my children are boys after all.

This pregnancy is a terror. I am five years older than when I endured the last one and the influenza was a setback. The other pregnancies may have troubled me as much at their end, but I have forgotten it. This one surely is now one protracted misery.

WEDNESDAY, DECEMBER 18TH.

I am obsessed with constant memories of my childhood and of Hammersmith. For days and days memories have been flocking, and I cannot get rid of them. I am not seeing the house and all the actual, visible things around me here, but visions of home and Mother. I am so weary and home-sick. I am like a little child who wants cuddling and petting. I want to be enfolded in loving arms, to lay my head on a loving breast, and weep out my heartful of troubles. I want to be loved. Do men ever understand love? Is it not always to them only passion and sexual gratification? How women weary of that. Where exists the quiet, steady, understanding love of friends? Not between husband and wife, that I know.

MONDAY, DECEMBER 23RD.

I sent Edward and Harold to town to finish some shopping at Macy's. This was their first trip alone. I was rather nervous about letting them go, but, as they must start going about sometime, I chanced it today. Edward seemed pretty sure of the route, and off they went. They managed perfectly, too. They reached home again safe and sound, laden with packages, and brimming over with excitement. They are both very tired and complaining of a headache tonight.

THURSDAY, DECEMBER 26TH.

Another Christmas safely over and the infant considerately did not choose that day to arrive. The boys had a good day.

We had a very simple dinner of steak, mashed potatoes, peas, and turnips. I did not dare plan for elaborate cooking. Ted cooked the steak. Mrs. Slocum presented us with a Christmas pudding, steaming in its cloth and with sauce to go with it. In the evening we all went to their house for tea. They had a large tree, which they really got for our boys. They are so kind.

After our dinner, I was so tired that I undressed and had fallen asleep on my bed. I was awakened at dusk as the whole Thomlinson family had arrived. I did not go downstairs, not wishing to be seen by Mr. Thomlinson just now, but I might as well have since he insisted on coming up to see me with the ladies and children. I was well covered by a big shawl, so it was not quite so bad as walking across the floor in front of him.

Today I am awaiting the arrival of Mrs. Terhune, who is to nurse me. That is why I am writing now: to say good-bye to this book and this year, for I shall not write anything as long as she is here. I am feeling very ill and frightfully crippled. The final agony cannot begin too soon to suit me.

Good-bye, old book. I am going to bury you with the others now and hide all my grumbles close.

Ruby did not always write regularly in her diary. However, after long inter-
ruptions, she often greeted her diary with the acknowledgment that she had
not written for a while. The last entry we have was written in December 1918.
We start again in March 1920 with no acknowledgment that time has passed.
Apparently, a volume has been lost.

In the elapsed time, Ruby gave birth to twin boys. Alfred Cuthbert and
Arthur Frederick were born on January 10, 1919. Alfred was called Cuthie by
Ruby and Sket by his brothers. Arthur was called Artie by his family and Fred
by his friends. Having twins was a great surprise to the family as well as to
the doctor. In those days it was not uncommon to discover multiple births
during the delivery itself. It took the advent of ultrasound in the late 1960s for
multiple births to be accurately predicted.

Also, the family has left Bayonne and moved to Bayside, New York.
They are planning to return to England and to buy a farm. The Bayside
house has already been sold and the family will live for several months with
Ted and Alice Taft in Bayonne until Ruby leaves for England.

Ted's sister Grace has married Jack Winmill. They live in Norwich,
England.

1920

The Cobble House
Wright Avenue and Palace Boulevard
Bayside, Flushing
Long Island, New York

SATURDAY, MARCH 20TH.

Nine P.M. The above is to be our address only a few weeks longer. Ted is downstairs in the dining room with Mr. Hill and the lawyers and they are settling the
legal business of the purchase and transfer of this house. So it is ours no longer.

MONDAY, MARCH 22ND.

It is no use pretending otherwise, I am in a panic. Here we are, having deliberately made ourselves homeless, and without possessions, turning everything
into cash, and I am getting sick with fright. No wonder I am cross: I am losing
my nerve. The money seems like nothing; the home we have broken up like
everything. Maybe we are doing a wise thing, but today I cannot think it anything else but a supremely foolish one.

When the children come in from school I shall go down to the church
and see if I can quiet down this churning fear inside of me.

TUESDAY, MARCH 23RD.

I have been fidgeting all day long. Mrs. Hill was here most of the morning with her decorator. In the afternoon, five different women came to look at our goods and among them spent one dollar. I was so nervous at suppertime I felt I must go out this evening, so I left Ted to mind shop and took Harold and John to the movies. By good luck, we struck a good picture and I feel better now and ready to sleep.

TUESDAY, MARCH 30TH.

Two P.M. We have just finished lunch, which was partaken of in an uproar. Johnnie is doing the dishes, under protest. Jim has gone to the bakery. Edward and Harold have the twins outside. I am sitting down to drink my second cup of tea in peace. The truth is that we dismantled this house too soon and the consequent living in it is very bad for all of us. Its cheerless discomfort is affecting us all adversely. Ted has taken to giving me a few more plain truths and their reception does not improve my temper in the least. It is a pity, because we were getting along so nicely lately. Poor Ted, he should have a woman like Blanche Sivell for piety, a woman like Edith Flemming for housewifery, a woman like Jessie Grey for brains, and a woman like Mrs. Utard for niceties and manners. I can't approach any of them and I cannot care. If I don't please, well, I don't please, that's all.

Mrs. Hill was here this morning, transplanting plants from her garden, and I had a few minutes' chat with her whilst hanging up the baby wash. She had a blue ribbon wound in her hair. She must be nearly forty years old, for she has a son of eighteen, yet she has the time and the heart to put a blue ribbon in her hair early in the morning. She has time to consider her appearance and to make herself as pretty as possible. It depressed me. When can I make myself look nice? When can I *be* nice, have leisure to look and to behave like a lady? Never, there is no time for me. My clothes must be drab and useful. I cannot wear the pretty things that women love, for the children will not let me take care of them. I have no time to fuss with my hair, no time to manicure my nails. My whole being is absorbed by house and children and I resent it. Shall I ever be able to live the kind of life I should like to live? Marriage is a compromise. Julia Ward Howe says it is a debt, like death, we owe to nature, and though it costs us something to pay it, we are more content and better *established* in peace when we have paid it. Yes, marriage is a compromise, alright.

WEDNESDAY, MARCH 31ST.

Nothing to do! The twins are sleeping, the washing is on the line, the boys have gone off to picnic, and the whole house was swept yesterday. Presently, I shall go and take a little sleep myself before the babies wake up.

I am feeling fidgety and restless.

When I anticipate farm life with Ted around all day long, I foresee trouble. Ted criticizes me when the boys get out of hand. What can I do with seven of them? They are regular boys, dirty, noisy, fighting, fooling. They are *not* sedate, dignified and polished, prunes and prismy as Ted seems to think I should have turned them out. They're just plain ragamuffin, rowdy, fooling, healthy *boys*. Someday I suppose they will turn into pleasant, respectable, presentable young men. Meanwhile I have to suffer their boyishness, but I do not think I should be held accountable for it. I am a fortunate woman, for Ted is good and faithful, the children are well, and we have money enough. But a happy woman? No.

I sat on the porch for a little while with the twins this afternoon. There was bright sunshine and a steady wind, with that same touch and tang of something in the atmosphere that I noticed when we first came here and which makes me remember old holidays of my childhood, spent at the English seaside. Very pleasant.

I have a letter from Vi Charlton. Only a note to tell me she had received my letters, but balm to me, for she writes as though she loves me. True, she hasn't seen me for eleven years, she hasn't had to work with me daily for fifteen, but she is a comprehending creature of my own sex. My friendships seem successful, even if my matrimony and my maternity don't.

THURSDAY, APRIL 1ST.

I have been chatting with Ted this evening, of course about England. He has had a letter from his brother Herbert today discouraging Ted about farming, but telling that farms usually change hands at Michaelmas term. So now we think it would be a good plan for me to go to England early in August and spend two months farm-hunting with the idea of securing a suitable place in October.

We spoke of furnishings. Ted seems afraid I should rush right in and purchase Circassian walnut, quite regardless of the bank balance. Stupid. I do want *good* things, but I am quite content to do without for awhile if I am certain of getting good things in the end. I don't want any more junk, thank you.

Ted also spoke about getting some of the paintings to England. Inside, I quailed. I emphatically do not want those oil paintings. If he loves them and wants them, I suppose I shall have to go on suffering such things in my household impedimenta. I want the simplest life, the simplest home. Too much bric-a-brac is a millstone on a woman's life.

We spoke of the adventure of our plan and how we can get much fun and happiness out of it if we keep the right spirit. Then he added that if I get a grouch and he gets a grouch at the same time, the Lord help us! So say I.

It has been a devilish morning with the boys. This scheme of getting so much work out of them is a nightmare. Thank heaven that neither in Alice Taft's house nor in Mother's will they have to scrub a kitchen or take out ashes, so I may have a little peace with them. They have been quarreling, disputing, and wrestling ever since they got up this morning. Such behavior drives me wild and tires me out. At this moment I cannot think of anything more tiresome than to suffer bad weather on a school holiday. Edward is particularly bad. He hectors and bullies all the younger fellows and makes trouble when otherwise there wouldn't be any. I shall gladly leave him in America with his father, for I need a rest from Eddie quite as much as from my other worries. He behaves detestably and seems absolutely void of affection. I guess the poor unfortunate has lumped all the bad qualities of both his parents.

I have a letter from Alice Taft, saying all OK for our arrival there on the seventeenth of April.

A rainy day for my last American Easter and I went to Mass and heard a good sermon by the young priest.

Just after noon, the Thomlinsons arrived. We went round to the Elsie Place Coffee House for a chicken dinner, leaving the children at home to get pickings for themselves. We used my ham with a salad and chocolate cake for supper at home. The party went home about nine o'clock, carrying a lot of my kitchen crockery, the last taboret, and all my wine glasses with them.

Ted was talking this evening about our future. He plans so surely for a large, comfortable house with a piano and paintings and so on. He speaks of the attainment, but what about the wherewithal, the actual farming? Ted knows as much about farming as I do about Greek, which is nothing at all. I suffered only half the trepidation about marrying him as I am suffering now about going farming. If Ted had failed me in our early days, I could have left him and gone out into the world and maintained myself. But now, if the farming should fail, and I am so much afraid of that, what can I do? I think I am fostering a lunatic in his lunacy.

The babies cry, Edward bullies, all the boys fight, Ted theorizes. My life is a weariness. Cuthie has an eye tooth. John has a toothache.

THURSDAY, APRIL 8TH.

I took Charlie to Brooklyn to take lunch with Mabel. I saw my bookcases and books and pictures in her house without much feeling about them at all. I suppose I am really so glad to get rid of all the material that cumbers me that I don't care a jot who has it.

MONDAY, APRIL 12TH.

Yesterday's sermon was on the Fourth Commandment: Honor thy father and mother. It was addressed wholly to the younger women. One point that the priest touched was about the necessity for obedience, a virtue fast becoming nonexistent in these days. He traced the present discontents, strikes, and upheavals of our time primarily to the lack of obedience in the home. He gave a definition about parents which made clear to me the authority for filial obedience. "You must obey me because I am your mother" never seemed to me a good reason nor a good argument, but the Church teaches that the parents are the representatives of God in the home and therefore obedience to them is a duty. This disquisition touched the surface of my mind, but not the core of my heart.

It is a damp, blowy night, working up for a storm. There are more political storms rising also. All the railroads are going out on strike. This will completely paralyze business and the city people. The president does nothing and says nothing.

WEDNESDAY, APRIL 14TH.

Mabel went to eight o'clock Mass with me this morning. When I went up to the railing, she also went. She also took communion! I could not stop her. I did not know what to do, so at the end of instructions, I went straight into the confessional and told the priest about it. I had not dreamed that she had any such desire or intention or I would have told her that she might not communicate there. She is an Anglican, took communion in the Episcopal church at Easter, has never been to confession in her life, and was not even fasting. The priest told me that there was no great harm done, as she was ignorant of the laws of the Church, and was devout and had good intentions, but that I must explain to her how it was wrong and that she must not do it again. I haven't done so yet. She will be back from Brooklyn to help me pack and travel to Bayonne with the children. This is a difficult and delicate subject to broach to her, but I must do it.

23 West 35th. Street
Bayonne, New Jersey

TUESDAY, APRIL 20TH.

Eleven P.M. Here we are in Bayonne once again. I intended to write herein tonight but was called into Alice's parlor to listen to the Victrola, until now, bedtime. Ted is out at a Credit Men's meeting but should be in soon. Bed now, with a book.

FRIDAY, APRIL 23RD.

Tomorrow I shall have been back here in Bayonne a week. I like to walk these streets. I find they have become nearly as dear and homey to me as Hammersmith streets. To the boys, of course, they are home. Bayonne is their native city. This week has been very crowded with unpacking and shaking down into new quarters and with seeing old friends. I had thought I should do much reading and writing whilst staying here, but now I think not. The days are full with housekeeping, with the children and friends, and at night Ted shares my room and bed.

Alice Taft is wonderful. Her house is overflowing with Thompsons, her kitchen and her routine are interfered with, yet she smiles all day. As an example of practical Christian Science she herself is a glorious "testimony." I love her.

TUESDAY, APRIL 27TH.

The other day I brought several of Amelia Barr's books from the library. They are all alike. I love to read them, and what I notice is that they are all autobiographical. It was the same with Ada Cambridge's books. Of course. We *can* only write what we know. Women like these two make wonderful profit out of the material of their own lives: the material happenings as the world sees them, and the introspective happenings of their interior lives, which are the life indeed.

So with myself. I could tell the story of my life in twenty different ways, and in tellings so different that only another craftswoman could detect the same model, the same theme, the same lessons, the same life. Shall I ever do it?

WEDNESDAY, APRIL 28TH.

I went to the old Bayonne Women's Club this afternoon to hear Mr. and Mrs. Edwin Markham. She gave a paper on women's poetry, and he gave a short lecture on poetry and then read some of his own poems. I liked particularly some quatrains and a magnificent poem on Lincoln. Markham laid a fresh fuse to my rubbishy bonfire heap of literary ambitions. Art is to convey emotion was his dictum, and I know I can write so that they who read can feel. I resolved that I would write without more delay. It was a very pleasant afternoon.

This evening while reading the Eighth Psalm, I was arrested by the verse: "When I consider thy heavens, the work of thy fingers, the moon and the stars, which thou hast ordained; what is man, that thou art mindful of him? and the son of man, that thou visitest him?" How very often have I felt just like that. I have felt that particularly this past winter when I would take a boy to the movies and then on our walk home see the wonderfully clear and deep winter's skies. Harold and John loved the stars for their beauty while Eddie regarded them more practically as guides in the wilds. I would trace out the Big Dipper with the boys, but my soul would be asking, how in the face of these heavens can God care for us?

Edwin Markham (1852–1940) wrote the immensely popular poem "The Man with the Hoe," inspired by Millet's painting. The depiction of the brutalized farmer was embraced by a reform minded audience who opposed the exploitation of labor. Markham's other famous poem was "Lincoln, The Man of the People," published in 1901.

SUNDAY, MAY 2ND.

Whilst returning home from the park this afternoon, I noticed the signboard on the door of St. John's Episcopal Church. It said Evensong was at 7:45 P.M., and I made up my mind to attend it. It was in that church that I was married fifteen years ago tomorrow, and I felt curious to go and look inside it once again and to say good-bye to it. After supper I told Ted I was going out to see Mrs. Norval. I couldn't tell him I was going to St. John's. I found her in the church and sat down beside her. The service meant nothing to me. The only possible Christianity for me is Catholicism. This is the second time recently that I have been to an Anglican service with the same result: emptiness.

As for the association, there was nothing much. I noticed the building badly need re-painting and decorating. I felt the lack of intensity in the sparse congregation. However, I looked at the organ and remembered how long Ted played it. I looked at the altar steps and had a vision of Ted and myself kneeling there fifteen years ago and the Reverend Mr. Taylor wrapping our two hands together in his stole and the churchful of curious and emotional women behind us. Fifteen years ago!

MONDAY, MAY 3RD.

Fifteen years ago today I landed in New York. Before I had been ten minutes on the dock a gentleman rushed up to Ted, who introduced him to me as Mr.

Hewetson. As soon as the introduction was completed this total stranger turned to me, eyes twinkling, and said, "Well, Miss Side, how do you like America?" I gasped in astonishment, for I was barely off the ship's gangplank. This was our dear Mr. Hewetson, a man who became dearer to me than my own father, and this was his first joke for my benefit. A few weeks later, when I had been questioned with that query a thousand times, he told me he had determined to be the first person to ask me it. I had no answer then but I have an answer today. I like New York very much. I like America, all I have seen of it. I am sorry to leave it. I could live here contentedly for the rest of my life. I am sad to think of going away. I have had good times and bad times in these fifteen years, but the bad times have not been of America's making. Ted never seems able to forgive America for not being England, but the differences between the two countries do not jar me. I can enjoy both. Will Ted be as happy in England as he dreams he can be? Shall I be able to live happily there when I suffer again its discomforts and its prejudices? Alas, England and I have become strangers and America I love.

SATURDAY, MAY 9TH.

Ten P.M. I am writing in the Tafts' kitchen whilst waiting for the kettle to boil, to make tea and baby bottles. Ted is with the Thomlinsons in Mount Vernon and a good riddance, for he was his most provoking this morning. When I came downstairs, Alice Taft was already in the kitchen and she immediately gave me a serious complaint about the noise the boys made in the room above her bedroom. I have never heard them, being in the back part of the house. She said they were all awake before six this morning and making such a noise that Ted Taft had to go and stop them. She also said they have been making noise early every morning this week since the May daily Mass began.

When I reported this to Ted, instead of questioning the boys and making them understand that such behavior must cease, he rounded on me and said it must be because I had not arranged a schedule and that if I would do so, he would see that the boys carried it out. Ted and his schedules! The same old talk! I get endless talk and criticism but no backing. The upbringing of these seven children is thrown entirely on me and I get no help about it. I am tired to death with the perpetual struggle of handling a family.

Then this: I said that the complaints were about this week, since the boys started to go to eight o'clock Mass, and since it was unnecessary and causing trouble for the Tafts, the Mass going had better be stopped. Ted replied that I had better understand that the boys will go to Mass every time they want to, even if we have to rent city hall to make it possible, even if he has to leave me to make it possible. He said for no reason shall they stay away, and I had better understand that. Oh, I understand it. The Church before everything is Ted's motto.

TUESDAY, MAY 11TH.

Ten A.M. The washing is on the line, the twins are abed, and Alice has gone to New York, so I have an empty hour before Charlie returns from school. I am feeling quite quiet, though tired.

Ted has been in a very amiable mood, all his bitterness of Saturday forgotten, so I forgot it too. Men are not supposed to suffer moods, but women know they do because they are the sufferers from their man's moods. Men "take it out" on their wives. All the same, Ted's nagging of me has got to be stopped. I accept my lot, I do my work, and I squeeze out little pleasures from life when I can, but I won't be nagged anymore.

Since this winter I have been reading the Gospels as I have never read them before and they *are* a revelation to me. Instead of reading them from the old Voysey theistic attitude of finding their historical discrepancies, I have been reading them to find the words of Jesus. The words astonish and humble me. I wonder how dear old Charles Voysey, wise and good man that he was, could so completely ignore the New Testament? He taught a passionate love for God. His theism appealed to people at a time when rationalism was rampant in the air. What I see now, but didn't see when I attended Voysey's church, are the teachings of Jesus about the *fatherhood* of God. I have come to see now that as men can only receive impressions about God through their humanity, the only possible way for God to reveal Himself to us is through Jesus.

THURSDAY, MAY 20TH.

I am overcome with despondency. At supper, Ted announced that he could get two adjoining rooms on the Cunarder *Royal George*, sailing July twenty-eighth, for twelve hundred dollars. He asked whether I thought I could possibly manage with only one room for six hundred. It took my breath away, and literally, for I felt like fainting. All I could think was that I didn't want to go at all. I was physically unable to answer Ted, so he got peeved and went out. Then I cried a little but shook myself together and went out too, to see Mrs. Norval for an hour. Now to bed, but with a feeling that I shall be dragged out in the morning to the electric chair.

FRIDAY, MAY 21ST.

A teeming, rainy day and Alice's laundress is here. I shut myself up in the bedroom with the twinnies all day and read *A Labrador Doctor*, the autobiography of Wilfred Thomason Grenfell. I feel more cheerful than last night and, since this English plan must be gone through with, I had better do it with a smile. I wrote to Mother and told her my ship and date of sailing. Tonight I helped Alice chaperone at a dance at the Y.W.C.A.

Nine-twenty P.M. I went up to the library just now and, coming back in the deep dusk, I looked at all the young people with sadness. Some couples were talkative, some were silent, but they all trod softly. I especially noticed one couple. The girl's eyes were shining from under the dark shadow of her hat. The boy, much taller than she, was holding her arm in a reverent way and stooping his head to look into her face. My quick thoughts jumped, "Poor things! Fifteen years hence they will be bothered and worried with children and perhaps their lives rent asunder by some caprice. Poor things, take your good times now. Nature is cruel: She will use you, torment you, and then throw you down like the rest of us." It is a true picture of Love that portrays him with wings. This tormenting ache for love; does there come a time when it ceases to gnaw us?

A very bad day. I've a raging headache and a raging temper. Edward is trying almost beyond endurance. He leaves the house at eight-thirty in the morning and does not return until six or later in the evening and then objects to do anything at all to help. He could come home when the high school is out and mind the twins for me for an hour, daily. It wouldn't hurt him and would give me a much needed rest from the babies, who are at their very worst stage for mischievousness just now. Edward never thinks of anyone except Edward.

Tonight I struck Ted in the face. He exasperated me beyond bearing with his theorizing upon training children. The last time he nagged me I told him that if he ever dared to call me "lazy" again I should pick up the nearest thing and throw it at him. Well, tonight he used "lazy" again. I was fixing the twins for bed when he came in and called my attention to the fact that Charlie had thrown his coat on the floor, upon which I had told *him* to tell it to Charlie. But no, he wouldn't, because it isn't his job to train the children, because he isn't here all day, and so on. I listened. Then we each took a twin upstairs, he steadily talking all the time about my delinquencies in child training. Then, as we were leaving the bedroom after putting the twins to bed, out came "lazy" again. I flared and raised my hand and struck him across the mouth. He could have killed me. He started to raise his hand to strike back, then remembered he mustn't, so laughed instead and said, "Now you have hurt yourself much more than you have hurt me, and now I know that you are not a lady."

We then finished our supper, I silent, but he trying to joke. At eight he went out to see a real fight, the boxing bouts at Melville Park, carefully kissing me before he went. Oh, Ted Thompson!

This last hour I have been drinking tea and talking with dear Alice Taft. Somehow or other I confided in her and told her of tonight's trouble with Ted, and she gave me a wonderful, helpful thought. I had said that it seemed to me that as time went on, after each spat with Ted, I cared less and less for him; that he made me indifferent to him, so that it would finally come to it that he wouldn't be able to hurt me, for you are not hurt by people you are indifferent to.

Alice said, "Yes. You will get to where he cannot hurt you. You are God's child. Ted cannot hurt you, Ruby Alice, this is going to work out. I don't know how. You are going through your hard times now, the very worst times for you with the twins and this breaking up of your home. Ted is too fine and good a man not to come out alright. I don't believe he knows when he hurts you or how much. You are both *trying* for adjustment. It must come right. God is good. It will be alright." Then she paused for a minute and went on, "My Ted doesn't hurt me anymore. He can't. *Nothing can hurt me.* I am God's child." What a thought!

TUESDAY, JUNE 1ST.

A wife who becomes her husband's servant ceases to be his love. When a woman must rise, waken her children, feed them, and get them ready for school, attend to her babies, dress and amuse them, and prepare her husband's breakfast, she *is* a drudge of all work. She looks like one, she is treated like one, and she hasn't to be conciliated because she can't leave. To do all these things sounds heroic in a story, but in real life it is damnable.

There is no pleasing Ted. And I get touchier and touchier. How can I continue to live with him? I have been thinking today that I would take the children safely to England, settle them amongst the relatives, and then disappear.

TUESDAY, JUNE 8TH.

I went to town and into St. Peter's for a few minutes. I came out refreshed in heart and spirit, determined that since I have put my hand to the plough (oh, how literally!) I will not turn back. It is unkind for me to say the discouraging and disappointing things of Ted that I do, and I will stop it. Resolutely now, I will expect good things of the English farming, and give Ted a cheerful and comradely acquiescence. God help me keep this resolution.

WEDNESDAY, JUNE 16TH.

I have suddenly seen what is the trouble with Ted. He is not housebroken. At fourteen he started at business, at eighteen he went off to the Klondike, and when he returned from there, he lived in a series of boarding houses until his marriage. Consequently, he has never learned to cooperate in the home. He has always taken the attitude of the boarder, the hotel visitor, a man who sits down, gives orders, and is waited upon. I have never seen a man who did less for himself, less for others in the house. He never fetches anything, never puts anything away. He never does anything for the children until I have first asked him. He never sees anything to be done. In short, he never helps himself nor anyone else.

This knowledge flashed to me this morning when he casually asked me for a spoon. His breakfast was waiting for him to eat, I was scouring the milk bottle so that Jimmie could go for fresh milk, the twinnies were waiting to be dressed and fed, and Ted calmly said, "I don't see any spoons: kindly get me a spoon, will you?" I got it, but suddenly saw how almost every other man in the world would have gone to the sideboard and fetched a spoon for himself. Ted regards his home as a hotel and simply calls for services. I am not the waitress as well as the chef and the nursery maid.

So with the bedroom trouble. Ever since we have been back in Bayonne and have had to share a bedroom, Ted has had a steady stream of complaints. I shake the bed when I get into it. I move in the night. I come to bed after him and disturb him. I have too many bed covers. I don't lower the shades sufficiently. I make noise when I undress. I see the fact of the matter is that he has never learned to share a room with anyone. My hopes that he would come to share my room in sympathetic comradeship will never come to fruition because all he sees in such an arrangement is inconvenience and that makes him peevish. In the next home I make I will see to it that he has his own monastic cell.

I write this calmly. I am neither angry nor hurt. I have merely discovered the cause of a great deal of our family dissatisfactions. He unknowingly, but all the same insistently, demands services he can never get. I am always wishing and hoping for the little trifling helps that he never perceives are needed. So there it is. He isn't housebroken.

Ted was very jocular tonight after we called on the Jenningses. I told him what sudden understanding I had of him today and he said maybe I was right. Now he is afraid I am going to "train" him. Well, I am!

WEDNESDAY, JUNE 23RD.

I had letters today from Mother and Gladys. Mother says Dad is sick with a stone in the kidneys and that Gladys has been home a week and is very fussy. Gladys's letter is full of righteous indignation. According to her, I have no business to go home. She sounds like a good Protestant old maid missionary, running true to form. If so, what a trial she is going to be for the family.

Ted says my sailing had to be changed. He has managed to get me booked now on the *Columbia*, sailing three days later, July thirty-first. This will mean a long and trying railway journey for me from Glasgow, but I suppose I shall manage alright.

WEDNESDAY, JUNE 30TH.

I have one more month to live under present conditions and am wondering where I am going to find the endurance to put it through. Alice Taft is unvaryingly dear and lovely about having us here, but the discomfort of the life is wearing on me. I long for my own home already. Possibly I shall find a suitable place by September, and then what bliss it will be to furnish it and settle in. But I am so broody about our affairs. Last week I was thinking brightly of them, chatting with Ted about all the gay possibilities. Today I am deep in the shadows again, so fearful, so regretful, so discouraged.

I received a compliment today that is worth remembering. Alice reported it to me when she came in from paying a call on Judge and Mrs. Lazarus. They had been talking about the Thompsons (it appears our affairs are a romantic piece of town news at the present!), and the Judge said he admired me very much and he considered me a "monument of magnificent fortitude." These people don't know me. I walk amongst them, apparently serene and cheerful, but inside I am really in a panic of fright and hopelessness. I fear and dread the future. I want to run away from my life. All of which is anything but fortitude.

SUNDAY, JULY 11TH.

American summer is now in full blast and we are all suffering the torments of the damned. I thought I should faint in church, which seemed quite without ventilation. There is also agonizing pain in the veins above my left ankle. Ted and I and the twinnies have two small bedrooms which are above Alice's kitchen. These rooms are the extension of the house and have a flat tin roof and sunshine all afternoon. Consequently, they are veritable ovens and we come to bed to scorch all night. The babies wake with the discomfort, Ted grumbles intermittently throughout the night, my vein jabs, my head aches, and my spirit flags.

TUESDAY, JULY 13TH.

I am feeling depressed and unhappy. I know that Ted is suffering from the heat and feeling the lack of sleep, the same as I am, but the things he says wound me deeply. I think it is high time we did have a short separation. What I feel today is that after enduring these fifteen years of sarcasm, cross-questioning, and "being improved," I shall never want to take up our mutual life again.

WEDNESDAY, JULY 21ST.

I have been writing letters all morning, including one to Sonnie and his new wife. Mother wrote that Aileen had secured a house in Shepherd's Bush, so Sonnie and his girl, Mabel, decided to get married forthwith and take Aileen's flat. Mother says the girl is nice and promises to make a good wife, but that she is Gladys's age, about eight years older than Sonnie. Well, they have had their way, so now there is nothing to do but be nice to the girl. She is another Mabel.

SATURDAY, JULY 31ST.

The expressmen arrived at seven o'clock this morning. They packed all the stuff for Ted's apartment on the front part of their truck and all my baggage on the back. We have nothing left in the Tafts' house except our hand luggage.

SUNDAY, AUGUST 1ST.

This is my last American Sunday. Harold, John, Charlie, and Jim went off in the rain with me to Mass. We had a delicatessen dinner at noon and then Ted and I took Charlie and the twins to a farewell visit with Mrs. Russell. She and her two daughters had bathrobes, rag dolls, and socks for the twins. We had a delicious supper and then left to put the twins to bed. I settled the children, did a final wash, and paid a last call on Mrs. Whitaker. Ted and I spent the rest of the evening in the Tafts' parlor with Mrs. Shaefer and Mr. Dryden. We didn't get to bed until two in the morning.

The Columbia

MONDAY, AUGUST 2ND.

Aboard ship. We had an awful scurry to get off this morning. We missed the train and had to hire a jitney to take us to the ferry. We reached the Cunard pier barely in time to get aboard. Mabel was at the dock, but I only had a moment in which to kiss her good-bye. I had to put Charlie to bed at three o'clock, and feel decidedly squeamish myself this evening.

TUESDAY, AUGUST 3RD.

I was feeling sick at breakfast time but was better at noon. I was able to eat a good lunch and supper. I got Charlie up on deck for a couple of hours this afternoon, but he was not able to eat anything. The rest of the children are perfectly well and are having a good time.

Ted, Eddie, and John stayed in New York in an apartment on Seventeenth Street in Manhattan while Ruby went farm-hunting in England with the other five sons. This arrangement was considered best for the children because Eddie was now in high school and could not afford to take a significant portion of the year off. Harold went to help Ruby with the younger children. The twins, Charlie, and Jim were considered too young to leave behind. John was in-between and stayed with his father and Eddie.

6 Angel Road
Hammersmith
England

FRIDAY, AUGUST 20TH.

I have been in England a week. I hate it. I am going to another estate agent this afternoon, but only as a matter of form for Ted's satisfaction. There is no home here, no matter how beautiful, that will ever induce me to live in it. I have got to get back to America.

Everybody is lovely to me, but I simply cannot stand the country. It is dirty and cold and the people are the same and drunken besides. Ted used to sing to tease me:

> Oh carry me back to Bayside,
> Bayside! Bayside!
> Oh, Bayside is the place for me!

Right, I must get back to America.

MONDAY, AUGUST 30TH.

Yesterday I went to Romford to see Herbert about the place I saw at Halesworth. I thought it was most suitable, cabled Ted about it, and got back word to buy. Herbert disadvised immediately because there was no arable land attached. He says we require twenty acres of arable land. I am going to write Freeman, the owner of The Grange, and decline the place. Next I am going to write to White-lock and make inquiries about Bournemouth. Then I shall take my letters to the post and cable Ted that Herbert vetoes Halesworth.

FRIDAY, SEPTEMBER 3RD.

I am making friends with Gladys.

TUESDAY, SEPTEMBER 14TH.

Joan left to join Mother and Dad on holiday at Margate. On my way home from seeing her off at Victoria Station, I bought some cigarettes. I am getting most dreadfully nervous, and now that I have the house to myself, I think I will try smoking and see if that calms me down. I have been to Sonnie's flat to supper. I had a good talk with him and Mabel. I am so glad to know Sonnie grown up.

Ten P.M. I am weary and troubled. Ever since I got here one or another of the children has been ailing. One by one they have broken out in a bad rash, troublesome and irritating, and about which I am very apprehensive. Charlie has had bad days with toothache and biliousness and now little Cuthie has been ailing, crying constantly and refusing all food. I am very worried about them all. As each day passes I see more and more clearly the lunacy of this English farm idea. I could cry my eyes out, but that wouldn't get me anywhere. I shall take some tea and a cigarette and look through my new books.

Going through the drawing room I picked up a little autograph album of Aileen's, and turning the pages I came across this in Mother's handwriting:

> "The purest treasure mortal times afford
> Is spotless reputation: that away,
> Men are but gilded loam or painted clay . . .
> Mine honor is my life; both grow in one.
> Take honor from me, and my life is done."
>   Richard II

I don't know what surprised me most: the lines themselves or the fact that Mother should quote Shakespeare. Yet, on reflection, neither fact is surprising. We used to think our brains were Dad's gift to us, but for some years I have greatly valued Mother's share of wits. As for honor: honor *is* everything to Mother. What has all her driving of the past been but a driving for right? Speaking to me of Alice Searle only the other day, Mother said, "I am always so thankful that all of you girls have turned out good." Poor Mother, what has she feared for us? Drunkenness, prostitution? Certainly those ugly, filthy sins are hidden here and there in the family and, perhaps but for Mother's carefulness, we might have descended to them also.

A long letter arrived from Ted about the real estate plans. When I read it this morning I felt antagonized immediately. Re-reading it tonight I see he was trying to be fair and just, trying to assure me of his confidence. Yet nobody makes me feel quite so alone as Ted. Nobody makes me feel that my love and sympathy is thrown back as Ted. Nobody makes me feel so utterly foolish and worthless as Ted. It is best not to say what I think tonight, but if ever there was a lonesome wife in this world, it is I.

SUNDAY, SEPTEMBER 26TH.

A lovely day sent especially for me. After going to Mass we all took the bus to Bungay and from there Grace's husband, Jack, hired a fly to St. James. The Freemans were surprised to see me, but gladly showed us the place. Jack took special notice of the land and decided it was a very good farm and just the ideal one for Ted's ideas. Therefore I took his judgment, as against Herbert's, and decided to take the place. I have written to Herbert tonight asking him to come to Norwich with me one day next week and settle the business.

MONDAY, SEPTEMBER 27TH.

I was unable to sleep last night for thinking of the Halesworth farm. I caught the early train for London, stopping at the Norwich Post Office to cable Ted that I had bought the Bungay place. I cannot realize it.

I took Joan to the movies tonight, where I fell asleep as usual.

WEDNESDAY, SEPTEMBER 29TH. MICHAELMAS

At Herbert's request, I went to Romford to talk over the Halesworth place with him. He is still inclined to think it unsuitable because of not having arable land. However, when he understood my decision was made, he sat down and wrote a letter to his lawyer instructing him to get in touch with Freeman's lawyer. I hope they settle it quickly now. I have written to Freeman myself since returning.

18 Willow Lane
Norwich

SUNDAY, OCTOBER 3RD.

I am writing this in Grace's back attic. Harold is sleeping on the landing, the twins are in a single bed in the corner, and Jim and Charlie are in the bed where I am going to sleep. I brought them here last Friday.

On Thursday Mother made such a scene that I determined I wouldn't stay in Angel Road another night. When she finished rowing at Dad and me (Mother is jealous of me, I think), I spent the remainder of the night packing. Early in the morning I went out and hired a taxi to take us to Liverpool Street and sent a wire to Grace that I was bringing the children to Norwich. Before he went to work Dad asked me to remain, but I could not.

The strain of Angel Road has been intense, and after the hell of a row which Mother made, I couldn't have carried on any longer. It was one of her old style rows: violent, unreasonable, raging. I won't accept that now. It doesn't have to be tolerated and I think it is high time her violence was met with a check. I was sorry to hurt her by leaving the house so abruptly, but I did it on calm, deliberate judgment, considering it the wisest, best, and only dignified thing to do.

Grace met me at Norwich and gave me a most loving welcome. So did Jack when he came home. Tomorrow I am going to The Grange again to see Freeman about taking over the furniture. I hope to get in there within a few days. How thankful I shall be to be in my own house again! This has been a weary year indeed.

THURSDAY, OCTOBER 7TH.

Mabel writes that Mother is hurt. Very likely, but very good. Let Mother savor the hurts she distributes. I know that Dad is a faulty man, and has always been far from the pattern husband and father, but I do not remember him ever hurting me. Dad is careless and rather indifferent about his children, but Mother takes an impossible attitude towards us. She has expected perfection and then made a tragedy out of every little imperfection. A pity. A proud, domineering, suspicious, unrelenting, unreasonable, violent woman is a bane to her family and to the world. God keep me from becoming such a woman.

FRIDAY, OCTOBER 8TH.

Eleven P.M. I am in Grace's attic, the four boys are sleeping soundly, and Harold is warm and safe outside on the landing. I saw Blake, Freeman's solicitor, today. He has heard from Herbert's solicitor and is now waiting for Freeman to bring the deeds in, which he expects tomorrow. Blake says they may be able to get a contract signed early next week so that I might take possession by the end of the week. I wish that might be, but I hardly think it likely.

I have been here with Grace a week. It is an imposition on her and I do want to clear out again quickly. I shall be so deeply thankful to be in my own house again. I have only been homeless for about six months but it seems like six years. Tonight, lonesome for America.

WEDNESDAY, OCTOBER 13TH.

I called on Blake again. There is no news from my solicitor. Tiresome. This will mean that I must stay in Norwich another week. Tonight Grace went to bed early, feeling unwell. Last week she had to take a day in bed. I am afraid we Thompsons are too much for her. What a predicament it is to have to live in other people's houses. Alice Taft accepted it the nicest of any, but Mother got wild and angry, and now poor Grace gets sick. How thankful I shall be to be in my own premises once again!

I had a good letter from Ted today, which is some consolation. He speaks of staying in New York until March to make and save more money, which is quite necessary, I think. He wants to know if I could settle the children with a caretaker and take a run back to New York for a few weeks. I do not know whether I should like to or not. I might find it too hard to tear myself away from America a second time. I am lonesome for America now and feel much more American than English. I should dearly love to see Ted and the other boys, but am afraid it would be too painful to come away again. However, I will think it over.

THURSDAY, OCTOBER 14TH.

Freeman and I met in Blake's office, where they were in receipt of the contract and Herbert's ten percent deposit check. I gave Freeman another check for fifty pounds on account for his linoleum and other goods. He said I could take possession any day I liked. I decided to go tomorrow but have found it impossible. After leaving Freeman, I went to the furniture warehouse, where I have spent the remainder of the day fitting up. I cannot move in tomorrow because the furniture cannot be delivered until next week. I am so thankful this is settled at last.

The Grange
St. James, near Halesworth
Suffolk

SUNDAY, OCTOBER 17TH.

Seven-thirty P.M. I am sitting in the room that is the library, having just come downstairs from putting Charlie and Jim to bed. The twins went off at six o'clock. Freeman has cleared his dining room ready for my furniture, putting his dining room furniture into this library. I sit now at his table with Harold playing patience on it beside me. I am writing by candlelight, but queerly enough this room has a little American stove in it, burning a nice fire now, too.

I came here suddenly yesterday. The alarming news with which Grace greeted me at breakfast was that the miners *had* gone out on strike and that the railroad men were expected to go out also. Before noon I telegraphed Freeman that, on account of the strike, I was bringing the children and small baggage by the five o'clock train. It seemed the wise thing to do; the imperative thing. Such a scurry!

I went to see the furniture man and asked him to hurry my goods for me. He said he would. He also most kindly offered to send a man to take my boys and baggage to the station, which I gladly accepted. A great covered wagon drew up at Grace's door and a big fellow came in to cord-up for me. Then I not only put the boys and the baggage aboard but I climbed up myself and rode off to the station in state. We swayed and bumped over Norwich cobbles and the twinnies were greatly amused. I sat on a trunk and held Artie while Cuthie stood just behind the driver and looked over the board. It was like riding in a gypsy caravan or a prairie schooner. We caught the same train as Mr. Freeman. He was surprised to see us and did his utmost to make us comfortable. The Freemans have not vacated the premises yet, and since I have no dishes or saucepans, I cannot prepare meals. We have been sharing the Freemans' meals until I can arrange to cook for myself.

It has been a queer day today: no church, no cooking, no washing, no dish washing, and nearly no boys. They have been outside all day long. I took a good walk around this morning and all I see confirms my first judgment that this was an excellent place to buy. There is everything here that one could want, both in the house and in the grounds. I feel Ted will like it and agree I have chosen wisely. If only we can keep it now and make it pay. I am thankful to be here and I pray God to bless the place for us.

SUNDAY, OCTOBER 24TH.

Young Freeman drove us to Bungay to church. We nearly froze on the drive but found a nice little church, St. Edward's. The back of the altar is all sculpted with angels. I like it.

Tonight I could have said curses on Ted and his English farmhouse. There is no hot water and the stove in this kitchen is practically useless. It gives no heat but makes a dirty mess. Yesterday I got desperate and ordered an oil cook stove from the hardware man. After my American kitchens, with their gas stoves and electric lights, this antiquated method of housekeeping drives me crazy. I simply cannot stand the dirty mess of this kitchen range and when it won't boil the kettle, well, I feel like saying things.

WEDNESDAY, OCTOBER 27TH.

This afternoon I have had a violent cry. Freeman, according to agreement, should be out of here the end of the week. I see no signs of his going, and moreover, he has not yet bought another place.

I feel I cannot stand this life very long. The house is too big a task for me. I cannot contend with this farm any more, the country life is intolerable. I must undo the purchase of land, house, and furniture and get back to America. Ted will lose his precious money. It will either be that or I shall lose my mind and have a breakdown. I suppose I rushed into buying this presentable place because I was so wearying for a home again. I cannot stand this English life, nor the climate. I have never been really warm since I left New York. I cannot stay here. I must go back. I must go back.

FRIDAY, OCTOBER 29TH.

I am determined to go back to New York. I have wired the furniture man to delay delivery of the remaining furniture. I shall see him about canceling the undelivered articles and buying back at a reduced rate what he has delivered. He might also buy my stove, lamps, and crockery.

Since Wednesday I have thoroughly exhausted myself weeping. Now I am stiffening and getting ready to fight. I have no more tears to shed. I can't concern myself about Ted's feelings in this matter. I am too desperate to consider him. I must get back to America. Ted will hold this up to me forever as a glaring instance of my fickleness. Let him; I don't care. He knows I never wanted to come over here in the beginning. I have only tried the whole thing to please him and I can't do it. His bugaboo is consistency, but when I know I am wrong I have strength of mind enough to be inconsistent. Because a wrong road has been taken it doesn't have to be followed to the end. Ted is like the donkey who never wants to turn back. I can.

I knew I was wrong about Loretta and I terminated that adoption matter quickly. I know we are wrong about an English farm and I won't do it nor allow Ted to do it. I shall be absolutely deaf to his arguments, his pleadings, and his bad temper. I reverse right now in my tracks and make for America.

Ted dreams of being a farmer. It is a wild dream. I am not dreaming and it is up to me to look out for the family and protect it from the dangers of his insanities. It would be as much silliness for me to give Ted his way about farming as to give gunpowder and matches to the twins. So there! That's all tonight.

10 Angel Road
Hammersmith

MONDAY, NOVEMBER 1ST.

I tore up stakes at St. James. I had the furniture collected from Norwich, packed trunks, and brought the children back to Hammersmith.

TUESDAY, NOVEMBER 2ND.

I went to Romford to see Herbert about The Grange. I have stopped the final settlement. I won't pay it. I will lose the deposit if I must but I won't pay another penny. We talked all evening.

THURSDAY, NOVEMBER 4TH.

A cable arrived this morning reading:

YOU MAKE MISTAKES DISREGARDING INSTRUCTIONS.

NOW REFORM AND REMAIN.

TELEGRAPH HOW MUCH YOU LOST ON THE GRANGE.

I cabled back:

REFUSE REMAIN. BOOKED ON SAXONIA DECEMBER THIRTEENTH.

LOST 175 POUNDS.

He is wild. He may be. I am wilder. He is disappointed over the failure of a dream. I am sick with the hardships of chasing his will-o-the-wisp. Nothing that he says, feels, or does will induce me to remain in England or go farming with him in America or anywhere else in the world. I feel quite indifferent to his disappointment and to his financial losses. If he must farm, he must do it without me.

Something has snapped in me about Ted. I no longer feel I must defend myself from him. I feel absolutely unscrupulous and callous about arranging my affairs as I want them. I am determined to get back to America and I don't care how many of my promises I break, nor how many people I ride over, nor what I lose to get there. I am fighting for my life.

FRIDAY, NOVEMBER 5TH.

When I said goodnight to Dad he kissed me and said, "Goodnight, my little sweet." This tenderness quite unnerved me. It excites again all my old excessive craving to be loved. This afternoon I was thinking of love and how it vanishes. Household companionship, marriage, and child rearing are not love. I was thinking what satisfying love is there except the love of God? Love: what immense capacity I have for it and what a little measure is granted to me.

Before I went to Norwich, Joan gave me a little bundle of manuscripts which I had written when a young girl, and which she had been treasuring. It had passed from memory completely so that it was like the work of a stranger to me. I noted the old cry. It was supposed to be the reverie of a young, religious girl wondering about the beauty of the world and ending in a passionate prayer for love. "Oh God! send me love ere I die!" Literal, I suppose, but it showed me the same lack and the same desire that I suffer under now. I have always ached to be loved and am loved so little. What makes me so unlovable?

SATURDAY, NOVEMBER 6TH.

Cuthie is sick and I have had to send for the doctor. Dr. Gaff says he thinks it is only a heavy chill, but he is coming again in the morning. Tonight I am sleeping in the kitchen with Cuthie all night. He is sleeping on the sofa and I am going to try to sleep in the armchair. These English bedrooms are so very cold, I will not risk taking a sick baby into one of them.

I went to town today to see about my passport and got it viséd by the American Consul. When I got into Cavendish Square and saw the Stars and Stripes, I cried on the street. Oh God, take me back, safely, to America and re-unite my family happily there.

MONDAY, NOVEMBER 8TH.

Cuthie is very ill with pneumonia. The doctor was afraid of meningitis but, thank God, it isn't that. We can fight pneumonia. It is almost midnight and I am going to sit up with him all night again. I have Cuthie in the back down-stairs sitting room with a good fire burning. The doctor ordered a teaspoon of brandy every four hours for him. He is very low. One thing I am most glad for, that I am not still up at The Grange. Had I been, I think the child would be dead by now. Here I can get warmth and aid, but up there I should have had neither. Mother is a wonderful help in sickness. She stayed up all last night. I was all in, so Mother took the watch. I am better tonight, and more cheerful in spirit now that I know it is not the dreaded meningitis. Little Artie is perfectly well, as are the other boys.

WEDNESDAY, NOVEMBER 10TH.

Midnight. I am sitting up with Cuthie again. Doctor Gaff says his illness will not take a turn until the end of the week. He is less feverish tonight, but more fretful.

I look around this room and remember that about twenty-five years ago I was sick with pneumonia in it. In Mother's occupancy of this house, this room has alternated as bedroom and sitting room, and as I look backwards, I see that I have suffered much in it. It was in this room I was shut up with scar-let fever and it was here I suffered through brain fever, sunstroke, and diph-theria. It was in this room, used as a bedroom in 1908 and 1909, that I longed and wept for America. It is here now that I am suffering with my little Cuthie.

THURSDAY, NOVEMBER 11TH.

This is the second anniversary of Armistice Day. Today the nation buried an unknown soldier in Westminster Abbey with the king attending as chief mourner. A two minute silence was to be observed by everyone and every-thing. I was nursing my little Cuthie at that time and he was crying. He is very restless and fretful, and has cried almost incessantly since I bathed him this morning. His temperature was down to 101° today but he keeps screaming sud-denly as though he is in sharp pain. He throws his head about a lot as though that hurts him severely, and that frightens me.

The discomforts and harshness of life in this house add so unnecessarily to the burden of living. I find there isn't a comfortable chair in the house to nurse a baby in. The lights are poor, the fires dirty, and when there are no fires, the rooms are damp and cold. Then the noise and the shouting! It is frightful. The table manners are disgusting. Dad eats audibly. Mother belches wind both upwards and downwards. I have to listen to the malicious evil speaking of those who are disliked, the tittle-tattle, slander, and backbiting. Eric irritates me. He strikes me as a most obnoxious boy: sly, lazy, greedy, and shiftless. I know this may be vile natural jealousy, yet I have known many other boys, and have not disliked them as I dislike this boy.

I long for time to pass away. Seven weeks from today I will be aboard ship, but that won't be the end of my troubles. I shall have a bad ten-day voyage and, when I reach New York, I expect a bad meeting with Ted. I will get through it somehow. Tonight I feel I cannot endure things any longer. Dear God, let Cuthie sleep well, make me thankful for a warm room, and for Mother and Dad. Help me and help my baby. For Jesus' sake, Amen.

FRIDAY, NOVEMBER 12TH.

Midnight. When I look at Mother, cooking for ten, waiting on everybody, planning for everything, I feel humbled and ashamed. I allow her little mannerisms to irritate me, I criticize her and it is a shame to me.

Cuthie is slightly better today. His temperature has dropped to 99°, nearly normal. I have developed a heavy head cold and am ceaselessly bothered with neuralgia. I think it may be due to the very heavy fog here again. I had forgotten these London fogs; though today I remembered that when I booked passage to America before, it was a densely foggy day. I remember I booked at an office in Trafalgar Square, and then made, as I thought, for Charing Cross Station, only to find myself in Whitehall.

SUNDAY, NOVEMBER 14TH.

Cuthie is better today: no fever, but extremely irritable and he has no desire for food. Doctor says I need not worry about him "quite so much." He also told Mother to send me out this afternoon as I was looking very pale. I did not go out.

I have a fresh worry tonight. When I first came home, Mother told me a long story about Dad having a holiday alone in Edinburgh two or three years ago, and after coming home, developing syphilis and then contaminating her with it. She was passionately angry when she told me about it. She was vindictive and full of hatred. At the end of my first week in Angel Road, all the boys developed spots and kept getting fresh ones all the time we were here. Jim, who went up to Norwich the very first Sunday, was the only one who escaped them. After Mother's tale, I felt sick and nervous about those spots. As soon as

I got the children up to Grace's the spots began to disappear and when I brought them back here, they had entirely cleared. Tonight, as I was undressing Artie, I found a fresh batch of them on his little legs. Then at supper Dad informed the company that he was going to go to the hospital because his "old trouble" was breaking out again! Now Dad has been nursing Artie every day!! This makes me sick with suspicion and worry.

I went to Mass this morning and received Communion. One thing in this miserable year I am glad of is the renewal of my Catholic faith. I don't think I could have gotten through the year and stayed sane without it.

It is possible, though rare, to transmit syphilis through household contact or kissing. It is more likely the children had contracted scabies.

MONDAY, NOVEMBER 22ND.

Mother told me her family history today and I want to include it in this book.

About 1800 there was a family named Thompson doing business as corn factors in Birmingham and Wolverhampton. One of the daughters married a man named Walford and had a daughter, Hannah. Mother has a framed sampler hanging on the drawing room wall which is the work of Hannah Walford, 1798. This Hannah, when an adult, was a woman of independent means and married a soldier *off the strength* of the army. This means that the marriage was not sanctioned by headquarters and that no allowance was ever made for the wife. She, however, having money, followed the regiment wherever it went. The soldier's name was Joe Beates. He was Irish and most handsome. In 1840 the regiment was about to embark but Hannah Walford Beates had to remain in lodgings at Pinner, to be confined. She was delivered of a daughter, Mary Ann, whom she left at Pinner whilst she went on to join her husband. The regiment went to Ireland but Mary Ann was left at the Pinner cottage and was not paid for. The cottagers, being too poor to keep the child and having a family of their own, decided to put the infant in the workhouse. This stirred the pity of a childless couple, William and Eliza Searle, who lived two doors away, and offered to take the child. They adopted her and brought her up as their own. Early in 1842 the Beateses returned to Pinner to look for the child left there in 1840. (What loving parents!) The Searles did not want to surrender the child, and as Hannah was about to be confined again, she was quite willing to leave little Mary Ann to the Searles. She traveled on to Birmingham to the Thompsons, the corn factors, and was delivered of another daughter, Maria. Maria was left with the Walford grandparents and Hannah and her soldier, Joe, departed gaily once again. However, very soon after this Hannah died, and that was the end of her.

Meanwhile, little Mary Ann Beates was being brought up as Polly Searle, and was idolized by William and Eliza.

William Searle was one of a large family at Cadbury, Devonshire, who came to London as a youth and joined the police. He married Eliza Rice, also a Cadbury woman. William was the police sergeant at Pinner, the place where the gay wife of the careless Irish soldier happened to have stayed for her delivery. The Searles were particularly thrifty and go-ahead and, one by one, the remainder of the Searle family came to London to try their fortunes, always making William Searle their pattern, and his house their headquarters. To them came John Searle, a lad of seventeen. This young John was a nephew of William and Eliza. He also joined the police and in 1860 he married Mary Ann Beates.

These two, John and Mary Ann Searle, were my maternal grandparents. Their first child, William (my Uncle Will Searle), was born in 1861; their second child, Eliza Alice (my mother), was born in 1863, and these children were always taught to call William and Eliza Searle grandma and grandpa. All this time, William and Eliza had kept in touch with the Walfords at Birmingham and had heard of little Maria, though the two sisters had never met. When Polly married John Searle and came to London, she sent for her sister and Maria joined them in Chiswick where John, now police inspector, was living in the police station. Maria set up a sweet shop in Glenthorne Road and that is the end of her for just now. I know her story, but it has nothing to do with this one of Grandpa and Grandma's, which is mine.

About the time John married Polly, William developed "chalk gout" (whatever that is!) and resigned from the force. He and Eliza left Pinner and came to London also. They "took a beer house" (something different from a public house, but I don't know in what way) near the new Metropolitan Railway works, which was just being built. Enterprising Eliza then took in lodgers and rented all the rooms to the men working on the new railway. She gave them beds on her top floors, cooked meals for them in her kitchens, and entertained them in her taproom at night. Mother says she can remember the taproom well, and can hear the noises of the dominoes now. Eliza must have extracted pretty nearly the entire wages of the men who came to her. She began to collect money and to lend it.

At this time there was a certain jerry builder, named Petter, who was always in difficulties for lack of ready money, and he used to come to Mrs. Eliza for loans to pay his weekly wages bill. In this way, Eliza began to get interested in real estate and to take up mortgages. When Petter couldn't repay in gold, he would repay in a house, so that gradually Mrs. Eliza began to pick up little shops and houses all over this western neighborhood. She had them in Notting Hill, in Latimer Road, in Brook Green, in Hammersmith, in Fulham, in Chiswick, and in Uxbridge Road, besides owning many shares in the National Freehold and Building Association.

I was the person who could have inherited the whole fortune had my fa-

ther only condescended to name me after her, Eliza. My mother was her favorite "grandchild" and she had intended to leave everything to my mother;
only Mother offended her deeply when she married my father, so she was dis-
inherited. When I was born, the old lady relented, came to see Mother, and
told her she would leave me everything if they would call me Eliza. My father,
a hotheaded youth, enraged in his dignity, said he would see her damned first,
and forthwith christened me Ruby. So that was the end of that affair.

As for the money, the old lady carefully split it up so nobody got much,
but all got a little. She left it to Grandpa Searle (John) and to his children, and
to Will Searle's boy (Cousin Will Searle). I got nothing. Mother got three
houses in Notting Hill. Mother tells me today that Eliza left nothing personally to my grandmother, the little Polly she adopted, and that Grandma was
always hurt about it.

Midnight. I have discovered why Mother gave me this rigamarole today.
She wants to claim credit for our brains. I missed one point of the story, which
was the telling of how the four brothers and four sisters Searle came to
London and *all* made their fortunes. According to Mother, they must have
had brains, education, and ambition. She is proud of the old Searle family set
back in Devon in the 1700s. She says the father was the village schoolmaster
and her great grandfather was the organist of the village of Cadbury. She instances the musical ability which has descended to Julius Searle and his
daughter, Maud; the brains of her brother Will, which developed in engineer-
ing; and the cleverness of her daughters. "It is a sure thing you don't get your
brains from your father's family," she says. So Mother has one positive satisfaction in life. She is proud of her daughters.

TUESDAY, NOVEMBER 23RD.

I am making resolutions today about the future. Now that my mind is settled
and plans are definitely laid about returning to America, my depression is beginning to lift. All these months I have felt so old and heavy, but today I begin
to feel I am not so old after all. I have given Ted love and service for fifteen
years and I am ready to give more as long as I live. If he won't accept it, I can't
make him, but I will not allow his attitude towards me make me miserable. I
cannot give him his English farm life, but if he is going to turn me down and
cease loving me, he will be a fool and the loser. Here I am: not ugly, only
thirty-six, easily made happy, affectionate, ardent, ready to make a comfortable home and ready to be happy with him. If he turns his back and goes into
his shell, he is an idiot and that's all.

FRIDAY, NOVEMBER 26TH.

I took Harold and Jim to Romford to stay until Sunday. Then I went straight to Herbert's office to see if my furniture had been delivered there. I brought away for myself the china dressing table set and the little yellow egg cups. Freeman's solicitors are threatening writs, but I cannot be served because I never signed the contract. Herbert signed as agent for Ted, so he cannot be served, and Ted's address is unknown, so he can't be served. Herbert has moved our money into his account so officially Ted has no money in England. Freeman bought The Grange for five hundred pounds, so he is not going to let us escape if he can possibly help it. I feel quite unscrupulous about Freeman. I don't care a farthing about his disappointment. I am out of the place and glad of it. Soon I will be out of England and gladder still.

SATURDAY, NOVEMBER 27TH.

I received a very curt letter from Ted. Also one from each boy, which I can see he has directly inspired. I am sorry for the poor boys. They have had a hard deal left on their own with Ted in a New York tenement. It has been hard for the poor chaps to cook, to wash, and to keep house. I am most anxious to have them under my wing again. I may have trouble with Ted. This is a very ugly letter. I can almost feel the hatred and cold anger in it. I am sure I have done the right thing, and he cannot make me feel a criminal about it.

WEDNESDAY, DECEMBER 1ST.

I have been sorting and re-packing my crates today. I did a lot of this work last week also. Sonnie is coming on Saturday to nail them up for me. I packed up a few tears along with the baggage.

THURSDAY, DECEMBER 2ND.

This week Mother is particularly nervous and irritable. The children get on her nerves dreadfully and then she shouts and scolds and it is Bedlam. Poor Mother has no business being bothered with my children. We are an imposition here. Thank God we are into our last month and in a few weeks we shall have started home. What trouble I shall find when I get there, I dread to imagine. I cannot write about Ted's letters. I shall tie them up and put them away with this book. When I am old I may re-read them, but now they are too painful.

It looks as if I have hurt Ted beyond healing. Sometimes I weep for it and sometimes I take satisfaction in it, feeling as though at last I have paid him back for all the bitter heartaches he has made me suffer for years and years. But I am sore of heart and troubled in mind. I do love him and I want him to love me. Why do we chafe and wound each other? It is foolishness. If only we could make an entirely fresh beginning, then there might be hope for us.

FRIDAY, DECEMBER 3RD.

This afternoon I bought a pudding basin and two cake pans. The basin is to have a Christmas pudding put into it for me to take back to America. The cake pans are to have shortbread baked in them to carry home. I enter these silly purchases here so that fifty years hence, when one of my grandchildren reads this record, she can see the all-round silly woman her ancestress was. Here I am, in spite of the tangle of my life, buying pudding basins and cake pans!

MONDAY, DECEMBER 6TH.

I have had American letters this morning. One from Mrs. Tidmarsh, saying Ted had spent Thanksgiving with her and they had discussed our affairs. She wants me to write and tell her my reasons and troubles and then, if I am not *too* unreasonable, she will take my side in the case! Thanks!

Ted's letter is harsh and insulting. He writes that he can "rely" on my good judgment in connection with Cuthie and his illness. Ted crossed out rely and substituted "hope." One of his letters last week said he was afraid it was too much to hope that I should be kind to the boys. What unnecessary unkindness! I am not the kind of wife he likes, but I am not deliberately a bad mother.

Then he goes on to suggest that I shouldn't write to my friends because they all criticize me, even Mrs. Nighman. Well of course people are talking and criticizing me. Deliver me from my friends, then. I think of Mrs. Hewetson, who always seemed without friends and so aloof. I wonder what miserable experience taught her not to give her confidence to anyone? Doesn't old Julia Howe somewhere recommend that we should give courtesy to all and intimacy to none?

THURSDAY, DECEMBER 9TH.

I went to Romford to get my last supply of money, and received good news from Herbert, who had a cable from Ted to remit his money to New York. From this I conclude that Ted must have found a house and needs the money to make a purchase. This would mean I have a house of my own to go to, and how thankful I should be for that. I never want to be a staying visitor again.

Herbert and Tillie were talking with me about Ted and his extreme fads: cold baths, cold air, thin clothing, and vegetarianism. Herbert said Ted was always an extremist. He spoke of Ted's extremes in religion. Suddenly I saw Ted for the everlasting crank that he is. I won't let his cranks and fads upset my daily life anymore. I had tried to fall in line with him, but it can't be done. I shall let him pursue his fads alone, but I'll train my boys to be normal men.

Tillie is Herbert (Bert) Thompson's wife. Their children are Bertie and Selma.

SUNDAY, DECEMBER 12TH.

Snow in England, which I had not expected to see.

I have been thinking over some of the remarks of outsiders about Ted. Herbert said Ted had always been a crank. Thomlinson once said I took Ted too seriously. Mrs. Hewetson once asked me if Ted was ever cross at home. She told me that when her Henry was cross she never paid any attention to him, because if he couldn't be cross in his own house, where could he be cross? She added that he had to be good tempered all day at business and if he couldn't let off his anger safely at home, what was a poor fellow to do? She advised me to pay no attention to a cross husband and not to worry myself about him.

FRIDAY, DECEMBER 17TH.

A letter came from the Cunard Company saying that *Saxonia*'s sailing has been delayed until January fourth. I have taken it hard. Where and how am I to screw up the extra patience and endurance for those five extra days?

SUNDAY, DECEMBER 19TH.

After Mass and a hurried dinner, I went off to the Tate Gallery with Joan, Harold, and Jim. It was a very dark afternoon so we couldn't see much. When we came out we walked up the Embankment to Westminster and Whitehall. We saw the Cenotaph. It was banked high up at its base with flowers, nearly all wreaths having cards attached, a most pathetic sight.

*The **Cenotaph** is a monument in Whitehall, London, erected in honor of English soldiers lost in World War I.*

SATURDAY, DECEMBER 25TH. CHRISTMAS.

Harold and I both received Communion at midnight Mass. I went to High Mass at noon, again, and to my immense surprise, Dad came with me. Joan came too.

Mother planned a family party for today with Gladys, Sonnie and Mabel, Aileen and William coming to dinner.

I received a most biting letter from Ted this morning, but on the whole, a good day.

1921

MONDAY, JANUARY 3RD.

My last English Day.

I met Vi at Charing Cross and had lunch with her at the old Florence Restaurant. Then we went over to the office and saw some of my old coworkers: Miss Annie Moore, Gertrude Hall, and Edith Duncan. It was pleasant to see them again.

There were more visitors in Angel Road when I returned, and Mother planned a farewell supper.

This time tomorrow my boys and I will be somewhere out in the Channel. At last the time is finished. Trouble is waiting for me in New York, but I would rather be unhappy in America than unhappy in England. I am weary and depressed, but whatever my personal life may be, still my American life attracts me. I like America best.

Ted is miserable and loathes me. Surely all the good and all the happiness there was in our first fifteen years will not be all destroyed by last year's folly. I pray for a good understanding with Ted and for a good new life.

Here another volume of the journals seems to be missing. The previous entry was written in January 1921, as Ruby was about to return to the States from England. She starts again in November of 1921, without mention of an absence from her writing. During that time Ruby and the sons who were in England have returned to the States and the reunited family has bought a home in Tenafly, New Jersey. In an attempt to appease Ted, Ruby is more seriously involved with the Catholic Church than ever before.

523 Knickerbocker Road
Tenafly, New Jersey

TUESDAY, NOVEMBER 1ST.

A year ago today I left The Grange and returned to my mother's house at Hammersmith. Now here I am firmly settled at Tenafly, New Jersey.

It is waning afternoon as I write. Presently, I want to go down the hill to the village, to get my Aquascutum coat from the tailor with whom I left it days ago for alterations. I wanted to have it altered, the fullness taken out of it, in Hammersmith, but Mother wouldn't let me, on the theory that you can't have too much of a good thing. But it was too heavy for comfort and I shall get along better with less of it.

SUNDAY, NOVEMBER 6TH.

In the night, after his satisfaction, Ted said, "There is only the body left for us now, isn't there?" I answered nothing, struck dumb by his tongue, as so often before. But this fact, if it is a fact, I do not know if it is good or bad. Sometimes I think, well, as long as we have that, it is something, I am worth something. Other times I am swept with revulsion, because if that is all that remains, I could do without it. If that is all he wants, it would be kinder to purchase it elsewhere. Oh, marriage, this hateful trap.

Tonight discussion came up as to English versus American traits. Ted, as usual, was belittling the Americans and I was standing up for them. I got cross. So silly. I don't have to fight the Americans' battles for them. Why can't I let Ted continue in his ideas that the Americans are inferior people to the British, and keep quiet, keep the peace? This is like so many of our differences. They are all about things that don't matter to us an iota.

MONDAY, NOVEMBER 7TH.

I have been thinking about religion again. Charles Voysey has long been dust, but Charles Voysey influenced my life for good more than any person that has entered it. The Catholic Church alternately attracts and repels me but I have never accepted it in its entirety. The idea of God that Voysey gave me, the idea of a personal and loving God who loved me, and to whom I could go for any help, for sustenance; this God lies forever at the bottom of my mind and soul. From time to time these memories well up and flood me. Then Jesus Christ fades away. The whole Christian story and scheme drops into limbo. I find God the Father.

I don't care how psychologists might explain it, charging it to my adolescence, and so on. I know that the conception of God that Voysey held is the only conception I have ever really accepted.

Ah me, this question of religion again.

TUESDAY, NOVEMBER 15TH.

I am writing at the red desk in the kitchen, Harold is behind me at the table doing home-lessons, all the rest of the boys abed, and Ted at a meeting. Quiet with only the kettle singing on the stove and the wind faintly moaning in the chimney.

I went to town today and extravagantly bought four books. I must have books; they are my only outlet, my only company. Saturday Mrs. Whitaker, exhorting me to study astronomy, spoke of the friendliness of the stars to her in her isolation. To that lonely woman astronomy is a diversion; to this lonely woman, philosophy.

WEDNESDAY, NOVEMBER 16TH.

I have just come in from the garden where I was hanging up my morning's wash. I have a large pan of ironing waiting for me but I am tired and shall not begin it till after lunch. John is at home with a toothache and is upstairs with the twins. On Monday I had to take him to a dentist, who gave him gas and extracted four six-year molars. The boy has been unwell and suffering ever since, so I am keeping him out of school for a few days.

My mind is incessantly running upon Ted and our domestic situation. Ted talks of economy. I think we have practiced too much economy and his economy is rapidly developing into stinginess. The other night he said we shall have saved two thousand dollars this year, and that next year we ought to save four thousand. But what good is that to me? Always I have to ask even for the house money two or three times a week. As to personal money, I have none. Even little Charlie has a dollar and a nickel every week, but I get nothing. What personal oddments I want I have to squeeze out of the kitchen money. A situation like this is simply galling to a woman.

I think Ted has driven me further away from him this week than ever before. You cannot love a person who won't let you love him. He is a peculiar person. I try to imagine his home and his parents. He has told me that every night they had family prayers, and every child had to pray aloud, *ex tempore*. They were strict and pious and puritanical and Ted took their stamp. Then I think of my own family, with everything so different: passionate parents, with religion in the discard, but excited about art and literature and poetry and politics, the theater and music.

I suppose only the certified respectable went to the Thompsons'. To our home came all kinds of people, from clergy down to mountebanks and prostitutes. Why, whenever I think of Kitty Abbot a little glow of remembered love goes through me. So, then, how can I be censorious, puritanical? I cannot. I can remember with pleasure many people who were absolutely outside the pale of respectability and religion. We all are as we are. I have a tolerance for those who are "sinful" that, to Ted, is incomprehensible, reprehensible; and he has a coldness and a narrowness that irks me nearly to madness.

So it is the old story: Marriage is a lottery and only one in a thousand can draw a prize. But once married we have to stay married, and I suppose peace and balance of mind comes when we can ignore the suffering in the personal relationship and see only the economic aspects and the safeguarding of the family. If we were all rich, or if we had no children, we could separate, and torment each other no more. As it is we must stay together till death us do part. The hard thing to do is to cease looking to each other for personal love and happiness. We have had such dreams of love and marriage it is hard to acknowledge that, after all, marriage is a snare, and that life must be lived in spiritual isolation.

Kitty Abbot was a friend of Ruby's parents.

SUNDAY, DECEMBER 4TH.

Ted and I spent the day in White Plains with the Bowes. When we got back home we found the house in a state of wreck. The boys had let everything go for the new snow and evidently had had fights both indoors and out. I found potatoes scattered in my bedroom and the top hall! I set to and cleared up the kitchen, made tea and sandwiches, got rid of the boys, and Ted and I enjoyed the papers in late leisure and peace.

I have been very unwell all week: neuralgia, backache, headache, toothache, leg-ache. I also have a great throbbing, a feeling of blood pressure behind my ears, which is distressing me.

The twins are little imps of mischief. This morning they got up on the dining room table, unscrewed the light bulbs, and broke all four of them. This afternoon, in the kitchen, they got at the flour bin and scattered flour all over the newly scrubbed floor. They drive me mad.

Now I am waiting for the water to boil to make tea for Harold, who has chills.

This afternoon I went to Englewood to the movies with Eddie. George Arliss, playing Disraeli: very good. Passing by the cemetery in the trolley, I noticed many little graves that looked like children's, decorated with bunches of bright red flowers, for Christmas, I suppose. That scene brought back memories of my mother going to the children's graves at Brompton. She used to take me with her, it seemed often. I had particular pleasure in running along the colonnade beside the mausoleums, and looking at the figures on the monuments. But today I was set to wondering what Mother's thoughts had been. She was always having babies, and losing them. Was it pleasure or pain for her to go to their little graves? To lose a little child: This is a grief I have never had.

This morning I washed a big tubful of clothes and finished the ironing. I also made a batch of raisin bread and two fruit cakes.

There was devastation in the chicken run today. The Smith's dog, Scotti, got in and killed four leghorns and wounded five others. Johnnie is very upset about it. "And besides, Mother," he said, "he's scared all the rest of the hens, and you don't know *what* damage he's done. Maybe he's spoiled their egg-systems!"

Eleven A.M. The house is clean, the big cooking is done, I have a quiet day. That is, as quiet as it can be with all the boys at home. In the night the temperature moderated and snow fell, and is still falling, which makes the boys jubilant. A white Christmas is their desire. They are now harnessing Dan to the big wagon, so as to go down to the village to shop. Not that the shopping matters to them, they are just simply wild to get out in the snow.

Three P.M. Johnnie reports that Dan fell three times going down the hill and twice coming up. Poor old horse. This is a brute of a hill but today, covered with icy snow, that hill must be awful. John says an automobile had skidded into the ditch halfway down.

I want a letter from Dad. I am thinking of him often, of the times when I was a little child and he must have been a young man, of him taking me walking the tracks to his cottage office. On our way we went to scores of places and met all sorts of different people. I am listing them in my mind. And as I look back I see how fond he must have been of me. He never took any of his other children about as he took me, never talked to them as he talked to me. Dear old Dad, passionate, selfish, a most un-model-like husband and father. And yet how much he gave me. He showed me the historical world I lived in and he showed me the way into the imaginary world that has no end. I wish I could make a story of it all. I think of Mother, passionate too, but passionate about persons and personalities. Dad was only passionate about the impersonal things, intangible things like art and literature, actors and politics. They are another pair who could never understand each other, another pair dissatisfied, unsatisfied. What *is* wrong with marriage that so few people can find it tolerable? Common courtesy will make daily living tolerable. But what heart is satisfied with courtesy any more than justice?

SATURDAY, DECEMBER 31ST.

All the boys, except the twins, sat up to see the New Year in, their first time. I served them hot cocoa and cake at eleven and they thought they were having a party.

1922

THURSDAY, JANUARY 5TH.

I finished reading *The Memoirs of a Midget* [Walter de la Mare]. Aileen sent it to me for a Christmas gift and wrote that she liked it so much. I can't see why. To me it is a nightmare, horrid. Another thing; if this kind of writing *is* writing, then I can't write and never shall be able to. This was wordy, involved, allusive, elusive, is hard reading and yields very little. It is clever, without doubt, and fresh, but nasty. Yet if it is the kind of book that sells, then the straightforward narratives I could offer would never find buyers.

I suppose in the future, if any literary granddaughter of mine should trouble herself to go through these "memoirs," she will exclaim: "Poor silly old gal! Always aspiring to write and never turning out anything except these ludicrous diaries. Old muff!"

Sometimes I am inclined to make a bonfire of all my diaries. It would probably be much better for my abiding reputation (if any of it abides) if I did. But I refrain. If I made a clean sweep of every word I have written today, I know I should only begin writing again tomorrow. I have to write. And I know I am inconsistent and I suppose all my world knows it very well too, even without my diaries to convict me by.

FRIDAY, JANUARY 13TH.

Last night, after the last boy had gone to bed, Ted invited me to sit by the fire. I knew this meant he wanted to talk. After awhile in silence, Ted began to speak of the Schaefers. "Have I ever told you," he asked, "what strange resemblances there are between me and Schaefer: in our ideas, and even in our circumstances?" He hadn't, and he went on: "The resemblance is carried even further, in the likeness between our wives. You two women think alike, accuse us of the same things. Schaefer showed me a couple of his wife's letters today and it was like reading your letters of last year. It was uncanny. I have often thought that Mrs. Schaefer was so like you; you think alike about life, and art, and morals, and conduct, and so forth. But when it comes to writing, the likeness is most striking. Her letters might have been *yours*."

I have only met Mrs. Schaefer twice and both visits must have been at least seven years ago. I feel I don't know the woman at all, but Ted knows her much better, from staying with them at Manitou. He told me he wanted to get my ideas on their story, in hopes, he said, that we might get some solution to our own problem, some light as to what is wrong with ourselves.

Briefly, the story is this. Mrs. Schaefer disliked the country life at Manitou, and he and she were at such general loggerheads that he agreed to her suggestion that she should take their boy and go to Europe for awhile, which she did, in 1920. (I remember, when I wrote to Ted how much I disliked England, he wrote back that Mrs. Schaefer was in Europe and liked it immensely; in fact, so much that she did not want to come back to America. I felt sore at that comparison because she was a rich woman living in hotels and with only one grown boy to take care of, whereas I had five little children with me, not nearly so much money, and was living about in relatives' houses.) Ted says now that Schaefer has been supplying her with fifteen hundred dollars a month to spend. Well, she settled in Rome and put the boy in the Methodist College there. Then Schaefer heard reports that she was flirting with other men and he went off to see her. This was this fall. Then, while he was in Rome, a young Italian officer shot himself, leaving letters to say it was because of Mrs. S. and because she wouldn't live with him. She went to see his body in the morgue! The whole affair was in the newspapers and Schaefer himself was in Rome at the time. However, she denies that she misbehaved or was unfaithful to her husband, but will not admit she was wrong in going about with men, or that she is sorry for doing so. This is what makes Schaefer so sore and hurt. Ted says that Schaefer doesn't think she is guilty, but he can't tolerate her not seeing that she could in any way be to blame, and not being sorry for her conduct. Now they are talking of arranging a divorce and Schaefer is looking to Ted for advice.

To Ted, our similarity lies in our stubbornness and blindness in not admitting we can be wrong. Mrs. Schaefer as regards her conduct with men; and me as regards my conduct about England and The Grange. But the crux of this lies deeper than instances. To Ted, and to Schaefer, I suppose, it is our mental attitude that is inexplicable. Well, it is and it isn't.

"Look at Schaefer," says Ted. "A good man, kind, generous, straight; what else can she want? She says he is self-opinionated, which is what you say of me. She dislikes the country, but he never made her spend the winter there. He has given her expensive jewelry, liberty to go abroad. What more does she want?"

"And she," said Ted, "A well-meaning woman, intelligent, clever, well-educated. But she says that 'she can't live her own life.' That's like you with your separate bank account. Like you said last night, that you have never really become Mrs. Thompson, like the women who, though married, want to keep their maiden names. What do *you* think is wrong? Why are women so dissatisfied? Where do men fall short? It is pitiable. I see it everywhere. Two good-living, well-intentioned people, and yet they cannot live happily together! What is the trouble?"

We spoke of other couples that we knew and their difficulties. "But aren't the *women* wrong?" asked Ted. I was able to admit that they are, but they can't help it. It is the times that are against them. "Feminism!" scorns Ted. Yes, it is feminism. The conditions of marriage have changed, changed in our time, but only for the woman. The man regards marriage as all his forefathers have regarded it; but the woman, no. It is not the same to her as even to her own mother. Marriage is no longer the sole career for women. Although women's ideas of marriage have changed, marriage has not changed, and so long as women will not accept it, so long they will be miserable in it.

So with me, and Mrs. Schaefer, and all the women of our time like us. Marriage was simply the consummation of a love affair: not a sacrament. We did not feel we were giving our lives away, and all the time we were. As the years pass we fight to get our lives back, our educated girlish lives. I am no longer Ruby Side, but I am Ruby Thompson, loath though I am to admit it. But I must admit it. Back in the summer, Ted said, "I always feel that you are against me." It was true. I suppose I have always been trying to keep my precious personal identity. I'll try not to do it anymore. I'll try to merge into him, into my family. I want to make him happy.

SATURDAY, JANUARY 14TH.

I received a letter from Joanie today, saying that on Christmas Day Dad gave his consent for her to come to me; but with the postscript, dated December 30th, saying that Sonnie's wife died that day. Mabel and Sonnie were to have spent Christmas Day at Mother's, but Mabel was taken ill with pneumonia and had to be removed to the hospital. Poor Sonnie. Mabel was a lovable and good, unselfish woman. I am glad I knew her.

FRIDAY, JANUARY 20TH.

Last year this time we landed in New York, so it is a year since we got back. At that time Ted met me with kindness, enfolded me with ardor, said he was giving me a second honeymoon, better than the first. Last night he said everything was finished between us. I think it is. He says he knows I am trying to please him but he can't be pleased. He says he knows he ought really to be thankful to me for affording him the occasion of abjection, but he can't be. *That* talk makes me shiver. He says that because of his bad feeling towards me he has to stay away from Communion, so his spiritual decline also is my fault. He says I have killed every refined sentiment he ever possessed, and that he is miles beneath the man he was twenty years ago, before he knew me. *That* talk makes my blood run backwards. I think this is spiritual conceit and selfishness that is colossal. I realize I have been a selfish woman in a thousand ways, but I don't think I should or could ever accuse another human being of corrupting my soul.

We talked from two o'clock until nearly six this morning, horrible, heartbreaking talk. Today I am dazed. He had no special complaint. I had done nothing definite to annoy him, only to be myself. How can I combat his attitude of mind? He says he knows I am trying to please him.

I am tired. My head aches. It is five o'clock and the twins need their supper. Good-bye, friend book.

SATURDAY, JANUARY 21ST.

I have just done my last job for the day and am sitting down for the first time today. I have been sweeping, cooking, baking, ironing, all of it standing work. Now my back feels ready to snap and I can feel my ankle freshly broken open. But in my spirit I am lighter. While thinking over my ironing today, wishing some wise outsider could shake us and sort us, something suddenly said to me, "You mustn't both be crazy." It was as though my crumples got ironed out. I'll just try and be normal, to keep sane. I am going down right now to sit in the parlor with him. I'll darn and if he wants to talk, I'll talk.

THURSDAY, FEBRUARY 2ND.

Last week I sent to Macy's for a book advertised as one that, "Should find favor with that large class of Catholics in the outside world who aim at reproducing in themselves the cloister virtues: humility, docility, patience, generosity, fortitude, and self-sacrifice." It has not yet been delivered, but I wish it would come, for if ever a woman needed advice on these virtues, I need it urgently! I am so alone. My children are company but they are not companions. My friends are far away. My husband, at best, is indifferent. All I have are my books and a pen.

Last night when Ted came in I tried to talk to him, but he would not talk. I inquired about his meeting but he replied perfunctorily and shortly. He did not want to speak to me nor be bothered listening to me. He undressed and sat up in bed and smoked a cigar before putting out the light. We might have been the world apart. In the darkness I lay and thought how love and happiness are delusions, only knowing that doesn't help any. But being sorry for myself won't help either. I've got to have fortitude.

Yesterday I was singing in memory "Just as I Am," "With One Plea," and "Jesus, Lover of My Soul." The great favorites of my childhood. But today I can't sing them. Today I am dazed. I don't think I have another tear left to weep. I can only have good intention.

SATURDAY, FEBRUARY 4TH.

This afternoon I took the trolley into Englewood, and went to confession in the church there. I felt secure and unknown and was able to speak freely and plainly and fully about my troubles. I have tried to get help in the confessional here in the Tenafly church but, because I only spoke generally, was misunderstood and got no help.

Today the priest happened to be sympathetic and, although much of his counsel is only what I have been counseling myself, still it was enheartening and steadying. I have come home feeling calmed, almost happy. "Patience, patience, patience," was what he said.

TUESDAY, FEBRUARY 7TH.

True love is everlasting.

With me, when Ted says he has not a particle of regard left for me, he turns all my past life with him to ashes, for I think then he never loved me. Only I can't believe it. I swallow my pride. On Saturday, the priest said, "Do not hide your own love and esteem for your husband. Behave as usual. Show your love." This is what I determined a couple of weeks ago: Go on as usual, loving and expecting to be loved.

MONDAY, FEBRUARY 13TH.

I am feeling crotchety today. The boys and the weather are on my nerves. The boys are all on holiday today for Lincoln's birthday, and there are too many of them around. Our boys collect all the neighborhood boys. There are about a score of them outside now.

TUESDAY, FEBRUARY 14TH. ST. VALENTINE'S DAY.

I want to find alleviation for my varicose veins, and generally to improve my health and strength. I live a laborious life but, I suppose, no more so than any other mother of a large family. I seem to tire quicker than other women. I want to do things. I want to enjoy my youth while it remains. I suppose the best years for a woman lie between twenty and fifty. Well, I shall be thirty-eight at Easter, so I ought to have another twelve years of modern youth and activity before me. I don't want to be crippled with these swollen and irritating veins if I can improve my condition. The Christian Scientists assert that they overcome maladies by prayer and right-thinking, and I think the earnest ones do. Then why not Catholics? Is this where the saints help? At any rate, I am going to try and help myself in this matter. I think Dr. Walsh has written a book on religion and health, and the next time I go to town I'll try to find it. It might be helpful and probably costs no more than a prescription.

WEDNESDAY, FEBRUARY 15TH.

I lack sleep. I am slow to fall asleep when I go to bed because my legs and ankles itch so much. I could give a ransom for a couple of nights of ten hours of solid sound restful sleep.

I am extra weary tonight from the fact of having had the boys all home and in the house all day. There is a blizzard and they could not go to school. But, oh how they get on my nerves. Their silly giggling, their sillier quarreling, their rough-housing, their penetrating voices, their general boyishness, how exhausting it all is. This place was Pandemonium and I myself presiding Lady Beelzebena. I am getting up to my last job now: put clean sheets on Charlie's bed in place of those he vomited over last night. If ever there was a woman who *wasn't* designed to be a mother!

WEDNESDAY, MARCH 1ST. ASH WEDNESDAY.

The first of the month and Ted has instituted early rising for the boys so that all can get an hour of work, between six and seven, before breakfast.

THURSDAY, MARCH 2ND.

Loneliness. That is what I have got to face and conquer.

Last night I asked Ted if he would come to the evening service with me.

He thought a minute and then refused. When the taxi came I thought he might change his mind but he did not. Mrs. Faley was in the car and I sat with her at church. It was hard not to cry. When I got home again, the boys were upstairs and Ted was reading. He did not say one word to me.

My life is becoming well nigh intolerable. For months Ted has never given me a name. He speaks at me. Things have been getting worse between us steadily for months. He is miserable and he makes me miserable. But I am getting more than miserable: I am getting angry. I am coming to a point beyond where I want patience and religion and resignation; I am coming to where I want freedom. Oh, to be free! When I suffer as I did last night I know it is only the little children that hold me to him. But for them I should go. As I lay wakeful last night, I thought of all the years behind us and grew angrier and angrier. I have been a fool, but surely not so much a fool as he. When I married I had the freak ideas of my time. I was a woman looking for love and happiness. I look back over all these years of ridicule and contention, never sympathy, tenderness, understanding, companionship. Oh, the struggle of it all.

SUNDAY, MARCH 12TH.

Twice in the night I awakened to find myself sobbing. It seems the tears I refuse to shed in the day weep themselves against my will when I sleep. This morning my lids were swollen and my lips have been painful all day. I must have bitten them in my dreams.

The differences the years bring. In the first year or two, after my marriage, I used sometimes to waken weeping in the night, dreaming of the pain of leaving home. Ted used to wake me and comfort me. Last night he never gave a sign.

I pray for indifference. An armor of indifference.

SATURDAY, MARCH 25TH.

It is really spring-like today. The children were outside practically all day. Eddie was busy on the roof doing something about setting up a wireless radiograph he is making.

Last week I went to the Englewood High School to hear a reading of John Drinkwater's "*Abraham Lincoln*." I got there early and watched all those boys and girls filing into the auditorium, chattering, laughing, careless, carefree, happy. My heart ached, for in a few years they will be carrying the cares of the world.

Last Wednesday night at the parish church there was a sermon on the sacrament of Extreme Unction. It only confirmed my conviction that *I* shall never make a death-bed confession. Never. I simply don't believe in that. It is the devil. I don't believe in the devil. I don't believe in confession.

I try to believe. I have little flashes of belief. But underneath, all the time, I am the same as I have always been: a theist, never a Christian. So in the Christian literature, what is it I fasten on? When the writers preach of God, I am attracted. When they preach of Christ, I am dull. Jesus Christ has never been real to me, not real as Voysey made God. I try to believe. Actually, truly, I am afraid I have never believed. I wish I could stop worrying about this subject, take it casually. Although Ted cannot know it, it is my resolution to *observe* Catholicism with him. Thank goodness there is no radio yet invented to detect what I think.

SUNDAY, MARCH 26TH.

I had to go to bed yesterday because of profuse and exhausting menstruation. But I'm glad, *glad*. I was beginning to be just a little afraid I had conceived again and how I should hate that. As things are now with Ted and me, I would rather die than have another child. I am going to bed now with a contented mind about my physical condition.

FRIDAY, APRIL 14TH. GOOD FRIDAY.

I have been spring cleaning. A new departure for me as there has always been some Vera or Bertha to do it. All at once in the new spring sunshine the house began to look mussy so I pitched in to the scouring. I have washed all the windows, curtains, paint, pictures, and bric-a-brac. I have swept all the walls and ceilings and polished all the floors and the furniture. My hands now are like boiled dough, but I've enjoyed it. It has cleared the cobwebs out of my brain and that is the best housecleaning of all.

I have been to town for the Easter shopping. I intended to buy a suit, but would not buy anything I saw. The skirts are narrower than ever and still too short. I simply won't wear such clothes. I have taken my roll of Indian cloth to a Tenafly tailor to have a suit made.

Whilst in town I bought a number of books. I have been longing for Dickens, so have bought *David Copperfield, Our Mutual Friend,* and *Dombey and Son.* I also got Dr. Copeland's new book on weight reduction and the Elizabeth Cady Stanton biography and letters, just out.

TUESDAY, APRIL 18TH.

The birthdays, thirty-eight for me, sixteen for Eddie. To celebrate, Harold invited us to see *The Three Musketeers* at the movies. We enjoyed it immensely. It was one of the best pictures I have ever seen.

MONDAY, APRIL 24TH.

I have been to town to buy *Bleak House*. I have been consumed with desire for that book. It is much in my mind of late because of the absurd Mrs. Jellyby. On the hill, walking home, came the memory of Dad saying to me when I was nine or ten, "Oh, you little Mrs. Jellyby, you!" My dear Dad, villainous, selfish, mean, irritable, erratic, but understanding and dear.

THURSDAY, APRIL 27TH.

I look at other people, and their lives, and see their faults of disposition and mistakes of conduct, and the remedies therefor; why can I not see the same for myself? I think I do, a little. At least I am resolving, in most serious earnest, to remedy my life wheresoever I can. The great thing I am striving for is thoughtful, humorous, sanity. I want to get away from the dreadful miasma of ponderous seriousness. Looking backwards over all the years of useless argumentation and lack of play, I see how drearily killing they have been. I am resolved I will have no more of them. In the future I shall stick to facts and tombstone my teasing mind and imagination. I have fretted and fretted because Ted hasn't loved me in the way I desired, but I won't do that anymore. He has loved me in his own way, and although he has been saying he doesn't, I know he really does.

We were talking about the Schaefers again. The story only comes to me through Ted's confidences. Schaefer claims he gave her a good life in Europe, but what of their secret conjugal life? She may be a passionate woman and he a cold man or vice versa. What was their fundamental relationship? It seems to me the story of the familiar case of the changing woman and the unchanged man. She is the new woman, the rebellious woman.

In the last twenty or thirty years women have changed fundamentally. We are *not* like our mothers. We do not look at life as they did and we will not accept it as they did. Our men have not changed. They are just like their forebears and they can't understand us. We hurt them in their vanities and sensibilities and then they hurt us back again. It is tragic. Yet how do we alter it? I can't see any way except in giving new ideas to our sons. Perhaps the youngsters will find out the proper way to change marriage.

Today women have a sense of separateness that is new to the sex. We regard ourselves as individuals, not as simply wives or mothers, not possessions. Men hate that. They call it disloyalty and that is the unforgivable Judas sin. We can't change *that*. The men must change their ideas.

FRIDAY, APRIL 28TH.

I have shut up, in an upstairs bookcase, my various Bibles and testaments and Catholic religious books. Out of sight, out of mind, I hope. I don't want my mind working in these ancient creedal phrases. Outwardly I am going to be a Catholic, but I am going to sweep my mind clear of the biblical and churchy fandango. I will no longer ranger the conduct of my life alongside these old myths and stories. The books are wonderful, yes, but they are tyrants, self-imposed, and I am going to shake them off. I have a feeling as though I am coming out on the highway after being lost in a wood; or a diver coming up to light and air from the hideous bottom of some cold ocean.

Just glancing through a couple of the books before I closed the door on them I noticed the recurring phrases: "We must not think God so-and-so." Or, "God meant us to so-and-so." Supreme arrogance of the saints, priests, commentators, speaking for God, explaining His meanings and intentions. I will be my own arrogant self. We are all but mere ants of human beings, and I am refusing to be entrapped, befogged, by any other ant.

I feel I have come to a new beginning. It was my birth anniversary last week and it will be my wedding anniversary next week, and a new time has come for me. In some sort of way I feel I am attaining a quiet mind, that troubles don't matter, that I may be natural to myself, that I can "play the game." I can become agreeable and conforming, exteriorly, because interiorly I have become indifferent. I have come to my own self and I am content to keep that self hidden. Why try to to make people understand you when it can't be done?

I don't mean I am posing as being un-understandable, because I am not. My kind of people, like Dad and Leila Cook, can understand me quickly and easily enough. What I mean is that I see it is hopeless to find an understanding friend among the people with whom one's life is lived. No, I cannot word it. This book is my friend. I write herein because I haven't a friend to talk to and I have to spill over. I am dreadfully alone because a married woman and a mother of children cannot go out seeking to make friends. But I can read and write and think. I hope my mind is never shrouded with piety again.

Leila Cook was Ruby's friend and co-worker at the General Post Office.

SATURDAY, MAY 6TH.

I am waiting for Mabel, which is the same thing as waiting for trouble, I suppose. She is sure to gush about England and the superiorities of the English, and Ted will get glummer and glummer.

So far, every morning and every evening this week, Ted has had a complaint to make. It is rather getting on my nerves, though fortunately I have been able to keep my temper and my spirits, until last night. I was very tired and at ten last night the three big boys were still fussing downstairs, arguing and threatening to wrestle. I scolded them and sent them to bed. Then *Ted* departed in a huff. I followed him and then he began to scold me. He said there was no excuse for shouting and my noise was worse than the children's. I let him rampage on and answered nothing. But I lay awake a long time, thinking. Part of his annoyance, I know, was from finding three Dickens books on our Macy's bill. He calls it selfishness for me to buy books, but he buys his books on gardening and so on. But what can I do but ignore his scoldings? Suppose he ever brought me a book? I think of the barrenness of my life and I resent it. All my life I have hungered for the tokens of love, the little daily showings of affection; the pet name, the spontaneous caress, the trifling gift, the silly compliment, and I suppose I shall hunger to the grave.

I am an ardent woman. I can love, giving and taking. I want pleasure, not asceticism. I do not shirk duties, only I want them clothed in cheerfulness. Ted says I am vulgar. It is an adjective he gives me on and off, and one he considers damning. Well then, I am vulgar, if being alive and facing life squarely is being vulgar.

Sometimes he checks my speech, corrects it for being unladylike, when really it is only forceful. He can't bear me to call a spade a spade. I know that I never use unseemly nor indecent speech. I love words, delight in phrases, revel in language. I try not to talk much in his presence, but sometimes when others are present, I forget him, often to have his hand raised in deprecation to stop my utterance, or else to get a certain lecture on it afterwards. What an affliction I am to Ted. Then I think of the thirty years or more that stretch before us!

But suppose last night Ted had come to my rescue. Suppose he had squelched the boys. Suppose he had guessed or seen that I was tired. Suppose he ever waited on me. Suppose he ever planned a pleasure for me. Suppose he ever saw the things I really do. Suppose he ever gave me my name. Suppose he ever petted me. No. It is impossible to suppose any of these things happening. Oh, I'm lonely.

THURSDAY, MAY 18TH.

Ted is going to take his vacation in his usual way again this year, one day off a week right through until September. This year it is to be Thursdays.

Ted loves this place and the life here, but it gets on my nerves frightfully. The monotonous routine of the housework and baby-minding does not satisfy me, in spite of all the dicta that it ought to. I could do so much more. It is uncongenial work. I wonder how many thousands of women today suffer from these disagreeables.

Marriage, as I know it, absolutely stultifies a woman. Look at my girlhood. Those years at Skerry's College and at St. Martin's le Grand: all full of talk and ideas, always full of something new, new people, new thoughts, fun, invigoration, life. And then to be shut up with a conservative pietist and ceaseless babies, 3000 miles from everything I know and care for, oh, how to go on any longer? But mothers have to. But I want my life; I want love and friends, recreations and stimulations. You see, one hour I think I am thirty-eight and too old; and another hour I think I am thirty-eight and too young, too young for denials and resignations. You are a silly fool, Ruby Alice.

SUNDAY, MAY 21ST.

I picked up the *Manual of Prayers* and carried it to Mass this morning. I amused myself by reading the service for the Sacrament of Matrimony. It is certain no woman ever composed it, not even a lady saint. I am not deriding prayer before marriage. God knows that if we ever need to pray it is at that time. I am deriding the distinctive and separate prayers and the assumption of man's superiority and women's thankful humility. Men and women are equals and this false Eastern teaching has got to be repudiated. How different the feeling and spirit and expression of mutuality is in the old theistic prayer book in its Service of Matrimony. Voysey must have been a feminist before the term was invented. Anyhow, he knew that all bibles and scriptures and religions were man-made, just as any government; and he surely looked upon women as men's equals before God, if not before the ballot box. For all I know, he might even have believed in votes for women.

Dear old Voysey, he certainly taught me true religion and I rather think has made me forever a theist. Though I may be outwardly uneradicably bound up with the Catholic Church, I think that inwardly, at least, I am uneradicably a theist.

All the same, I had a bad moment in church this morning. At Communion, Ted went up to the railing. This is the first time for him since New Year's. As he goes back to the sacraments I fall away from them. I *want* to be one with Ted, and yet how impossible it is.

MONDAY, MAY 22ND.

I am writing at a new place. On Saturday, when I was cleaning downstairs, I rearranged the library and parlor slightly, moving the couch into the parlor and putting the big writing table into the library. This house, so far, has had no agreeable, convenient corner for me. I have done most of my reading and writing at the big red desk in the kitchen. But I get tired of the kitchen; it is too much my general workshop. Also, in this house my bedroom is not my own. This is the first time Ted and I have shared the same room since Eddie was born, and though I want that arrangement, it does have its drawback in lack of privacy. It is not my room anymore. So I thought I would try and make this little library into my special sanctum, for I do want to write. I do so want to get at the story of Dad and my childhood.

Charles Henry Side. c. 1881.
Ruby's father as a young man. It was probably his classical education at Charterhouse
School that prompted Charles Side's lifelong
exploration of ideas. He found a willing student and companion in his eldest daughter,
Ruby. She adored him. Charles Side was
a clerk with the London Transport Railway.

Eliza Alice Searle Side. c. 1881.
Ruby's mother at eighteen. Eliza is presented by Ruby as a force to be reckoned
with. She was self-centered, arbitrary, and
explosive. She had six children who sur-
vived infancy. Eliza taught Ruby to read and
encouraged Ruby's interest in the theater
and the arts.

The Thompson Family. c. 1895.
Back row from left to right: Benjamin Thompson, Ted, Herbert, Emily, Sarah. Front row: Grace, Arthur, Billie. Ted's family was a presence in Ruby's life throughout her marriage. Ted's brother Arthur and sister Grace lived with the newlyweds in New Jersey. Sister Emily's well-being and baby brother Billie's progress were continual concerns for Ted. During the England years, Bert became Ted's employer as well as a friend to Ruby. Ted's father, Benjamin Thompson, was a house painter and devotee of General Booth, founder of the Salvation Army. Little is known of Ted's mother, Sarah, except for Ruby's belief that it was her strength that kept the family together through hard times. The Thompsons were fundamentalists and Ruby believed that Ted's early religious training contributed to his later religious fanaticism.

No. 6 Angel Road, in the Hammersmith district of London, England.
Ruby's parents moved into this house when Ruby was a young child.
Charles and Eliza Side lived in the house the rest of their lives. It was then
willed to Ruby's youngest sister, Joan, who, widowed early in World War
II, lived here until her death.

Ruby, Aileen, and Gladys Side. 1896.
The three older Side sisters, taken on Aileen's first birthday. As a young adult, Gladys
won a scholarship to London University and earned her degree in astronomy. She then
headed a school for girls in India and, after the Great War, she returned to England,
where she authored several geometry textbooks and taught school. Aileen married
and quickly divorced. She was an avid reader and traveled in the Bloomsbury set. She
later remarried, emigrated to the United States, and became an editor for the Book-of-
the-Month Club. She is the author of a biography of Virginia Woolf, *The Moth and the
Star*, 1953, written under her married name, Aileen Pippett.

Edward Thompson. 1897. Ted at sixteen, the year before he left England. He had finished school at fourteen and worked in an insurance company office for four years. It is at this time that he became an agnostic and a socialist. He stated in his biographical notes that he was "willing to work to reform the world and had arranged to go a socialist colony in Paraguay." Instead he went to the Yukon with his brother Bert to look for gold.

Jack Holiday, Ted, and Bert Thompson in the Yukon. 1898. Three young men from London's East End posed in their gold rush garb. They did not strike it rich. In order to pay for his return fare to the east coast of the States, Ted worked in saw mills in Washington's lumber district.

Ruby Alice Side, 1903.

At nineteen, Ruby had finished her formal education at the Flora Gardens School and the Skerry Business College in London. She was then employed by the civil service and worked in the General Post Office. She describes the Telegraph Section, where she worked, as an elite department made up of women employees. This is the period when Ruby was being introduced to the London literary scene and when she was exploring religious and philosophical ideas and organizations.

Ted, 1901.

Ted at twenty-two, when he was working at the Royal Exchange Insurance Company in New York. This picture may have been made while he was in London at the time of his father's death.

Ruby. c. 1904.

Ruby at twenty, when she was working at the London General Post Office in the Telegraph Section. This is the year she met Ted Thompson. In New York he had seen a letter she had written to *The Clarion,* a Fabian weekly, and a correspondence developed between them. Ted returned to London to see his dying mother, and Ruby agreed to meet him on the steps of the post office. She observed him from behind a pillar before she made herself known to him.

Ruby Side Thompson. 1905.

At the time of her marriage, Ruby was twenty-one. The Sides did not approve of Ted Thompson so, on her twenty-first birthday, Ruby booked passage to New York and she married Ted in Bayonne, New Jersey, on the day of her arrival.

Thompson's
A Little Ovation
given
by
Their friends to
"WARM the HEARTH"
of
The New Home

1913

Party invitation,
including the Avenue A house
in Bayonne, New Jersey.
"We had been here just two weeks when last night our friends gave us a surprise party for Halloween and a house warming. It was the greatest, greatest fun and I enjoyed it immensely. I don't think I ever enjoyed an evening so much before." (Saturday, November 1, 1913.) This house was the first one purchased by Ted and Ruby.

Ruby with Charlie. 1916.
Two-year-old Charlie, nicknamed Chili, picking roses in Bayonne with Ruby.

Ruby and her sons. 1919.
Ruby holding the twins, Cuthie and Artie, and surrounded by, left to right:
Charlie, Jimmie, Harold, Eddie, and Johnnie. Bayside, Long Island.

Ted. 1920.

Ted at the peak of his career in New York as comptroller of Saks Fifth Avenue. He was the father of seven sons, the family was living on Long Island, and he was hoping to return to England to take up the life of a gentleman farmer.

523 Knickerbocker Road, Tenafly, New Jersey.

Ruby, Ted, and their seven sons moved into this house in January 1921, after the disastrous English farm purchase. They lived here until Ruby, Ted, and the three younger sons returned to England in 1927. The four older sons continued to live either in this house or in the cottage behind it until 1939. This is the home in which John and Ruth lived with their two daughters when Bonnie was born.

Ruby with six of her seven sons. 1925.
Back row from left to right: Harold, John, Ruby, Jim.
Front row: Cuthie, Artie, Charlie. Tenafly, New Jersey.

Family snapshot. 1925.
Ruby with Artie, John, Cuthie, Jim, Charlie, and Ted. Tenafly, New Jersey.

Ruby. 1926.

The Thompson family was living in Tenafly, New Jersey, in 1926 but the record is sparse because several journals of this period have been lost.

Ruby. 1927.

Ruby's serene look masks the turmoil she was experiencing in 1927. She, Ted, and the three younger boys were about to return to England to live. It was Ted's desire to retire there. The four older boys were to remain in Tenafly. This division of her family created a strain on Ruby and her marriage for the rest of her life.

Ted. c. 1927.
This photograph was probably taken shortly before returning
to England with the three younger sons.

Eddie.
Tenafly, New Jersey, 1929.
Eddie worked for the Defense Department during World War II and eventually became a salesman and manager for Moore Business Forms. He and his family settled in Batavia, New York.

Jim.
Tenafly, New Jersey. 1929.
Jim became the editor-in-chief of the real estate section for the *New York Herald Tribune,* then for the *New York Times,* and eventually for *Architectural Forum* of Time, Inc. He wrote under the byline s. g. thompson. His second wife was Dorothy Barclay, who wrote a weekly child development article for the *New York Times* magazine. They lived in New York City.

Harold and John.
Tenafly, New Jersey. 1929.
As an adult, Harold worked for the *New York Herald Tribune* in the business department. He then supervised contract negotiations for the U.S. Navy. He eventually moved his family to Ogden, Utah.

John became an actuary and worked his way up in the Metropolitan Life Insurance Company, retiring as vice president. He was the most athletic of the boys and especially excelled in tennis. He was nationally ranked number eight in correspondence chess. John and his wife, Ruth, raised their family in Tenafly and moved to California in 1957. They now live in Ojai, California.

80 Eastern Road. Romford, England.
Ted and Ruby lived in this house from 1931 to 1940
with their three youngest sons.

Ted and Ruby in France. 1932.
"We have returned to London this morning. I have had the most enjoyable holiday of my whole life. Moreover, I have fallen in love with the mountains. Argentière is the most charming place in the world. The Utards were charming. Paris was hot as Hades but perfect as ever." (August 28, 1932.)

Four generations. 1935.
Ruby with Harold's wife, Kay, their children, Dick and Sheila, and Ruby's mother, Eliza Side, in Romford.

The Thompson family tree

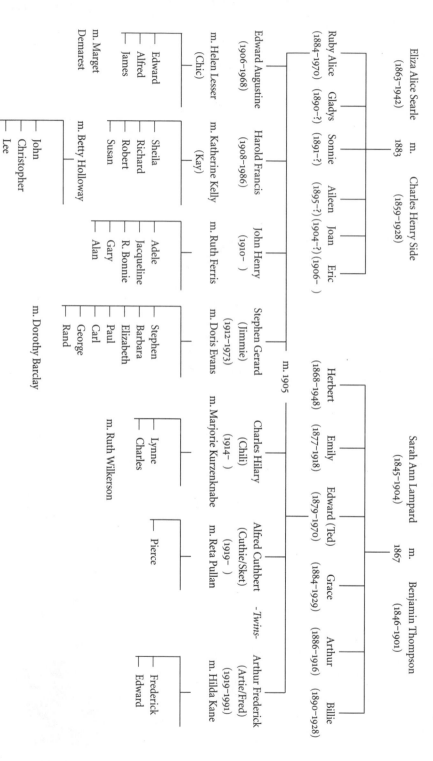

WEDNESDAY, MAY 24TH.

Ruby Side Thompson. From now on that is my name. From today I take back my maiden name. It may not be my legal name, but it shall be my name just the same. Ted makes out checks to me as R. A. Thompson, but that will be only my business name. Anyhow, it is customary with American women for them to retain their original surname at marriage and merely add to it the name of the new husband. I think it is a good custom and only wish I had observed it in the beginning. Certainly I am Mrs. Edward Thompson, but just as certainly I am Ruby Side.

Ted laughs at women's names. He says they have no names, if not a husband's they must use a father's. Quite right. But a father is a natural and inevitable relation, whereas a husband is often unnatural and never inevitable. Fathers and daughters: mothers and sons. Perhaps they are the only satisfactory relationships in life. My father understood me better than my mother did. Some day my sons may understand me and love me without reason.

But as for now, I will again use my father's name. Side. I know the Sides. A bad lot but brainy. I don't know the Thompsons very well. They are all so respectable, so colorless, so restrained, so pious. Not me. I am red and yellow, flame, ruby, beside their white and gray.

SATURDAY, MAY 27TH.

Last night I had a foolish outburst of talk with Ted. Why do I ever speak of anything except the superficialities with him? And I cannot arrange my life without this man. I have to live with him. I cannot change myself. I cannot change him. Yet the children hold us indissolubly together. My God, what women pay for their children.

Freedom? There is no freedom for married mothers. And many don't want it. But for we who do, what a torment life is in bonds. Oh, to be free. It isn't the work we mind, nor the pain. It is the spiritual imprisonment, the isolation of heart and mind. I must find something congenial to do.

Now I go to my day's ironing. It is a task I dread, because it leaves me so much time for thought, and this morning I am full of hateful thoughts. I am angry and miserable. I should like to go out and forget myself, but it is impossible. I have an accumulation of two weeks' starched clothes waiting for me and they simply must be done.

And why do I stop to write? Because writing is the only relief I can get, this book my only friend.

THURSDAY, JUNE 1ST.

Today is my father's birthday. I think he must be sixty-four today. Dear old Dad.

Ted is at home today and happy working outside. I am busy indoors and very much troubled with my veins. I have had to apply hot fomentations and go back to both high shoes and bandages. Last night I had raging inflammation and pain and could not sleep for hours. I think the greatest boon I could crave of a fairy godmother would be forgetfulness of my feet and legs. I can hardly remember what it is like to walk around and not remember at every step that one is walking.

SUNDAY, JUNE 11TH.

I've been abed with bad varicose veins. I've had to hire Black Maria, who rents the cottage, to help in the kitchen. The boys don't approve of her cooking. Eddie brought me my supper, turned up his nose at some tapioca pudding, and exclaimed, "Well, Ma, I hope to tell you, *you're a good* cook, you are!" Compliments from my eldest. I suppose ten years hence he will be following domestic tradition and asking his wife for dishes like mother used to make.

SATURDAY, JUNE 17TH.

I must have become that tiresome creature, an excellent housewife. At noon I went downstairs for the first time since I took to my bed to mend my legs. When I saw the rooms I was desolated: I could have sat and wept. Everything was exactly as I had left it twelve days ago. The same flowers stood withered in their vases, the same newspapers lay scattered in the parlor, the same measuring cups stood exactly where I had left them in the kitchen. The place had seen neither broom nor duster. It was a hideous mess. Coats, shoes, blankets, caps, encumbered all the chairs, and the closets were a dirty piggle. I ate some bread and potatoes, took a cup of tea, and then commandeered my forces. I made the boys take up the big rugs and beat them on the lawn. I set Maria to sweep the bare floors. I tackled the dishes, mountains of them, but the easiest job for me as I could stand still at it. Then I straightened the closets, though I could not stop to clean them properly. Then I washed the mirrors and the kitchen windows, all filmed with smoke. My only helpers of the boys were Eddie, Jim, and Charlie. John has gone to take the exam for the St. Peter's scholarship and Harold has taken to bed with a poison ivy foot. My foot and leg are tightly bandaged, but beginning to nag. What a life!

TUESDAY, JULY 4TH. INDEPENDENCE DAY.

"The Bunch" arrived about two o'clock, about forty of Ted's clerks. The married men brought their wives, and the married women their husbands. We had planned to picnic in our woods, but the weather was too bad for eating outside, so we served refreshments in the house. We managed to crowd all at once into the dining room. It was lots of fun. Ted had planned races and games, and was able to get these off in between the showers, and awarded the prizes in the parlor after supper.

And now I am going to get something to eat myself as I was too busy serving to eat with the crowd. It was such a good day.

WEDNESDAY, JULY 5TH.

Twice yesterday Ted called me "Lady." The first time he has used the old name since I returned to America. Perhaps it was only forgetfulness. He was happy giving happiness to his young clerks. Perhaps he forgot his grievance against me. But I shall listen alertly to hear the name again.

TUESDAY, JULY 11TH.

In the ardor of the night, exciting me to all abandonment, surrendering him-self to all the sensations of delight that I could give, Ted whispered, "What else shall I do to you?" "Kiss me." "No. I have never kissed you since you came back from England." "I know it." On the instant, passion died in me.

There are things that should never be said. There are things that should never be written. I know it, but I'm hurt, cruelly hurt. The crudeness and bes-tiality of conjugality is intolerable unless it is suffused with the sentiment of the soul. A man who will use every atom of a woman's being for his gratifica-tion, yet all the while withholds his reason and affection in judgment, can I understand him, excuse him, love him? No. It's too much for this wife.

WEDNESDAY, JULY 26TH.

I have been thinking so much this summer of all the pros and cons for English versus American life for this family. Sorting through the confusion of my per-sonal thoughts and feelings about our present life, I have been trying to decide what is the best plan to make for the future.

This country life irks me dreadfully; its isolation is almost unbearable. We are too far from the village for me to walk to it comfortably, and at night I cannot walk out on the dark roads. I stumble even on our own paths. Week after week I have no society but that of the children, all boys. Visitors are al-ways out-of-town people who mean overnight work and I am already over-worked. I want neighborly society, women who drop in and chat an hour, reachable houses where I can call-in, people passing my windows so that I can see there is something alive in the world besides trees. Isolation, physical and mental; it is a strain I cannot stand much longer. I know this place is rest and recreation to Ted, but he leaves it everyday, mingles with his own kind, has speech with men. I know this is an excellent place for the boys to grow up on. I also know that thousands and thousands of boys are as well raised and as happy without ten acres of home-ground to roam in. I know this is a good home, but it needs servants. For me, working alone in it, it is a brute of a house, unmanageable, killing. I want an obscure life among friendly people.

Ted complains that I have no hobbies, that I do not play games like tennis or cards or chess. That is my natural taste. As a child I did not enjoy running about and now it is rather impossible. Besides, after housework, I am too tired to run after a ball. Parlor games bore me. I can play cards, but I never enjoy doing so. "Your idea of recreation is a lazy one," Ted scorns. "You want to buy a ticket for something: to sit in a chair and see other people doing things." Well, what of it? Everyone to his taste. "You won't even play the piano," says Ted. Well, we haven't got one now, but when we had one he made a derision of my playing and singing, so that I naturally stopped that to protect myself, just as I stopped reading poetry, or expressing opinions. Ted has killed me with ridicule. He doesn't know it, but I have shut away piece after piece of myself, just so as to save my soul. Maybe I am too sensitive, but Ted's belittlement and derision feel like being flayed alive.

Ted speaks now and then of plans for the future, a future here. He speaks of buying fruit trees, of replaning out the garden, of hiring a man and raising produce for sale. About business he also has plans. He speaks of trying to make more money when he renews his contract with Saks.

Withal he speaks continually against America. Almost daily he quotes me from the newspaper instances of American foolishness or inefficiency. England and the English remain his ideals of perfection. He exasperates me. And it makes for a permanent isolation for the whole family. We do not belong anywhere. We are neither English nor American. We are a family without a country. Logically, Ted should either take out his papers and settle down properly as an American citizen, or he should leave the country and return to his heavenly England.

Ted does remark that few women like a country life but all the men hanker after one. Yes, it's true, but how unfortunate. And yes, I know this is a good place to raise the boys on, but how unfortunate for me we have only boys. Do you know what? I begin again to wish for a daughter. One little girl, one little woman, one little comprehending creature of my own kind. Foolishness.

SUNDAY, JUNE 30TH.

Another fine day to be thankful for.

Eddie did not come home last night, as he said he would, and while Ted and I were talking about him, and worrying a little, and deciding to ring up the Bayonne police if he didn't show up this evening, he and Farley drove up in a taxi. Their Point Pleasant Camp had been burnt out last Wednesday; nobody was hurt but everything was destroyed. Eddie was in a borrowed suit with long pants and looking very manly. I suppose we shall have to put him into trousers now, and I have a man among the boys already. I am so thankful no one was hurt.

Nearly seven years elapsed between the last journal entry of June 1922 and this next section, which starts in March 1929. Late in 1927, Ruby, Ted, and the three younger sons returned to England. By that time Ted had retired and planned to live the rest of his life in frugal comfort as an Englishman. He had considerable savings and investments in both real estate and the stock market. He returned to work in the real estate office of his brother Bert only after the stock market crash of 1929.

The four older sons stayed in Tenafly, and began their careers. The large house at 523 Knickerbocker Road was sold to a Mr. Hoffman, and the four boys lived together in a cottage on that same property. Although always referred to as "the cottage," it was a five-room, two-story house. Eddie, Harold, John, and Jim, formed a corporation and entered into a contract with Ted to buy the cottage by paying him a monthly quota.

Also in this interval, Ruby's father died of cancer at the age of sixty-nine. Sonnie, whose wife Mabel died in December 1921, married a woman named Edith.

As we resume, the twins are ten years old, Charlie fifteen.

1929

Oldchurch Road
Romford, Essex
England

WEDNESDAY, MARCH 20TH.

I went to the American Consulate to apply for a six months' extension on my Re-entry Permit. After a visit to Jo Tibbs, to see if she'd make me some frocks, I went to the theater to see *The Beggar's Opera*. I did not enjoy it particularly. For one thing, matinées seldom have pep, and for another, I kept thinking of Tenafly and my possible and probable return there this summer.

After the theater I went to Sonnie's house. Mother is there with Edith, who is awaiting her first confinement. Edith is looking splendidly well and happy. She will never be so happy again in her life as she is now. She had tea ready in the parlor, but before we could drink it, Mother had one of her paroxysms to upset us. Answering their questions about my day, when I said I had called on Jo Tibbs, Mother flung herself back in her chair and commenced swearing. She said I must cancel the sewing request because if I went into Jo's house she never wanted me to come into her's. Edith and I were flabbergasted. I made one or two attempts to reason with Mother but couldn't get in a word. Mother raved against Jo, who has the audacity to live next door to her, and insisted that I should not give her any work. I thought Mother would have a stroke, she was so enraged. Nor would she leave the subject alone, no matter how Edith and I tried to alter the conversation. I think my mother is the most exasperating and most unreasonable woman in the kingdom. Finally Edith took me away upstairs to show me her baby things.

What demon drives Mother? When I think of the patience attained and practiced by Dad, himself a high-tempered man, my hat's off to him. We children all left home as soon as we could to run away from the fighting. Dad stuck it out and learned not to answer back. Poor Mother, we've all escaped her now but she can't escape herself. And what bad luck that no one ever stood up to her. Because we all got out of her way, she got her own way so much that she just naturally thinks she is entitled to it, no matter how wildly unreasonable. She makes herself miserable.

MONDAY, MARCH 25TH.

There are troubling letters from Eddie and John about the corporation. When we left our four oldest sons on their own in America, Ted formed a corporation with them by signing over the Tenafly property to them. He gave them the deed and left them saddled with a pledged monetary indebtedness to him, a quota, which was to be paid monthly. Eddie was twenty-one, Harold nineteen, John seventeen, and Jimmie only fifteen. I know Jimmie was under school-leaving age, and we were scared the authorities would find out. It was a crime to leave those boys by themselves and to collect money from them. Now, Eddie and John are making accusations against Harold. This whole situation is serious.

WEDNESDAY, MARCH 27TH.

Last night I had a very vivid dream about my books. Aileen was showing me her bookcases and she pulled out three books in red bindings and said, "Of course you know *these*!" They were my novels. I opened one and distinctly saw the printing, the style of the book, and the illustrations. From childhood I have dreamt I was writing, but never before has a dream shown me the finished product.

Nine P.M. Ted has gone to Ilford for one of his Catholic Evidence Guild meetings. I am feeling thoroughly fed up with these meetings. They have taken two evenings a week for this last twelvemonth. This is too much.

I have been preoccupied today with the early days of our married life. In those days life was real. Ted was not lost in religion but was living for his wife and his child and the sweetness of life for its own sake. Not until after we had left Thirty-fifth Street did he begin to be intrigued with religion. He was acutely interested in it from the time we went to live in Avenue E, and he joined the Church whilst I was on my first visit back to England. It must have been his innate temperament expressing itself in reverting to the religiosity of his parents. But how the children and I have suffered since. If I could go back to Thirty-fifth Street and pick up the actuality of living that ceased there twenty years ago, then perhaps I could be a sane and happy person. But there is no going back except in memories. We remember what is no more.

*The **Catholic Evidence Guild** is a lay organization within the Roman Catholic Church whose members speak on street corners and conduct classes in Catholic teachings in order to bring new converts into the Church.*

TUESDAY, APRIL 16TH.

I am re-reading *The Life of Olive Schreiner*. I began it feeling I wanted to get in touch with women's work, and brooding again on my old desire to write. It gave me a feeling of forlornness, slapping me in the face, as it were, with the fact of my old age as I read of her abiding enthusiasms. There is an account of her loves in art and literature, especially her passionate love of Browning.

This makes me heartsick, makes me sorry for myself. Where are my en-thusiasms now, I ask? Where are my ideals, my passions, my dreams? Evaporated, the whole lot of them. A sort of resentment rises in me, a facet of the old resentment against Ted. He destroyed such things of mine years and years ago by his deadly ridicule. I loved Browning when I was a girl, but Ted's ridicule of poetry, and of me for liking it, made me put it away and now I have forgotten it.

Everything I loved he mocked. I remember I had a copy of Rossetti's *Beata Beatrix*. I thought it beautiful and I brought it from England with me. I hung it on the parlor wall; Ted took it down. I hung it in the dining room and then in the bedroom. Each time, Ted took it down. This was he, the young bridegroom. I wept, but I put it away. I was a fool. I should have kept on hang-ing it up daily, until the walls were full of holes, until Judgment Day. But I gave in, as I always gave in.

Olive Schreiner (1855–1920) was a member of the Fabian women's circle who studied the condition of women in South Africa and England. She examined unemployed women in Women and Labor. *Her mystical writings and her first novel,* The Story of an African Farm, *brought her additional acclaim.*

WEDNESDAY, APRIL 17TH.

I received a birthday letter from Harold this morning and a packet of books from "The Four." One was inscribed, "To the one and only, from the 4 given, 4 saken, and 4 closing sons, Ed, Harold, Johnnie, and Jimmie."

THURSDAY, APRIL 18TH.

Forty-five years old today and I look every minute of it.

I went to the hairdresser's and had my hair cut, shampooed, and waved. My hair is still beautiful, not gray at all, but oh, my face! A beautiful young girl, about twenty, attended me and as I watched her face above mine in the mirror, the comparison was more and more striking. She so blooming and I so faded.

What grieves me is not that I am so definitely in the middle ages now, but that I didn't joy in my youth when I had it. I was a very beautiful and very clever young girl. Many told me so, and looking back I know I was. I married at twenty-one and then was lost in matrimony, smothered with babies and domesticity, perplexed and bothered by religion, and all the starch and pride taken out of me by Ted's everlasting sarcastic criticism. I grew to think myself worth about thirty-five cents, whereas I was worth a million dollars but didn't know it. And now I am worth only thirty-five cents. If only I could have my time over again. Do we all feel like this in our forties?

I had letters from Grace, the Aunties, and Mother. Mother sent me her brown silk jumper suit and a couple of nightgowns. At breakfast Ted presented me with another of his necklaces, a blue and gold one this time. It is very pretty. Tonight we are to go to Ilford to the cinema.

Mother's letter gave me sad news that Uncle Will has died of liver cancer. This deadly cancer again, torturing and consuming us. What a devilish thing it is.

SATURDAY, APRIL 20TH.

The effect of *The Life of Olive Schreiner* is to send me forthwith to attend to my religious duties. I am a rotten poor Catholic but I cannot live without the Church. I've been swimming along in Emerson lately but he doesn't *do*. He is exhilarating at first, but tiring later. I don't want to paddle that canoe; the ark of the Church is much steadier, safer, roomier. I am not young anymore. A solitary canoe in the Hudson would be too strenuous for me. I need the crowded ferryboat today.

WEDNESDAY, APRIL 24TH.

I have finished the books sent by the boys. What strikes me about them is what disagreeable women the heroines are. I think about the women I want to write stories about: Em Copus, Mrs. Kennedy, Bessie Wottan, Auntie Liz, Flora Terhune, old lady Norval, Bertha Hludenski, and Mother. Em Copus and Mrs. Kennedy particularly. I have been brooding over them for fifteen years or more. In the lives of all these women there is passion and beauty, fighting and loving, fortitude and generosity, betrayal and triumph, loss and gain, death and glory. All these women were and are ardent and vital, and I should show their stories to be the romances which they are. Why in thunderation don't I begin? I have made a couple of beginnings but they won't do. The real story is that of the mother's struggle, but she is too old to be acceptable as the heroine of a novel. To be popular a novel must be focused on, and from, a young person. I must begin again and write it from the standpoint of one of her children. Em would be easier to start on, because I do know her beginnings in her girlhood, but I think I need to feel happier in my own life before I could tell the tragedy of hers. Beautiful Em! She was one of the persons I loved when I was a child.

TUESDAY, APRIL 30TH.

I am feeling unwell but menstruation does not begin. I have been very erratic and irregular in my periods ever since I came to England. Whether this is the change of climate, or the change of life, I do not know. I am also much troubled with my bones and I think that is due to the chronic dampness. My knees are particularly painful, and I have to place two feet on every step going up and down the stairs. Well, what is this but English rheumatism? How I long for dry and sunny Tenafly.

I do nothing else but think of America. It is in the back of my mind, waking and sleeping. My passport is not back yet, and I think if I am prevented from returning to America this summer, I shall lie down and die.

A postcard has just arrived from Mother saying Edith had a daughter yesterday. All well.

FRIDAY, MAY 3RD.

Our twenty-fourth wedding anniversary.

My passport arrived in the first post. I picked up Aunt Lizzie in town and went to Walham Green to the cemetery. I bought some daffodils to put on Dad's grave and said good-bye to him. I don't think I shall ever see his grave again.

Ted and I went this evening to see *Hamlet* at the Old Vic. This was an excellent presentation, I think the best I have ever seen. Ted gave me a bracelet. I'd really like to have some earrings but my ears are not pierced. It was a good day.

MONDAY, MAY 27TH.

On Saturday Bert told me how much Ted was like his father. The family was living in Whitechapel when [William] Booth started his preaching and Salvation Army work. Bert said his father used to go out with and for Booth, preaching to the poorest people in the toughest slums of the East End. Then the father switched to temperance work and used to go about preaching tee-totalism, but he himself drank too much. He stopped it for a time, but he returned to the drink. "You know that was Dad's great failing," said Bert. I didn't know. Ted has never told me any such thing.

There has been much troublesome correspondence with the boys this month. They quarreled among themselves over the corporation work. The quota was held up, Harold resigning as treasurer, and nobody banking. The main scrap was between Harold and Eddie. Eddie, as usual, has his father's condemnation. I dread to see Eddie's letters arrive. Ted's comments on them are bound to hurt me. From Eddie's babyhood Ted has never had patience with him. Eddie is too like me, and Ted's scathing condemnation of either of us is to say we are just like the other.

Harold wrote recently to me to say that he and John and Jim would sub-scribe my passage to New York. This upset Ted, and when Harold had to write later that he couldn't do it yet because he'd had a motor smashup and had broken a fire hydrant to boot, Ted said he would pay my passage if the quota was paid up. I wrote to Eddie and asked him if he would give me a month's pleasure money to put in my purse for the journey. I received a cable from Eddie saying the quota was paid and for me to sail immediately. He also sent a letter, enclosing a money order for fifteen dollars and apologies that he couldn't send more. He had just paid out sixty-seven dollars to have his tonsils out.

Ted doesn't like this either. Firstly, it's a waste of money to cable. Secondly, it's a waste of money to buy money orders and pay for the exchange. Whatever Eddie does or does not do is wrong for Ted. It always has been and I suppose always will be. I went out this morning and sent a reply cable to Eddie and told him that it was impossible to sail before August. I am determined that he shall not waste his affection, and if he is looking for a hasty reply he will have it. Eddie needs loving, like some of the rest of us.

Ted now says he did not say I could go if the quota was paid up. He *did*. I expected him to start being obstructive and sure enough, he's begun. I've got to keep my head and not talk. Ted always wins with talk. I will go ahead with preparation for my departure, for I *will* go. Oh, how I wish I could talk to Mrs. Nighman!

The Salvation Army is a charitable group organized on military lines for the evangelizing and social betterment of the poor. It was founded by Catherine and William Booth in 1865 in Whitechapel, London. The difference between the Salvation Army and other evangelical groups was that the Booths shared the way of life of the poor. There was equality between women and men at all levels of the organization.

THURSDAY, MAY 30TH.

This is General Election Day. Ted and I can vote this year but I shall not. I intend to become an American citizen and will cast my first vote in America.

Last night Ted asked me if I had written to Eddie. I told him I had written and said that I could sail after the due quota was paid up. Ted jumped on me and said I was all wrong. He said that after the quota was paid, any extra money the boys advanced to me could be charged to writing off the standing debt. He also explained that he meant *full* quota, and that had not been paid all this year. This is a pretty Shylock business. It makes me sick with sheer, cold rage. Ted's flourish of magnanimity was an empty gesture.

I long for a friend. There isn't one person in this country whom I can turn to for love or encouragement or understanding. I am solitary indeed.

In England, women gained the vote in 1928.

SUNDAY, JUNE 9TH.

Eight P.M. Ted has gone off to Forest Gate for his Evidence Guild work. His paramount interest in life is Catholicism. I resent and hate it. Here in England he is more and more religious, *unbearably* religious. Fanatical.

Last Monday he did not get back from his "class" until after midnight and then he prayed abjectly for fifteen minutes at the bedside. It is unnatural. Mass every evening, street preaching one night a week, class another, and organ playing for extra services at the church.

A Salvationist at least goes out for love of God and man and preaches love and repentance. The Catholic Evidence Guild worker goes out to *argue*, to *prove* something: to prove the Catholic Church is right and every being outside of it is wrong: not zeal for souls but zeal for an argument. This is fine fun for the disputatious and an excellent showing off field for the intellectually vain. When Ted comes home and reports with glee how neatly he has scored off hecklers, I just feel sick. This isn't even religion. It is merely Edward Thompson and I am tired of him. If he knew that *my* constant meditation was how to get away from him, would he change? I don't think so. Will he ever return to a normal life? I'm afraid not.

MONDAY, JUNE 10TH.

Eight P.M. Last night I did a very foolish thing. Ted came in about ten o'clock and we had a pleasant half hour over coffee, but afterwards upstairs he began asking questions about his clothes closet and moths. He was not satisfied with

my answers and got angry. Getting into bed he got angrier with the bed-
clothes, flung them off, jounced over with his back to my place and said something ugly, and looked uglier. Vehement rage flew through me but I did not
say one word. I stood a minute and looked at him and then took my things
and went off into the yellow room. There I spent the night. I felt such an em-
anation of hatred from him that I could not lie down and spend the night beside him. I did not weep. I have not wept. I simply feel finished.

It is incredible that I should be still hoping and wishing for love, like a girl,
but it is true. I think Ted has never really loved me. I know he has never loved
me as I wished to be loved, nor accepted love from me as I wished to bestow it.

> "Do not ask for the hands of love or love's soft eyes:
>   They give less than love who give all, giving what wanes.
>   I give you the star-fire, the heart-way to Paradise,
>   With no death after, no arrow with stinging pains."

Yes. Where is the man who once said that to me? If he's alive he must be
seventy by now, but he'd still have a poet's heart. But dead or living, he's lost to
me, and has been lost all these marriage years. "I love the free in thee, my
bird," he used to say to me. The free! Well I'm caged now, alright. I long for the
free spirit, the free mind, for beauty, for love, for friendship. I have nothing
but a weary soul and a broken heart. Frustration and futility.

TUESDAY, JUNE 11TH.

Early in the dawning Ted turned to me for loving and our quarrel was ended
without speech. Why doesn't he love me oftener?

THURSDAY, JUNE 13TH.

A letter from Johnnie to Ted arrived this morning. He says that Edgerton reports there is going to be a shake-up in the Credit Men's Association soon and
there are good chances for Ted to get the secretaryship. I asked Ted if he would
apply for it. He answered that firstly, the post wasn't open yet, and secondly,
Edgerton knew weeks ago the conditions on which he would consider it.
Pressing to know if he would accept if nominated, he said he would because
that would make life in America financially possible. Also, since all the family
wished for that, *if* the job came his way he would try it. He thought it was extremely unlikely the job would come his way. Anyhow, this is something. At
least a concession that he might return to America.

THURSDAY, JUNE 20TH.

I have been to the doctor today. Last night Ted told me of a woman who
claims she is being cured of varicose veins by injections. This is a new treat-

ment and is being administered by Dr. Woodhouse at the hospital. I determined to see Dr. Woodhouse this morning to see if such a treatment would be good for me. However, he was on a month's holiday so I saw Dr. Green.

Dr. Green examined my legs and said Dr. Woodhouse would give me the injections if I wanted them, but he didn't think much of the treatment. Dr. Green advised me to stick to bandages and to rest every afternoon and not to walk. There is no diet that helps varicose veins, as they are a mechanical defect. If I could lose weight, he said, the veins would not be so troublesome, but it was extremely difficult to lose weight. I might be the type of person who was naturally heavy, and if so, dieting would reduce my strength much more than my fat. Fatness is something naturally assigned to people, like tallness or shortness or longevity. Only a few people were fat from gluttony. Moreover, my age might have a great deal to do with my weight. I told him that I did watch my diet very carefully, cutting down the starches very rigorously and fasting until I felt faint, but I simply got heavier and heavier. He then examined my neck and decided I might try some thyroid tablets to see if they would have any effect on reducing.

From there I went straight to Boots and bought some new crepe bandages and I also got on the scales. They recorded two hundred and thirty pounds. It is shocking. I know this isn't due to food, for I haven't eaten differently from what I usually do.

Maybe this is one of the ways the change of life is working on me. If so, maybe when it is all over I shall return to my normal weight, which is one hundred fifty-four pounds. Until my third child was born I never weighed more than one hundred thirty and sometimes less. From 1910 to 1924, when I was forty, I weighed one hundred fifty-four without varying at all. Since forty I have been getting heavier and heavier. What can I do about it?

Ted says exercise. He means gymnastics. Housework does not count as exercise according to him. I think gymnastics is only a man's remedy. A woman of my age can't become a contortionist. Exercises and drills may be all very well for young girls, but not for middle-aged women. Anyhow, I simply can't do them and I am not going to try. Ted also says walk. The doctors all say, "Don't walk, lie on the couch whenever you can and keep your legs up." I think the doctors are more apt to be right than Ted. Now Dr. Green gives me thyroid tablets. Maybe a month hence I'll weigh two forty. My goodness, it's awful!

TUESDAY, JUNE 25TH.

This morning I received a letter from a priest in Southwark asking me to come and see him. He says Will Mears is trying to receive an ecclesiastical annulment from Aileen on the basis that she was not baptized. Will has become a Catholic since the divorce. This is Aileen's business and I don't know what to do about it. I love Aileen and I don't want to hurt her by touching her most private affairs.

John reports that Will Mears was abusive to Aileen. She divorced him after a short marriage, vowing never to remarry.

FRIDAY, JULY 5TH.

I went to Bishop House, Southwark, to give a deposition about the family. So far as I know, Aileen was never baptized. A queer episode. I met Aileen for lunch and told her about the priest's letter. That aside, we had a jolly good talk. I like Aileen very much.

I then took a train to Sonnie's house to get my first sight of the baby. They have called her Monica. She is a lovely, darling baby.

Yesterday Ted got a cable from Eddie saying Connolly was out and telling him to cable Strickland. Ted said that practically meant that he could have the job. I cried about it. If there is really a job at last, and Ted can get it, and will take it, that means home to America. What joy! It also, however, means holding my plans to visit America. If we are to return there to live, no need for a visit now by me.

MONDAY, JULY 8TH.

I took Aileen *Andy Brandt's Ark* [Edna Bryner] to read, and told her to find Mother in it. I think the mother in that book is the nearest thing to our mother I have ever come across in print. I told Aileen that Gladys had read it and utterly failed to see the likeness. "Of course," commented Aileen. "Gladys has a mother fixation. The ambivalence of Mother sticks out all over her." Discussing Gladys, who at present is in a very bad way nervously, Aileen presented a theory that Gladys is, and always has been, a victim to me. I was dumbfounded by the idea. This is the case as Aileen presented it. "You have a father fixation, Ruby. It's perfectly obvious. All your remarks about Mother show it." "But what has that to do with Gladys?"

"See here. You were the first child, weren't you? A daughter. Of course you'd naturally have a love fixation on the father, anyhow. Well, you're not an ordinary child at all. You're queer, you're odd, you're bright, you're very clever, and you're very nervous and highly wrought. And you're original. None of this Mother understands, but all of it endears you to Dad. Then along comes Gladys: another girl and one who should naturally have the father fixation. But you are already in possession of the father's affections so she fixes herself upon Mother. But Gladys is very different from you. She is an ordinary normal, healthy, pretty, placid, commonplace baby and she just gets the attention such normal children receive. But this does not satisfy: indeed, it enrages her.

"Wherever you go you attract notice and admiration. You supersede and eliminate her and she hates you. She determines to supersede you. As I see it, Gladys's life has been one incessant struggle to prove herself as good as you. And you ignore her. For you, she doesn't exist. She's always tense. You're always easy.

"Well, then I came along: another girl. I was very delicate and ailing. Nobody wanted me. I was a nuisance. A nuisance to Mother too. I transferred what should have been my mother fixation *to you*, Ruby. I thought you were the perfect being in the world. My one ambition was to be like you. You scarcely knew I was alive. You came and went about your own affairs but I adored you. I was totally unaware of Gladys. I can't even remember her in the family at all. I've no recollection of her in the house even until one day when she was about fifteen, when she came home from school and said this: 'I've got a scholarship. Nobody thought I was clever, did they?' And the thing is, she isn't clever, you know. But she works and has will. Will and work will pull you through exams. But it's a strain on her, always has been.

"You're brilliant. Wherever you are you shine and you don't even know you're shining. You're born clever. You have wit and everything is easy for you. For Gladys, everything is a struggle. She will not take herself as a normal, healthy, pretty female. She makes herself compete with you, but it's a strain. She has achievements, but they exhaust her. And all the time you go careening about, getting blame and criticism but getting admiration too. Whatever you do, wherever you go, you receive admiration though mostly you're quite oblivious to it. You see, you've got *personality*, but Gladys has only her will.

"Yes, Gladys has always been sacrificed to you. You have first place and she can't wrest it from you. You are the eldest child, you have the father's love, and she has to make do with the mother's love and it never satisfies her. You have brains, beauty, love, admiration, adventure, achievement, personality: everything she wants.

"So she fights herself, you, and destiny. That's why she's exhausted. She's on the verge of a complete collapse now. From the accounts that Mother recently brought back from Plymouth, I think she's getting near the madhouse if she doesn't watch out.

"She has a grudge against me, too. She thinks I'm vain and that it's her duty to correct me. She has an obsession that I wear my shoes too small and frequently tells me to buy larger shoes. The first remark she made to me when she came home from India was, 'You've been peroxidizing your hair!' She's afraid I might cut her out on looks, and we never meet without her making some kind of a would-be mortifying remark to me. Yes, Gladys is the victim in the family, but most particularly to you, Ruby."

Well, that's how Aileen sees the family.

FRIDAY, JULY 26TH.

Ted received a letter from Strickland this morning saying his formal application for the Credit Bureau Secretaryship had been received and forwarded to the special committee, where, no doubt, it would receive very serious consideration. That's all. I feel rather let down, afraid Ted isn't going to get that job after all.

Charlie went off to Norwich on his bicycle for a week. He has finished the school year third in his form.

THURSDAY, AUGUST 1ST.

Ted has received a letter from Edgerton saying that Ted will probably not get the secretaryship job because of objections about his bureau experience. Ted says this is only Edgerton's private opinion, but it does look as though he won't get the job. Another set of men is now in control of the bureau. I feel down, but refuse to surrender all hope.

SATURDAY, AUGUST 3RD.

No American mail has come in and I am feeling fretty. Ted has given me a pair of earrings. They are large sapphires surrounded by small diamonds and are very pretty.

MONDAY, AUGUST 5TH.

I have been reading Kathleen Norris again. Some of her books are twaddly and thin, but some of them, the long crowded California stories, are very clever and extraordinarily alive. Cinderella books, nearly all of them, but delightful. The plots are fairy tales but the telling is good realism. I hear, smell, taste, feel, and see all through these books. I go into those kitchens, eat those meals, iron those frocks; I make those beds, wash those dishes, endure that heat, worry that worry, and weep for that joy. Kathleen Norris is as clever as Balzac in individualizing ordinary houses. She doesn't need a chateau or a Fifth Avenue mansion to work magic. She can take any house, any woman, and presto, you're keenly interested. Of course, her men are all shadows.

In *Little Ships,* she exhibits the Irish. It brings Mother's Irishness to me. I forget the existence of Joe Beates in our family. Of course, he was Mother's grandfather and a full-blooded Dubliner. Surely Mother's habit of always having a grievance, always feeling a martyr, is absolutely Irish. Mother, spoiling for a fight when things have been peaceful too long, is Irish. Positively.

Gosh, why don't I get busy with some of my stories!

THURSDAY, AUGUST 8TH.

One year today since Dad died.

A disturbing letter from Eddie came today. It makes me realize how imperative it is I should be home in America. Ted and I took a walk this evening to get away from the children and have a talk about it. Ted talked in his usual style that the boys are going to the dogs because they have left the Church and that is my fault. I said little, but my conviction is that the boys are going to the dogs because they have no home, and that's *our* fault. We left them.

SATURDAY, AUGUST 24TH.

Ted received a letter from Eddie with an enclosure from the Credit Men's Association. The job has been given to a man from Pittsburgh. So finale to that.

I feel very down. I did not know I had really banked so much on Ted's getting it. He doesn't mind at all, apparently. I suspect he will now be more set than ever on staying here in England, and probably argue that that is the evident will of God.

I'm not going to stay here. There is no will of God in this for me. I shall go to America as soon as ever I can.

FRIDAY, AUGUST 30TH.

I intend to go to Angel Road to make some farewells there. Ted has agreed to my early departure for New York, now that his return is not going to happen and that the boys are going to put up the necessary money. Johnnie sent me a hundred dollars and Eddie has cabled that he is sending me a hundred. Oh, this is good.

This afternoon I took the twins to the Super Cinema at Ilford. They enjoyed their first "talkie" there: *Black Waters*, a mystery melodrama. We also saw Lon Chaney in *Laugh, Clown, Laugh.*

SATURDAY, SEPTEMBER 7TH.

I secured my passage this morning on the *American Banker*, sailing on October fourth. In a month I shall be well away.

There was an argument at dinner between Ted and Charlie over Henry VIII and the English Reformation. Ted with his political statement that Henry threw over religion because he wanted a young Anne, and Charlie saying that the Reformation would have happened anyhow, Luther having started things, and that public opinion was with Henry or he could not have created the English Church. But Ted, of course, saying and believing that the English people were bereaved of their religion arbitrarily, by one man's will. They went on and on. I get impatient listening to this futile talk.

TUESDAY, SEPTEMBER 17TH.

I received a cable from Jimmie saying he is coming to England and will travel back to New York with me. This means I shall be in England two weeks longer than I had planned. Jimmie will have three weeks here. What a lot of money he must have saved.

WEDNESDAY, SEPTEMBER 18TH.

Charlie and I went to the Ilford Cinema to see the movie-talkie *Showboat*. It was a very good performance. Ted declined to come along because he refuses to take a train just to see a movie. Charlie commented afterwards, "I'd just as soon he didn't come, then he can't knock it. If he saw it he'd only have something more to criticize. He'd pick it to pieces, like he always does, and try to spoil it for us."

THURSDAY, SEPTEMBER 19TH.

Ted received a letter from Johnnie regarding the property. He writes that the four of them wish to draw out. I wish they would. I think this corporation business a cursed thing. To listen to Ted, you would think it was a great benefaction he had bestowed upon his children. He can talk away to the crack of doom, justifying it, proving it, praising it, and explaining it but he will never change my judgment: It is wrong. I am ashamed of it and ashamed of Ted and ashamed of myself for allowing myself to be persuaded to it in the beginning.

SUNDAY, SEPTEMBER 29TH.

Jimmie got in about four o'clock. He has grown to resemble Harold.

SUNDAY, OCTOBER 6TH.

We all went to eight o'clock Mass and Communion. Then Ted took Jim out in the Storey to practice driving and Jim smashed it up. He forgot the left-hand rule of the road, turned out of our lane the wrong way, and collided with a double-decker bus. Jim was not hurt but Ted has a cut face. Aileen came in about four and we had a jolly evening.

The American Banker

FRIDAY, OCTOBER, 18TH.

I sailed with Jim from Royal Albert Dock at nine this evening. Charlie and Ted came to see us off.

MONDAY, OCTOBER 28TH.

We landed in New York at four in the afternoon. Harold came aboard with the immigration officials. Eddie, John, and Ruth Eason were on the dock to meet us. There was no trouble with customs. We had supper at the Easons' and then to bed in the cottage at Knickerbocker Road.

Ruth Eason was the next-door neighbor to the 523 Knickerbocker Road home. Her house became a second home for Eddie.

Old Church Road
Romford, Essex
England

THURSDAY, DECEMBER 12TH.

I landed in London last Monday. Very, very much has happened in the last two months. The Thompson affairs are still in a muddle, but I am more contented now than I have been for two or three years. Maybe at last I am sailing home.

MONDAY, DECEMBER 16TH.

Ted received a letter from Johnnie saying that the boys had elected him to come and talk to Dad about the corporation; that he had a leave of absence from work, his passport, and expected to come and sing "Adeste Fidelis" with Dad at Christmas. Something has begun. The boys planned this move before I left them and apparently it is going through.

Meanwhile, here in England, Ted bought another house! It is a house on Eastern Road and he had planned to be moved into it before my return. I went to see it yesterday and sat on the top stair and felt like fainting away with shock and disgust. It is another of Ted's bargains, somebody's discard.

What am I to do with this man? I sat in the debris in the cottage in Tenafly and the consummation of my life and the vista of the future looked like nothing but desolation and the end of the world. I thought I had finally assented to having to surrender my sons. I saw they felt I had taken myself out of their lives, and that they had come to live without a place for me. I acknowledged their reaction as just and natural, and I thought I accepted it with stoicism.

I return from America, where I cannot resume the pattern of my days, and I find in England another home to be demolished around me. A new home has been selected again and all I may do is accept it. But I don't accept it, I choke. This is what I have come to at forty-five: a demolished home, a scattered family, a broken life. I choke.

WEDNESDAY, DECEMBER 18TH.

Seven-thirty P.M. I am alone in the house. The boys are at a Scout meeting and Ted has gone to Forest Gate with the Catholic Evidence Guild.

When I look at Ted, to really see him, I have to admit to myself that he has become passé for New York business. He has grown a beard whilst I was away and it is a horrible disfigurement. It makes him look like a tramp en route to the workhouse and it hides all the beauty and character of his face. Still, that could be shaved away. He wears an air of tiredness, of being finished. I cannot see him becoming alert and snappy again, smartening up, being vivid and energetic as he used to be. I saw Spencer Smith in Tenafly. He is several years Ted's senior, but he looks, and acts as well, as smart, as young, as ever. He hasn't let go of himself. Ted has.

I realize again myself as woman: mere female, tagging along behind my man. Philosophies, religion, power are for men no matter what may be declaimed about the rights of women. Wives are still in the harem. I might just as well have been born in Turkey for anything I can do as long as I am Mrs. Edward Thompson.

Listening to Ted's conversation this week, my spirit goes flatter and flatter. I think of the company of people on the boat: artists, writers, travelers, and actors. The weather was abominable but the company was delightful. What conversations, what repartee! Socially the trip was one of the most enjoyable times I have had in my life. Then I come back to Ted, who puts a prick in every bubble, who doesn't understand bantering, persiflage. For him, every scintilla of wit must be strained through the mesh of Catholic theology. And yet I love him, at times with passion. Why must I be bound to this man?

I have written to a Mrs. Wallace, who was a fellow passenger. She has a cousin at Forest Gate and writes proposing to call on me. I have written to make excuses. She is a professional society entertainer, "Madame Isis," a crystal gazer, an astrologist. She is delightful and amusing, but fancy having her to tea with Ted!

The boys provided me with a bagful of books before I left New York, but I read very little on the boat. The company was so charming it was a waste of time to read. So now I have those books to enjoy.

THURSDAY, DECEMBER 19TH.

Three-ten P.M. I am baking cakes and waiting for the last one to come out of the oven. The boys are at school, and Ted is attending Bert's auction.

Whilst on the boat I read Somerset Maugham's *Of Human Bondage*, with enjoyment, though I thought Mildred overdrawn, made too vile. One thing struck me about Philip, and that was where he realized he spent his life waiting for an imaginary future. That brought it home to me that that is what I do.

I daydream about what might, could, or should come to pass and it never comes to pass.

For a year or more I thought that if I could only get back to America I could pull the family together again. I saw myself getting a house, setting it in order, resuming a routine life with the boys, and then drawing Ted and these boys to me. A dream. I get to America, but I find nothing can be resumed. The elder boys do not desire a return of parents or any return of the old status quo. They love me but they can live without me. I've been six thousand miles and spent five hundred dollars to find out there is no going back in this world. I knew it before, theoretically, but now I really know it.

FRIDAY, DECEMBER 20TH.

Johnnie arrived this evening. Ted guessed he'd be sailing on the *Berengaria*, if he was planning to arrive by Christmas, and met him at Waterloo Station. Johnnie was immensely surprised to see his father there.

SUNDAY, DECEMBER 22ND.

Bert came over this morning and opened his eyes when he heard Ted was at church for the second time today. He inquired if Johnnie would go and I said no, and that Ted was unhappy about that defection. Bert remarked: "Well, that's alright. Let him be unhappy. Folks have to worry about something, I take it. Ted's worry is religion and how his boys don't go to church. Let him worry. It's a darn sight better to worry over that than thieving or murder, isn't it? Folks have got to get themselves a worriment of some kind or other. Leave 'em to it, is my motto." Then I mentioned all of Ted's extra services for the Christmas season, and Bert said, "That's alright. It amuses him, don't it? It don't hurt anybody. It's his hobby, like." True. Sensible Bert.

FRIDAY, DECEMBER 27TH.

We have had two very charming days at Bert's. Tillie is the perfect hostess and makes everyone comfortable. We came home to sleep, late on Christmas Day, but returned to them again in time for dinner yesterday.

Ted has been cranky with me all through the holidays. It is a pity. I'm sorry I can't suit him, but I fail him in piety as he fails me in passion. Early this morning I woke with desire and turned to him for loving but he would have none of it. Why did we two have to marry? I need a lover; he needs a saint.

1930

THURSDAY, JANUARY 2ND.

On New Year's Eve Bert, Tillie, Bertie, and Selma came here to see the New Year in. Yesterday John and I had a day in town shopping and visiting. We went to Mother's for supper and found Gladys, Eric and Malvin, Sonnie and Edith, and the baby, Monica, there. Mother served a sumptuous dinner of roast goose and plum pudding.

I stayed in bed until eleven this morning and am now feeling fine.

SATURDAY, JANUARY 4TH.

Ten P.M. This has been one of my bad days. I had to go to the house on Eastern Road to see the plumber. This house does not invite me at all, and when I think of all the work involved to make it into a home, I quail. What a task! And the results so dubious. Also, I have just been sewing chevrons and badges on Boy Scout uniforms for the twins, and that depresses me. I hate this standardizing of patriotism and this training to the soldier idea.

Johnnie left with Charlie last night for Paris. I am glad he can get a few days there, but this departure brings closer the ultimate departure for New York, and I could fret so easily. I feel so sad tonight.

MONDAY, JANUARY 6TH.

A cable arrived to Johnnie from Harold and I opened it. Harold states that Hoffman is offering the house back to us for six thousand dollars and that he favors the proposition. Ted does not.

TUESDAY, JANUARY 14TH.

John and Charlie returned from Paris last week. Charlie is sixteen today. He, John, and I went to the Ilford Cinema in the afternoon.

Ted and John had a long talk tonight about Tenafly affairs.

Ted has sold the Eastern Road house. Thank goodness.

SATURDAY, JANUARY 18TH.

John left Romford this morning. I said good-bye to him in the house, but Ted and the boys all went to the station. The boat leaves Southampton at two o'clock. Good-bye, Johnnie.

SATURDAY, FEBRUARY 8TH.

Three P.M. All the boys are at football and Ted is at the office.

This has been a full and exciting week. On Sunday Ted was talking about a house at 80 Eastern Road which is for sale. He said he had been to see it, liked it, and asked me to go to see it and let him know what I thought of it. On Tuesday I went to look at it and liked it very much. It is bigger than this house and has a pleasant garden besides. Ted asked me if I thought I could take care of it, and I said I thought I could. He has made an offer for it.

Ten P.M. Ted and I had tea alone and he was speaking disparagingly about the boys. He received a letter from Johnnie reporting that Eddie and Harold wanted to withdraw entirely from the corporation, and that Harold was very disappointed that Ted would not take back 523 Knickerbocker Road from Hoffman. Harold wanted a home, and missed and needed a home more than any of them. Harold wants to give the cottage and the property back to Dad and end the corporation. Ted does not like this. He says the boys have no sense of honor and that that would be welching. He says he can't expect them to have a sense of honor or to be ethical since they have given up their religion. I do not like this. I detest the assumption that only a Catholic can be honorable, trustworthy, and good.

I think the boys have been abominably treated. I think that as parents Ted and I are a pair of duds. If we had died in 1927 that would have been a satisfactory ending to family life, both for us and for the boys. But we didn't die, we merely moved out. Ted shuffled an American life of thirty years off his back, cleft his family in twain, and left those four on their own, saddled with a pledged monetary indebtedness to him. I think of the cottage and the boys' horrible bachelor hall life there: no comfort, no care, and paying quota. But they have property, says Ted. True, the cow fields, the wood lots, the cottage, and they are fed up with it all. They are aching for a home.

Think of it, four young sons, three thousand miles away, and always to be so except for a few vacation weeks here and there through the years. Why be a mother? What a cruelty. It does not bear thinking about. I can't change anything or anybody. I'm here and here I must stay. I must get interested in here and quit thinking about *there*.

MONDAY, FEBRUARY 10TH.

Ted bought 80 Eastern Road today. We have been measuring around and surveying its possibilities. I like it very much and I am sure we shall be much more comfortable there than in this house.

SUNDAY, MARCH 2ND.

Grace and Jack Winmill are in Romford because Grace has come for a medical examination. It seems she has had a lump in her stomach for nearly a year. Dr. Green examined her this morning and she is to go into the hospital in a few days for an operation. Cancer, I suppose. Ted's mother died of cancer and so did Emily. Billie and Arthur of T.B.

MONDAY, MARCH 3RD.

Grace went into Cottage Hospital today. Dr. Green presumes the lump is a tumor and that it probably weighs seven or eight pounds.

I notice that quite frequently women who won't have children have tumors. If told, Ted would never believe that Grace ever practiced birth control. She is nearly as pious as he is, but Dorothy has told me how Grace asked her for knowledge of methods to prevent conception. Dorothy gave her the information. Medical authority states that very few women are naturally barren and no women are born old. But Catholics, as well as Protestants, avail themselves of birth control and not, one is sure, by the permissible and devout abstinence from conjugal intercourse. Being a devout Catholic is a sustaining diversion, but really obeying the Church is something else again, and only to be indulged so far as convenient.

FRIDAY, MARCH 7TH.

I went with Ted to visit Grace last night. No doubt she is gravely ill. I gathered a serious impression that she is making her peace with the world. I felt she had withdrawn her attitude of criticism and antagonism to me, and when I bent to kiss her goodnight she kissed me with an affectionate fervor I had never experienced in her before. When death is imminent all barriers fall, all jealousies evaporate.

THURSDAY, MARCH 13TH.

Three-forty-five P.M. The kaleidoscope of the past continues to revolve in my dreams. Why don't I begin to write a story? Perhaps the greatest holdback now is my complete lack of values. I believe in nothing and no one. There was a time when I longed for reality. Now that I flounder in it, I long for illusion. Once I longed for knowledge and determined to acquire it. Now I am horribly wise. I know too much. Yet if I could lose myself in scribbling again I might find it an anodyne.

We are in a hole again for money. The boys have paid in no quota since last October. Ted is thoroughly dismal about it and murmurs against the boys daily. I listen and say nothing. If I began to speak I should swear and say much too much. I should begin to tell Ted what I think of him and I should probably end in the divorce court or the penitentiary. Ted sits and mopes, criticizes the boys, and lays all their errors and misdemeanors to their lack of religion and their leaving the Church, which is my fault. I should think they would leave the Church. His showing of the Catholic life is no recommendation for sanity, affection, or manliness. His religion is an insistent self-indulgence. He is a neurotic.

Well, that doesn't get me anywhere. That is only another stating of cold facts.

THURSDAY, MARCH 20TH.

Eleven-thirty A.M. Grace is mortally ill. At first there was a slight hope that she would recover sufficiently to leave the hospital, but now there is no hope at all. She is dying. This thing was a cancer, of course, and it weighed eight pounds. At the beginning, Dr. Green informed Jack that there was no earthly hope for her. If she got over the operation, the cancer would return again in a few months. So if she can die now, so much the better.

Yesterday I received a cable from Harold saying he had deposited one hundred and thirty in the account, so that has eased the money worry, at least.

Monday I wrote at length to Dorothy Nighman and now I wish I hadn't done so. I spilled over to her, very foolishly. Extra foolishly, as I knew yesterday when my long-delayed courses appeared. I had not had a period since Johnnie was here, nine weeks ago. These last few weeks I have been growing more and more moody and fretful, finding living absolutely unbearable, and behold, as per usual, my courses have begun and I am restored to sanity and serenity. But the unlucky, ranting, hysterical letter to Dorothy went off just the same. What a fool of a woman I am.

MONDAY, MARCH 24TH.

There is tension in the house again. Before Ted went out this afternoon he affixed a large printed placard to the parlor window announcing a forthcoming mission at St. Edward's R. C. Church. As soon as I found it, I took it down and burnt it in the kitchen stove. I have never yet had any kind of a notice appearing on my house and I never will have one. These are the gratuities of tenement dwellers or the tactics of those who have something to sell, advertisers, and neither stunt is for us.

When Ted came in at teatime he asked me about the placard and I told him I had burned it. He told me I was selfish and that he would be out very late tonight and "at least, I shall not hurry home." He returned from his Monday class around eleven and was surprised not to find me downcast at all but enjoying a visit with Mrs. Barkham, who had happened to call.

Ted is martyred over my religious shortcomings as usual. I would have removed any placard he might have put up, only this one dealing with the church notice makes my crime of independent action all the greater. Are wives people? No, not in England.

Unforgiven. When I wakened this morning I was coming out of a dream and had absolutely forgotten last night's crime. I was feeling happy and turned towards Ted, slipped my arm under his neck, and threw my other arm across his chest, but he gave me no response at all. He was awake but he did not give the slightest sign. I kept still until he arose, too proud to withdraw myself.

Aileen's review of *Kristin Lavransdatter* [Sigrid Undset] is in the *Herald* today. One sentence arrested my attention. She has written: "One may lament the sense of sin that cripples every character in this book." Exactly, the sense of sin that cripples. I've never been aware of a sense of sin and I don't suppose Aileen ever has, whereas Mother is one of the people who is obsessed by it, and Ted is another. Mother, feeling absolutely righteous in herself, is obsessed with the delinquencies of all the rest of the world. Ted, chockful of religion, mourns his own sin, but cannot refrain from commenting on the sins of the world and correcting the people who belong to him. Mother scandalizes but Ted interferes directly with people, urged by a passion for correction. He doesn't call it correction. He calls it Justice and Truth. Lord deliver me from a just man.

Mrs. Wallace, the astrologer on the *Trader*, asked when my husband was born. When I told her, she made a little moué and said he belonged to a watery planet and that I probably didn't have a very harmonious time with him. I laughed, but she didn't know how she'd hit the mark. Several of the things she said were surprisingly correct. She guessed that I had had trouble with my scalp. This was an extraordinary hit, for I have had the birthmark on my head removed three times and she couldn't possibly have known anything about that. Another very lucky guess concerned my taste in food. She said that since I belonged to a fire planet, I will like sunshine, hot baths, and food much hotter than most people. She said I was exceptional in not liking raw foods such as salads and fresh fruits. That is quite correct. I like fruits and vegetables cooked and warm. One of Ted's perennial jokes is about my asbestos lining.

I might as well note what else Mrs. Wallace told me. She said my lucky day was Sunday. Comment: I rather dislike Sundays, as there is always too much work for the housewife. She said my lucky number was seven. Comment: Not that I'm aware of. I have seven sons, that's all. She said I was careless about money and that I would never be rich nor in want. Comment: I can never worry about money, so she's fairly right. She said I should have good luck with anything to do with oil or oil wells. Comment: That doesn't mean anything. She said my colors were black, white, and pink. Comment: I've always looked well in black and white. I have always hankered after pink, but have rarely worn it because I thought it clashed with my red hair.

Mrs. Wallace and her husband were genial, cultured people, quite sane and very charming. Everybody on that trip was charming. I think I shall remember them all.

THURSDAY, MARCH 27TH.

Yesterday I finished [E. F.] Dakin's book on Mrs. Eddy [*Mrs. Eddy, The Biography of a Virginal Mind*]. I found it extremely interesting, but I thought it rather too severe on the lady. For all her faults, she did have a vital apprehension of God, and God as Love and Righteousness. She was a rebel from New England Calvinism, and she addressed herself to her contemporaries, who also had grown up crushed by Puritan theology. She presented them with an idea of God and the soul which was new to them, and which was extremely satisfying.

Turning her pages in *Science and Health*, I began to pray. Flooding back came my own belief in God, intense, real, and suddenly linking up like fire with all my Catholic knowledge. Everything began to fall into place. That dreadful hatred of my life lifted, that sense of loss and hopelessness began to drop away. I think I have come to faith, something I have never known. Something I have apprehended at last, a glimpse, a gift.

SATURDAY, MARCH 29TH.

Joan, in Baluchistan, Pakistan, is to be married today.

I have been reading Saint Jane. It is incredible to me that her works had already been in the world for two hundred years when Mrs. Eddy was born. I suppose Mrs. Eddy never even heard of Saint Jane, nor any other saint, except those in the New Testament.

When I was fretting in the summer of 1928, at the time Dad was dying, my thoughts jumped to Mrs. Eddy for a time. I thought she might have something to say to me. I was so sick of man's world, and man's religion, that I thought Mrs. Eddy would understand me as a woman. I went to the Christian Science Reading Room in Sloane Street and borrowed some of their literature, and I attended a couple of services in their church. But it did not please me. Somehow, it did not ring sincere. I did not want to join.

As for now, do not think I am not aware of myself as a woman at her climacteric. As youth is definitely going, perhaps I am clutching for erotic satisfaction, like any other poor fool woman. Very likely old Dame Nature is playing her tricks on me. All the same, I do know this, that I am again aware of

God, and not as an abstract idea or scholastic theory, but as a living being. I want to let go of all the past. I want to begin a new life, to be a new creature. I love God as I used to when I was a girl, catching fire from Voysey.

Joan married George Godfrey, a career soldier in the British Army.

THURSDAY, APRIL 3RD.

Grace died last Saturday.

TUESDAY, APRIL 15TH.

This morning Ted shaved off his beard. This is a positive joy to me. He has a beautiful face, and I hate to have him hide it with a beard.

I went to the hairdresser's today and had my hair cut, shampooed, and water-waved. As the spring opens one certainly does feel like furbishing up a little.

Tonight I have recommenced my story about *Nine Row*. This time I have begun it in the first person. I shall tell it through the character of a young girl, though she is not my heroine. If I'm to aim at the popular market, I must appeal to the young.

TUESDAY, APRIL 24TH.

The cold weather and Mother's Easter visit seem to have taken every bit of vitality and spirit out of me. Mother is simply devastating. Probably I am very much like her, positive, vehement, domineering, and insofar as I'm like that, I'm sorry for Ted. At least I try to curb myself and always have done so.

My earliest recollection of Mother was of somebody *not* to copy. I got away from her. All her children got away as fast as they could. Although she can no longer interfere in our lives with her tempers, her beatings, her swearings, her obstructions to all our privacies and plans, still she interferes with her overwhelming inquisitiveness and her dictatorial ways about how we run our lives. How we cook our meals, open our windows, take our baths or our physics, where we buy our clothes, what is in our correspondence; really, there isn't a detail of our lives about which she will not dispute and try and make us perform it otherwise.

Grace used to say she found Mother so refreshing because she took such a keen interest in life. I simply hate it for anyone to take such a keen interest in my life. I want to be left alone, to pursue my business in silence. Fussiness and censorious talky-talkyness do not refresh me, they only drive me mad.

With me and Mother, I suppose behind everything, lies the indelible memory of my childhood and girlhood. She has forgotten it all, but I haven't. I suppose she thinks she loves me, perhaps she does. We always observe the standard mannerisms of loving parent and dutiful child. She, no doubt, because she is incurably conservative and observes all fetishes, and I because I loathe friction and differences and because I follow the rules of polite society and quarrel with no one. I know she considers herself a perfect mother, she says so, but I remember hell. Those first twenty hellish years remain the root of my life no matter what changes have followed. The fact is, I do not love Mother. I endure her and with cheerfulness. It is only in this scribble that I moan.

FRIDAY, APRIL 25TH.

I've cheered up. Last night Charlie came home from visiting Gladys in Plymouth, and the weather has improved. Ted and Charlie have been working in the Eastern Road house all day and I went over this afternoon to have a look around. I think it will be pleasant living there.

THURSDAY, MAY 1ST.

Charlie and the twins went back to school today.

Tomorrow I expect to go to town and to take Selma with me. I shall take her to the Tate Gallery and try to make her see a few pictures. Selma is really underdeveloped. No one has ever taken an interest in her or taught her how to use her brain.

I intend to go to Straker's whilst in town, to buy a new manuscript book and also some foolscap. Mother dried up all my enthusiasm for my *Nine Row* story but I shall get to it again soon. Oh, I wish I could comb Mother out of my mind and regard her with just natural animal affection.

Saturday is to be our silver anniversary.

There is an eighteen-month gap between the last journal entry and where we now resume. Probably one volume has been lost, or perhaps destroyed.

During this period Ruby worried that Ted was having an affair with a Mrs. McTurk, a neighbor. Ruby referred to this episode as "Ted's summer madness of 1930." She believed that the one thing that might keep Ted from acting on his flirtation was his Catholicism. On October 1, 1931, Charlie, age seventeen, left England and returned to the United States to live with his older brothers in Tenafly, New Jersey.

1931

Holmwood
80 Eastern Road
Romford, Essex

WEDNESDAY, NOVEMBER 25TH.

Ted was in Wimbledon all day, attending Dorothy's sale. He has brought home an oil painting, a sunset scene in Wales that hung in his father's house when he was a child. Bert says he can remember when their father bought it. So now I know where Ted gets his taste in pictures.

Dorothy has given me twenty-eight volumes of Balzac which were Billie's. Some of them duplicate mine, but I'm fully pleased to get them. I first read Balzac when I was a bride in Bayonne. There was a complete edition in the public library, and I read practically all of it. I had nothing to do in those days so I read my fill. What a revelation he was to me! No one has ever surpassed him. He is the supreme master of them all.

Dorothy Thompson is the widow of Ted's brother Billie, who died of tuberculosis in 1930 at age thirty-eight.

SUNDAY, DECEMBER 6TH.

It has been four years today since we landed in England. For me, four years in purgatory.

This is how we spent today. Ted and the twins went to the eight o'clock Mass whilst I cooked the breakfast. Then Ted sat in the parlor whilst I cooked the dinner, which consisted of roast lamb, roast potatoes, and cauliflower, followed by apple tart with whipped cream and coffee. I did not go to Mass. Then, in the afternoon, the twins went to Sunday School whilst Ted and I occupied the parlor in silence. He read *The Catholic Times* and I read Balzac until I fell asleep. Then at five o'clock I set out tea. Before we had finished, Dorothy came in. At six Ted left for church and Dagenham. Dorothy and I talked scandal in the parlor till nine-thirty and then adjourned to the kitchen for coffee and ham sandwiches. At ten Ted came in and very soon after Dorothy left. Ted and I returned once more to the parlor and this time he read *The Catholic Universe* whilst I smoked a couple of cigarettes. At eleven-fifteen he went up to bed, and when I thought he had finished his prayers, I followed. I found him on the bed violently doing the scissors! After which he did a lot more arm and leg exercises standing nude in front of the mirror. He never spoke and I never spoke. What a day!

There is more and more trouble: nasty, niggling, bad temper, troubles. I've come to the conclusion it is because Ted is fasting too much. Since the beginning of Advent he has been fasting and he's like a bear with a sore head. He is as steadily disagreeable as he knows how to be. He has stopped smoking, too, and is almost unbearable. I am in continuous disgrace, of course.

Christmas passed away pretty well. Ted and I went to the midnight Mass and to Communion side by side. I was not moved by the mass but was content, feeling at peace with Ted.

Early this morning Ted awoke me for loving and we knew a bliss like that of twenty years ago. He fell again into a deep sleep but I lay wakeful, content, soothed, happy, and with a clear, stilled mind such as I have not known for a long time. It was as though all the muddied sediments of my unhappiness, follies, and lacks sank down in a quiet settlement and a clear stream of sensible and philosophical life ran above it all. In that clearness I saw the truth, which is this: Primarily, we are animals. The man needs the woman, the woman needs the man. Ted and I need each other. Our desire is to each other, and together we can still find the ultimate harmonies.

Each life pursues its own course. I left my parents and ruthlessly went my own way. If I had not left my sons, ultimately they would have left me. I left them too soon, too abruptly and quite selfishly. Yet so much time has now passed by that all of that has become *old* trouble. It will remain as a story and its consequences will remain; but it will not remain as a grief, only as a memory of grief. Time cures all things.

I've got to keep the knowledge that Ted does love me in spite of all the friction that rubs on the surface of our lives. We tease each other, we hurt each other, but we do love each other.

1932

Eleven A.M. Watching the pots.

Today is Charlie's birthday. He's eighteen. We had a letter from him last week, saying he had started work in the Metropolitan Life Insurance Company at a salary of eighteen dollars a week. He also said he went to midnight Mass on Christmas Eve but did not know if he should continue to go to Mass because he did not know whether or not he believed in religion. This upset Ted pretty considerably. He did not eat for three days but has pulled back into cheerfulness now. Charlie was a silly boy to write so to his father. I wish he hadn't. We can't change Ted about re-ligion, so why make him miserable by insisting on our lack of it? It is never necessary to tell all we think, and thank God for that.

TUESDAY, JANUARY 19TH.

I had a shock today. When at the dentist's this morning, he suddenly laid down his tools and told me the teeth were rotten. I had pyorrhea and had best have the teeth out. Of course I had to accept his judgment. He suggested that I have a proper anesthetic and have them all out at one go. I agreed. He said I had better see my doctor and then communicate again with him.

So this evening I have been to Dr. Marjorie Munro and had the heart and blood pressure tests. They, very happily, are quite good. She then telephoned to Dr. Ritchie and together they made an appointment, here at the house, for next Tuesday. I feel decidedly nervous.

Pyorrhea is a gum disease in which inflammation and degeneration of the gum tissue surrounding the teeth leads to loosening and eventual loss of the teeth. Until about twenty years ago, and the introduction of flossing, this condition was difficult to treat and the loss of teeth was common.

THURSDAY, JANUARY 28TH.

Well, my teeth are out. Dr. Munro gave me a hypodermic injection of goodness knows what. Then she prepared my bed, fixing it so that my head would be at the foot of it. Ritchie then came in, bringing a nurse with him, and I got more and more scared. Dr. Marjorie had made me take off dress, shoes, and corsets and get into a dressing gown. Then they laid me down and gave me ether.

About two hours later, when I returned to consciousness, there was nobody there but the nurse. The doctor came in around four o'clock and said Ritchie had taken out thirteen teeth, all very bad ones. This seems to have surprised them, as it does me, since my teeth looked so good and strong. She said that probably I shall be in much better health very soon, and most likely my leg trouble will clear up considerably. Well, that remains to be seen.

Last week, too, Ritchie said that I must be a very robust woman because the toxic state of my teeth was such that it was a wonder I wasn't laid on my bed with a complete breakdown. He thought a less strong woman would have become very ill long ago. I listened with a smile. We have heard so much of this talk about bad teeth causing severe bad health these last few years, and I don't know that I believe any of it.

I have twelve teeth left in my head. I feel pretty good today, though my mouth feels queer and I can neither eat nor talk. Yesterday I felt rather rotten, because the ether hangs about and hangs about. I can have a temporary denture pretty soon, I'm told, and shall not have to wait through toothless months until the gums finish shrinking and hardening. One advantage I can reap out of this is I can be excused from Saturday bridge and Sunday visitors! I absolutely decline to see anybody until I have some teeth to talk with.

MONDAY, FEBRUARY 1ST.

Last Friday both Ted and I each got a very brief note from Harold announcing his engagement to a girl called Kay Kelly. His letter to me says briefly, "This will break the big news to you that I have renounced all obligations to the family, to man, to God, and beast in order that I may get myself engaged to one whom I shall marry as soon as I can save enough money to put a roof over her head. I'm abandoning the ship."

The note was theatrical but the news is serious. What about his corporation quota? What about his promised assistance to Johnnie in financing the house deal? Not that Harold hasn't the right to marry whomsoever he pleases, but what about his previous pledges to his family? And who is *this* girl? He has had so many hot affairs. Is it that this is a girl clever enough to pin him down? I feel stunned at the news.

Anyhow, no matter in what light I consider it, our son is marrying a girl we have never heard of, and we are not there. It's crazy. Our whole family hash-up is crazy.

MONDAY, FEBRUARY 8TH.

Eight-thirty P.M. Ted is out tonight, and I have just come from the scullery where I have been mixing up parkins, now in the oven. I feel frightfully restless. I don't know why I suddenly made cake at this hour, but there it is.

I had two jolts in this morning's mail. One was a wedding announcement from Flushing.

Mr. John J. Kelly
announces the marriage of his sister
Katherine Veronica
to
Harold Francis Thompson
January Thirty first
St. Joan of Arc Church
Jackson Heights, Long Island

The other was a piece of advice from Charlie. He wrote a nice long letter, but sandwiched in it is this:

> You're funny, though: I mean not realizing how well off we were here until you got back to dear old England. You say you were not as jolly as the rest on Christmas. May I suggest you look at it this way. You were there, you thought of what you would like better and knew you could not obtain it, at least for the moment. That's the position. Now you can't change it, so please forget it and get all the fun you can. You worry about us and figure you would like to be amongst us. The idea has struck me that the first is your nature, and the second is thinking about yourself. The natural tendency is to grow selfish and let the wish of what you would prefer become stronger than your concern. Of course, it would be wrong of me to suggest that you let it happen, but the idea came and I'm intending to be honest with myself, as regarding religion, but I'll come to that. Forget last New Year's. Let me reiterate. Forget yourself and the future and what you can't better, and have a good time.

That's Charlie, eighteen two weeks ago and a bare four months away from me. He advises like an old father confessor. Well, I do sit up and take notice. Yes, I was considerably jolted, but not to my knees. This family mess-up isn't God's affair. I felt and heard the door to America shut with a bang, and I remain on this side of it indefinitely, perhaps forever. The only gesture I could make was to buy an English cookbook.

I wish I could take my life and wring it free of all these distressing problems of religion, of love, of country, of fidelities, as I wring a dishcloth free of dirty water. But I can't. I have to go on living my life *as it is*. But then, how? And tonight I'm baking parkin whilst Ted is at the Friary studying theology. What a world. What a life!

WEDNESDAY, FEBRUARY 10TH.

It is a cold and very snowy day. I went to the dentist's this afternoon, who, after examining my mouth, asked me to let it wait till April. He says my gums are still full of poison and it is better to leave them free rather than to fit any kind of plate yet. Well, I really do not mind, for this gives me a good excuse to extend my retreat from the world. I'm glad for another couple of months with no visitors and no visiting.

TUESDAY, MARCH 1ST.

Four P.M. Too emotional. It is partly menstruation, I suppose, but there are distressing facts as well to endure. I have had a nasty letter from Eddie. However, against this I can place a photograph of Harold's wife; she looks pretty, good, kind, and sweet.

Last week I had to write to Jimmie for his birthday. He'll be twenty on the eighth, and I was distressed to find how little there was to say to him. I had just two letters from him in the whole of last year. I no longer know the boy. There is nothing to say to him. It is like death between us already.

WEDNESDAY, MARCH 30TH.

I was very wakeful during the night and lay seeing myself horribly clearly. I am a muddler.

The longer I live, the more sure I am that the personality of a human being never changes. We are what we are, the same, from the beginning of our lives until the end. We do not know ourselves all at once, and in some things we never know ourselves at all. But those we live with will know us, and though we may deceive ourselves, we cannot deceive our intimates.

To me it seems that the basic fact in Ted's character is timidity. The most arduous acts of his life, like his trip to Alaska, were his most determined efforts to overcome it. But he never really overcomes it. He was afraid of business all his business life, and, as soon as he could, he made excuses to quit the business world. He was afraid of his sons, his power to dominate them, as soon as they became men, so he left them altogether. And he is afraid of hell and that is what drives him into the Church. That it is the Catholic Church is incidental, really. He thinks he accepts it from rational conviction, but I don't think so. His parents were very pious evangelicals, bringing up their children with all the old Puritanical taboos. Upbringing is never overcome. After a spell of rebellion from our parents' codes we nearly always go back to them. I was brought up in skepticism and I go back to skepticism, if, indeed, I ever forsook it.

What is the basic fact of my character? Is it un-morality or inertia or amiability? I'm sure I don't know, but I should guess that it is amiability. But a foolish kind of amiability, resting not at all on a genuine sweetness of disposition, but on a hatred of discords. I grew up in such a hellish atmosphere of rancor, fights, and hatreds that my prime necessity is peace, peace at any price. There is the difference between us: Ted's dominant desire in life is for security; mine is for peace.

It is this silly amiability which will most probably take me to Mass next Sunday. I run away from disputes. It is easier to do what the other fellow wants than to stick out for my own want, to follow his inclination rather than to tag away to my own. I assuage my pride by remembering that I can always think my own thoughts. I never feel that truth must be stated. It is enough for me to know it.

I see myself becoming more and more like Dad as I come well into middle age. I cease to contend with the disagreeable world which surrounds me and which I cannot change, but I retreat further and further into indifference and silence.

Ted wrote in a brief autobiography that in 1897 his brother Herbert, who was working in New York, invited Ted to join him in a trek to the Klondike to look for gold in the Yukon territories. With Jack Holiday, a friend from Romford, Ted sailed to Halifax, met Bert in Montreal, and then all three went off to Skagway and the Chilkoot Pass. They packed three thousand pounds of supplies on a sled and got as far as Lake Lindeman. Disenchanted, one by one, they dropped out to return to New York City. Eighteen-year-old Ted was the last to leave, selling what was left of the equipment to the next wave of gold-rushers. Ted then worked in Washington sawmills and lumber camps to raise the railroad fare back to New York. He said he arrived in the city with fifty cents in his pocket and, unable to find his brother, spent his first night in the Bowery.

Although Ted was a success in the business world, it was not his pleasure to be part of it. He always dreamed of early retirement and wished to live a life of frugal comfort as an Englishman. He also wished to have the leisure to attend Mass every day.

MONDAY, APRIL 4TH.

Today I received a good letter from Charlie. He tells me he has had a raise of two dollars a week. He also describes the life in 523 Knickerbocker Road during the weekends. It all sounds jolly. He also says that Eddie is happy most of the time and has just got another organ. I take heart from this report, concluding things are not so bad as Eddie's letters would make out. Presumably Eddie writes to me when at his gloomiest, so I must remember this and discount at least fifty percent of his woe.

MONDAY, APRIL 18TH.

Eight P.M. Alone in the kitchen by the fire. This is my birthday. I am forty-eight and Eddie is twenty-six. I had a good letter from him. I think Charlie has gauged him correctly. I will try not to worry so much in future when I get gloomy letters from him.

TUESDAY, MAY 3RD.

Our twenty-seventh wedding anniversary. I have lived with Ted now six years longer than I lived with myself.

I was thunderstruck by his remarking that *I* was the horrible example which made him join the Church. He said he could see that my ideas were crazy and that you couldn't live that way, so there was nothing else to do but accept religion. Really. I made no answer to this. What would be the use?

FRIDAY, MAY 13TH.

I am either ill or mad, or both. Experience teaches me nothing. I am either the biggest fool woman in Christendom or I am such a neurotic that I am virtually mad.

What *is* the matter with this family, anyhow? The other day Mother was telling me about Mary Searle and said, "Mary had such rages. Her temper was ungovernable and she was always making rows, swearing, and carrying on something awful."

I did not comment to Mother, who seems to have forgotten her own rages, but I did add Mary to the shrews of Mother's side of the house. Luckily, Mother didn't pass on her violent temper to me; or if she did, I have hated the exhibition of unrestrained temper so much that I rarely give way to mine. But I really don't think that I have that kind of temper. I am melancholic, not virulent. Mother's rages were so awful to me that I *cannot* give way to passionate anger, but Gladys does. She was a fighting spitfire all through our childhood and all her culture has been insufficient to make her control herself. Since I have been home, I've heard of her pulling the tablecloth off the table and destroying a whole meal upon the ground. Then there were Mabel Barnsbee's rages. I've seen her foaming at the mouth in sheer rage, and she had to be restrained by the police from damaging Kitty's shop window.

The Searle women are mostly an ungovernable lot. Where did that awful fighting temper come from? Joe Beates, the Irishman? I wonder. I think I have Dad's temper, which is a morose one. Anyhow, I find myself more and more like Dad, and I'm afraid he was a neurotic,

Probably if I were a rich woman, and could go to a great psychologist, he would tell me that all my disharmonies, mental and physical, arise from the violence I allow to be done to myself: violence to my mind in coercing it into Catholicism; violence to my heart in the breakup of my home and separation from my sons. Well, I know that, don't I? How do I correct it? How do I surmount it?

I cannot leave Ted and try to recreate the old life. I am tired, utterly tired. I want to write. Only in writing can I forget myself. Last week I wrote a very long letter to John and it pleased me. It was not just a tabulation of events, but ideas. I want to give them ideas.

I want to go away. I want never to have to keep house anymore, never to order or cook another meal, never to receive another guest, never to have to pay another call. I am tired, utterly, thoroughly tired. I should like to go to bed and stay there, never to have to speak to or listen to a human being again. Mad, of course. But only mad enough to wish it, not to really do it.

We have been to Antwerp since last writing. Ted suggested going on an excursion, so we went. I had a very pleasant time, not too tiring. Both nights were spent aboard ship, so I was able to undress and sleep properly. The weather was showery, but as most of the sightseeing was in museums, churches, and castles, the dampness was no inconvenience. It was a day I shall remember.

Three P.M. Disturbed and unhappy. I have been reading and enjoying D. H. Lawrence's book *Apocalypse*, but I think it has upset me. Such books as this one, full of beauty, adventurous thought, and free spirit, exalt me whilst I am reading them. They give me keen pleasure, but, when I have finished them, I am more sickened and disgusted than ever by the drabness which surrounds me and the Christian bigotry from which I can never escape. Then why read them? Why does a drowning man clutch at straws?

Ted seems to me more reactionary than ever. Frequently he will pontificate about a wife's duties. So English! So Pauline! He is quite bucked because the new Gaspani Catechism states simply, explicitly, and dogmatically that a wife should obey her husband. And when he comes in from rent collecting he invidiously sings the praises of the cottagers' wives because they suffer poverty cheerfully, and faithfully whiten their doorsteps. He told me recently of a woman who had made one hundred thirty pounds of jam and he thought it wonderful. Did he think it wonderful all those years when I used to put up fruit and make jam and can vegetables, from the first spring rhubarb to the late fall peas and pumpkins? Of course not. Nothing I have ever done has earned his praise, but I have heard his adverse criticisms pretty continuously. To be a house-drudge, ceaselessly working for her man, that's the English idea of the perfect wife. Comradeship? Understanding? Sympathy? No, not between man and wife, only lust. Deep down in his heart the Englishman still regards his wife as his chattel.

Well? I am fidgety. I want to get up and go. I want to run away from the disagreeables which enchain me. It is Joe Beates, or Mrs. Joe Beates, popping up again, I suppose.

Ted was employed by his brother Bert as a rent collector and sales agent for his real estate business. In England at that time, the rent was collected on a weekly basis and in cash.

Today is Ted's fifty-third birthday. I went to Mass and Communion with him this morning. But I guess my religion is about as thin and weak and invisible as a tightrope thrown across a Niagara of unbelief and skepticism. If I can keep my balance along that rope, I shall get across to the other side. I'll try. I am trying.

WEDNESDAY, JULY 27TH.

I have not been to town today because Gladys is coming up from Plymouth to visit Mother this evening. Today I received a charming Russian jumper, hand embroidered, from Aileen. I saw her on Monday. She had flown back from Paris that morning. It is very seldom that I receive a present, and this is a beautiful one.

THURSDAY, JULY 28TH.

There are a few ideas I cannot get out of my mind. Visiting Mother, riding back and forth through the city, vividly brings back my whole girlhood. There are scenes in which I struggled with my youth, and lots of incidents, long forgotten, are being churned up into recollection. From girlhood I go on to memories of my early married life, and from there arise my dreams of old Bayonne and the old friends there.

Evening. A concert was relayed from Edinburgh on the radio and one of the numbers was "Softly Awakes My Heart" from *Samson and Delilah* by Saint-Saens. As the music came into the room I recognized it as an air that Dad used to sing, and my soul took a deep breath of surprise. Surprise at how much, how very much, Dad knew.

What was Dad? He was nothing but a poor railway clerk. It is true that as a boy he went to Charterhouse School, but only until he was fourteen. After that he had to work. But think how he educated himself, and how he educated me! Books, pictures, poetry, philosophy, the Greeks, Plato; archaeology, sculpture, astronomy, even theosophy; drama, the theater, and music. Was there any field of the imagination and the soul in which he did not stray? He opened my eyes to the world around me and behind me, and the things he showed me I still can see. But I did not glimpse, until this afternoon, how much he must have known and loved of music alone. He was not a musician, but I guess he loved the beautiful wherever he could find it.

Yet think of his life. Angel Road and everything that connotes. Nearly fifty years spent with Mother, an absolute and virulent materialist. Not only do his grandchildren not know him, his younger children do not know him, never knew him. Only Gladys and I, and perhaps Aileen a little, knew him. After I left home he must have drawn into his shell more and more, for Joan and Eric have no comprehension of him whatever. Joan even hates him. What a story is wrapped up in his life. If I could unfold it I would.

Charterhouse is a leading public [private] school founded in 1611 on the site of a charterhouse of a Cathusian Monastery in London. In 1872 the school moved to Surrey.

FRIDAY, AUGUST 12TH.

Trouble. We received a disturbing letter from Jimmie in which he speaks of marrying next spring. He will be twenty-one in March and the girl is nineteen this month. A long letter and a saddening one, leading to a melancholy conversation with Ted.

SUNDAY, AUGUST 14TH.

Last week Tillie said she thought I was happier of late, and more happy than I used to be with Ted. In these last few days of melancholy over Jimmie's plans, I have had a feeling that she is correct, I have been quieter and more at peace with Ted. I had thought this peace had come from philosophy, but maybe it is only a rhythm of happiness and unhappiness we perpetually live through. Anyhow, I am *not* worrying at his criticisms and sarcasms. I acknowledge to myself that I am not, and never have been, the perfect wife and mother, and I let it go at that. Why do we tease and fret each other with our defects of character and idiosyncrasies of personality? I accept his, he must accept mine. Why fret because the other one is imperfect? Let us stress what we agree upon, and admire what we can in each other, instead of fault-finding. This is a strange new mood for me, God grant that I can keep it.

MONDAY, AUGUST 15TH.

I want to note an ever growing intensification of my desire to write, and an ever sharpening clarification of *what* I intend to write. Frequently, composition flows clearly and definitely in my mind, especially in quiet hours when I am traveling or while sitting in church. I rarely feel devotional at Mass, but set free for an hour from house and family, my imagination begins to work and my mind composes steadily. My ambition is twofold: to make a little money, and, primarily, to make a record for my descendants. I should like my children and my grandchildren to know what life was like whilst I was living it. I am more and more convinced that, except for the historical novelists, no writer writes other than what he knows. Practically all of Balzac's life is wrought into his *Comedie,* and the same is the case with Dickens, with George Eliot, the Brontës, and D. H. Lawrence. Practically all of them write themselves from outside and from in. One can only write what one knows.

I have been thinking of Sigrid Undset's *Kristin Lavransdatter* series, of Marcel Proust's *Things Remembered,* even of *Jane Eyre,* and I have come to the conclusion that I will write *my* life, or will try to do so. My life is quite as authentic and typical as any portrayed in any of these books. Sigrid Undset portrays the entire life cycle of a Viking woman of the early Middle Ages. Proust portrays the neurotic invalid of nineteenth-century Paris. Charlotte Brontë portrayed (and betrayed) the love-hungry Victorian spinster. What of my life, is it not as romantic as any?

I begin to see what I will do with it. Instead of taking chunks of it, I will take it in its entirety and make one long chronicle of it, much as Miss [Dorothy] Richardson has done in her Miriam stories. Not as autobiography, for I am nobody and have done nothing, but in fiction guise from the crowded kaleidoscope of my own particular life. Surely I ought to be able to draw a picture and an interpretation of the ordinary bourgeois woman of my own times. Yet perhaps not quite ordinary, for though the outward setting of my life has been ordinary enough for these past thirty years, the interior life has been anything but ordinary.

I do not consider my parents ordinary. Both of them were violent and excessive people, and they have given me a messy character and a cursed temperament. Aileen and I were comparing notes about our childhood in Angel Road and we agreed that for "respectable" people, our milieu was astonishly crowded with the disrespectable, the violent, and the bizarre. If I could write the actual truth of Angel Road, and of our particular family, nobody would believe it, for it is incredible.

Dreaming through the mass on Sunday, my dream book began to take a definite plan. Using Whitman's phrase, I shall call it "A Backward Glance O'er Travel'd Roads." I shall divide the book into four seasons. Spring shall be my life until 1905, when I married. Summer shall be my life in America. Autumn shall be my life from 1927, when we returned to England, until when? Until some final adjustment and resolution into stability and peace. Winter shall be in the form of essays, the distillations of all the various wisdoms I shall have learned in enduring life. I see a clear way before me now and I can follow it.

Dorothy Richardson (1882–1957) was an English writer who preceded James Joyce and Virginia Woolf in constructing a stream of images in her character's mind. She labeled this "interior monologue." Her most important work is Pilgrimage.

SUNDAY, AUGUST 28TH.

We returned from France this morning. I have had the most enjoyable holiday of my whole life. Moreover, I have fallen in love with mountains. Argentière is the most beautiful place in the world. The Utards were charming. Paris was as hot as Hades but as perfect as ever.

WEDNESDAY, SEPTEMBER 14TH.

I am visiting Joan in Tidworth. George was on maneuvers yesterday, but today we three went to Stonehenge. This fulfills the ambition of a lifetime, or at least one of them.

THURSDAY, SEPTEMBER 22ND.

I was surprised today by the arrival of Mother. I was very pleased. A spontaneous visit like that makes me feel that she really cares for me, as me.

TUESDAY, SEPTEMBER 27TH.

Three-thirty P.M. I am falling back into my mood of wretchedness and ennui. I've been having worrying dreams every night and woke up last night crying.

I'm feeling fretful, too, with Ted. He approached me for loving last night and, though I loved him, I fell asleep in tears. He doesn't realize an old wife needs wooing. I long for a lover's kiss, for a word of tenderness or endearment, for a close and tender embrace, breast to breast. I hate his matter of fact attack upon my lower person. I feel like a cow, tethered for the bull. I am a fool of a romantic. I cannot stomach cold, dispassionate sexuality. I want romantic love even at my age.

THURSDAY, SEPTEMBER 29TH.

Four-thirty P.M. Just a word to note that I am happy and released from my black mood. What has happened? For one thing, I have read Freud's book, *Civilization and Its Discontents*. When I meet a book like this, a mind like this presenting such an argument as this, I get excited and my spirits rise. It makes me feel myself, the mind that I am, instead of the mere domestic machinery. These are the thoughts that I think and would never dare to express. These are thoughts that Ted would abominate and castigate.

I've also had a successful love encounter. Last night we went to the movies. The picture was a version of *Dr. Jekyll and Mr. Hyde*. I think the pictures act as aphrodisiacs on us, for in the night Ted was ready to love. I was ready too. I loved without any of those miserable mental reservations, taking what I could, giving what I could, and being sensibly happy. What has happened? Activities of hormones, phagocytes, sex glands, ductless glands, God knows what. The result is positive cheerfulness for awhile. I know it will only be for awhile, but I thank the gods just the same.

SATURDAY, OCTOBER 1ST.

I went to my return visit to Dr. Woodhouse this morning. Two weeks ago I saw him because I had been told that he had a special treatment for varicose veins. Then he put some special medicated bandages on my legs. Today, when he had cut off the plasters, we were both pleased to see that the legs were much improved. He says that when he can clear up the eczema he will try injections in an attempt to shrivel up the bad veins so that they will never bother me again. I hope he can do so.

He says the condition is an hereditary disease. The walls of the veins are too weak and break down. No diet, no medicine, no exercise, can help the condition. It is from a constitutional defect, not from wrong living. I think of Ted boasting if *he* had bad legs, he'd bet he'd cure 'em! By willpower or by prayer, I wonder.

Varicose veins are a condition, not a carelessness that can be corrected. Varicose veins descend to me, the same as my red hair does. I sought neither, and I have to put up with both, besides a lot of other accidents as well. When I said to Woodhouse that I supposed I would have to endure them to the end of the chapter, he replied, "Not necessarily." If he can shrivel up the particular bad patches, they will never trouble me again. I hope he can do something about them.

MONDAY, OCTOBER 3RD.

I had a queer experience this morning. I had to go to one of the big trunks to take out some blankets, and at the bottom were some of my old diaries. I took one up and began to read it. It was the year 1916, the year Gertie got married and Mabel Jackson showed up. Much that the book contained I had entirely forgotten: events, people have faded from my memory. But much of the book is the same old Ruby Alice, the same fool, only incredibly young. I realized what wisdom and what stability I have attained as the years have gone by. I'm not such a fool as I was, so I can thank God for that, anyhow. And I do.

THURSDAY, OCTOBER 13TH.

Today is the anniversary of Arthur Thompson's birthday. If he had lived he would have been forty-five today. Ted remembered it and we spoke of when Arthur was twenty-one. What a household we were! I was twenty-four and had two babies, Ted was twenty-nine, Arthur, twenty-one, and Grace was twenty-four. With the exception of Ted, we were all children, and Ted was youngish too. No wonder the Bayonne people were so interested in us, remember us always. We must have been the romance of the town: plunging about between England and America, getting converted, having babies. What a time!

THURSDAY, NOVEMBER 10TH.

Ted's been so damnably British these past few weeks, I feel annoyed with him. With all the newspaper comment about Franklin Roosevelt's election in America, he keeps haranguing the twins on how lucky they are to live in

England. He extols the Englishman, the excellence of English politics, and the glories of English history, and all the time he sideswipes America.

I have listened to so many radio speeches of late that I say to myself, Well, they're brewing up another nice little war. Strikes, hunger marches, taxes, destitution are the same that I've seen since 1916. There are too many people in the world and talk does nothing. When I survey the political situation, I don't wonder religion is such a failure. Religion was ineffectual against the war and is equally ineffectual against the worldwide Depression.

Yet Ted insists on saying that what is wrong with the world is the Reformation. All men need to do is to go back to Catholicism. No wonder I feel depressed. For there is no answer to Ted's frame of mind. He has put himself safely away in a closed system of thinking, in a little fairy tale, and he won't let anyone in unless they'll play fairy tale too. He never sees that his fairy tale is too simple.

MONDAY, NOVEMBER 21ST.

Three P.M. I am very very tired and I am afraid it is due to frustration and anger rather than to any extra physical exertion. I am longing for America and I have a distaste for England.

I made a fool of myself on Saturday night at Arden Cottage. I didn't want to go there, but Ted insisted. Well, we began the infernal cards. On the radio were old melancholy songs of the war period, and I found them perfectly harrowing. Presently "Queen of My Heart" was sung and that I couldn't stand. I heard Dad singing it, and I felt choked. I had to excuse myself and go out into the hall, sit on the stairs, and conquer my tears. Then, of course, I had to return to the room and continue the game.

Tillie is really a very nice sister-in-law, and Bert I like alright. He is quite a nice old fellow, and I can get on with him very well; indeed, I can get along with all of them. But is my life to be spent with my in-laws whilst my own sons are enjoyed by someone else? No, this isn't good enough for me. And now Dorothy has written asking for further financial help. Last year we helped her but if there is any spare money in this house I want it for my sons and not my sister-in-law.

So, I am cross and irritated and I expect that's why I am so tired.

Arden Cottage is the name given to Bert and Tillie Thompson's home at 55 Junction Road, Romford. In England, buildings frequently have names in addition to street addresses.

THURSDAY, DECEMBER 5TH.

I thought at dinnertime today what a pet example for Freud's theories I should be if he could know me. The image of my father returns to me over and over again. I can see that my father is the only human being I have ever unqualifiedly loved. I hear a tune, I see a place, I read a book, or a speech, or I have a dream and it all leads back to Dad. Today, for instance, we were talking of dates and Cuthie said that perhaps he would be alive in 1999. I said he could be, and how exciting it would be to see the year 2000. Ted, of course, didn't think so. I asked if he hadn't been excited when 1900 came in and he said, "No." I was, and then I remembered it all and talking with Dad about it. I have a distinct memory of walking down Bluck's Road with Dad, his arm resting on my shoulder, and talking with him about it. He was listening, assenting, and smiling at me. It seems to me that all my intellectual and emotional life was bound up with Dad.

TUESDAY, DECEMBER 20TH.

I am going to town today to see Mother, and I will go into a church some-where and try to pray. The Church isn't all bad because Ted's a fool. I mustn't let him take away from me what little religion I have got. Before some altar, I might be able to feel the presence of God. I need God. The longer we stay here in England, the more Ted falls into the English frame of mind, which is that a wife is not a person, she is chattel. The war, the suffrage, have made practically no impression upon the historic mind. In this country there is no equality of the sexes. A woman may be a decoration, but she is usually only an undis-chargeable servant.

The idea that marriage is a sharing of life with a beloved woman is not held by any Englishman that I see or know. England exists for the English man. The woman only exists for him, just the same old Miltonic conception as ever.

This is not for me. I am an intelligent and a civilized human being, not a slave nor a concubine, nor yet an English wife. I will never be one, so help me, God. Get me to America! Patience, Ruby Alice. Patience.

WEDNESDAY, DECEMBER 21ST.

Well, my emotional storm has passed over, but what devastation I have strewn in my tracks, God alone knows.

Going to Hammersmith sobered me. I did not go to church, which shows yet clearer my further attainment of sanity. When I got to town and saw all those millions of people, religion vanished. For me it is impossible to hold any emotion in a crowd. In a crowd I am only aware of acute discomfort and an abysmal dislike of human beings. And when I cannot love human beings, I cannot conceive how God can either, and immediately churches and orga-nized religions become very no-account. It may all have belonged legitimately and naturally to the past, but most obviously it does not belong to today. So any secret thought I had that I might find comfort in a church vanished in a twinkling, and so completely that I even forgot I had had such an idea. So I went straight to Mother's.

Angel Road. Well, number six could be labeled "hell." Since it is not quite so bad as it used to be, at least "purgatory." Mother is detestable. I was there for several hours and Mother fussed incessantly. I got dizzy watching her and listening to her. She scolded me, Sonnie, Aileen, and even Malvin. Each for our own good, of course. She is the most intolerably overbearing woman that ever breathed. But it is Mother's temper which cured me of mine. She explodes wordily so that the whole world is aware of it. My temper simmers away in a smothered silence, only finding expression in this book. But it is the same temper. "My passion," Mother calls it.

Well, I reflected last night that I'm really no better in myself than Mother is. I avoid expression of my passion just because I have always hated it so in Mother, but I've given way to my passion just the same, inside. Although my family has suffered less from me than Mother's family suffered from her, still I've suffered more from myself than Mother has suffered from herself. In fact, I don't think Mother has ever suffered from herself at all. She has always exploded her "passion" on her world. Her world has suffered whilst she found release. Indeed, she enjoys her rages, though of course, she couldn't conceive that, and is even proud of them. "My passion."

Well, looking at her in one of her senseless "states" yesterday, it flashed home to me that I'm quite as senseless, and realizing that, animosity left me. All that insane and destructive self pity, gone. I came home mentally sobered.

I still will go to America as soon as it can be arranged, for I am sure Ted and I are too close together. We need a separation.

1933

MONDAY, JANUARY 2ND.

I am writing with a new fountain pen, Ted's Christmas gift. I have worn out two pens these last five years.

I came through Christmas serenely. We all went to Arden Cottage for the celebration as usual. I went to midnight Mass with Ted on Christmas. Yesterday the Bert Thompsons came here to celebrate the New Year.

THURSDAY, FEBRUARY 9TH.

Three-thirty P.M. I was surprised at noon by the arrival of Eric. He is in Romford today working on the plans of the new National Provincial Bank which is being built here in town. He will be coming back for tea, so we shall have a very argumentative evening. Ted likes Eric. Nevertheless the same peculiar characteristics of youthfulness, when exhibited by Eddie, annoy Ted considerably. Isn't it odd?

Two weeks ago I received a couple of copies of the *Christian Science Monitor*, sent by Alice Taft from Miami Beach. Today I received a packet of them from Boston. Alice must have paid in a subscription for me. This pleases me. The papers are good, as even Christian Scientist detractors will admit, but the thoughtful gift of them pleases me. Very few people ever give me anything. I seem to strike people as one of those rocks in the desert, who never needs anything. Ted, of course, laughs at the *Monitor*. Moreover, he had the audacity to say that as a Catholic I ought not to read it. What restrictions his Catholicism would impose, if it could. If his bigotry could prevail, we should have new Luthers springing up all over the world.

I shall never be a good and complete Catholic, or ever the good and complete anything, I suppose.

Eric, Ruby's youngest brother, is an engineer. He was the baby of the family, and Ruby thought him their mother's favorite. He is married to Malvin, and both are radical socialists.

MONDAY, FEBRUARY 13TH.

I have had a very enjoyable day with Aileen. Then we taxied to her flat and Roger Pippett had tea ready. How we talked! One of their questions I have brought home with me, and I keep turning it over, but can't find an answer to it.

"The thing is," said Aileen, "have you got anything to make a personal life of? You see," she explained to Roger, "Ruby has never really had a personal life. She's been swallowed up all these years by her family. But now, if she stayed in America, if she didn't have Ted, what would she do with her life?"

"*Could* you stay in America?" asked Roger. "What would you do if you were me?" I asked them. They were terribly noncommittal. "If I were you, I should *be* you," said Aileen, "but you see, I can't imagine myself allowing myself to be in your position. I should have done something about it years ago. The thing is, have you anything left to make a personal life of?"

Well, have I? I can't make a life out of reading, that's only dope. I can't write. I can't make a life out of embroidery. What *can* I make a life out of?

Aileen is now living with Roger Pippett.

THURSDAY, FEBRUARY 16TH.

Today is Mother's seventieth birthday. She is still in Plymouth with Gladys, so there is no party to attend and no meeting of the clan. Eric was in to tea and we fell to talking about Mother and Dad, especially Dad. Eric doesn't know the Dad I know; he hasn't a suspicion of him. Someday I must write it all down.

Ted had a letter from Eddie which gives us the information that *we* are now grandparents. Harold has a daughter. Somehow, it makes me weepy; not because it has advanced me a generation, but because I feel so out of it all. Here is Harold becoming a father and here we are, three thousand miles away. Here we are running after dreams, whilst all the real things are happening to our real children. It's a crazy world.

I am so homesick for America! I am going to take a book and sit by the parlor fire and doze, like the regulation grandmama, I shouldn't wonder. I shall visit my American children this summer.

WEDNESDAY, MARCH 1ST.

I am flirting with Anglicanism again, or rather the idea of it. I have been looking around the house to see what I could find about the Church of England, and except for my old prayer book and a small Bible, there is nothing here. We have books about Unitarianism and Theism, about Theosophy and Christian Science, about Deism and Free Thinking, about the saints and by the saints and scores of books on Catholic apologetics, and likewise missals and prayer books. I don't want one of them.

The Church of England may be as irrational as all its detractors declare. I care not. I understand it and I love it. I understand the Roman Church too. I have actually been a Catholic longer than I have been an Anglican. But Catholicism has never been anything but a painful veneer upon me. Anglicanism is in my bones, at my roots, and nothing will change that. I have *tried* to change it, tried for a long time, but it cannot be changed. Arguments are useless. Desires are useless. Policies are useless. Expediencies are useless. Even loyalties are useless, because beneath all lies the inescapable loyalty to myself, the woman I was born. I was not born a Catholic.

THURSDAY, MARCH 30TH.

Tonight Ted suggested going to the movies and we saw *Sherlock Holmes,* but it wasn't very good.

What did impress me immensely was an educational film which showed a battleship being maneuvered by wireless. Not a man was aboard it, but it sailed about, shot off guns, increased and decreased speed, overtook other boats, and got in blockade formation. It was worked entirely by wireless orders sent from another battleship. Photographs of the machinery at work, and also explanatory charts of the electrical devices, were given. I could not understand the technology, but the mass of machinery and the working of the system was obvious, and weird.

Sitting there, watching that mysterious picture, I was shot through with the thought: What has God got to do with this? Above all, what has church and theology got to do with this? The answer is: nothing. This wonder is the work of man, man's brain, skill, and ingenuity. Insofar as man is the work of God, this might be linked with God, but to link it with the practices and beliefs of Catholicism is impossible. This is Science. I was immensely impressed.

SATURDAY, APRIL 1ST.

Seven P.M. Ted has just left to attend a meeting of the Romford Social Service League. I have orders to go to Arden Cottage *early* and he will follow after the meeting.

Yesterday I went to town and bought myself a prayer book. I said I would and I've done so. I'm an incongruity. I belong to two churches, just as I belong to two countries. The theologians would probably dispute it, saying I must be either Anglican or Roman, one or the other. But they would be wrong. The fact is I do belong to both churches. I was baptized and confirmed in both of them. I understand both of them. And each of them can help me sometimes.

I am *not* going to Arden Cottage early. I'm going to read for an hour. I have D. H. Lawrence's *Letters* and am enjoying them greatly. Also, I have my *Book of Common Prayer*, and I am going to read this evening's psalms.

SUNDAY, APRIL 2ND. PASSION SUNDAY.

I went to late Mass and sat in my usual state of indifferent response. However, I was surprised to find Father Arendzen there, asking all to attend a retreat next week. I shall go. Father Arendzen is a clever man, and somewhere in the week's talk he may have a fruitful word for me.

Today's sermon was picturesque and forceful, but it could not touch me. His subject was the meaning of the crucifixion. Christ on the cross means God came into the world, in human form, in order to redeem souls. Mankind was lost and God wanted to buy it back. The price: his own blood, and he paid it.

I think the crucifixion wasn't such a horror as the preachers paint it to be. Jesus was dead in three hours and not a bone was broken. Countless men have suffered far more agonizing deaths than that. Moreover, if Jesus was God, whatever he suffered was infinitesimal, because He knew He was redeeming souls, which was the achievement of His plan. Mere men suffer tortures and die, *for nothing*. If Jesus was God, he couldn't suffer. Anyhow, what are three hours or three days in Eternity? And if he wasn't God, then the argument doesn't hold. There is no proof that God loves individual souls, loves me. How could He want me, one atom in the eighteen hundred million now inhabiting the globe, or one of all the trillions of people that have been, and that are to be? It is this individual personality of Christianity which I cannot get. God and myself, no, I cannot get it. I do see, and know, that it is just that importance which Christianity gives to souls which makes life endurable for so many unfortunates.

The importance of self, self-reliance, is something we must have. I can feel important in myself, without God at all. The kingdom of God is within you, perhaps that is it. I do know myself, my powers, my own soul, and I'm not asking Jesus to redeem me or to love me, because I don't feel any need for his love or his redeeming. Pride, of course, but I can't be any other way.

TUESDAY, APRIL 4TH.

Three P.M. When Ted came in at noon he said he had made reservations for me on the *American Trader,* sailing on April twenty-eighth. I am so glad. I have been holding my breath for weeks, ever since little Sheila was born. I was getting afraid he wasn't going to do a thing about it.

TUESDAY, APRIL 11TH.

Eleven A.M. I am waiting for Mother and in my usual state of nerves at such an awaiting. My heart is thumping, and I feel sick at the pit of my stomach. It's really awful.

She is coming to sew for me. I asked her to come, yet I literally dread her visit. What she must have done to me in that so far away childhood, that my body is still afraid of her and my instinctive impulse is for flight.

I'm most miserably and sickishly tired. Three weeks from now, D.V., I shall be well out on the Atlantic. Meanwhile, I've got to continue to behave properly and to keep hold of myself. I can.

THURSDAY, APRIL 27TH.

Four P.M. I open this book to write the last word. Then I shall lock it away and forget it.

Mother has gone, the dressmaking is done, my hair is curled, my legs newly plastered, and tomorrow I sail away. My trunk went off yesterday, and now I have only little odd cabin stuff packing to do and a few farewell calls to make. I shall probably play bridge at Bert's tonight. He is driving me to the dock tomorrow. I should reach New York on May eighth. This is another ending. Good-bye.

Although there is a long break between these two entries, no journal is missing. Ruby did not write while on this six-month trip to the States.

On September 1, 1933, John and Ruth Louise Ferris (Glaser's parents) secretly married. They kept their wedding plans from Ruby because they knew she was looking forward to a tour of the western United States with Bill

Berry and his mother. Bill Berry worked with John at Metropolitan Life and was living with the boys at 523 Knickerbocker Road. John and Ruth felt that if Ruby knew of their plans, she would cancel her trip in order to attend their wedding. The marriage was kept secret because during the days of the Depression Metropolitan Life would not permit two members of the same family to be employed by them. Ruby liked Ruth and had expressed her wish to John that he marry her.

THURSDAY, NOVEMBER 16TH.

Here I am back in England again. I bought this book in Macy's, back in the summer, but I have not opened it until today. I have been opening various other books, but this is the one I need now. I am not unhappy, but I am not happy. I am restless, bored. The terrible fact is that I do not like England and that I am not glad to return to it. Before the boat reached Ireland I knew I was dreading landing. But here in England, right here in Romford, I have got to live, so I had better do something sensible about it. I have been back here only a little over two weeks, and already I feel confined. I look in the glass and see that I look old, and I feel twenty years older than I did a bare two months ago. What has happened to the Ruby Alice that was the *me* of summer? I am swallowed up in the domestic round again and I am discouraged.

FRIDAY, NOVEMBER 17TH.

My environment irks me. I want to be back by Niagara Falls, across the Plains, up in the Rockies, in the desert. There I could feel the presence of God. Here I am just dull and miserable. Ted is good: good and intolerable. I suppose I was spoiled all this summer. The boys and my friends gave me admiration and lavish affection. I was well and beautiful and gay. I thought that health and happiness would last. I thought when I got back here I should be able to laugh at Ted and all his scornings and teasings. Alas, not so. He squelches me as easily and steadily as ever. He checks my spontaneity.

I want a friend, and I haven't got a friend in all of England. Only Aileen, and she's so inaccessible. Mother was over here last week, but Mother isn't a friend. I can't talk to Mother. I want a friend with whom I can be my spontaneous self. What am I going to do with my life here?

SUNDAY, DECEMBER 10TH.

I visited Aileen and had a good talk with her and Roger Pippett. It left me wondering, again, what in the world I am going to do with my life. What in thunderation am I going to do with it? I am also resolving, again, not to talk. With Aileen, what ease, what pleasure, what affection. But here, mockery, derision, criticism, scorning, deprecation. Well, what's to be done about it? Isn't it queer, outsiders can like me and love me, but Ted can only tease and scorn and belittle. I am tired, soul tired.

Aileen has loaned me some books about Taos. My dreams and day dreams are continuously of New Mexico and my summer there.

1934

TUESDAY, JANUARY 16TH.

When I first wakened early this morning my inner woman was saying, "more and more loitering and tomorrow the same story, always and always more and more dilatory." It was a paraphrase from Goethe, probably thrown up from the old subconscious by last night's reading of Anthony Trollope and meditating about him and his mother: especially noting again that Mrs. Trollope was fifty-two years old when she put out her first book. And then thinking about my books, which I *don't* write.

I picked up my old Goethe and see that Dad gave me this book in 1901. I casually turned through it, staying to read only the lines I had marked. These show me I was such a serious girl. Well I was, wasn't I? This year Elizabeth Bowes, talking of me when I was a bride nearly thirty years ago, said that I was the most serious young woman she had ever met. "Too serious," she said. Yes, and still serious, too serious.

However, there is this advantage accruing to having been born in the eighties: one positively understands the Victorians. No one born since 1900 can possibly understand us. Not only do sympathies change, interpretations do also. I was thunderstruck by a criticism on Ibsen in the *Times* this morning. The critic writes of Nora in *A Doll's House* that she tries to escape from reality by leaving her home. Well, I gasp at that. My generation always thought Nora was trying to escape from unreality. We hailed her as a bold feminist, a rights-for-women girl, but lo, today the critic regards her as a shirker. So, not only do ideas change, the whole emotional evaluation changes. We admired Nora as a noble heroine, but now, evidently, she is regarded as a slaking duffer. Enough of Nora; I guess her door never stops slamming.

SUNDAY, JANUARY 28TH.

I have begun to read Adolf Hitler's book, *My Struggle* [*Mein Kampf*], which Ted has brought home from Boots. One bothersome effect of reading this book is that it has driven to the forefront of my mind the fact of my own particular rootlessness. I do not belong anywhere. No country, no church, no family. What a denudation.

Yet I haven't the strength of mind to put an end to it all. I ought to take a firm stand and say to Ted, I am through with your ideas and your way of life. I will not put up with your domination any longer. I cannot live this broken and destroyed life any longer. I cannot pretend any longer to believe what I do not believe. Let me go. Let me go.

But I shall never say it, not a word of it. I shall only go on secretly grousing and fretting. I am a fool. Why can't I take myself by the shoulders and shake myself until I shake some sense into my addled pate? The root of my trouble lies, I suppose, in my sex. Feminism is only a delusion that we can be free. Our men own us, body and soul, just the same as in the days of savagery. Maybe we have a few more yards of leeway on our rope, but we're tied just the same. But it is all so wearing. I look ten years older than when I landed three months ago. Yes, I really do. Some days my face shocks me. I cannot believe I'm the same woman that I saw in the mirror last summer. No, and I'm not. Then I was my own woman, free, happy, and well. Now I am simply Mrs. Edward Thompson!

SATURDAY, FEBRUARY 17TH.

Eleven A.M. I have something very strange to set down today, something frightening. Yesterday was the first Friday of Lent and when Ted returned from church, and we were all at breakfast, I suddenly saw around Ted's forehead a circlet of red marks, some bloody and all looking very sore. For a moment my heart stopped beating, I fell into such an anger. I asked him what he had been doing and he said he didn't know what I was talking about. Then I told him of the marks and he blushed and began to tremble. He got up to look in the mirror, for the twins were also saying that they saw the marks. Then he said that it was extraordinary and that today is the special commemoration of the crown of thorns. His forehead looked as though it had been pressed with nails. Horrible. He tried to laugh it off, but he showed his pleasure. I said no more. I could only sit still in a panic, screaming inside, I'm not going to have this!

Later I rang up Father Bishop and asked him if he had done anything particular to Mr. Thompson that morning. He said he hadn't seen him. I told him what I had seen and he, too, seemed to grow angry and said he wouldn't stand for anything like that. He was dead set against unusual mortifications, and then asked if I had noticed anything else out of the ordinary. I said only that Ted was spending more time than ever in church in the mornings. Father Bishop said I was right to let him know, and if I noticed anything further I should tell him at once. He told me that long ago the Church did celebrate different items of the Passion, and that the first Friday of Lent was given over to the crown of thorns, but that this was a devotion that had been dropped.

I am over my fright, but not over my warning. Ted's religion! His accursed religiosity.

THURSDAY, MARCH 15TH.

Three P.M. After tea last night Ted wanted to talk over the quarrels we have been having lately. What he should have said was *he* wanted to talk. Well, he talked till bedtime. He mentioned all the items that he had forgotten the previous nights. I tried to defend myself, but I cried too much. Weeping is a damnable failing of mine. I don't *want* to weep, but I *can't* prevent myself. However, I suppose we did talk ourselves out, for we finally ended without anger. When I came to bed he did turn to me and kiss me goodnight. Today we are quiet. I suppose both of us are exhausted.

I suspect we two have no more troubles than most married people: maybe fewer. It is marriage which is so terrible: the permanent living together of two people of the opposite sex, the most difficult thing in the world. Men against women: women against men. Eternal sex antagonisms. We thought we could overcome it! Or at least I thought I could.

MONDAY, MARCH 26TH.

There is nothing like a good stiff dose of a heretic to fasten me securely into the Church. The result of seven or eight hours of Dorothy's company will be to send me to do my Easter duty. I have been miserable for weeks. Too much winter, too much Lent, too many arguments, so that I have been feeling very irreligious, and especially very anti-Catholic. My rebound from Ted is always a rebound from the Church. At fifty, I had been thinking to myself, I will begin a new life again. I will go back to the church of my fathers. I'll be a Church of England woman.

But Dorothy shows me I can't do that. Outside of Rome, it's chaos. I've joined the Church, once and for all, and without it I'm a mess. When I regard a rudderless woman like Dorothy, or an undisciplined woman like Mother, my intense desire is *not* to be like them. I know that authoritative Catholicism is the only thing that can guide and discipline me. I hate it, but I hate chaos more. So again my heart and mind is submitting, and some time or other this week I will go to confession and I will try again, sincerely, to conform.

THURSDAY, MARCH 27TH.

Eight P.M. It seems that making a resolution over a mental conflict doesn't resolve me into peace, it simply leaves me stranded. Evidently a worry is a better occupation for my mind than suffering ennui.

There is no one to talk to, nothing to read, nowhere to go. There is no conversation with Ted, and, of course, if we don't talk we can't quarrel. But oh, the emptiness. One must agree with him. The only time we can be jolly together is when we can join mutually in a derision, which is horrible. Chitchat, spontaneous wit, the tossing back and forth of fooleries, discussion of the arts, expression of opinion on current events, all are taboo with Ted. Criticism, censoriousness, bigotry from him is all that gets spoken here with my yes-yessing when I can. There is never easy companionship, fun, pleasant or exciting conversation. It's awful. No wonder I am tired and bored. This state of things is likely to go on for another twenty years. What am I going to do?

MONDAY, APRIL 2ND.

Ten A.M. I am in a state of quiet, simmering anger but funnily, an amused anger. Ted, of course! Last night, as I anticipated, as the finale to all his Holy Week austerities, he indulged in loving. Queer compliment.

Also, I had a queer eye opener last night. I actually went to church with Ted last night, and after Mass one of the parishioners, Mrs. Butcher, asked us to go into her house for a little while. It was my first visit. Ted introduced young Ted as his namesake! Mr. Butcher and the other children, Georgie and Frances, were there also. Obviously Ted was very much at home, and there was an air of intimacy and comradeship between Mrs. Butcher and Ted. She portrayed several of the attitudes of a love-interested woman. The daughter was watching me very intently and curiously. The men, of course, were quite unconscious of the atmosphere, except that Ted once deliberately sidetracked the conversation when Georgie began to reminisce about some experiences of last summer. I made myself as agreeable as I knew how, but I saw and sensed things which I am evidently not supposed to know.

I came home with the determination in future to stick to Ted like a leech. This morning we went to Mass together. Ted took up the collection. I was sitting at the back of the church, and as I watched him working up the aisle, I thought him the handsomest man in church. Obviously, other women think that too. I also remember that the other week he told me that some woman had told him that she thought he was a bachelor. Evidently I've got to be seen. I've got to go to church and all the damned parish affairs to keep my man, as well as save my soul! Well, I *feel* like fighting.

THURSDAY, APRIL 5TH.

There is news from John and Eddie. They are working on 523 Knickerbocker Road, painting and papering with intent to put it on the market and sell it if they can. Also, John expects a baby in August so I presume he wants to get rid of the house before Ruth is confined. It seems that last year was the best time for me to have gone over.

WEDNESDAY, APRIL 18TH.
MY BIRTHDAY. FIFTY TODAY.

Last night, as I was falling asleep, I was brought back to wakefulness by hearing the church clock strike twelve. Then I said to myself, Now you are fifty.

At dinner time Ted brought me a pretty gold ring, set with a cluster of five garnets. Selma brought me a bunch of red tulips, and she and I have been sitting listening to a variety show on the radio. Ted was out to a Catholic Federation meeting, the twins at a Scout meeting.

MONDAY, MAY 14TH.

Last night I had confused dreams again of packing and catching boats. This is my everlasting nightmare. But last night's were more tiring than ever, for I was driving the car through milling crowds and I had lost Ted in the crowd. It was imperative that I should find him, especially as we'd got to go to my funeral before we caught the boat. How I was to be buried, and yet drive away and sail away, was not divulged nor worried about. What would Freud make of it all? Could he promise me that my secret woman is intending to bury her past? Such dreams tire me as much as actuality.

TUESDAY, MAY 15TH.

I was dreaming of Bertha Hludenski this morning and we were traveling, of course. This time it was trains. It is extraordinary how often I dream of Bertha. Why does *she*, of all people, come into my dreams?

It must be twenty years since Bertha Hludenski came into my house. She came when Jimmie was a baby. She stayed with us between three and four years and was the best servant we ever had. I wish I had her in the kitchen now. Maybe she is wishing herself there. Twenty years ago we were both young women. Perhaps she is a grandma now, the same as I am. If I could go to Bayonne someday, and go prowling around the Hook section, I wonder if we should recognize each other if we met. Perhaps. We did like each other. We were friends once. Bertha from Vilna, making the best lemon meringue pies in the world, whilst I frittered time away with my megrims and my scribblings. That's when I was writing *Hamlet House*, a lifetime ago.

SUNDAY, MAY 27TH.

I went alone to Mass and was overcome with happiness there in church and it has lasted all day. There is one thing a sung mass does for me: It releases me into dreams, my thoughts marshal into orderly battalions like soldiers, and composition begins to flow.

I sat there dreaming of Johnnie and Ruth, of Harold and his baby, of Eddie and Bill Berry, of Charlie, of all my sons and their friends and lovers, of last summer, of Santa Fe, of the Indians, of Mary Austin, of Aileen and Roger, even of Mother. Everything was suffused with peace. A wonderful hour, the peace of which has lasted all day.

Mary Austin (1868–1934) was an American novelist who wrote of New Mexico and the West. She is known for her sympathetic interpretations of Native American life in her book The Land of Little Rain, *and her play* The Arrow Maker. *After Ruby visited Santa Fe and Taos she became an admirer of Austin.*

THURSDAY, MAY 31ST. FEAST OF CORPUS CHRISTI.

Four P.M. This is the evening when there is the Procession of the Blessed Sacrament in the convent gardens at Upminster. I do not know whether I will go or not. It seems like such a childish game to me. On the other hand, I think it policy to keep myself on view. I think it advisable that all the dear good Catholics of the neighborhood should remember that a Mrs. Edward Thompson exists. I shall probably go.

WEDNESDAY, JUNE 6TH.

I have just finished the upstairs cleaning and must now go down and cook. I am expecting Mother and am in my usual panic. When I woke this morning I was in a cloud of dread simply because Mother is coming. I could not eat any breakfast. I feel sick to my stomach and have pains in my bowels. Queer. An emotion I don't want descends on me in my sleep and I awake ill. I look shocking. Ted remarked it, and he knows the reason. "It's funny," he said. "You two are as alike as two peas and yet you can't agree. But I expect, really, that is why you don't agree." Well, we do agree, because I will not disagree. But alike? I don't think so. And I'd hate to think so. Well, she's coming and I shall get through alright. Fifty, and still afraid of my mother.

WEDNESDAY, JUNE 27TH.

Mother left after tea this evening. Thank God. No doubt she is an estimable woman, but she wears me out. Ted is staying home from class this evening to celebrate. He finds Mother amusing, and so do I, in spots. But Mother, in toto, is devastating.

There is one great thing about Mother: she is fundamentally *real*. She's overbearing but she's essentially sincere. She never pretends anything, and that's a wholesomeness about her that is a tonic and that makes me ashamed. I am living my life on the bias. To be real, as Mother is real, to be unafraid, to be unashamed, that would be to be well, to be happy.

I got my new spectacles today. I had Aves retest my eyes last week and as I thought, I needed new glasses. Aves says after forty, the sight is always changing, right up till the age of seventy-five. He says my sight is very good and is likely to remain permanently so. I was afraid I might need spectacles all day long, but he says only for reading and writing and so forth. I consider this jolly good news. I would hate to be a granny in glasses all the time. For "men don't make passes at girls who wear glasses," as Dorothy Parker said somewhere. Who can possibly wear a becoming hat over a spectacled face? Aunt Lizzie is eighty-two and only requires glasses for reading. She never wears them to the movies and I don't have to either. Hurrah.

FRIDAY, JUNE 29TH.

When I was walking down the street this afternoon, thinking of Johnnie and the coming baby and hoping it would turn out to be a girl, I saw one of the great lacks of my life: feminine love. My mother never loved me and I've never had a daughter to love. I've had women friends, but never a satisfactory mother and daughter love. My mother is so damned self-sufficient that she never needed anyone. Ted is self-sufficient too, and never needs tender love. I've always had love to give and nobody wanting it. Gosh, it's a lonesome world, and for all of us, I suppose. No wonder we take to drink or gigolos.

THURSDAY, JULY 5TH.

Happily, I am in good temper, laughing. It is not often a diary records laughter. It is mostly a record of gripes and mortifications. I think Tuesday night's movies acted as an aphrodisiac for Ted, and yesterday we both got up serene and released from tension. Since it was the Fourth of July, I suggested that we go to Arden Cottage for a surprise game of bridge. Bert remembered it was the glorious Fourth and brought out champagne to celebrate. After that we drank gin. Why can't we be casual and silly oftener instead of fussing so about our immortal souls?

THURSDAY, JULY 12TH.

Three P.M. One of Ted's criticisms of me, and also of Eddie, is that I am fooled by words, led on by words, led astray by words, lose my head over words. I get intoxicated with words, he says. Maybe. So did Dad. Like father, like child. I do live by words. I ought to work with them. It is only over language that I have any mastery and only in writing that I have any skill. But if words intoxicate me, they also sober me: If they lead me astray, they also lead me aright.

Ted talks and I write. Words. Nothing but words for the pair of us. It is to laugh.

MONDAY, JULY 16TH.

I am again in an uproar. I am aching and fretting for my boys, particularly Eddie and Harold. I'm coldly anti-Christian and especially anti-Catholic. I'm broody about Hitler and the terrible massacre of June thirtieth in Germany. I think since Hitler is a Catholic, I certainly won't be. I am wondering what possible application of Christian doctrine could be offered to the surviving victims of his savagery to assuage their desolation, or to the world at large to rationalize it. There isn't any answer to that.

On June 30, 1934, a widespread purge of early supporters of Hitler was carried out by the S.S. On Hitler's order, Goering, Goebbels, and Himmler directed the murder of thousands of men, many of whom had been the storm troopers and Brown Shirts who had brought Hitler to power.

THURSDAY, AUGUST 2ND.

Rain in the night brought coolness and sanity. I woke in a more casual frame of mind then I have known for a long time. Through the morning various thoughts of various men came to me, in various ways, but all building for stability.

First I thought of Uncle Bradley, saying the last time I saw him that he no longer belonged to any church, but that he helped them all because they all were doing the Lord's work. Every year he opened his beautiful house and gardens for any church that cared to use them for their treats and festivals.

I thought of old Bert Thompson saying about Ted, who was away preaching, "I don't understand the Roman Catholics and I don't want to." He said he was christened in Whitechapel Parish and he would be buried in the Church of England. He thought Ted funny, overenthusiastic about religion. He said that we do learn a little sense since nobody's burned at the stake anymore. He thought it a good thing to have varieties of religion so that nobody can bang the other fellow. "Let's have all kinds and then we're all free, and nobody bossing."

Then I thought of Tomlinson and his remark to me on the old Liberty Street Ferry. It was when I was going to New York every day and teaching, so that Ted could go off to the war. Bluff old Edgar said, "You know, Ruby, the trouble with you and Ted is you're both too serious. Nothing matters as much as either of you two think it does. Why don't you stop thinking and start playing a bit?"

And I thought, true enough and well I know it.

FRIDAY, AUGUST 3RD.

A letter arrived from Johnnie in reply to my distress letter to him of last month. His letter was even more sobering to my mind than old King Solomon. He gave me eight reasons as to why he couldn't do as I asked him, a sermon on being contented with my lot, and criticism of my character. Also a postscript which had the grace to say, "You must think this a terrible letter. You ask 'Bring me over' and I reply, 'No.' Sorry, John."

Of course he said "No." I expected him to, but the sermon makes me cynical and the criticism rankles. It may be just. I don't know. It is true I have often criticized my mother, but never to her face, either in speech or writing. As a matter of fact, Johnnie was rather critical of me last summer.

Well, I wrote to him this afternoon. I told him I was sorry I had posted my previous letter and I hadn't expected him to act on it. I agreed that he was quite right, wished him well on his exams, a safe confinement for Ruth, and sent my love.

Children! Are children a blessing from God? Anyhow, his letter was a cold water douche and tonight I'm absolutely sane, drowned in sanity, in fact.

SATURDAY, SEPTEMBER 1ST.

Johnnie's first wedding anniversary. I forgot to record their daughter was born on August twelfth. A year ago I started on my trip out west with Bill Berry.

WEDNESDAY, SEPTEMBER 26TH.

Ted and I quarreled dreadfully on Monday night. Why, oh why don't I keep my mouth shut? A woman of my age can't afford to quarrel. It is *saying* things that's so silly. Think what you must, but keep your mouth shut. Ted said things, too, of course. He said he spent his time trying to forget me. He must hate me because my presence here is a reproach to him. He can't escape me. He has spent his life running away: from his parents, from his work, from his sons, but unluckily he cannot run away from me. And what is his religion but one vast escape? All the worries of our times: poverty, war, revolution, assassination, are conveniently covered by original sin, and the panacea is subordination to the Catholic Church. What a madness.

I get so cross, so wild. This week the issue was that I didn't go to Mass last Sunday. Ted has his ways of compelling me to go to church. I shall have to go. I am trapped, simply trapped by my sex and my age and this enduring marriage. It's infuriating. It doesn't bear thinking about.

Happily, I'm no longer vitally concerned with the need of believing church religion. I can go to Mass and go through all the motions, but use my secret mind on other things. Fortunately, no certificate of having gone to confession is required. I can behave, but how one longs to be real! How one longs to be free! How free can an aging woman of fifty, with no money, be? The only happy women in the world are believing nuns and independent, healthy old widows.

Ted said I was just like my mother, an overbearing, intolerable, domineering woman. He was sorry for the old blighter, my father, and what he must have suffered. I expect I am like her. We each want our own life. Mostly she got her own way, but I don't get mine. Ted arranges our lives to suit him and I have to put up with it. He is devoted to church, to social service, to preaching, to the Knights of Columba, and to argument. Query every statement and prove the other fellow a silly fool, seems to be Ted's first axiom for the conduct of life. Argument. Always the supercilious talking. Twist the other fellow in knots and then be gleeful at how clever you are. It's wearying.

There's one thing Ted's religion can do for him. He can regard me as his penance, his cross, his opportunity for practicing the virtues of patience and forbearance, and, in finale, his earthly purgatory. I expect he does.

This is what young love comes to. Seven children together and thirty years of marriage and all that is wished for is the breaking of the bond. It is sad. It is unutterably, deathly sad. Failures, the pair of us, and I thought I could make a success of marriage. To try and to fail is a bitter dose.

What is left? Only expediency and proper behavior. Sounds easy enough. The mind can assent to it and the will can direct it, but when the hungry heart beats too violently, what then? When the primitive soul runs amok, what then? Let's keep a chain on that monkey.

Down, Ruby Alice, to your kitchen, your marriage bed and board. Down, girl. You damn fool girl.

THURSDAY, SEPTEMBER 27TH.
Three-thirty P.M. It is a beautifully perfect day outside: inside only trouble. To begin with, my day started badly. I found a little crack on my ankle and in each leg a patch of thrombosis, so I had to put on my bandages again. Then when the family came in to lunch, I mentioned seeing Lois Harris whilst out shopping. Ted began his quibbling. Shouldn't Miss White and Lois be introduced to each other since both are middle-aged spinsters, said he. I protested, saying that Lois is thirty but that Daisy White is nearly my age. Then somehow we were in a quarrel about the differences between what was old, elderly, or merely middle-aged, and what was a girl!! I snapped. I said I wasn't going to quarrel over such a trifle and he said I was, but he was only laughing. I said I was tired of his laughter.

I had to go out and fetch the dessert, and then I was really cross, for Toby, the cat, was nibbling at my tapioca custard, which I had put out to cool. I shouted at him and chased him out. Ted got wild at the noise. He threw a knife down and broke a plate, he took up a fork and rattled a cup, and he banged his fists on the table. "How about a little more noise?" he said. I said nothing. I served dessert and poured the coffee. He rose and went out to the garden. At two o'clock he came back in the house, kissed me good-bye, and went off to the office. I hate these kisses. I hate his affiliations, his pieties, his religiosity, and his busybodying. I fight it down but it surges up in me like a nausea.

Evening. At teatime Ted said to the boys, "I wonder if I have any engagements this evening. If not, could I take Ma to the movies?" I smiled. This is Ted's gesture of apology. Well, we've been to the movies and another reconciliation is brought to pass.

Clearing the decks. I am full to overflowing with thoughts and notions. I should particularly like to express something about women and religion. The whole assumption in theology and in the scriptures is still, and continually, Turkish. All philosophy is built upon the unquestioned supremacy of man over woman. But why? I have been thinking of the Garden of Eden story, and assenting to it, but I still ask, Why?

Woman must have some value for her own self. She can't always be secondary or a mere incident in man's life. Over and over again women are alluded to as simply animals, creatures without minds or souls, only bodies, which are sometimes pleasurable, sometimes useful, but oftener hindrances, necessary nuisances.

What of woman herself, with her sensibilities, her thoughts, her longings for God, and her sufferings? What of God and woman? All the religions and philosophies are full of God and man. I ask, What of the women? The Virgin Mary? No answer. She was too docile, accepting conditions imposed on her, masculine impositions. What of a woman like me, a woman as conscious of her ego as any man could ever be?

The King of Yugoslavia was assassinated yesterday. Franco's forces had successes against the rebels in Spain yesterday. Opening the winter relief campaign in Berlin yesterday, Herr Hitler exhorted the more well-to-do classes to prepare for "sacrifices" in the interests of the community. The Sultan of the Maldive Islands has been dethroned by his ministers.

Nice little world! Everything safe for democracy. Bloody little Europe, almost every day presenting us with another assassination or revolution. What times we live in. How can a man be important or a woman bother about her soul whilst these things happen?

Last night I listened to a radio play where all the action took place on board ship and all the characters were men. It struck me that many of the radio plays have no women parts in them. I talked about this with Ted, and we think we have discovered the reason. At bottom, woman is only concerned with the passions of love, and this position must be portrayed with visibility. One must see the charmer to believe in her. Hence the masculine radio dramas.

Like it or not, woman has no importance in the world except so far as she can please a man. Her knowledge, her wisdom, her experience, her talents, are all tinsel decorations. What she must have is youth and beauty. No wonder women hate to grow old. No wonder they patronize the beauty parlors. The wisest woman is the woman who keeps herself as young and beautiful as she can. The woman who neglects herself, who grows dowdy and careless, is a fool.

I have been thinking of the New Woman too. How that idea fooled us in the nineties. When woman stepped out to fight for equality with man, she simply cut her own throat. Look at women working all over the world. Financial independence? No, it is only wage-slavery. Women have to work, whether they like it or not. Which is better, to be dependent on the job and the boss or to be dependent on the father, husband, or son? The only financial independence comes from safely invested funds, and only a tiny minority of people have it, men or women.

Meanwhile, I found myself thinking maybe women should stay at home. Of course, the home is a restricted place. And such a tiny place. But old Joe Beates is raising his head in me and stirring up all my inherent Irish restlessness and carelessness. I survey this house and I am wearied by it. I do my housekeeping job and I am bored to death with it. I want to walk out and to walk away. I want to be roaming. The old Sides are stirring in me, too. All their wildness and gaiety and sensuousness is asimmering.

I went up to bed feeling randy, like a silly girl mooning for a lover. I thought as I closed my eyes, I *don't* want to be huffed off with the Holy Ghost! That's how it is with me. I want to play.

TUESDAY, OCTOBER 16TH.

Four P.M. We moved the sofa last week. The effect is to bring Ted and me together, side by side. Rather pleasant, I think. Last night, for a wonder, Ted did not go out to his class, and we sat there, on the sofa, reading. Then we talked, really talked, about Russia, about art, about St. Thomas Aquinas. A good evening. Then early to bed and pleasant sleeping.

Evidently the exhilaration of the evening plunged me back into my girlhood. I was dreaming of Dad and myself as a young girl of seventeen. Dad was there so plainly, sprawling in his yellow blazer, dawdling over the papers. He was visible in all his laziness of figure and all his blazing activity of mind. Syd Whitelock was there and Will Hooton, and so incongruously, Bill Berry. I was young and shy, lissome and dancing, innocent and ignorant, and full of craving for life. I was athrill with the expectation of love, both wishing for it and dreading it. There was no Mother in the picture, only indulgent men. All day I have been thrilling to that dream. I could fly.

Syd Whitelock and Will Hooton were two of Ruby's suitors. Will Hooton is the mysterious W. H. who is mentioned again and again in the diaries as the love of young Ruby's life. His full name is noted only this once in all of her writing.

SUNDAY, NOVEMBER 11TH. ARMISTICE DAY.

Last night over at Bert's we heard a Salvation Army program on the radio. Old Bert turned to us and said, "I can remember when my old man used to go out with General Booth himself, and spout on the street corner too. Sanctimonious old bloke, he was. Good old boy too. Didn't last, though. Too fond of drink, he was. That was his failing. Beer. Well, he paid the price for it too. Died early. He was soaked with it, so when he got the cholera that summer, he died like a fly. All men to their taste. Spouting and drinking was his." Ted made no comment, only looked very sour. You could see that he hated Bert to publish these facts about their father.

TUESDAY, NOVEMBER 13TH.

The damnable fact is I am old. I am so tired I could cry. I was baking this morning, apple pies, treacle tart, gingerbread, sentimental pie, and I can't stand up anymore. Oh, I don't want to work anymore. This house is big and the work is too much. I should throw down my tools and walk away. But I can't. Here I must stay, and here I must carry on, willy-nilly. But I am crying out damnation, damnation. To hell with it all! And here's the dreadful winter ahead of us. There was a thick fog last night and this day's darkness is already descending. Grayness and gloom; how I hate it. And Ted is so chirpy I could knock his block off! What a mess I am, what a fool of a woman.

MONDAY, NOVEMBER 18TH.

Fog: inside and out. Fog in the house, and fog in the mind and the heart. I am angry and I want to write my anger out and get rid of it.

I have heard stories over the years of long-married individuals who wish their spouses dead or who rejoice at such a death. That's what marriage does to married people and that's why I say marriages last too long. In my temper, which is both mounting and deepening, I am growing afraid of coming to a similar hatred of my husband. If I am not careful, scrupulously careful, I shall hate him. In moments I do loathe him; but if those moments grow in duration, how awful it would be.

The trouble is, in this "retired" life Ted sees too much of the domestic machinery. He fusses about trifles. He comments on the way the floor is polished, the towels hung, the linen aired, the kettle boils, the cupboard opens, and so on. None of this is any of his business. Now that winter is here he fusses about the fires and is always nagging at me about them.

Along with the fires, he has been critical about the placement of my wardrobe and the fact that I moved some empty bottles from the pantry to the garden shed. He says he will train me and punish me for wanting my own way and for not doing things according to his own lights.

Is this Christian? This man who goes to daily Mass, who prays abjectly every night, yet who teases his wife, nags like a shrew, plays the petty tyrant, and disputes like a fool. I'm fifty years old, and he brags how he'll train me and punish me. Christian marriage? Is it any wonder that I long to be free of him? If I had money of my own I would leave him tomorrow. To be free, to be my own woman, that is the deepest desire of my heart. Money, and only money, gives freedom. If we had money we shouldn't stay together and get on each other's nerves. We shouldn't be fussed by paltry things like wardrobes and empty bottles. The machinery of life would be invisible. What I want is *my* life and *my* self. It is infuriating that a woman like me can be so prevented and constrained.

SATURDAY, DECEMBER 1ST.
Today was a leisurely day, less cooking than usual, and I feel much the better for it. Also, I actually enjoyed Arden Cottage tonight. Bertie's engagement to Peggy Coppin was announced.

I have been reading *A Backward Glance*, the autobiography of Edith Wharton. She ends her book by saying, "Life is the saddest thing there is, next to death; yet there are always new countries to see, new books to read (and, I hope, to write). . . ." She is a wealthy woman of leisure. She has money and time, and I have neither. But new books to read; Yes, luckily I have that pleasure. If I didn't have books I should die.

FRIDAY, DECEMBER 7TH.
Aileen has sent me the first two volumes of Proust's *A la Recherche du Temps Perdu: Swann's Way*. I am very excited about this. I have come across references to Proust for years past, but never yet read this tremendous work. Aileen writes:

> Here are the first two Proust volumes. Try them and let me know. I'd try them more than once if I were you. Because if you can "get" Proust, he is an addition to one's mental life. Of course he's a snob and a liar and a pervert and a hypochondriac: but he's also an artist of amazing integrity and astonishing sensibility, and a truth seeker, even if he shows a fly's eye view of the world. And a humorist, though this is not apparent at first glance. I think I like him because although his people and his

world are poles apart from mine, he knows how one sort of beauty links with another, so that the flavoring of a bun, or a seascape reflected in the glass of your bookshelves, or a piece of tooled leather, or a patch of sunlit wall in the corner of a picture, or a similarity of names (or almost anything, in fact) can transport you in an instant to a timeless place.

So that's Aileen. And she warned me on Monday that it went on forever. All the better, I say. When I am lucky enough to find a work I can relish, I want it never to come to an end.

I have been brooding on an idea to try to write my own account of *things past*. It seems to me that if I could sweep into one continuous stream all the various separate tributaries of my thinking, I could perhaps fashion a little river on which some other minds could glide along. The things *I* know of time with my woman's viewpoint. There is no philosophy for women; no religion for women; yet we have experience, and at least enough mind to deal with our experiences. Why don't I say clearly what I know? Perhaps I shall.

Mother is due tomorrow for a stay.

THURSDAY, DECEMBER 20TH.

Alone again and I thank God for it. Mother has returned to Angel Road once more and now I'm breathing freely.

I've listened to Mother now ten days on end: tales of the neighbors, of relations, of the past, and the one concrete conviction that comes to the forefront of my mind is the necessity of a practical daily religion for the living of the good life. I don't care what church. Of all the tales of disaster and disgrace, of unhappiness and failure, that Mother has related to me, not one of the people has had any religion of any kind. They are pagans, the whole lot of them. No, not even pagans, for the old pagans had their gods and observed their religious rites. They are heathens, white heathens. If we were all highly cultured humanists, or if we were all saints, the world might get along very well without churches. But being what we are, overriding, self-loving egotists, we must have religion of some sort. I used to think that the churches existed to persuade us to seek the supernatural life. I was mistaken. I now think the churches exist to teach the good natural life. Without the churches, there is a human life alright, but precious little goodness. The noble savage is still Rousseau's fiction. The discipline of the policeman is not enough.

Mother's tales are of "ordinary" people. There are millions and millions of them. I am an ordinary person. I have lived for fifty years trying to find out how to live and what have I found out? I shall try to say. Myriad books have been written about the extraordinary people: the saints, the sinners, the geniuses, the fools, the poets, the artists, the kings and the statesmen, the scientists and the players: picturesque and unique, all of them. But who has written about the ordinary people? Dickens? No, he was a caricaturist. Balzac? A little, but in a bygone period. Shakespeare? Not as I can recognize as ordinary. Proust? I don't know yet.

Why not a woman's book? Not one of wish fulfillments like the Brontës', but one which truthfully states life as any obscure woman can see and feel it? Why can't a woman speak for women? Women and men do not look at the world alike. Man's validities are not mine. I think as a woman and, by God, I'll write as a woman. Indeed, I can only write what I am conscious of, but I want to write more than my immediate private story. I want to write also what I have seen of others and what I have guessed at. And I shall write.

THURSDAY, DECEMBER 27TH.

Three-thirty P.M. The holidays at Bert's passed off better than I anticipated. Young Bertie's fiancée, Peggy Coppin, was there. She seems a nice sort of girl, and the twins like her very much.

Ted was cross and critical this morning, but when he came in at dinner time he was full of praises for the poor cottagers again, their virtues of house-wifeliness, of thrift, and of cheerfulness. He made invidious comparisons with my deficiencies in the same virtues. I was too tired to feel a shred of resentment, but Artie was indignant at all the implied detractions. After his father had left for the office he said, "Those women! They've only teeny twenny little bits of places to take care of. Seems to me Dad ought to have married a char-woman, then he might have been suited."

1935

WEDNESDAY, JANUARY 9TH.

Ted and I have been quarreling again, and last night I suffered again a sense of finish. Before I settled to sleep I happened to put my hand to my cheek and was surprised to feel how soft and how cold it was. Suddenly memory flooded me of my first winter in New Jersey and how Ted used to kiss my cold cheeks and say he loved them when they were cold. We were young then and he was in love with me. And now?

Love is the cruelest thing in the world and the greatest delusion. There is only one true love: that of a mother for her child, and even that fails. And that, too, is a torture. Perhaps the reason I fell ill on Saturday was because of the news we received from Charlie. He said he had got a job in Colombia, South America, would be sailing in January, and would spend his majority on the water. That was a blow to me. So long as Charlie was in New York, he was there with the rest. In South America he is lost to me indeed.

THURSDAY, JANUARY 10TH.

This is the twins' birthday. They are sixteen today. Artie has started back to Liberty today. Ted and Cuthie have gone to town to have an interview with the Dean of Queen Mary College. They are also going to see the Dean of the London Medical College.

Nine-fifteen P.M. Ted and Cuthie returned from the city at teatime and Cuthie is now enrolled as a student at Queen Mary College. He starts classes next Tuesday.

SUNDAY, JANUARY 20TH.

Ted came along with me to Mass. He was very affable, and I thought, walking along, what a fool I am to fight with this man. I've got to live my life with him, so why don't I take it easily?

The gospel for the day happened to be the account of the wedding feast at Cana. Father Bishop followed it with a discourse on Christian marriage. It was all to order, a beautiful thesis, only not according to facts. I had a hard job to keep a smile off my face. It is amusing to hear a priest talk about marriage. What does he know who has never been tried? Eye wash. That's what it was: theology. And what does Father Bishop know of the real problems of marriage? I suppose he can't even guess them. Marriage ought not to be a sacrament, for it is a destruction.

MONDAY, JANUARY 21ST.

Eight-fifteen P.M. I have just finished reading *Testament of Youth* by Vera Brittain. I want to note her feminism. Here is a woman only ten years my junior, so practically my contemporary, but one a hundred times more able to manage her own life. I regard her achievement with envy. Here is one of the things she says that I like. "They (her parents) understood now that freedom, however uncomfortable, and self-support, however hard to achieve, were the only conditions in which a feminist of the war generation and, indeed, a Post-Victorian woman of any generation, could do her work and maintain self-respect. After the Armistice my father, with characteristic generosity, had made over to me a few of his shares in the family business, in order that I might pay my own college bills and be spared the ignominy of asking him for every sixpence after so long a period of financial self-sufficiency."

There is one item that I thoroughly agree with. Freedom and financial independence are factors in life which I ceaselessly crave. In America Ted did at least approach the American man's attitude to his wife, considering her at least his pal and his equal. With his own business to attend to, he did at least give me the freedom of the house. Back here, he more and more assumes the

Victorian man's attitude. That attitude assumes that a woman is inferior to a
man, that a wife should be thankful that her husband supports her, and that
she must be satisfied with his ideas of how she should be supported. It will be
incredible to my grandchildren, but it is true, that I, a woman of fifty, have no
money at all, and that *every week* I have to ask for the necessary household
moneys. It revolts me that every week I should be expected to be grateful for
my maintenance. Have I not earned it? Do I not still earn it? I am the working
housekeeper, and my body is still used for pleasure. To be free, to be my own
woman, that's what I long for.

Vera Brittain did marry. I like this excerpt she gives from a love letter to
her future husband. "Just as you want to discover how a man can maintain a
decent standard of culture on a small income, so I want to solve the problem
of how a married woman, without being inordinately rich, can have children
and yet maintain her intellectual and spiritual independence as well as having . . . time for the pursuit of her own career." And this: "If marriage made
the whole fight harder, so much the better; it would become part of my war
and as this I would face it, and show that, however stubborn any domestic
problem, a lasting solution could be found if only men and women would
seek it together."

Fine words. She was about thirty-one when she wrote that, and felt like
that. She was only just about to marry, not in the fray. And I am nearly fifty-
one.

*Vera Brittain (1894–1970) was an English novelist, feminist, and pacifist.
She is best known for* Testament of Youth, *a novel depicting the horrors of
World War I.*

SUNDAY, JANUARY 27TH.

Ted read my Boots book, Albert Halper's *The Foundry*, and commented on its
nastiness and vulgarity. Then he said, "I love you, but I don't want to see you
in the bathroom, and watch what you do there any more than you want to see
me there." "I love you." Casually, quickly, but factually, and my heart leapt. He
never says he loves me, but he should say so. Women want to hear the words,
as well as experience the union. I am very happy over this.

MONDAY, JANUARY 28TH.

I am still happy. This morning before Ted snapped off the light to go downstairs and out to Mass, he leaned over the bed and kissed me good-bye. This
was so unusual, but quite spontaneous. Oh, if he would only show me more
love, and the church less. I'm happy about it, anyhow.

WEDNESDAY, JANUARY 30TH.

I am still quite happy. I know that I do not believe in the Church, but I can go to Mass for Ted as I can cook him his dinner. It is a chore. Now and then I apprehend God for a moment: in that hour of the sun's eclipse, alone on the topdeck of an Atlantic liner, alone in the street on a starry night, watching Niagara, climbing the Rockies, lost in our New Jersey back woods, feeling my child in my womb or at my breast, in the mud plaza of the Indian church at Taos, listening to solemn music, even sitting in the sunshine and peeling potatoes. I have been wrapped in the certainty and feel of God in such moments of extreme aloneness as these.

But I can go to church. That, after all, is only one of the politenesses of life, and evidently, for me, one of the little necessities, like washing my face, or combing my hair. So long as Ted loves me, I can do it. At least I think I can.

TUESDAY, FEBRUARY 19TH.

At breakfast Ted was reading from the obituaries in the *Times.* "In memory of my adored husband," he read, and then said, "Will Ma ever say that about me?" He received no answer from the twins, nor from me, who was standing over the frying pan in the scullery. Ted thought the use of the word "adored" irrational. I answered, "What people see of a marriage is only what they see. You know perfectly well that the state of affairs between husband and wife is never seen. How we really feel to each other is never known to anyone but ourselves. It is feeling which determines us, and that is not founded on reason. Affection is irrational." Ted said, "I don't think so. And anyhow, it ought not to be. Our conduct is founded on right and wrong, and so should our affections be." I responded, "But they are not. In matters of affection we cannot help ourselves. If marriages were founded on rationality they would never last at all. It is because feeling endures that marriage endures and nothing else." "Well, I shouldn't have thought so," said Ted, "but perhaps you're right, Lady." And then breakfast proceeded in silence.

MONDAY, FEBRUARY 25TH.

Yesterday in church I was asking myself what earthly credibility or usefulness is there in Christianity. Christianity is man-made and that's why it is so useless to a woman like me. All the masculine philosophies, whether Plato or Epicetus, or Jesus or Paul, or Augustine or Thomas Aquinas, or Kant or Spencer, are really useless to women. Men and women are different. They can feel together but they will never think alike. All those Christian virtues, meekness, forbearance, humility, obedience, charity, which they preach to us, they are very convenient for the men, aren't they? Do I intend to practice meekness, humility, and all? Of course I don't. I've as much right in the world as any man has, and I'll never humble myself. By force of circumstances, the muscle and the purse, men can control women, but they cannot think for them. A woman like Mrs. Eddy comes along and tries to give women a new religion for their own. So does Annie Besant. And their new religions are alluring on first sight, but very quickly one sees they are only using, revamping, the old men's religions. Mrs. Eddy revamps Plato and Emerson. Mrs. Besant revamps the Brahmins. What's the use of that? But what is woman's philosophy and why does no woman state it?

Auntie Liz, Grandma, Em Copus, Mother. They managed their whole lives without the slightest regard to the Christian myth because they didn't believe it. They knew it was only talk. Men's theories, men's talk, men's reasons. We smite at them because they don't work. Maybe they work for men sometimes. Men idealize, but we realize. We have to, we endure. We endure our own lives in our own bodies, and think our own thoughts in our own minds. When men suffer menstruation and childbirth then maybe I'll credit some of their speculations about God Almighty. I know what I know, and men's philosophies and theologies are not for me. They are not for any free woman.

Annie Besant (1847–1933) was the leader of the English Theosophy movement. Theosophy was a mystical cult that originated in New York in 1875. Buddhist and Hindu teachings were at its core, and Theosophists believed in reincarnation. Ruby met Besant in London when she was exploring religious ideas and organizations.

FRIDAY, MARCH 15TH.

Have I said that we invited Kay and her babies here for the summer? This morning we got the final word from Harold about their sailing. He also stated that he had heard from Eddie, that he would be coming on the same boat, but is going to France first.

WEDNESDAY, MARCH 20TH.

This morning a letter from Eddie arrived but, instead of giving notice of his sailing, he wrote that 523 Knickerbocker had been badly damaged by fire, and would Ted send power of attorney to Harold, as he is the first mortgagee. There aren't any details but presumably the house is completely burnt out. This *is* a shock.

THURSDAY, APRIL 18TH.

I am fifty-one today. I have had letters this morning from Mother, Auntie Liz, and the twins, but no one else remembered it. Ted has given me no good wishes today, probably because he cannot mean them. However, it is only four o'clock. He may yet remember the day before bedtime.

The twins went off to Plymouth to visit Gladys. Kay and her babies arrived a week ago. Sheila was two in February and Richard six months yesterday. The children are good, but looking after them is rather fatiguing. When the weather warms up they can live in the garden most of the time, which will make it more comfortable for us in the house. Joan is coming to spend Easter with us, and Eddie is in Dieppe. He will be in France for another two months. He is twenty-nine today.

I look the old woman. Having a young woman in the house is considerably deflating. So long as I am the only woman on the premises I think I am not so bad, that I still have a modicum of beauty and charm, but with a young woman daily beside me, oh, Lordy, there is no mistake about it, I am obviously in the dowager class. I don't like it. Not that I grudge Kay her youth, but that I grieve for mine, so utterly past and gone. I hate to be old. There are *no* compensations on the downside of the hill, and I don't care what anybody says. "Grow old gracefully?" It simply can't be done.

THURSDAY, MAY 2ND.

Three P.M. I am afraid I have bitten off more than I can chew for this summer. The children tire me dreadfully. Sheila I find particularly exhausting. Little Richard is a very good baby, but Sheila is spoiled. She does not cry, is good tempered enough, but is self-willed to the limit. Kay said Eddie did not like Sheila and said she was a pest. One evening when she was cutting up in the parlor, Ted remarked, "Well, if Eddie said Sheila was a pest, I think his remark was most moderate." As a girl, Kay took a course in child psychology in college, but as a mother, she is no disciplinarian and allows the child to rule her. The American child, I suppose. We shall only have her for a few months, so can endure smiling for that short time. She is a nice child. If I could have her to myself I could train her.

Tomorrow Mother is coming to help with the babies, her great-grandchildren. It is also our thirtieth wedding anniversary. Awful.

MONDAY, MAY 20TH.

We received a letter from Eddie from Paris. He will be coming to London in a week or so. Ted has not seen him since 1927.

Last night on the radio we heard of the death of T. E. Lawrence, Lawrence of Arabia. He died from a collision with a pedal cyclist. Lawrence was born in 1888. He has died in his prime, a great gift. He will never have to sink into fatuity and puerility. He will never lose his friends and his loves, nor his enthusiasms and ambitions. He will never have to contend with increasing infirmities and ugliness. He will never suffer the torment of growing old and living too long. Lucky Lawrence.

MONDAY, MAY 27TH.

The postman brought a letter from Eddie saying he will be at Victoria Station at five this evening. When Ted came in to breakfast I showed him the letter. He said that he had planned to go to Forest Gate tonight. He added that Eddie could find his way himself since he'd been here before. I asked him to go to meet Eddie, he hadn't seen him for eight years. He refused and he concluded with: "There will be plenty of time to see him. He hasn't written to me anyhow. Your atheist son!"

Then, to make things worse, when Kay came down she said she knew Eddie expected his father to meet him. Kay said Eddie told her that he wouldn't bother to write to his father because, he was such a wonder, he knew all the times of the trains and he would be sure to be there.

I gave Cuthie some money and asked him to go to Victoria after classes, and I phoned Bertie because he had previously said he would like to know Eddie's time of arrival.

Did Ted ever love Eddie? Did he ever love me? No, all Ted loves is his own soul, his own self-righteousness, and his religion. He is the detestable Pharisee, praying on the street corners that he may be seen by men, but within, another picture.

TUESDAY, MAY 28TH.

Three P.M. In the middle of the night Ted took me for loving and I am assuaged. What a fool a woman is. Last night Ted left for Forest Gate, and thirty minutes later Bertie drove up with Eddie, Peggy, and Cuth. At eleven o'clock Ted came in. "Hello, Dad." "Hello, Eddie." They took hands, and they kissed. So everything is alright. We sat talking until midnight. This afternoon Ted has taken Eddie with him to Brentwood. All well.

MONDAY, JUNE 17TH.

Last night Ted came in from his retreat very chipper and then he proceeded to argue with Eddie. I went into the dining room with a book, to get out of his way. He was teasing and teasing, trying to make Eddie look a fool.

But after we had retired, I boiled over. Whilst he was undressing he began on me, my misdemeanors, and when I looked at him, he had such a nasty, sneering grin on his face, suddenly I smacked his face. He was flabbergasted and so was I! He dropped his pride and grabbed my wrists and said, "What are you doing? Say you're sorry. Are you sorry?" "No!" "Then I won't say another word to you." "I don't want you to, you holy man! You little Jesus! Great God, save me from such a man!" I went off to the bathroom. When I came back he was on his knees by the bed, eyes closed, head down, beating his breast. My impulse was to go and kick him, but I didn't. I undressed as quietly as I could, put out the light, and got into bed.

This morning he began at breakfast badgering Eddie. As so often, it was an argument over mere definitions, but Eddie had to be squelched. Ted hasn't seen Eddie for eight years, yet all he can do is get elated because, to his own satisfaction, he can prove Eddie wrong.

I try to keep quiet, but anger and hatred are churning in me like butter in a churn. I don't want to hate Ted. I want a proper husband, an old pal who can smile at my foibles, seeing he has known them for thirty years. I want a friend who will draw closer as life draws in. I want a lover, a true husband, a good man. Instead I have a religious neurotic, an ascetic, an inquisitioner, a common scold.

THURSDAY, JUNE 20TH.

Harold arrived this evening. Young Bertie drove to Waterloo to meet him, taking Kay and Eddie along. Harold looks very thin and tired.

THURSDAY, JUNE 27TH.

Eleven-twenty-five A.M. I am in a bad temper and feeling completely mother-in-law-ish. Kay is in bed. At any moment Joan will be at the door. I have a roast veal dinner in the course of cooking. The breakfast table is not yet cleared. *Harold* is doing the baby wash! The hall and kitchen are needing to be swept and all the downstairs rooms to be dusted. But Kay lies abed. She is tired!

FRIDAY, JULY 12TH.

I have a headache. I'm sleeping badly, the weather is hot, the children wear on our nerves. I need loving. I look at Ted at night, absolutely nude, saying his prayers, and in the morning, I feel him flop out of bed and immediately fall to his knees, praying. I am consumed with impatience and scorn. Every nerve in me is shrieking *for a man* and *this* is what I get, a praying mantis! That wartime summer that I was in the cable company, I overheard one man say to another, "Fancy a fellow wanting to go to war and leaving a woman like that. He must be mad!" Well, that was a long time ago, but I still want to be loved, need to be loved. All I get are the leavings. Imagine! I'm jealous of the Blessed Virgin. Yes, I am. I don't want plaster images, devotions, ideals, ideas. I want a flesh and blood man.

I have thought a great deal lately of all my refusals and discardings. I look at Eddie, and Kay and Harold, and distressing regret arises in me for 1927. We should have never left those boys, never. Their failures, their poor marriages, are due to us, the parents who abandoned them.

I think of all my abandonments. First, I left the Church of England for free thought and theosophy. Next, I left England, my parents and home, my friends, my job. Then I left Protestantism altogether, joined the Roman

Church, and abandoned my secret integrity and all that my past stood for. Ultimately, I abandoned America and all my American life and meaning: my American home, my American friends, and my American sons. All self-willed losses. What a mess!

When a piece of knitting becomes mis-stitched and tangled, one simply rips it all out, rewinds the thread, and begins the work again. With a life, one cannot undo the past, but suppose one could put oneself back in one's true and original position. Could one correct the present and improve the future? Seeing I now have to live in England; seeing I am an Englishwoman, in blood and marrow, in tradition and education; seeing I have no living part in a tradition and religion forced upon me; could I find integrity and peace of mind by returning to the integrity of what I was born to? I wonder.

THURSDAY, JULY 25TH.

Bertie's wedding day. He and Peggy Coppin were married in the parish church this morning. Ted did come, but it was touch and go right up to breakfast time. Afterwards there was a reception at the King's Head, with refreshments and champagne and about ninety people there. Very bourgeois, the first wedding of this kind I have ever attended. About one o'clock Bertie and Peggy made their adieus and drove away in Bert's car. Another marriage begun.

MONDAY, JULY 29TH.

Three P.M. My Americans must be just about pulling out of the dock at Antwerp. It is a beautiful day here, and I hope it is the same for them. I was surprised last night by a sudden onset of violent grief. Partings are always horrible, but as the night wore away this one seemed to become worse and worse. I especially feel the wrench of parting with little Sheila. This child has been pretty much of a nuisance, but I have loved her. And she loved me. I want her. She will forget me. I shall fade away in her memory, quickly as a dream fades.

I grieve all over again for my American life. I *ought* to be in America, in actual touch with my children and their children. This English life becomes more and more of a tragic mistake. We ought not to be here.

FRIDAY, AUGUST 16TH.

On Monday I went to London. My intention was to see Mother, but I went first to Notting Hill. I mooched around, found Charles Street, and then was launched in an escapade. I called at the houses that had once belonged to Grandma Searle. I talked to the various tenants, pitched a yarn about being an American tourist who had come to see the house where I was born, and got the people to show me over the premises. I enjoyed myself hugely and they enjoyed it all too. I stayed a couple of hours or more in that street. It was a silly thing to do, but I am sure that it was good for me. The mere excitement and fooling of it pacified some misery in me and it *has* arranged something in my mind. For in all my absurdities and shilly-shallyings of mind and mood, I do keep hold of my intention to write books. This is what I want to do, and have always wanted to do. Charles Street has intoxicated me like champagne.

FRIDAY, SEPTEMBER 6TH.

A beautiful autumn day, so Ted suggested we might go somewhere in the afternoon. We went to town and walked along the Embankment to Westminster Bridge and there took a riverboat to Kew. It was a very nice outing, something which happens so rarely with us.

SATURDAY, SEPTEMBER 7TH.

This afternoon I went to Cecilia's to get my hair set. Whilst there I got into a conversation with Mrs. Perry, the proprietoress. Somehow we began talking very seriously and intimately about religion, and about the lives of women. Remarks about the present likelihood of war began it, but whatever it was, we were really conversing, "making friends." My hair was finished but still Mrs. Perry and I sat there, talking like old cronies.

Somehow the talk veered to Christian Science. She said she was not a member, but in belief, she seemed to be a natural Christian Scientist. Then we talked of how mothers must teach religion to their children. We talked of the problems of older women, and what they could and should do with their experience. We talked of marriage, of men, and men's love. I've come home pleased, lifted out of my cussed self.

MONDAY, SEPTEMBER 9TH.

Eight P.M. I have just finished reading *Trial by Virgins* by David Larg, a book about Rossetti. I have enjoyed it, but I don't think it has been good for me. I find I am trying to fend off one of my misery moods, probably a discontent aroused by thinking of the past. This book deals predominately with his association with Elizabeth Siddal, and it has jerked to the front of my memory those years when some discerning people saw me as a replica of Elizabeth Siddal and, in fun, christened me *Beata Beatrix*. Some of the physical descriptions of Elizabeth Siddal in the book were of her flaming head, of heavy drooping lids over blue-green eyes, of lightish brows, an obstinate chin, and a straight nose. As to her character, Elizabeth is described as one who was lazy, remote, ambitious, and without faith. Her charm and her weakness was her detachment.

There is the picture. Cold, self-centered, solitary, cynical, unbelieving, lazy: not a pretty picture. Elizabeth Siddal. Ruby Side. This book makes me remember my own ambitions, all unfulfilled, which I prefer to forget. My life teases me. It is not the life I wanted, meant to have, planned for, dreamed of. It is an alien life and I detest it.

Elizabeth Siddal was the wife of and model for Dante Gabrielle Rossetti. One of the founders of the Pre-Raphaelites in 1848, Rossetti painted the Beata Beatrix.

FRIDAY, SEPTEMBER 13TH.

I went to call on Peggy, the bride. She showed me through her house. This latest fashion of emptiness and neutrality and lack of all decoration makes me feel lonesome and cold. She has one picture only, a wedding present, which hangs above the dining room mantel. However, in a little spare "junk" room I had a shock. Stuck up on one of Bertie's files was a small framed picture of the *Beata Beatrix*. I voiced my surprise at seeing it there. Peggy said that it had belonged to Billie and that Bertie likes it so he brought it to their house. I am just finishing Violet Hunt's *Wife of Rossetti*, so this is quite a coincidence. The blessed damsel!

MONDAY, SEPTEMBER 16TH.

I am homesick. I want my boys. I want to be in America.

I have been reading St. Francis de Sales again today, so I am tranquilized tonight.

When I was a little girl, perhaps about nine years old, I once found in the bottom of Grandma Searle's breakfast room cupboard a little black book which became a great treasure to me. It was small enough to live in my pocket, and it contained several little texts and verses for each day of the year. I cannot remember one of them, nor what the plan of the arrangement was. Nor did I ever read it consecutively, nor in its daily sequence. I used to open it at random, looking for light. I would pull it out of my pocket at any urgent moment, dip into it, and fish out of it some counsel or refreshment or other. Most vividly, I can remember one occasion when I was standing in the corridor outside the seventh standard room in Flora Gardens. I can't remember that moment's need, nor its gratification, but I see myself there in the cold corridor, reading in the little black book. Funny child.

That habit has persisted in me. I always seem to think there is a book somewhere which will tell me exactly what I want to know. I have only to open it, anywhere, and I shall find something for my need. It does happen that way sometimes. When it fails I am always disappointed. Today, St. Francis satisfied my restless mind.

St. Francis de Sales wrote in The Introduction to a Devout Life *that piety is found in the familiar experiences of daily life, the life of family and neighbor,*

*rather than the asceticism of the solitary or introspective believer. With his
friend St. Jane de Chantal, he conceived the idea of an order of nuns who
would combine the contemplative life with visiting the poor and the sick. It
was an unusual idea for the time (1641) and was born of one of the great spiritual friendships of the Catholic Church.*

SUNDAY, OCTOBER 6TH.

I have finished reading *Constance Markievicz,* a biography by Sean O'Faolain.
What a wild woman! I got very bored with all the Irish politics, but I wanted
to find the woman. She was one of the women to whom the Dunlops often
likened me. The other one was Isadora Duncan. Both these famous women
were friends of the Dunlops, and I never met either of them, but I have always
wondered what it was the Dunlops saw in me when I was twenty that made
them think of these wildcat women. Perhaps there was something which
made them smell out my Irish ancestry, something ardent, turbulent, melancholy. Nobody knows now.

    This reading and thinking causes much remembering, especially follow-
ing my recent reading about the Rossettis. This frames me as I must have been
thirty-five years ago, a lovely and romantic heroine: but not me, the battered,
old woman I am today. I look back at that girl I was and she is a stranger, a
beautiful and exciting stranger, but pathetic in her ignorance and her help-
lessness. I am sorry for her. I love the poor thing.

    *Constance Markievicz (1868–1927), an Irish patriot arrested for her role in
    the Easter Rebellion of 1916, was a member of the Sinn Fein Parliament.*

    *The **Dunlops** were friends of Ruby when she was a young woman. They
    introduced her to William Butler Yeats, G. K. Chesterton, George Bernard
    Shaw, and others in London's literary circle of the turn of the century. Ruby
    appears to have been a protégée of the Dunlops. Daniel Dunlop, O.B.E.
    (1868–1935) worked for Westinghouse in London. He is best known for his
    leadership role in the World Power Conference, London 1929.*

FRIDAY, OCTOBER 11TH.

Three P.M. I woke this morning in a cloud of misery. I had been dreaming of
America, being there in the midst of my family, and being ignored. All the
young wives were getting first attention and I was being shoved in the background. I was not miserable in the dream, but when I wakened I knew this was
my old subconscious talking, telling me what would be the facts of the case.

    I have been worrying for letters for some time. Harold has not written
since he returned in July. John and Jimmie have not written since early spring.
Eddie has sent only one letter since his return, though I hear Reta Pullan gets
letters regularly from him. Not one of them has answered my letter of

September except Charlie, saying he could and would take care of me if I went there in event of war. Now this morning I get a nasty, brutal letter from Eddie. A sort of telepathy, for it confirms my dream.

He begins:

> I firmly believe that all your ideas about coming over here on account of war, and wanting Sheila over there, are nothing but an outlet for your own frustrated life. You are not tackling the problem by running away from it. The trouble is between you and Dad and if you don't tell him where he gets off, I'm sorely tempted to do it myself. You are an absolute bundle of repression and frustration. Hence that talk about raising Sheila; Sheila means nothing to you and you know it. Can't you, for once in your life, calmly figure out for yourself, your rights and needs as a human being. Stop trying to please other people by trying to be another person. Be *yourself* for once and remain yourself. You have legal rights, ethical rights, and any religion that doesn't give them is a mockery. If the Church won't give them the State will. When I make money you can have all you want. If your husband won't take care of you I will. But for heaven's sake clear up your mental atmosphere because one lunatic per family is plenty. If you don't tackle your problems I'm tempted to do it myself. You'd better write soon before I do blow up and do so, and that would make the air pretty blue over there.

So, not any son to any mother: my eldest son to me. The severance is now complete. We left them, and now they don't want us. Natural enough, only it makes life blanker than ever. What to do with my life? That is the question. What to do?

Presently I'm going out to meet Ted, and we are going to our weekly movie. This is another kind of dope, and I know that too. I shall look in the shops on the way. I want some new dresses, and I think I'll try to amuse myself by making some. They will give me something to do, something to think about. Filling up emptiness with clothes: what an occupation for a supposedly sensible woman!

MONDAY, OCTOBER 21ST.

Three P.M. I had been sort of fighting with Ted about churchgoing. I asked him again to give up the C.E.G. Because he was friendly, I went further, and told him that it was because of all his excessive zeal for guilds and societies that I could not go to church at all. I reminded him of Mr. Utard, a really devout Catholic, who persistently and firmly declined to join any church associations either in America or France. He went regularly to Mass, he maintained Catholic viewpoints, he gave to charities, but he simply would not join societies. He wouldn't even buy a Catholic paper. I ventured to ask Ted why he couldn't take his religion like Mr. Utard, in a sober and gentlemanly way. I also said that if he went less, I might go more. Ted took me up on this, but alas, we got nowhere. It all ended up in a wrangle.

This turmoil has all subsided, but I'm tired and bored with chores and in-laws and I can't change anything. What's to do? Act like a cat, I think. I'll curl up in all the warm spots I can find, completely indifferent to the surrounding world, and lash out with a spit and scratch whenever I'm annoyed. But how to be indifferent? That's the difficulty.

I need to keep reminding myself: Ruby Alice, you are a nobody, you have nothing, you are nothing, and you never will be anything or anybody. I need to hammer this in and then some. Then all my tortures, past and present, would become nothing too. Then doubtless I should attain cathood: sleek fur and purring on the hearth. If only I could forget, then life would be easier to endure. If I could forget young love, America, my sons, and my home, all vanished.

I long for a home, for a resting place, for a friend, for a belief, for a conviction, *any* conviction. To give worth and sense to living I fight, trying to retain beliefs, illusions, an old husband. Why cannot I be simple? Why can I not forget the sufferings of my heart and soul and mind? I want peace, inner peace. I want indifference.

TUESDAY, NOVEMBER 19TH.

Movie night and we saw a film of the *Call of the Wild.* It showed the Klondike gold rush and was really made in Alaska. Ted enjoyed it, though he could see its absurdities, such as wrong packing and clean trails. I enjoyed the mountain scenery.

Last week I dragged Ted to the Laurie because there was a picture advertised as *In Old Santa Fe.* It wasn't Santa Fe at all, just old cowboy stuff. I am weary of Romford and of the domestic round. Weekly movies: minor distractions, these. What I need is an earthquake.

THURSDAY, NOVEMBER 21ST.

Nuns on the doorstep again this afternoon; presumably the same two as earlier in the week, and again I did not answer the door. Then lo, at teatime, young Father Atlee comes calling. What the dear Catholics of this town want to do now, is to "get after the cinemas." Ted is asked to watch them for twelve weeks and then report on all the immoralities. Actually, Ted said he couldn't see anything much wrong with them, morally, and said he thought they were quite clean nowadays. Mrs. Taylor wants to press the matter. Mrs. Taylor! Mrs. Taylor is a very plain woman in late middle age whose husband has left her for another woman. She is another of the self-righteous ones. I listened to Father

Atlee, trying to find something to do; he was quite nonplussed because Ted said he saw nothing to interfere about.

THURSDAY, DECEMBER 5TH.

Three-thirty P.M. These last two nights I have been dreaming very vividly of Doris Whipple. I was back in the Avenue A years and we were as we were then: young, excitable, dashing about in our cars, playing at the club, down by the bay. I wonder why memory persists in throwing up this particular woman, and whether the darned old unconscious isn't handing me a nice warning. After all, weren't Doris Whipple and Ruby Thompson rather similar idiots? I can see her now, so clearly: young, rich, with a charming husband and two beautiful children, one of the best houses in town, and a swell car. Yet all the time, Doris was fretting herself into misery, worrying about God, nagging at her husband, being moody, refusing to play. I wonder if the old Freudian censor is throwing her at me now as a horrible example, and warning me to behave. I wonder.

Doris Whipple was one of Ruby's friend's in Bayonne. They shared an interest in religious ideas.

SUNDAY, DECEMBER 23RD.

The American mails came in this morning. As usual, I find they give me a kind of sick, sinking feeling. The fire damage to 523 has been repaired and John and Ruth have moved from the cottage back into the house but have quarreled with Eddie, Chili, and Jimmie. Harold and Kay have gone back to Long Island. Jimmie and Doris have taken a house in Bergenfield, and Eddie and Chili have gone to live with them. John's second child was christened on December first, and Harold stood as godfather. Ruth was away on a trip to Havana with her brother whilst John was left to mind the babies *on his own*. As Jacqueline was only born in September, and Adele was only a year old in August, what kind of a mother is Ruth? Doris is expecting her second baby in February.

What have we done for our children? We've cast them loose, left them to shift for themselves and make silly marriages. We've left them to be poor struggling clerks, always to be poor. We've plunged them into a struggle whilst we've run away. I think of our boys becoming fathers, worrying about money, and I think of Ted absorbed in religion. What about fatherhood? What about manhood? Oh, why talk?

Midnight. Big Ben has just struck twelve, so it is Christmas Day. Ted and the twins are at midnight Mass, but I have stayed home because of icy slush in the streets and a cold rain. The weather is very bad.

This morning Peterson delivered *three* cases of wines and spirits. I was speechless. The bill must be ten pounds if it is a penny. Ted selected one large bottle of claret and wrapped it up for Father Bishop. I managed to keep quiet, but I am angry. Not one gift, not one penny, not even a Christmas card has been sent to the boys or their babies on the other side. On the other hand, Ted has written to Johnnie for money due. Johnnie had a confinement to pay for in September, and Jimmie is going to have one to pay for in February. Ted's been scolding at me for months about pulling down bills, and yet he goes and buys three cases of booze. He's crazy, but I am hurt.

Now he will go and daydream about the Babe of Bethlehem, but the real babies, Sheila and Dickie and the rest, he will ignore. This ignoring and neglect of his own children and grandchildren, this preference for strangers and religious fantasies, puts me into a passion.

SUNDAY, DECEMBER 29TH.

We got through the Christmas orgy alright. On Christmas night, Ted loved me but alas, his loving left me with a sense of humiliation. There is no tenderness or affection in it, no kiss, no loving word, only earthy beastliness. I loathe it. In the king's speech on Christmas Day, he alluded to the queen as "my dear wife." It made me think of Grandpa, of Mr. Utard, of old Mr. Eason, old men who lived, and do live, contentedly with their old wives. Ted never thinks of me like that, and everybody knows it. Yet, in spite of that knowledge, I still wish for his love and am miserable because I have not got it.

Last night he deliberately hurt me by alluding to my figure and by companying me, sneeringly, with my mother. How cheap. The comments may be true, but how rude, and hurtful, just the same. My body has been at the disposal of his lust for over thirty years. I have brought seven children to birth and suffered a miscarriage. I have worked as a housewife. My figure now resembles that of most of the women of my family. We all have the same physique and we thicken in the same places. Auntie Lizzie, who had only two children, Auntie Mary, who had none, and Gladys, who is an old maid schoolteacher now in her middle forties, are my build and pattern. All of us are tall and big hipped. Ted jeers at me because I am no longer a thin virgin. He has been looking at all the young women over at Arden Cottage through Christmas, only to compare me with them to my great disadvantage. How unfair and unkind. He is always belittling.

This morning I am calm. I am writing this out, trying to get rid of it. But church is a million miles away from me. Ted went out to the early Mass, but I think, what is religion worth? I think it is worth just about nothing at all.

1936

Last night we had the usual see-the-old-year-out party here with Bert and Tillie, Bertie and Peggy, and Selma. Everything passed pleasantly, and the visitors left about one o'clock in the morning. But the party was only an interlude. Ted and I are quarreling worse than ever, but I am so angry that I have begun to do things. I simply cannot and will not continue with Ted as he is now. Unless some satisfying adjustments between us can be made, and quickly, I shall take steps to secure a proper separation. I mean this. I am infuriated with him, and I will not endure the humiliations he places upon me any longer.

On Monday morning, I made a startling discovery. I was cleaning up the parlor in anticipation of New Year's Eve, and began sorting papers on the desk and came upon a receipt from the Propagation of the Faith Society for ten pounds. It was dated the twenty-first of December. I found another for the Catholic Truth Society. Then I went through Ted's coat pockets, a dishonorable action, but I had begun to fight! I found receipts from the Catholic Missionary Society, the convent on Western Road, and also various letters from the nuns thanking Ted for playing Father Christmas to the children who otherwise would have had nothing.

I nearly fainted away. I don't think I have ever been so angry in my life. I have to ask for household money and I have no money of my own. My bills are scrutinized, and I am told I must economize. He doesn't know how we will manage. "Don't go to the oculist, go easy on the expenses, Lady, go easy on the spending." Like hell, I will!

After dinner, I went to town and had my eyes examined and ordered two pairs of new glasses. I then went down to the convent and spoke to the mother superior. I said I had called on an urgent matter and that as she knew, things were not always what they seemed, and people not what they appeared. I said that Mr. Thompson had lost his head a bit over Christmas, that he had given away excessive amounts of money which he could not afford, that he had embarrassed his family, and that I was asking them to kindly refrain from notifying him of any more deserving causes. I added that I intended to see Father Bishop about the matter. The little nun seemed rather scared and said she understood and would pray for me.

Later in the evening, as we sat in the parlor, I took up the matter with Ted. He was surprised and at first refused to answer my questions. He said he didn't care to discuss financial matters with me. He finally argued that he had every right to give his money away and not to tell me. I did not tell him that I had been to the convent, but I did tell him that I was going to see Father Bishop about the matter. We talked ourselves out and went to bed.

Yesterday I laid the whole case before Father Bishop. I began by telling him that I was thinking about seeing him about myself. I told him everything: the draw-back to Anglicanism, my visits to Anglican churches, my hatred of the C.E.G., my homesickness for America and my boys, the three cases of booze, and Monday's discoveries. Everything that burns me up. I told him I would endure this marriage as it is no longer. If matters could not be arranged amicably between us, I would go to a lawyer, go to the courts, and sue for a legal separation or a divorce. As I will. I am deeply angry.

I got two satisfactions from the priest. One was his expressed impatience with the nuns. They are never supposed to ask for money and any they do receive, they must account to him. "I shall have to look into this," he said. "This is wrong and I won't have it. I shall have to speak with Mr. Thompson about this, for he has no right to give them any money. I am the almoner in the parish. Any charities are at my discretion. I know better than the sisters where the proper cases are." So the dear sisters are in for a wigging.

I had asked Ted what exactly he had done for Sister Joseph, since she had sent him letters thanking him for all the kindnesses he had bestowed upon her since she came into the parish. He told me it was none of my business. I told him I might enjoy myself citing her as co-respondent. He was pained! He asked me what could I get out of that? I said I could get it in every penny illustrated paper in the kingdom and it would be a lovely sensation for the British public. I am angry.

I asked him if he had sent any gifts or money to America for his children there. He said, "What children? No, I didn't." No letters, no cards, nothing. But forty pounds for "religion."

After I kept asking and asking questions, I got this information: Ted had sold the London Road shops, and it was a principle of his to give ten percent of any profit or raise to God. A private principle, of course. I exploded. More anon.

THURSDAY, JANUARY 2ND.

Ted and I had further serious talk last night. The outcome is that he is going to think over my suggestions, and he will let me know what he will do.

I state that as his wife I am entitled to his confidence. It is my right to know exactly what our income is, and to be in agreement with him as to how it shall be budgeted. I am entitled to receive moneys for household disbursements without having to ask for them, and without petty criticism as to how they are spent. I am entitled to more than mere maintenance. I am entitled to a private allowance. I ask for a sum of money equivalent to the amount he has given to outsiders. I ask for a bank account in my own name. I demand that Ted make a fifty-fifty division of all moneys remaining after our expenses are paid, half for him and half for me. I demand that he donate to his charities out of this private allowance, not the family income.

It is ridiculous that a wife of a man of Ted's standing should have no money in her own right. All my sisters have money, even Joan, the wife of an ordinary soldier. I demand the satisfaction of having money of my own. I demand to be treated as an intelligent woman, and not like a child. I demand to be treated like a lady wife.

I agree that it is a virtue to practice charity, but not at the expense of one's family. I maintain that none of these moneys should be expended without my consent, as I am an equal partner in this marriage business. Any excess money that Ted has to disburse should go to our sons, young husbands struggling with growing families.

Meanwhile, the next thing for me to do is put myself right with the church. Ted is a bigot, and he antagonizes me into a hatred of religion and the church, but Thomas Bishop is a calm parish priest and brings me back to reason. I told him of my excursions to the Anglican churches and about going to Communion there. Father Bishop said that was not a matter for the confessional. He understood that I was distraught and that I was not apostate, nor against the Church. He said, "You believe, alright. Anybody could understand that action. It's quite excusable." When I had told Ted about it, he damned me straightaway for a heretic and apostate. When I told Father Bishop that I hated the Church, that I cursed the day it came into our lives, and I cursed all religion because it had been a curse to me all my life, he quietly said, "No, you don't hate religion. You are only hating the misapplication of religion." I felt a sense of relief at that. It must be true.

So tomorrow I shall go to town to church and Saturday I shall go to confession and then I shall go to Communion on Sunday.

SATURDAY, JANUARY 4TH.

I went to confession this morning, and was helped more by Father Bishop than I have ever been before. He knows everything, and he gives rational advice. He recommends some philosophical readings for me, and says they will suit my mind. He tells me not to bother with sentimental piety and pious gush. They are definitely not for me, and I am to ignore them. He told me to remember that, even in religious practices, one man's meat is another man's poison.

WEDNESDAY, JANUARY 15TH.

The faithful Mrs. Page came to tea. She is a beneficent distraction from my dreadful moods. I was so distraught this morning, suffering with nameless longings and desires, I could hardly bear myself. In the wholesome commonness of Mrs. Page I come to earth, and tonight I am serene.

TUESDAY, JANUARY 21ST.

King George V died last night.

WEDNESDAY, JANUARY 22ND.

I listened to the broadcast from St. James's Palace of the proclamation of the prince of Wales as the new king, King Edward VIII. It was very moving. How marvelous that these actual words can be picked up practically everywhere in the world; the remotest squatter in the Australian Bush, or the settler in central Africa, or the friend in Chicago, all could hear as clearly and distinctly as those who stood next to the actual ceremony. What an age!

SUNDAY, JANUARY 26TH.

I went to early Mass and Communion. Ted was beside me. Happy.

MONDAY, JANUARY 27TH.

Last night the memorial service for King George and a concert, which included the *Eroica*, were broadcast. I wanted to listen to the music carefully but instead found myself plunged backwards to a memory of when I must have heard the *Eroica* for the first time. It was a snowy, rainy, wintry afternoon and W. H. took me to Queen's Hall. I saw myself there, a shy and timid girl, stunned by the music, and frightened of the emotion holding between me and this man. Then I went deeper into the past, and felt again that old love affair. I felt it: the whole turbulence and frustration of that love we could not bring to a culmination. I thought of that night when we stood on Hammersmith Bridge. We kissed, and St. Paul's clock struck midnight, sounding like an admonition. We went down on the Mall, swooning, suffering. Then we went home to Angel Road, to the hell there, and Mother in her fury. I thought: no, W. H. will never be dead whilst my mind and my nerves remember like this. And Ted in his armchair, clattering with the poker, chattering about Beethoven, was eclipsed into a stranger, the mere successor of a dream. Then the music ended and I was nothing but an elderly woman knitting.

How clearly last night I saw that young girl. Not the young girl as Victorian romanticists saw her, nor the girl as the cinema presents her today; but the girl *as she was,* ardent, quivering in fear of life, ignorant and innocent, struggling with circumstances and with dreams, and above all, frightened.

I feel now that I can write my books if I could get the time. I think I have the gift of composition, but there are two stumbling blocks in my way: distraction in my outer world and diffuseness in my inner world. My daily life is filled with family, house, cooking, and visitors so that is almost impossible to find free hours in it. My mind is so crowded with images and ideas, ever enlarging circumambient memories, and dreams, that it is paralyzed, and does not know where to try to begin. I get lost in the woods.

Think how rapidly image succeeds image in the mind. Only a little while ago I wrote down "the Mall." My mind immediately made a picture of what it was thirty-five years ago, and as it is today. Then the scene unrolls like this: I think of the river, of William Morris as I knew him when I was a child, then of the river as a holiday place of my childhood and early girlhood, and of Auntie Liz's camp. Then all at once I think of another man who kissed me by the river, a man whose name I have forgotten. But I remember his black mustache, and his very sudden and surprising attempt at lovemaking, and my irritation and fright. Then my mind jumps forward to fairy-tale possibilities. I am thinking, supposing I had married *that* man! Why, I might now be a publican's wife, drawing ale in a four-ale bar. Equally, I might have married Clarke, and gone to live in Inverness, and baked griddle scones every day of my life. Odd, that we are all so crazily adaptable. Odder still, that I won't adapt to what I have chosen for my lot, or that I won't do it with good grace.

All I know is that my thoughts are just constantly gnawing in my mind and that I am happy today.

MONDAY, FEBRUARY 10TH.

Last week we got in touch with the Pullans. The Eddie and Reta affair is a serious one. Mr. Pullan has received an "official" letter from Eddie, asking if he has any objections to Reta going to America. He is a cautious, canny Scotsman, and will not agree to Reta's going until Eddie can show a fairly good, reliable income on which to keep the girl. Eddie has written that he has good prospects in a three-man partnership with a publicity agency business. Mr. Pullan remarks, "More wishbone than backbone, perhaps." The Pullans give us to understand that there is no hurry from their side, though they are perfectly agreeable to the match.

I am afraid that Eddie will sell the land, which isn't his, because of his eagerness to marry Reta. Johnnie has written that Eddie is threatening to do so. Yesterday, in a money talk with Ted, I suggested that he go to New York and attend to family and financial matters. Surprisingly, he said he would think it over.

WEDNESDAY, FEBRUARY 12TH.

I am in a state of general discontent with my appearance.

Last night I had a lovely dream. In it I was meeting again with W. H. I was looking for him and afraid. Then I came to his hotel and met him in the vestibule. It was not the young man, but himself, as he might have appeared had he lived into his sixties. He was handsomer than he was when young, as a man of his type would naturally have become. He took my hand and everything was bliss. In the dream I was as I was in 1932, and wearing the clothes I had that summer, the figured silk suit and the black shady hat.

When I got up in the morning and saw myself in the mirror, I had a spasm of disgust. I saw a tired and dilapidated old woman. Gosh, it's awful. To be beautiful is woman's abiding desire. Yet with every day she lives her beauty wanes. The philosophers would have us accept that waning philosophically. Well, it can't be done.

SATURDAY, FEBRUARY 15TH.

Yesterday I went to town and bought some American cookbooks. I am crazy with homesickness for America and the nearest approach for relief is to read American cookbooks and also to cook American dishes.

I then went to Selfridge's grocery store and bought American foodstuffs. I also ordered yellow and white cornmeal, Karo Syrup, Baker's Chocolate, Welch's Grape Juice, marshmallow cream, assorted Jellos and spices, and Maxwell House coffee. Probably the things will be delivered next week, but when they do come I'll have a real home meal: hot Johnny cake with syrup and good coffee.

SATURDAY, FEBRUARY 22ND.

Today Ted took up the question of domestic finances. He will give me three pounds a week to feed the family. He concedes I need not keep a detailed account of it and if there is any left over, "You can keep it for yourself, and God bless you." I am still to keep an account of all other expenditures, such as gas, laundry, charwoman, cobbler, drugs, etc. He will reimburse me for these. In addition, he will give me a personal allowance out of which I am to cover *all* my own expenses: clothes, doctors, postage, carfare, gifts, holidays. Everything. He refuses to give me a lump sum of money. He then went through my account book, deducted what personal moneys I had spent from the sum of six pounds, which he reckoned was for two weeks, and gave me the difference. So I now have almost two pounds in hand: my private capital.

It has been arranged with old Bertie that Artie is to take a six months' business course at Clarke's College and then start in the office next September. He is to work his way up to five pounds a week. Not too bad.

TUESDAY, FEBRUARY 25TH.

Three-thirty P.M. Here is something funny. At dinner time I asked Ted if we were going to the movies tonight. He said alright and then asked who was going to pay? What a question! He thought I ought to pay since I was the one who wanted to go. I told him he ought to pay because a husband always pays when he takes his wife out. He agreed to pay, but did not think it fair.

As time goes on, Ted has less and less use for me. He looks elsewhere for friendship and companionship. He looks too eagerly. He spreads himself to strangers, and to young people, avid for admiration. He soaks it up. He has developed some kind of mental and moral vanity. He has the same sort of enthusiasm as an adolescent, searching for sympathetic friends and admirers.

I suppose he endures me, as I endure him. What a joke.

WEDNESDAY, FEBRUARY 26TH.

Last night I reached the Laurie before Ted, so I bought the tickets. I shall not do this again, nor shall I ever again ask him if we are going to the movies. Should he ask me to go, I will go and he can do the paying. Otherwise I shall go alone to a matinee or I shall go off alone some night when Selma has settled herself on the family. I'm not going to endure much more of Selma.

THURSDAY, FEBRUARY 27TH.

I am in a bad way. My head and my womb are creepy with desire and I have an inner trembling I cannot still. All my morning work is done, but no work wears away this misery.

Last night I was thrust into anger by a rebuff. At the bottom of half my troubles lies unappeased eroticism. Ted spends his passion and his romantic imagination on religion and the Church, whilst I consume myself. He gushes a devotion to Mary, the Mother of God; but for Ruby, the mother of his children, there is no devotion, only depreciation of her motherhood. If I were a frigid woman I might appreciate his "chastity" and "purity." I might even be thankful he was like that. I am not a frigid woman. I am ardent and full-blooded, and I require both affection and passion to live happily. Ted's neglect chafes me, whilst his passion for religion enrages me. His piety, his sanctimoniousness, his perfect self-satisfiedness, and his occasional cold lust, infuriate me.

Since 1920 there have come times when in the desperation of my physical unease I have been driven to secret masturbation. This should not be, I know, but it has been the only way in which I could ease myself. I should have taken a lover. I didn't. The regret of my life, now that it is too late, is that I never did so. Life has been a constant warfare: with him, with myself. I am trying to presume the appearances of graciousness. God help me.

FRIDAY, MARCH 6TH.

Eleven A.M. I had a very full day yesterday. I went to Hammersmith to break the news of Mary Searle's death to Mother. Cousin Will had called me on Wednesday, reporting the news of his sister, and asking me to tell Mother. He met me there.

The official cause of Mary's death is put down to pneumonia, but what she really died of was drink. Mary had been a very heavy drinker for many years. Willie said she practically committed suicide by drinking herself to death. Mother wouldn't have that, and said she had never seen Mary the worse for drink. Naturally, a habitual soak doesn't behave like a rolling drunk, and Mary had plenty of money so neither her house nor her person ever showed neglect. Mother and Willie went off into a debate as to whether Mary was a drunk or not, and lots of family history came out, all of it disgraceful.

Here are the facts. Mother's own mother was a dipsomaniac and so were both of Mother's sisters. And so were, and are, all of Mother's nieces. Many of the Searles are loose morally too, beginning with Mother's mother, who ran off with a lover when Uncle Harry was a baby. Her sister Belle had an illegitimate child, who fortunately died at once. Young Alice Searle, Mary's sister, has been a light lady from the beginning, and Mary herself has been under suspicion more than once. At present the family doesn't even know where Alice is. She and her husband parted several years ago, she went back to "business," but lately lost her job. Occasionally she visited Maude, but never left an address. Willie thinks she is living with a man, but Aileen and Nellie say they think she is living with twenty men. She is a very beautiful woman, but she must be nearly forty by this time.

Here's a beautiful story. Last week Alf Little, Maude's widower, told Mother that Alice had accused his daughter of murdering her mother. Alice said that she and Mary were going to have Maude's body exhumed and they were going to prosecute. Nice, sweet ghouls! Alf had been to the police and to the coroner. Sweet, sweet family, muttish beyond everything.

All thanks to Joe Beates, I say. His daughter, my Grandmother Searle, started that wild Irish blood in the family. Of her children, only Uncle Will and Mother were intelligent and respectable. Uncle Will resembled Grandpa and was good, decent, and kind. Mother's problem was her bad temper; she has been a violent shrew all her life. Only young Willie has turned out well of Uncle Will's children. He is another good Searle man. Mary was protected by a good man or else she would have been as bad as her sister. As it is, as soon as her husband died, she slumped with a rush right into her death. Mother's children are a violent crew, but, thank God, the Side blood flows in our veins. Though we suffer and are often fools, we can all manage our lives to a certain degree satisfactorily.

I want to record something very pleasant. It is the discovery that Cousin Will holds me in a deep affection. He spoke of our childhood together and all the pleasure it was to him. "I was always happy here with you, Rubby," he said. "I often think of those days when we were children, and what good times we had together. I tell my children about them, too. Those were good times." "Rubby," he called me, a pet name I had forgotten. Under it all ran warm affection. I thought, here is somebody who really likes me, for myself. I am pleased. Real, true love.

Light lady is a term used for a loose or wanton woman.

Muttish is an English slang expression for a stupid person, a blockhead.

SUNDAY, MARCH 8TH.

This is Jimmie's birthday. He must be twenty-four today. His second child, a girl named Barbara Doris, was born on February 13th. I don't think I've recorded it before. Still another girl in the family, and not one of them yet named for me. I am disappointed and it's foolish, but it's so.

SUNDAY, MARCH 15TH.

I am feeling that I do not want to go to church. I am also feeling that the pope ought to do something about the Italian-Abyssinian War. He never says a word. He's an Italian, and I suspect he's afraid of Mussolini. Nevertheless, if he is what he claims to be, God's representative on earth, he ought to denounce this war, he ought to reprimand Mussolini. He ought to denounce all war.

Another great European war seems near. The Christians do not bother about what Jesus said about love and forgiveness. He might never have lived at all for any impression his teaching has made on civilization.

SUNDAY, MAY 10TH.

Last night Mussolini announced that the war in Abyssinia was over. So is the prestige and honor of Italy. Tonight the radio reports tell us that throughout Italy the Te Deum has been sung in all the churches. Italy praising God. Does God smile, or does He vomit? Throughout this outrageous war the pope has never raised his voice against it. I should think that this will annihilate every last pretension for papal authority in the whole enlightened world.

SATURDAY, MAY 23RD.

In the news tonight, from Prague, came this item. A couple who have just celebrated their diamond wedding aniversary have sold their house and possessions, divided the money equally between them, and have applied to the courts for a dissolution of the marriage. One wonders how long they have secretly waited for a death to release them. Sixty years of marriage and finally they decide to part. They cannot bear it to the end. Hateful marriage.

WEDNESDAY, JUNE 10TH.

Eleven A.M. Ted left this morning to sail to New York. He made up his mind suddenly on Monday and now he's off. He plans to return on the *Aquitania* at the end of the month.

I am glad he has gone. I think he should have gone long before. I hope he will achieve something good and useful, and something helpful for the boys. Mother is still here. Two weeks so far.

At a quarter of five this evening I have an appointment with a Harley Street eye specialist. My eyes have been bothering me all year, and last week Dr. Munro said I must see a specialist. I have something which she calls, I think, thromboidal cysts, and these have to be cut out from under the lid. Today the job is to be done. I shall ask Mrs. Page to go with me.

SUNDAY, JUNE 14TH.

No Ted, no Mother, no church, and no cooking. This is what I call a perfect Sunday.

My eye is beginning to look more normal. After anesthetizing and probing, Dr. Smart decided that the cyst was a "hard" one and he would probably have to do a dissection on it. This means an operation and a hospital stay. I am to see him again next week.

THURSDAY, JUNE 18TH.

Eleven P.M. I am to meet Dr. Smart at the Victoria Hospital tomorrow afternoon. I have written to Mother and asked her if she will stay with me a few days. I do not know how much pain and trouble I shall have after the operation. Presumably the eye will have to be bathed and dressed frequently until it heals. I expect she will come.

FRIDAY, JUNE 26TH.

Eleven-thirty P.M. This should be Ted's last night in America. I wonder what has happened over there.

As for me, I have not been able to extract the joys from his absence which I might have done because of this trouble with my eye. Dr. Smart is satisfied with the progress of my eye so far, but he wants to see me in a month's time. Meanwhile, I am to bathe the eye three times daily with a special lotion he has prescribed. I have something which he calls a sub-acute infection of the meibomian glands.

Dr. Munro has been dressing the eye wound daily since the operation, and she explained the condition to me. It is an inflammation caused by a germ. When I asked what caused that, she said, "Perhaps excessive weeping, only of course you are not a woman who weeps." I told her that I wept quite a lot. She replied, "You surprise me. You always look so calm. But why weep? After all, there is nothing in this world worth weeping over." I told her that I knew that, but that sometimes one cannot help oneself and she agreed that that was so.

Mother has returned to Hammersmith, and her going leaves me just one week to myself. Now maybe I can find myself. No one can call her soul her own when Mother is around. I did want to think things out a bit during Ted's absence. I want to find out what I really think, feel, and believe. I also want to find out what I really mean to do and not do. Where, exactly, am I, and what, exactly, am I? Since I would have life differently, how would I have it? Who and what is the true Ruby Alice?

TUESDAY, JUNE 30TH.

I went to Snelling's this morning and had my hair done. Snelling is a good hairdresser, but a nasty little man. Once my hair grows properly long, I'll never go into *his* shop again.

I went to tea with Mrs. Page. We had strawberries and cream, quite a fiesta.

I received a letter from Ted today. It was a nicer letter than I anticipated and it made me feel quite friendly towards him. I have been thinking of him returning, coming nearer and nearer to England, and having a nasty feeling about it, not wanting him to come back, wishing I need never see him again. But this is quite a nice letter. I guess I get too broody about him. He enclosed snapshots of the family. Two are of himself with all six babies, those incredible six grandchildren.

WEDNESDAY, JULY 1ST.

Nearly midnight. I've had a self-revelation alright, but not the sort I was look-ing for. Tonight a couple sat next to me at the movies. Something about the look of the man puzzled me. He reminded me of someone I knew, but I couldn't remember whom. When the lights went up I opened conversation with his wife and naturally fell into talk with him too. We spoke of a piece shown on the news about communists in Russia. That was all.

But inside, something happened to me. For that was my type of man, and my blood recognized him immediately. I could have grappled him to me and merged with him in ecstasy. Large, dark, clean, rugged, calm, strong, serene, content; I don't know what, but everything I've always missed and wanted. I know nothing about him. I shall never see him again, but just to see him quickened me. Sheer animalism, but irrefutable.

But I *am* quick, not a dead one yet. I could still love. I regret that I have never taken a lover, a man of this type tonight, who could have complemented me, made me whole, and loved me properly. All the good years I have wasted, when I might have found a true lover, and now it is too late. Ted fooled me with his Apollo Belvedere face. It is his lack of strong masculinity which has always exasperated my essential womanhood.

Now he is coming back with his eternal *talk*. I won't let him hypnotize me into his futilities. Divine Mothers, Heavenly Bridegrooms, Gentle Jesus, and the Holy Saints, no, I can't fool myself with those dreams. I want realities. I want a real man, a real lover. I intend to remember this evening's self-knowledge every time I find myself drifting back to theology and the Church. I regret, from the bottom of my heart, that I never tried to find a lover whilst there was still time. *That's* what I found out tonight when instinct spoke with *its* infallibility in my blood.

*The Belvedere court of the Vatican, now a museum, contains a garden of ancient Greek statues with a special niche built to contain the **Belvedere Apollo**. Apollo was the sun god in Greek mythology.*

THURSDAY, JULY 2ND.

I went to town to visit Cousin Will and Nellie. They are pleasant people, but what I heard from them about the Searle family in general was disgusting. It is the old story of drink and debauchery, *in the women* of the family; in Mary and Alice of downright sexual rottenness, lasciviousness, pornography, and prostitution. I also heard of meanness, lying, trouble-making, and violent tempers. It's in the blood, that damned black Irish blood of Joe Beates.

I am shocked by these things. I shudder away from it all, and all the possibilities of these sins in my own character. For they are sins, and if staying in the Church is the only course that is going to keep me from committing such, then I'll have to stay in the Church. I, too, am a granddaughter of Polly Searle, and all the Searle women are a bad lot. It is only the brains that Dad passed to his daughters which prevent us from acting as such muttish fools as the Searle girls. Joe Beates, curses on you and your wild Irish blood!

So I am arrested again in what I was about to do. I'm not sure now about leaving the Church. Perhaps the Church is exactly the kind of policeman I need behind me. My personal, secret hypocrisy is a very minor sin. I don't know. As usual, I don't know!

FRIDAY, JULY 3RD.

Ted arrived home tonight and we have had a pleasant meeting.

MONDAY, JULY 6TH.

Four P.M. This morning I scrubbed the kitchen floor. This is such an event it must be recorded. In fact, I don't think I ever scrubbed a kitchen floor before. Not on my knees, which I could not have done, but by using the long-handled brush and mop I bought at Selfridge's. At dinner time both Ted and Artie noticed the clean floor and commented on it which, childishly, pleased me very much. Since I had done a good job of it I was pleased with it myself. Somehow, I am in a more normal and more housewifely frame of mind than I've been in ages.

I've been thinking. If Ted's worst failing is talk and disputatiousness, mine is brooding and imaginativeness. None of the imaginary conversations I evolved with Ted to take place on his homecoming have taken place. So why the devil don't I stop dwelling in the dark cavern of my imagination? I'm going to try to stop it. Ted and I have actually come together again as friends and lovers, and I'm glad of it.

WEDNESDAY, AUGUST 19TH.

Three-thirty P.M. I am in my room, serene, nothing troubles me, wondering why I am so compelled to write this journal. Why do I do it? Isn't it because it gives me some release of chagrin and malice and misery which I can get in no other way? Probably I libel everybody I mention herein, but it doesn't matter, for none of them knows anything about it; whereas I am definitely set free, discharged of my venom, so that in the outside world I can always maintain my amiability. Actually, my reputation is for affability, patience, and good-heartedness.

It must be that these books serve as my mental dustbins, into which I can throw all the rubbishy discard of my mean and hateful self. Anyway, I hope it is that way. This writing out, this writing down, is purgative; it truly is, even though absurd. I know it's absurd, but I also know it works, so I write on and shall probably do so all my life.

It is like swimming across a river. In midstream, one just keeps on, stroke after stroke, until one reaches the other side. So with me. I just write, and keep on writing. I have to.

MONDAY, SEPTEMBER 21ST.

Three P.M. I am writing in the parlor. Mrs. Prior, my new char, is cleaning upstairs.

American letters arrived this morning. One from Marjorie Kurzenknabe, tells me she is engaged to Charlie. He has given her a ring, and the engagement is announced. A nice letter and a nice girl. One from Eddie. He was offhand and disagreeable. Anger whips up in me, not so much against Eddie as against Ted. Eddie is a very successful man, has attained his own ends, but his family pays the price. When I look at my life I could swoon with despair.

Eight P.M. I am simmering down after being angry with Ted. The root trouble with me is feminism. I hate my subjugation as a woman. I long for the emancipation of my sex. I resent the assumption and the practice that, merely because he is a man, Ted is entitled to the satisfaction of his wishes. Then why not I to mine? I crave the equality of freedom for the pursuit of happiness. Whilst we were in the States the force of environment, I suppose, caused Ted to allow a certain degree of equality of the sexes. There he did regard me as a human being in my own right; but *here*, no. Here I have become the traditional female, the secondary being, of most secondary importance. Only last week he had the rudeness to say to Artie, "Of course, Mother doesn't realize that a lot is excused to her simply because she is a woman. We have to remember she is only a woman."

Yes, actually that. I resent it. I resent the entire attitude. If his maleness was in itself more satisfactory than my femaleness, I might tolerate it, even admire it. But as things are, his maleness is so inadequate that it infuriates me. That *he* should dominate my life is hateful beyond everything and yet it has to be endured.

Sex is not a privilege, it is an accident. No man, pope or king or saint, is a better human being than I am merely on the accident of being a man. I'll never admit it. I loathe the control of a husband. My life, that's what I want. Myself for myself. To be free!

THURSDAY, SEPTEMBER 24TH.

Three-thirty P.M. Last night, surprisingly, Ted loved me with lovingness, and today I am a new woman. He is not the most unendurable man in the world to live with, because I do endure him. But he is the most exasperating. His censoriousness, his constant tutelage, his argumentativeness, his crusading, his prosy talkativeness, his eternal rightness, all this wears me down till I can't bear him another minute. Then there will come an hour when he'll forget his overwhelming evangelicalism and his passion to challenge every statement made, forget his animosity against the Protestant mind and against America, forget his precious soul and the earnestness of salvation, and he'll be just a normal adult man, reasonable, cultured, and charming. And when he is charming, he is the most charming man alive.

Possibly someone could say to me, "Isn't it strange that you have such difficulties in your relationships with both your mother and your husband? Isn't there something seriously wrong with you, maybe?" Maybe, but I don't think so. Nobody can get on with Mother. All her life she has been quarrelsome and overbearing, and everybody gets away from her eventually. It is impossible for anyone to live peaceably with Mother, because she won't have peace. But I loved my father, and I get along well with my brothers and sisters.

And my husband? After all, I do "get along" with him. It is marriage that I hate, the dependence. It is freedom that I want, freedom to be myself, and to own myself. So I long for the impossible, which is much more wearing than longing for heaven.

SUNDAY, SEPTEMBER 27TH.

This evening, talking about belief, and about conduct, Ted told what I thought a very funny story. He said *his* conduct always depended upon his belief. He said when he was a socialist, he made up his mind never to give anything whatsoever to a beggar, because he thought the sooner the beggar's lot became unbearable, the sooner there would be a social revolution, and all poverty would be abolished. He said he kept this rule for years, long after we were married. I laughed to myself at this idea of his conduct hastening social revolution, and then at the comparison with his resolution to give ten percent of his income every year to charity.

But that's Ted to a T. Extremist about everything and everything tied up with private vows. What a man!

FRIDAY, OCTOBER 16TH.

Joan has been staying with us for the past ten days. She left last night, and I have been fretful and moody all day. There is affection between us two, and today I feel bereft.

Joan is in trouble. She and George are quarreling and he sent her up to town so that their mutual bad feelings may simmer down. She is under a promise not to return until he sends for her.

She tells me of their difficulties, and I listen to her. Then I say what I can, but she cannot really hear me, for she is wrapped in her wounded self-love and her anger. No rational words can sink in to her understanding.

The simple trouble is that they have come to the end of romantic love. George seems ready to adjust himself to the prosaic life but Joan isn't ready, nor is she even going to try. As I listen to her, I am appalled at her likeness to Mother, the likeness of a common termagant. George is not another passive Dad, but a man who himself has a violent temper. Apparently, on her own showing, Joan has goaded him too far. So they have parted for a little while, perhaps forever, for they are talking of a legal separation.

I am shocked. I see the damned family character asserting itself again. There is not one female descendant of that accursed Joe Beates who is a decent character and can live sanely and soberly. I have been brooding on the gang all day. Here's the list. In 1839 Joe Beates married Hannah Thompson of

Chester. They had two daughters: Mary Ann, who became my grandmother, and Maria.

Maria was seduced in her girlhood, and gave birth to an illegitimate son, Ernest, who grew to manhood, enlisted in the army, and died of enteritis in India. Maria lived until 1928.

Mary Ann married William Searle in 1860, and gave birth to William, Alice (my mother), Ellen, Isabel, and Harry. Whilst Harry was still a baby "in the cradle," she ran away from her house and was "lost" for a couple of years. Ultimately Grandpa found her in Brighton, quite destitute, and "took her back." She lived to be fifty-four, dying when I was ten or eleven, a sodden, dirty drunk. Her eldest son became a first-class engineer, but married my Aunt Rose, a nonentity. Their first child was a boy, my cousin Will Searle, a decent man; but all William's daughters turned out badly. There were four of them: Mary, Maude, Beatrice, and Alice. Mary and Maude have already drunk themselves to death, and Beatrice and Alice are on the same tack. Alice, a most beautiful young woman, is now an abandoned wife, and presumably has become a common prostitute.

Ellen Searle eloped with Jack Hedges. She had three children: Eva, Jack, and Marion. Again, the boy was the only decent character. He took to the sea, and when last heard of was a ship's steward. Both girls went to the bad, and Eva was thrown from a trap somewhere in Australia and broke her neck. She was drunk at the time. Ellen drank herself stupid, and was shut up in an asylum before she was thirty. Luckily, she died there after a few years.

Isabel Searle went on the stage, but had an affair with a married man and gave birth to an illegitimate child before she was twenty. Luckily, the child died. Then she married George Jackson. After a very checkered career she died at fifty, a victim of chronic alcoholism. Her children are Mabel and Eva, George and Bob. The boys are decent, respectable, fairly successful men, but again, the girls are pills. Mabel came to the States, married Alec Barnsbee, and became a regular virago. Like Mother, she created a little hell wherever she happened to be. Eva, more good-natured, went to Australia, but became a drinking slut. Before I left the States, Mabel, too, had begun to drink.

Harry Searle was a decent character, but a stupid man. Grandpa first articled him to an architect, but he couldn't make the grade. Then by influence Grandpa got him into the police force. He never rose above the rank of a constable. He had one son and two daughters and again, the boy is the best of the bunch. He began life as a telegraph boy, and has now risen to be a chief-sorter. His sisters are very stupid, common girls. However, though without brains, they do not drink. They have married poor men and are lost in the working classes.

And Alice Searle's children? Look at us! Dad gave us brains and gentility, but Mother cursed us all with her contrary blood, her damnable Irishness. Not one of us is normal. We are all a violent lot; unreasonable, unbalanced. Our brains only make us aware of our inharmony. We should have been less miserable had we been born stupid, like the Searle girls.

Gladys has always been violent-tempered. As a schoolmistress she is concentrated acerbity. In general society she is an ambulating vinegar bottle. Aileen is good-tempered nearly always, but sometimes lapses into a great rage. Her marriage to William Mears ended in divorce after only a few years. Eric's marriage was a disaster from the beginning, and now he is living with a typist. Sonnie is a very violent-tempered man, and his marriage would most likely go on the rocks if it wasn't just luck that Edith is a particularly sane and tactful woman. She makes their marriage work, not Sonnie. Their little Monica, so far, is a neutral child, but Eric's Karina is already a little liar and poseur. My children? Maybe I should thank God I have no daughters.

Now Joan is mismanaging her life. I listen, and I see what I used to see when I listened to Mabel Barnsbee raving. It is the lack of code, the lack of discipline, the lack of early training, the lack of religion. The stupidest Catholic woman has a rule to measure by and return to, a direction for rightness; but Joan has nothing. Mabel had nothing. Mother at least had the god of respectability, but such a god is only another dead dog in our times. We are all "emancipated" women today. What a mess!

MONDAY, NOVEMBER 16TH.

Again, I'm in a hurry to write, but the domestic round keeps me from it. I go to make soup. I am a housewife: a cursed housewife, trying to escape domestic dementia. Actually, I am seeing a redheaded, sober-faced brat sneaking into the Hop-poles, saying, as she places a jug on the beery counter, "Half a pint of porter, please," and tendering a penny. Then walking away with the foaming pitcher and a horribly sticky farthing for change. Then in the house being accused of spilling the filthy liquid, but not answering, afraid she will vomit before she can wash her hands clean from the reek of the sticky handle and the beastly farthing. That was me. Who would believe it?

There was a period when Mother had an infant at the breast, and as soon as I got in at noon from school, I was sent off daily with a jug and a penny to buy her dinner porter. I was about ten years old and I hated that errand. I can still smell the stink of that bar!

But for now, I must attend to my soup.

Hop-poles is the name of a public house near Ruby's childhood home in Hammersmith.

TUESDAY, DECEMBER 1ST.

I just returned from the library. I have brought back *Green Hills of Africa* by Ernest Hemingway, and the *Letters of D. H. Lawrence.* Aileen loaned me the Lawrence when it came out in 1932. Ever since I read the notice that his *Phoenix* was published, I have been unable to forget either Lawrence or Taos. I am sick for New Mexico, and I want contact with the mind of Lawrence. I suppose he has been the most potent force in the artistic world in my lifetime. Even the people who hate Lawrence cannot ignore him. He gives me some sense of being which nobody else does.

SUNDAY, DECEMBER 6TH.

I dutifully went to Mass today. The news report is that the pope is very ill, with dropsy, gout, and asthma, but I don't care a bean. He is old, has had his day. I have no allegiance to the pope. His authority is one of the points on which I never was a Catholic.

There is great excitement in this country this weekend concerning the king, who has expressed his desire and intention to marry a Mrs. Simpson, who is not only a commoner and an American, but a divorced woman into the bargain. This has created a grand political uproar. Most of the poor and common people are for the king, but the great bulk of the "respectable" population, the conservatives, the old, and the middle-aged, are against him. The greatest factor against the match is the fact that she has had two divorces, and her two former husbands are still living. What she might be *in herself,* how exactly she might suit the king, how well she might be able to act the part of a proper queen: none of these points is thought of, only her divorces. What is apparent here is the old primeval and medieval idea that *men own women,* and that every bride must be a virgin. It makes me sick.

I also hate all this damned class distinction. King Edward, poor devil, can't help being king, he was born for that fate. I wish I were in America, where there is classlessness, and no man can be born better than another. No wonder communism spreads.

Then there is this damned divorce nonsense. Only last week a Bill for Easier Divorce was read for the second time in Parliament. The English Church is not officially against divorce, any more than it is officially against birth control. A divorced person has a legal right to be married in church, and to receive Communion, and no parson, whatever his eminence, can refuse either right to him. Supposing the king doesn't mind that the lady has had two previous husbands, why should his subjects object? Presumably she suits him on every count, and he regards her as a human being, not as a piece of property. But no, Parliament won't accept the lady of his choice and there is talk of forcing his abdication. He must choose between the crown and the lady.

Last night old Bert infuriated me with his comments. He thinks the whole British Empire will collapse if the king persists in marrying her. Herbert believed in divorce when he was a young man, for he divorced his American wife in 1899 and married Tillie in 1900. His children don't know he had a previous wife to their mother. What humbug, what hypocrisy, what insincerity! Most Englishmen haven't got beyond the slave-owning mind and, at bottom, still regard their womenfolk as on a par with their cattle.

This tacit assumption of Englishmen that all women are secondary creatures gnaws my very soul. Some women accept the idea too! This infuriates me to the limit. I'll bow to no man, be he husband, king, pope, saint, nor Christ himself. I am myself. I possess true being, in my own right, and I will give place to no one above me. God the creator I will adore, but I will never hold myself subservient to any one of his creatures. I am constricted by my limitations, but I am not constrained in my soul and in my spirit. I never will be. I stand for the equality of human rights, men *and* women born free and equal, and I always will.

Here's an absurdity I want to note. There was a Catholic Service Broadcast from Oxford on the radio. Here is the choice bit from the priest's sermon. He said that there were four kinds of intelligence in this universe. There is the intelligence of God, of the angels, of man, and lastly (I thought he was going to say the intelligence of animals, but no!) the intelligence of woman. I was startled into laughter, and had the giggles for the rest of the evening.

MONDAY, DECEMBER 7TH.

When Ted came in at dinner time he was full of comments he had received from his morning rounds about the king's proposed marriage. Ted said only two women he talked to were in favor of the king having his desire, and even those two didn't like the lady. What do they know of her? Of all the millions now so righteously declaiming against her, how many have ever seen her? All we know is that she is a rich American woman who moves in high society, has been presented at court, and has friends amongst the English nobility and royalty. What she is *in herself* nobody knows. In her pictures she is pleasant looking, and presumably the king's judgment is that she would grace the throne.

What she is in herself is of no account against the fact of her two divorced husbands. Her right to a private life is denied her. Two dead husbands wouldn't have been against her, but two living ex-husbands is unforgivable. It isn't "nice." What does the world know of those men, of her troubles? What does the world care? It's the damnable double standard again. The whole world knows the king had many love affairs; too much wine and too many women, like his grandfather. But who cares about his morals? But the lady's divorces? Oh no, impossible to accept those. She is a divorced woman! Ted said one old Irish woman had summed up the situation very neatly. "Isn't it a pity," she said, "that the likes of him should waste his time running after the likes of her: the leavings of two other men."

So very neat, isn't it? Here's the assumption again of the terrific importance of virginity and celibacy. Exaggerated importance, of course, but true importance since men will have it so. Why *do* women accept these ideas of men? It's this crazy social world, wherein money is so important, and women are so moneyless. By accepting the ideas of men about themselves they keep up their market value. Damnation.

TUESDAY, DECEMBER 8TH.

Eleven A.M. At breakfast there was more talk about the king's dilemma. Ted remarked that he would hear the opinions of all the old women at Factory Terrace today, and he expected them all to be against the lady. He said, "After all, the king himself asked if there could be a morganatic marriage arranged. Why? Because he himself realizes that the dame isn't fit to be the mother of a future king of England."

My insides turned over with anger. Memory flashed back to Bayside, when the twins were babies. Ted said to me: "I think God has been specially good to me in not sending me daughters, because you are not a fit woman to be the mother of girls." Men's minds. Men's insults. I haven't calmed down yet. My insides are still churning.

Three P.M. It is dark already. Today is the Feast of the Immaculate Conception. Well, I know darn well I don't believe that. Am I a Catholic? Ask the priests. Because Mary was to be the Mother of God she was created without original sin on her soul. That's the idea. Something and somebody special again. No sir, I won't have it. If Mary wasn't an ordinary mortal, and Jesus wasn't an ordinary mortal, then their lives as human beings are not of the slightest value to me. And why pay tribute and honor to someone because they *were born* superior to the rest of us? I won't do it, I can't. I will pay respect to man or woman who proves by their life and achievements they are superior to me. For the accident of birth, never. It is this old medieval world that I hate: kings, holy virgins. Give me America, the new world, where man is proved by his manhood, a woman by her womanhood, and nothing else.

Young King Edward is writhing in his personal anguish because he's a king. He musn't marry the woman of his choice because his subjects decide she isn't good enough for him. They refuse her as queen. He does his public job of kingship well. Why can't he have his private life in peace? Well, I'm sorry for him, but isn't it time all kings were done away with? I can't do away with the king, but I can do away with subservience of worship to the Virgin

Mary. If she ever lived at all, she was a woman as I am a woman, neither more nor less.

FRIDAY, DECEMBER 11TH.

Yesterday the king abdicated. King Edward VIII is no more. Tonight he is to broadcast to the nation. After that he leaves the country, probably to return no more.

So the hypocritical politicians have won. They have pushed him out of his place, and put on the throne his brother, the "respectable" Duke of York. I think this a pathetic and loathsome event. God help Edward Windsor.

SATURDAY, DECEMBER 12TH.

At three o'clock we heard the Proclamation of the Accession to the Throne of His Majesty, King George VI, broadcast from St. James's Palace. I wept. Early this morning ex-king Edward left Portsmouth in the battleship *Fury*, and crossed to Boulogne. He has gone to his love, poor fool.

MONDAY, DECEMBER 21ST.

I went to town and spent nearly four hours shopping in Selfridge's. What a disgusting and silly orgy this Christmas shopping is! Afterwards, I had tea with Mother in Hammersmith. I had some sad news for her.

The doctor's report on Selma's X-ray is that she has a spot of tuberculosis at the apex of the lungs, and must go to a sanitarium for at least six months. Supposedly, she has caught this germ from her mother, who is definitely T.B. This is a shock to all of us. Tillie has not been told yet. She does not look at all good. Once she was more beautiful than ordinary. Poor old Bert is really upset.

1937

THURSDAY, JANUARY 7TH.

Am I becoming more and more jealous of Ted's religion? Yes, I am. Ever since he became a Catholic, Ted has been deteriorating as a man. I have needed a man, but I have been compelled to endure a saint. Ted has not lived for human love and affection, but for Christian reflection.

I am neither lewd or lascivious, but the major part of my sexual life has been a torture of inadequacy and unfulfillment. This is not because my husband was impotent physically, but because he set his mind against love. The flesh became something to conquer. I became a sort of demon. Ted had swallowed the medieval mind, and a woman was nothing but temptation, to be resisted, or when resistance becomes impossible, to be repented.

The root and core of the whole problem is that I married the wrong man and Ted married the wrong woman. It is as simple as that. Endlessly simple: endlessly sad. And there is nothing to be done about it. If Ted wasn't so thoroughly Catholic, we could arrange a divorce, and each of us go our separate ways in decency and peace. But that will never be. Ted regards divorce as a mortal sin, so he will never commit it. I want him to love me, but if he ever did, he's forgotten it. Why do I write this today? This is no new discovery. I must be very tired.

SUNDAY, JANUARY 10TH.

I went to Mass today and it did me no good. I was thoroughly repelled by a missionary, begging for the Society for the Propagation of the Faith. His talks were absurd. What they would make evident to anyone who stopped to think for a moment was that the heathen Chinese needed education and a job with a living wage, not a prayer and a ha'penny from good Britishers. What's the good of converting the Chinese or Hindus to Catholicism if they still haven't got the means of livelihood? Why not instruct them in birth control so that they do not need to drown or abandon their unwanted infants? What about the goodness of God in these cases? What of the infant He allows to be born so that it can be destroyed immediately?

These missionaries make me sick.

FRIDAY, JANUARY 15TH.

Last night I went through my old American cookbooks. They are, sort of, a record of my American life via the kitchen, and it gives me satisfaction just to read baked beans and crullers.

This morning, after dreaming all night of the old American days, I awoke forlorn and sentimental. I wanted Ted to hold me in his arms, but no, he goes off to his rendezvous with a wafer.

This afternoon I went to the the Laurie to see *San Francisco*, featuring the earthquake. In the dark I shed a few tears, not for the picture, for myself. Eddie was born the day of the earthquake, April 18, 1906, the day I was twenty-two. My poor Eddie hasn't yet found himself, whilst I'm lost, lost in Romford.

WEDNESDAY, FEBRUARY 3RD.

Ted is concerned about Tillie, whom he went to see yesterday. Tillie is dying, she is frightened, and she is suffering what can only be described as a deathbed repentance. She is turning to Ted for help, he being the only religious person she knows. He has been to see her several times now, and every time she wants to talk to him about religion, being saved, doing good, forgiveness of sins, and so on. She confesses *to him* the wrongdoings of her life. She has lived all her life without religion and she will certainly die without the consolations of religion. She has only the fears of some vengeful tyrant who is going to punish her good and plenty for all the sins of her life. She is scared to death of dying. Well, Tillie is dying; Selma has to go away to a T.B. sanitarium. They've their troubles: I have my own. I *can't* care about other people. I grieve for the lacks in my own life.

Two-fifteen P.M. Mrs. Page telephoned to say that her husband thinks he's found a buyer for his last house, and they "are holding their breath" about it. I congratulated her, and sincerely, for I can be glad in other folks' gladness where I cannot grieve in their sadness. I'm going out to buy some fish for tea. I intend to make a habit of going out everyday. I'm sure I stay in the house too much.

THURSDAY, FEBRUARY 4TH.

Selma was in to tea yesterday and said that Tillie had asked to see a faith healer. The faith healer came and left some books with Tillie, but the books only give her a headache. They only worry her. They are about how God will never forgive the unbeliever and being "born again." Like Nicodemus, the saying worries her, and like many Protestants she thinks it means you must experience an upheaving emotion of conversion. We tried to explain to Selma that it meant simply *baptism*, but we couldn't get it over to her. What Tillie needs is a simple elementary catechism, simple enough for children in the first grade. But you can't give that to a dying woman of seventy. It would only be an old dry bone. Tillie is hungry for spiritual nourishment, and she can't take it any more than she can take ordinary nourishment.

In speaking of what a help it would be for Tillie to think of the Blessed Virgin, I told Ted of my experience in St. Mary's, Bayonne, before Eddie was born. At that time I used to walk along the waterfront every day and once, feeling tired, and somehow knowing Catholic churches were always open, I went into St. Mary's to rest. Without thinking, without reason, I went to the statue of Mary and I fell to my knees and I prayed to her. To me, she was as I was, the pregnant girl, alone among strangers, afraid. I asked her to succor me. At that time I was not only not a Catholic, I wasn't even a Christian, but the idea of Mary sort of lassoed me, and brought me into a security. It was like that, but I had never told Ted before.

THURSDAY, MARCH 4TH.

Eight P.M. I am going to visit Tillie this evening, a dying crone. I am restless and nervous. I have bad dreams and bad awakenings. All my dreams are of losses. I am going on journeys and I have lost my baggage, or my taxi, or train, or ship, or I have moved and lost my furniture or I have been shopping and have lost my parcels. It is loss all the time, fact of my life and the old subconscious keeps hammering in.

The fact is, every atom of me is shrieking out for erotic love and there is none for me. When I wake in the mornings, warm, full of desire, and I know Ted is awake beside me, I will him to hold me and love me, and nothing happens. He lies still until the alarm goes off, then gets out of bed, flops on his knees for a minute, then goes off to the bathroom. He dresses and goes out to church. Every day is like that. Piety. How much longer am I going to be able to stand it?

TUESDAY, MARCH 9TH.

Our *Times* correspondent from Rome reports today that the pope has blessed and presented the Golden Rose to the "Queen of Italy and Empress of Ethiopia." This constitutes the first formal recognition of the new Italian Empire made by the Holy See.

Grand, isn't it? The queen of Italy is no more the empress of Ethiopia than I am. The pope is evidently afraid of Mussolini. He is sure of the "faithful," but he is not sure of Mussolini, so he formally recognizes the conquest of Abyssinia. And what a conquest! Will I admit that he holds any jurisdiction over me, or pay him any allegiance? Never.

WEDNESDAY, MARCH 10TH.

Last night we went to the the Laurie to see *The Great Ziegfeld*. I thought it would show scenes of New York, but was disappointed; it was nearly all show business. However, in spite of Ted being bored by it, it evidently acted as an aphrodisiac for him, and in the night he loved me. But what a loving! It was no good, and worse, it simply made me angry. "Do you want the back?" he asked and I shook my head. "No," he said. "You know it's wrong, don't you? We mustn't." In an instant I was as dry and cold as a stone. So even in his loving he must bring his damned religion, and my passion passed immediately into anger and hatred.

These things shouldn't be written, of course. I write them because they exist, because they are just as much a part of us and our life as going to church, or going to the movies, or reading the paper, or eating our dinner, or anything else. If Ted is going to start talking ethics even in his very lovemaking, well, I simply can't stand it. Was there ever such a man?

FRIDAY, MARCH 12TH.

After seeing a picture of the pope and the queen of Italy in the *Catholic Herald*, Artie asked his father about the pope's seeming approval of the Italian-Abyssinia War, and why the pope crawls as he does. Ted answered, and laughing, as though the matter was so simple and childish, "Well, the conquest of Abyssinia is an accomplished fact, isn't it? The pope can't change that, so, not to acknowledge it, and the queen as empress, would simply be rude. He is merely observing good manners." My God! So the dear pope must be polite, must he? God's representative on earth mustn't be rude to a conqueror and a thief. No, he must always be polite and remember his manners!

Old Bert came to lunch today, to eat his promised dish of scallops. He sent me a message last night asking me to buy Tillie a red shawl for her birthday. I had Stone's send me some assorted shawls on approval and since they don't have any red shawls, they sent a velvet dinner jacket in red. When Bert looked at the selection, he immediately chose the red velvet jacket. "May as well get her something she can wear when she gets up again," he said. He simply doesn't see she's dying. In fact, he goes so far as to say the doctors don't know what they're talking about. "Why Tillie's no more got T.B. than I have!" he said. Queer, isn't it, how we won't see what we don't want to see.

SATURDAY, APRIL 3RD.

News came this morning from Mother that Eric is sailing for Singapore next Friday. So I went to Hammersmith to say good-bye to him, but did not see Eric. However, I did see Gladys and Sonnie, who followed me in, with Edith and Monica. I thought Sonnie looked ill and quite old, like a man of sixty, yet he won't be forty until October. I did not see Joan, either, but heard bad news of her. All the muscles of her leg are completely exhausted, and she must henceforth wear an instrument. A contraption of iron and leather, with straps and bolts, is being made for her, and she will probably have to wear it the rest of her life. These damnable family legs.

So I have missed Eric. Mother's baby. Mother's Bolshevik!

SUNDAY, APRIL 4TH.

This afternoon I've been reading a Kierkegaard book I bought on the strength of a review in the *Times*. I am disappointed in it. The review is much more interesting than the author. Kierkegaard does not strike me as a great religious philosopher, but as a great raving male egotist, and a dialectician, most extreme and unconvincing. Further, his mind works only in a man's world. Women are absolutely of no account in his universe.

Soren Kierkegaard (1813–1855) was a Danish philosopher who wrote on religious topics. His writings influenced the existentialist movement of the twentieth century.

Today I got down to letters. I wrote long letters to Eddie and to Ruth. Ruth expects a third baby in May. I've been thinking about her, and about Mother and Tillie, and about Kierkegaard, and thinking that his disregard of women is only normal. It is only while her sex value lasts that woman's value lasts. So long as a woman can attract lover or husband, so long as she can bear a child, so long as she must mother it and rear it, so long she is someone and has her place in the world. But after that, what use is a woman?

We women who like to think we are exceptional, that we have brains, intelligence, education; we fool ourselves. Our brains are a torture to us, for when our youth and beauty vanish, we are as significantly destroyed as any brainless fool of a woman.

I look at the old women passing down the street and I shudder away from the whole lot of them. Mother, Tillie, still thinking they're important, trying to make themselves important. It's horrible. Those women who die at the climacteric, those are the lucky ones, did they but know it. True, after fifty, money and the admiring affection of her family can give a woman a little prestige and a little gratification, but very few of us have money and most of us lose our families. Time and the world scatter families. Old age is a curse, not a blessing.

I was dreaming of Avenue A towards morning. I was spring cleaning there with Bertha Hludenski. In the dream I was in my old bedroom, with the great replica of the *Christian Martyr* over the mantelpiece. I was thinking how Eddie was frightened of that room, because of that picture, and how when he saw the original in the Metropolitan Museum of Art he got excited, thinking it was ours, stolen from us! I am haunted with a sadness all morning. Oh, these reminiscences.

Noon. In the kitchen. Selma came in last night. She has been in town just two days to say her adieus to her mother. She is tanned, but does not look well and said she is returning to the sanitarium today. Later, Artie joined me in the parlor to listen to the radio. He wanted to listen to dance music, and lying there on the sofa in the summer twilight, I did a lot of thinking. There was a section of Hawaiian music, very sensual, and it set me to dreaming of love, and our own early love-days. I remembered how Ted used to waylay me for love in the Somerville woods, on the Avenue A stairs, before the parlor fire, on the stoop. Suddenly, I realized how then Ted, too, was young. A young man passionately in love with his young wife. He was not in love with the Church then, that was only incidental. He was in love with me.

Then into memory came a tale Mother once told me about Auntie Belle. It was a complaint against Uncle George. Auntie said that while they were living at Maidenhead, and Uncle had long days in town, she would have a late supper ready for him and for comfort, she would set it out in the drawing room. When Uncle had had a good day, he would bring home a treat, a bunch of asparagus, a bottle of whiskey, an Aylesbury duck, ready cooked. This was fine, but after supper, she said he used to take her, there in the drawing room, on the rug before the fire. She thought he was a horrid man. To this, Mother's comment was, "the dirty old beast." I lay there smiling to myself about those funny Victorian prudes. Evidently George was a man who knew how to be a lover, and they couldn't appreciate him. What a waste!

MONDAY, MAY 10TH.

Tillie died at six o'clock this evening. Bert phoned us the news soon after it happened.

WEDNESDAY, MAY 12TH.

Coronation Day and a general holiday. The whole ceremony came over the radio faultlessly. It was very impressive, lasting about four hours. Ted and I listened to it all. Womanlike, I wept.

I was impressed by its stupendousness, and its sacredness. It was a sincere religious consecration, and it penetrated the air as such. It made me feel my indelible Englishness, which usually I forget, and it made me feel again my rootedness in the English Church. If I am any kind of a Christian at all, I am an Anglican one. However, my tracks are laid somewhere else.

FRIDAY, MAY 21ST.

Three P.M. I am having hot flashes again. They began last night, and keep going on today, so many I have lost count of them. In addition, I have a small discharge. Looking up the calendar, I see it is the full moon on the twenty-fifth, so this would be my time for a period, if I was still having periods. Anyhow, I feel decidedly unwell and queer. This probably accounts for my mental stress too.

Last night I was suddenly enveloped in one of those distressing moods of melancholy and boredom. I have known such moods since girlhood, when I simply did not know how to endure them. When I was a girl, I used to go and sit on the top stairs, and watch the street through the fan light, aching for a letter, for something. So now, if only something would happen!

THURSDAY, JUNE 3RD.

Three P.M. Today, the Duke of Windsor marries his lady love. The bishops, of course, are all making an uproar, trying to forbid any religious ceremony for the pair. I think the English bishops, and particularly the old archbishop of Canterbury, are a slimy lot.

News came yesterday of the birth of John's third child. It is another girl, Ruth Louise, born May eleventh. When I read the name I dropped a tear. This is the fifth granddaughter to be born, but not one has been named after me. Silly, I know, but I do feel it. John and Ruth are calling the baby Bonnie, after Bonnie Blue [Butler] in *Gone with the Wind*. Ruth was reading Margaret Mitchell's book when she began labor. Charlie's Marjorie wrote me the news. She adds that she is expecting a baby in July.

Marjorie and Charlie have been housekeeping in Dumont since March. They were married last summer, but kept it a secret, because Marjorie wanted to finish her nurse's training and get her degree. I don't think I've mentioned this before. I like Marjorie very much, but why couldn't they write me of the event when it happened? The news came rather as a blow, but there it is.

I have been feeling dowdy, so this week I've had my hair cut again. I went to a new young woman who has her shop in Carlton Parade. This newcomer, Miss Young, first chopped off the length, then she rubbed hot oil into the roots, then heated the head for twenty minutes, and then shampooed it. Next, she trimmed it, layered it, and put it into curlers, and permed it on a new Realistic machine. Then it was washed again and set. The result is charming. It is neat, stylish, becoming, and youthful. It has eliminated the dowdiness which is so aging. I feel thoroughly happy about the result, which is a rare thing for me to be able to say.

When I got back to the house, the boys and Ted were still at the table, arguing about war and pacifism. They didn't notice a change until Cuthie rose to leave the table. Then he suddenly saw me, and this was his exclamation: "Gee whiz! Who the heck do you think you are? Hepburn?" Then they all laughed, but as I received no adverse comments, I guess they like it alright. They razzed me, but it was a bouquet for the hairdresser. It does look nice. It really does.

TUESDAY, JULY 20TH.

Cuthie left for Devon for a cycling and camping holiday. Ted left for Dublin. A letter arrived from Marjorie and Charlie tonight saying that the baby was born on July 4th. It is a girl: Lynne Ellen. What a name!

The radio news reports Marconi died in Rome today.

SUNDAY, JULY 25TH.

I have been reading a book about the Tolstoys all day, *The Final Struggle*. Well, it is one of those books which is saying much more than its producers imagine. This book has been put out by one of the Tolstoy sons in conjunction with the eternal Aylmer Maude. Two men, and cranks at that.

Tolstoy has always been one of my aversions. He is one of those rich holy men, like Ruskin and Lubbock, who volubly tell the poor how to be happy and good. I hate those smarmers. I liked his novels. They were great, but his preachments, how fantastic. When I was a young girl back in 1900, and Aylmer Maude was to be seen any day at Ludgate Circus selling three-penny booklets of Tolstoy doctrine, even then, when I really didn't know what he was talking about, even then I sensed the stuff as rubbish. I felt there was something queer about his enigmatic preaching about "purity." I have wondered ever since how many marriages it has destroyed. Like Christian Science. Old man Tolstoy, old woman Mrs. Eddy, denying sex only after it has denied them. Why listen to the celibate condemning birth control? These fools speak of they know not what.

The editors, in this book, accuse Mrs. Tolstoy of being jealous. Of course she was jealous. As she and Leo became old, with all passion spent, he simply disregarded her. That is, he disregarded her as a person and turned to outsiders for excitement and admiration. This was belittling of her essential self, a cheapening of her whole life. An old husband does not understand this. But to the old wife, it is a daily torture and a slow death. The man is oblivious, immersed in his own interests, preaching, teaching, the pursuit of his own sanctity.

Mrs. Tolstoy was a countess, her husband a great genius, but my obscure life runs somewhat parallel with her experience. I understand her sufferings and know exactly how she could not help suffering as she did. Tolstoy accuses her of having no religion. Exactly. And I should like to know how many wives of religious men have been able to have any religion for themselves. I don't think it can be done. The longer a married woman lives with her husband, the more clearly she sees through his preposterous theories. They listen to him talking, but they know what he really is. You can't fool women. But you can exasperate them and you can destroy them.

Tolstoy was an exasperating old fool. Tolstoy was a genius but his wife's life was a tragedy.

Aylmer Maude was a devotee of the later (nonviolent, simple life, Rousseauian) Tolstoy. He wrote the Life of Tolstoy *in 1931.*

MONDAY, JULY 26TH.

As Artie sat down to lunch, he said with a smile, "Isn't it nice here when Dad isn't around?" I rejoined, "Yes, it has been a happy week, hasn't it?" And it has. No criticisms, no sarcasms, no arguments, no corrections, no disquisitions, no platitudes, no theories, no scriptures, and no moralizings. It has been a blessed rest, my mind is at ease.

Artie and I spent the entire evening in the kitchen, listening to the radio, me with my sewing, he writing letters: both of us happy.

TUESDAY, JULY 27TH.

I finished the Tolstoy book. What people!

They all wrote diaries: husband, wife, sons, daughters, visitors, peasants. And they all wept, with sobs, on the slightest provocation. I'm sure one could gather up a bucket of tears out of this volume alone. Neurotics.

The basis of the story rests on the eternal adage: "Man's love is of his life a thing apart. 'Tis woman's whole existence." This is quite true, but something the modern feminist hasn't found out yet. The one wail of the book, which twangs all the way through, is Sonya's anguished longing for the signs and the touch of her husband's love. When he is kind to her she is happy. When he is aloof, she is downright suicidal. And he is eighty-two, she is sixty-four, and they have been married forty-eight years. Yet she still craves his love and he simply runs away from her. Funny, isn't it? No, not by a damned sight! This is woman's tragedy.

Leo Tolstoy considered married life a mistake because married life hinders spiritual life. Of course it does. I ask you, is it possible to be Christian in the love embrace? Unfortunately, this was a belated consideration to fall upon a married man. He had had a conversion and everything else in his life had to go down before that. I know all about this. The correspondences between the history of the Leo Tolstoys and the history of the Edward Thompsons are many. When men "get religion," it is a disaster of the first magnitude. It seems to me the only way it can be endured, and be forgiven, is for it to be considered as a disease. No healthy or sane man could behave as these men behave. And *nothing* ever shakes their convictions that they are right and everyone else is in error, or in sin.

But as I read this book, discounting their funny Russian ways and exaggerations, I think the countess was really the sanest one in the whole mad outfit. She certainly was the practical one and did all the real managing and controlling. She managed the house, the estate, the business, and the family. What she most ardently wanted was normality and there wasn't one normal person near her. What a lot!

Love and religion: woman's two perpetual curses from man.

FRIDAY, JULY 30TH.

Three-thirty P.M. About half-past seven this morning I was wakened by my door opening, and there stood Ted, home again and with a pink rose in his hand. My instant feeling was pure pleasure. Simply, I love him.

After breakfast, he went off to the office as usual. He says he will take two days off later on. Tonight we are to meet at the Laurie, where *Green Pastures* is playing.

SUNDAY, AUGUST 15TH.

This is the Feast of the Assumption and I did not go to Mass. I remember once in Tenafly on this feast day, Ted was at home and he had a fit of passion for me, there on the Tenafly porch. Then a thunderstorm came up, and we had to go into the house. I don't know where the boys were. One summer's afternoon.

WEDNESDAY, AUGUST 18TH.

On Monday morning I went to the library especially to get a book about the Quakers. I nearly committed myself to writing to the Quaker Society to inquire for the nearest Friends' meeting house. Luckily, I had sense enough not to do so. I think the particular trait of damnable Irishness which persistently rises to the top in me is the Celtic love of being miserable. Well, I won't have it so, not when I can recognize it.

Turning from *Quaker Ways,* I have turned to St. Francis and St. Jane again, and again they have stayed my mind. These great two talk sense, they satisfy my intelligence and pacify my fretty feelings.

When Johnnie was a little boy he was noted for *his* awful faux pas. Once, when visiting the Utards, he very clearly and loudly made this reply when asked if he would like a second helping of chicken: "No, thank you, Mr. Utard. The last lot you gave me was all skin and bones." This came to mind as I read along in *Quaker Ways.* There is some nutriment there, but no satisfying meat, nothing to chew on, nothing to sustain one, and no flavor. We always thought chicken unsatisfactory eating. Something, yet nothing. So I return, with satisfaction, to the solid beef and juicy steak of Catholic theology and devotion. I have been realizing how much time I waste fretting. I worry about war, about Spain, about China and Japan, poverty and unemployment, the pope and politics. How silly. How futile.

I am determined to make the most and the best of what I have. Because Ted's fanatical evangelicalism gets on my nerves, that's no reason to throw away what the Church can and does give me. It does give me something: something of serenity, something of direction, something of beauty. The channels of my mind will never hold Jesus, yet they will always hold God the Father and God the Holy Ghost. I will take what I can in Catholicism, and ignore the rest or reinterpret it according to my understanding and needs.

SATURDAY, SEPTEMBER 11TH.

Eddie is married.

This morning Ted received a letter from Kay giving the information, and enclosing a newspaper clipping. The announcement was to the effect that: Ellen Margaret Lesser, daughter of Dr. and Mrs. Lesser of East 96th St., New York, had been married to Mr. E. A. Thompson, son of Mr. and Mrs. Edward

Thompson, of Romford, England, at the Church of St. Francis de Sales, on August 31st.

Kay said she didn't know when Eddie intended to tell us, but if it had been her son in such a case, she would have liked to be told. She said Harold acted as best man on a half hour's notice, and that she met the girl, known as Chic, at the church. I am stunned.

Reta had long since faded from the picture for Eddie but she and her parents continued a long friendship with Ruby, Ted, and the twins.

MONDAY, SEPTEMBER 13TH.

I am in misery. I grow lonelier and lonelier, and all my life behind me seems more and more dead. With Eddie's marriage, the last door on my American life, and my young life, has closed. Now I am definitely an old woman, a lump of junk.

Here is an irony: When I read that Eddie had gone back to the Church, at least far enough for his marriage ceremony, and when I noted that he had been married at the church of St. Francis de Sales, my specialty, I thought I would go to church to hear a Mass for him. However, our bedroom clocks were wrong and I missed Mass. Then this morning I felt so restless, so unhappy, so lost, I thought I would go to the cathedral in town and say the Stations there, but who should come in but Mrs. Jude! She stayed all afternoon so I never got to town. And now I don't know whether I am sorry or glad.

After she left, Cuthie and I went to a Marx Brothers movie at the Havana. Walking home I thought, at least let us thank God for the movies. Their absurdity does shift the glooms.

Tonight I am going down and down again. Ted is away to his evangelizing. I want comforting. For two pins I should weep. I want someone to hold me and love me. I want it to matter to someone that I am still alive, still here. I'm weeping for Eddie, that's what it is, Eddie.

SUNDAY, SEPTEMBER 19TH.

I am miserable about Eddie. I've lost Eddie completely, and America too. Now that all five boys are married, I feel that America is shut to me forever. The boys will belong to their wives, and I shall never be other than a casual visitor sitting in their houses. I should have my own American house, my home should be in their midst. Now I am weeping again. I ought not to weep, as weeping weakens and lays open my eyes to infection, but I can't help crying. I cry for my lost sons and my lost life. I am an old woman in exile. Old age is inevitable, exile isn't.

Ted is happy. Happy with his church and his guilds and his England. I can't bear it. This is what marriage comes to: desolation.

FRIDAY, SEPTEMBER 24TH.

I received a compliment from the man who comes to read the electric meter. "Well, and how are you today, Ma?" He always addresses me as "Ma." "Oh, a little older than when I saw you last." "Well, you don't look it." "But I am, just the same. I have eight grandchildren now." He shook his head as though he did not believe me. When he left he commented on the beautiful day and asked if I'd be out taking the air. I told him I seldom go out because I have to walk with a stick. He then said that it was true, he had not seen me on the street. "Of course, it would be very hard to miss me on the street: a woman as big as I am, and walking with a stick. There are not so many women as fat as I am," I said. "Plenty, plenty, and lots more much bigger, too. Lots."

I shook my head with a smile, and was about to close the door. He was already at the gate, but came back quickly, lowered his voice, and said, "Allow me to say, Ma, most respectfully, they're all so ugly. Now, if they carried themselves like you: so straight, so upright, and if they smiled as pleasantly. You know, I've told my wife about you, of all the women I see, you're the prettiest woman in this town. And that's true." "Oh, thank you, thank you," I said, and nodding and smiling his affirmation, he went away.

Well, only a poor public servant, nevertheless, one person in the world who can still see me as beautiful. Silly to be pleased, but I am pleased.

MONDAY, SEPTEMBER 27TH.

Noon. I am in an awful mood. I received a letter from Ruth, enclosing snapshots of all the children, every one of them except Charlie's new infant. The pictures are all taken by the big maple, with the background of the house. I'm just sick, sick, for Tenafly.

TUESDAY, OCTOBER 5TH.

Mother has been here and she told me one illuminating story about herself. I had told her that probably my eye trouble came about through too much crying, and that I must try not to weep in the future.

"That's right," she said. "I remember when I was a girl that I cried too much once, and I made a resolution I would never cry again. I never did. It was when I was only twelve years old and I had had a lovely holiday with my grandma in Tavistock. When I came home, I stood by the dresser and cried and cried. I can't remember what had upset me. It was some disappointment, I suppose. Everything at home seemed wrong after that lovely holiday. I cried all night, and I made myself downright sick. All the next day I was ill. I had such a headache, and my eyes were so sore and for what? Nothing had been changed, everything was exactly as it was before. So I made a resolution. I vowed I would never cry again, and I never did, never. When things went wrong I did this (and she made a grimace, biting in her underlip, setting her jaw, and frowning). I never cried even when your father upset me. I wouldn't. I wouldn't let him see he had me beaten. Besides, I always remember what old Mr. Side said to my father on our wedding day. 'Alice will be alright,' he said, 'so long as she never lets Charlie know when he has conquered her.' He never did know. I was bad-tempered, I know, and I nagged, but my tongue was the only weapon I had. I wasn't going to cry, and you know, I never did. So don't you cry either. Crying achieves nothing, only injury to yourself. I was only twelve when I found that out, and I made that resolution then, and I've stuck to it forever and shall do."

When I come to think of it, I never have seen Mother cry. The easy tears of sentimentality which she sheds at the movies, yes, but tears of grief or anger for herself, never.

MONDAY, OCTOBER 11TH.

Ten-thirty P.M. I am in a state of exasperation, which I've got to weaken down. I suppose exasperation is the keynote of my whole life. Anyhow, I've rung up the hairdresser and made an appointment for this afternoon. A couple of hours in the hairdresser's hands can soothe me as well as anything.

All Friday night I seemed to be dreaming of Taos and Santa Fe, and of love. When I awoke in the morning I was asking myself how long this torment of this insatiable craving for love was to go on.

Ted was at his most prosy, platitudinous, repetitive, and talkative. He seemed more silly than ever. I see the limitations of his intellect as plainly as anyone can see Selma's. Mother suffered because she married a man too clever for her. I suffer because I have married a man too stupid for me. Oftener and oftener I can see Ted only as one bloody fool. I wish to God we could arrange our lives so that Ted could go into a monastery and be done with it.

I am reading *The Flowering of New England* by Van Wyck Brooks, and enjoying every page of it. It covers the period 1815–1865, and I am surprised to find how much of it I "have." This, of course, is thanks to Dad. He gave me that American literature like he gave me so much other culture, and I "had" all that long before I went to America. As a matter of fact, I read John Motley and William Prescott when I was a girl. I got William Ellery Channing, Theodore Parker, and Oliver Wendell Holmes via Swallow Street. As for Emerson, Dad gave him to me long before I left school. As for the poets Longfellow and Whittier, I remember being surprised to find out they were not Englishmen.

Now I must go and prepare vegetables for lunch, but I'm a good deal calmer than when I sat down, thank heaven!

Van Wyck Brooks won the Pulitzer Prize in history in 1938 for his Flowering of New England.

MONDAY, OCTOBER 18TH.

Mid-morning. I've got hold of a new idea for myself. In Saturday's *Times,* three separate centenarians were noticed, and suddenly I've got back my determination to live to be a hundred.

Do you know how much life of my own I have had? About five years at most. It is thirty-three years ago since I met Ted and just about this time of the year that we were courting. I was twenty, and I expected everything good of life. I had health as well as youth, and good looks and talents above the average. I was violently alive. I had only known myself, and owned myself, a very few years out of my twenty. The first ten were hazy in childhood, the next six had been spent in intensive education, so only those years from sixteen to twenty, when I met Ted, have I really held in my hand. We married the next year and I have been "his" ever since, most damnably his. If I can live long enough, I can outlive him, and then, like so many widows, I will begin to live, to begin again to live. My own life.

Meanwhile and from now on, I will set myself to the good preservation of my life so that when it does become mine, if it ever does, I can enjoy it. I will look after my health and do all I can to extend my looks and activities. I will not become a valetudinarian. I will set my mind to health. Nor will I become a crank. I will set my will to sanity.

I will resume some sort of outside life, instead of moldering away in this damned house. I will go about to the picture galleries, the museums, and the theaters like I used to do when I was a girl. I will go in spite of my bad legs. I will make myself move about. I will buy clothes. I will seek and seek and try to find a friend. I will go places and I will do things.

My griefs I will put behind me, most resolutely. I cannot undo the past. I will forget it. I cannot change Ted, but I can change myself. I can dig down into myself and find my essential woman. I'll resurrect her, and assert her. I'll protect her, and cherish her so that after another thirty-three years she may enjoy another five years of vital and joyous being before the grave swallows her forever.

I will pretend I died last week in Madrid or Barcelona. Now, this moment, I am born again. Here I take up my new life: my life.

TUESDAY, OCTOBER 26TH.

Eleven-thirty A.M. I am so tired, so miserable. Partly my distress is physical. Very mundane, but true. At the bottom of my distress is sexual distress. Ted does not "love" me enough. Last night I awoke myself tearing at myself, trying unconsciously in sleep to allay gnawing desire. Ted lay there as cold as a stone. I dare not make advances to him. He would repel them. "Loving" must be only at his wish, never at mine. It often happens that he has desire when I have none, but no matter, he desires and he takes. So I suffer.

I was born ardent. He was born cold. We married and now there is nothing we can do about it. I do the suffering, not he. My anger at his religion is because it takes his affections from me. Indeed, I have come to think that Ted has no human affections at all. What does he care for his wife and his children? I may misjudge him. He may love us dearly, but certainly he does not show his love, or not in any ways which we can recognize.

WEDNESDAY, OCTOBER 27TH.

Ted has been lying around the house most of the day. When he came in at teatime yesterday, he said he had had two back molars out. This amuses the boys. "What?" says Cuthie. "What did you say? Dad got something the matter with *his* teeth! Dad got to go to the dentist! Howcome?" Also, he has got a cold. I've been fixing him bread and milk, and boiled onions, and chicken broth, but I cannot feel sorry for him. I really cannot.

MONDAY, NOVEMBER 1ST.

Mrs. Jude came to tea, and stayed till ten o'clock. Ted went off to Forest Gate. Alone in the parlor with Mrs. Jude, I found myself telling her the story of the Grange, and the history of 1920. I left the Grange on this day in 1920. After she had left, suddenly I had an illumination.

All at once I saw that this English life is some sort of punishment for me for 1920. Considering Ted's iron will, and his willfulness, and his vindictiveness, and his spitefulness, and his secrecy, I can see these last ten years as Ted's deliberate revenge and satisfaction. He meant, always, willy-nilly to return to England, and he finally came. I imagine that from the moment he got my cable refusing to stay in England, he determined to break me. I think, in addition, all these past ten years, in secret he has been gloating over all the deprivations he has imposed upon me. All this time he has been "getting his own back." I destroyed his dream. He destroyed me. That program of his in 1920 was the only thing I have ever refused him. I thought that I was right to act as I did, and I still think I was right. If that episode could be lived again, I would still refuse it. Suddenly I see, he is going to make me pay for it for as long as he lives.

THURSDAY, NOVEMBER 4TH.

Eleven A.M. Towards morning I was dreaming of love. I was back in my girlhood with Sydenham Whitelock. We were walking along Bournemouth Sands, going towards Parkstone, and we were both waiting and waiting for an embrace. But we never could escape people. We were walking arm in arm, hand in hand, closer and closer. Then I had to get up and see to breakfast.

FRIDAY, NOVEMBER 5TH.

Again last night I was dreaming of Sydenham Whitelock, and of his mother. Mrs. Whitelock was asking me not to repulse Syd, but to be kind to him, and to take him. She was reminding me that he was shy, and assuring me that both she and Mr. Whitelock dearly desired me for a daughter-in-law. Then I was dreaming of that spring day when he and I stood on Barnes Railway Bridge. Oh well, all dreams.

Yesterday Ted and I went to town together. There was an easement paper to be signed before the American Consul. This easement was for the town sewer in Tenafly. My name as well as Ted's was necessary on the document. In America, a property belongs to husband *and* wife.

Then, walking down from Hyde Park Corner, up Park Lane to Grosvenor Square, traversing that old district on foot as I did hundreds of times as a girl, I found myself in a mood of aloofness and very agreeable and rational detachment. I was back somewhere at the core of myself. That self I used to be. Ruby Side.

WEDNESDAY, DECEMBER 1ST.

Fresh trouble in the family. Cuthie has sent in a letter of resignation to the college, and this morning Ted received a letter from the dean asking him to see him and have a talk about the boy.

So Ted went to town. The college report is that Cuthie has been absent for weeks, and has been slacking (whatever that means) for twelvemonths.

Meanwhile, at home, Cuthie talked to me. He says he wants to join the air force and that he has all the necessary qualifications for a commission. Asked why he wants to leave college, he says mainly because he can't stick living at home *under his father* any longer. He longs to get away from Ted, and to be independent of him, and free.

There was much more, but too much to write down. The whole point is that Cuthie is miserable, and he wants to get away.

MONDAY, DECEMBER 6TH.

Two-thirty P.M. It is ten years today since Ted and I and the three boys landed in England. It is just such a day as it was in 1927: dark, cold, and frosty. Where have these ten years brought us?

Charlie is back in America, married, and the father of a daughter. Artie is a junior clerk in the family firm. Cuthie is in open rebellion against his allotted career. Ted and I are ending. Between us there is an ever-widening, ever-deepening chasm of differences. We have become almost completely antipathetic to one another.

If it had been Mother and Dad, who hated and fought each other from the beginning, it wouldn't be surprising. But that we two, who loved and were friends, that we should come to this antipathy, that *is* surprising. We may have to live still another twenty years together. God help us!

I feel I live with a cold stranger. The Ted of my early life is as defunct as my grandparents. He lives only in my memory, as they live only in my memory; but whereas I can think of them with pleasure, I can only think of him with pain. He is a man lost whilst he is still living. He has receded to places where I can't reach him.

As for me, these ten years have been a long process of denudation. I have lost all the qualities and emotions that gave life savor: romantic love, common affection, parentage, country, patriotism, religion, friendship. Nothing is left to me but an aging body, scalding memories, an abiding animosity, and complete loneliness.

Seven-forty P.M. At twenty-six past, Ted comes in to his tea, and before the clock strikes the half hour he has found fault with the three of us: Cuthie for speaking in the wrong tone of voice, Artie for the loudness of his radio, and me for having my chair in the wrong place. When we hear his key in the door we all stop what we are doing, so as to be ready for him, so as to protect ourselves from his criticisms. Is it any wonder that in the summer Artie said, "Isn't it nice here when Dad isn't around?"

I want Ted to take my hand and say, Well, old girl, here we are, ten years in England now. I'm sorry you don't like it, but at least we have each other. But of course, no such thing. That's only a sentimental dream I have, and a dream that will never come true. But I can't stop dreaming it. Ted's a bigot and I'm a fool. What a combination.

The family firm, Westlake and Hammond, was a real estate company owned by Bert Thompson. Ted started to work there after the stock market crash of 1929. Artie worked for Bert both before and after the war.

THURSDAY, DECEMBER 9TH.

Cuthie has decided to carry on and to return to his studies. Both he and Ted are writing to the dean and asking shall he return now, or not return until the beginning of the new term.

FRIDAY, DECEMBER 31ST.

Ten-twenty A.M. We got through Christmas passably well. Mother, Bert, and Selma spent the day with us. Ted was very amiable all through the holiday, but since Wednesday he has been getting peevish again.

Two weeks ago, when Ted went to town, he had lunch with Bewley, and he brought back the news that Mrs. Bewley was dying. Bewley was grieving. He said, "My dear wife. All I hope is that I shan't remain long after her. When she goes, life will be worth nothing." Ted commented on it as strange, and especially strange because Bewley is what Ted describes as an atheist. I said that I thought it was lovely. The Bewleys have been married almost as long as we have, but when one is to die, the other does not wish to live. Not so with us. Love. And still all is not written about love.

Fairly recently, on one friendly, talkative evening, Ted told me about the nun who was in the French hospital in New York when he was there. He told me about her at the time. She was in for an operation, and when she was convalescing she used to come and sit by his bed. I knew he liked her, but now he has told me, in reminiscing, that that nun was the most lovely woman he had ever met, and that she liked him too. He knows she fell in love with him and if she hadn't been a nun, God knows what might have happened. At that time I was big with the twins and I was visiting him in the hospital every day. He had a relapse, and one night I found him delirious, and he nearly died. But he could fall in love with a nun just the same. Well, well, my man, my crazy man.

1938

THURSDAY, JANUARY 6TH.

On the whole, I have got through this Christmas splendidly. I think it's because I feel so easy in my mind about Eddie. Every letter I have received, whether from the family or friends, praises the girl he has chosen, and says how well suited she is to Eddie. He writes happily, and I have had a nice letter from her too. Yes, I am happy about Eddie. And I am well except for my legs.

FRIDAY, JANUARY 7TH.

Selma came to see me this morning and was in the doldrums. She suspects a flirtation between her father and her Aunt Dorothy. She is scared her father might want to marry Dorothy. Then, about four o'clock, Dorothy called here. She said old Bert had proposed to her. He had written her a long letter, telling her how he stood financially and what he would do for her and for Peter. Dorothy said that Bert says he has always loved her.

From a business point of view, the marriage would be a good thing for Dorothy, but she says she couldn't, "I know he's a dear old soul, but marriage! Oh, no, I couldn't go to bed with him." She's going to refuse him verbally after tea, and she swore me to secrecy.

At nine o'clock they all came calling. Selma looked like the day of doom. Dorothy was at her most vivacious, and for a woman who intended to refuse a man, she was most free in her touches and taps of old Bert.

When I went into the pantry to get glasses, Dorothy followed me in and said that Bert wasn't going to take "no" for an answer and that he was giving her four months to make up her mind. She made me promise I would not say a word.

Naturally, I haven't said a word, and neither Ted nor the boys can guess what I am laughing at. I'm laughing at Bert, and at marriage, and at love's young dream. I'm laughing at men.

THURSDAY, JANUARY 13TH.

As I woke this morning I was dreaming of Mary Tidmarsh. It was a lesbian sort of dream. I was with her in the Avenue A house, and there was a positive sense of concord between us, as there always was. Then we were in each other's arms. I was pushing her vest aside so that I could lay my face upon her breast, skin to skin, and she was stooping over me, kissing me. Everything was suffused with warmth and peace, love and joy, and understanding. It was only a dream, but the sentiment is valid.

Mary Tidmarsh was a friend of Ruby's and Ted's in Bayonne.

SATURDAY, JANUARY 15TH.

Dorothy paid me a visit this evening, mainly to talk about her affairs. I conclude that she is making up her mind to accept Bert's proposal. If she did not mean to take him ultimately, she would not temporize so kindly now. Yet she says the marriage is impossible. She could not bring herself to go to bed with him. Nevertheless, she speaks of him as her lover. We shall see. The romance progresses.

TUESDAY, FEBRUARY 3RD.

Dorothy came round here and told me that today she finally said "yes" to Bert, and they will probably be married in June. She knows it is a good match for her, declares that she has told Bert all the objections against it, and against herself, but he persists. She said he cried dreadfully when she first told him she couldn't.

Bert came to fetch her around nine o'clock and he was all happy excitement. Dorothy told him she had told me. "What do you think of it?" he asked. "Do you think we'll make a go of it?"

"I think you're very lucky," I said, "both of you." When Ted and Artie returned from playing billiards, I told them the news. Ted thinks it funny, but he thinks Bert an old fool.

FRIDAY, FEBRUARY 4TH.

At breakfast this morning, Ted laughingly remarked, "I wonder how goes love's young dream this morning. I think Bert's a fool to take on Dorothy and when she buries Bert, who's next, I wonder. I know one thing jolly sure, she won't get *me*." I said, "If I were alive she couldn't, could she?" "No, and if you weren't she couldn't either. I couldn't stick Dorothy at any price." "How do you know? If I died, you too might look for consolation." "No, Lady, never! Not consolation. If you died I should call for a bottle of whiskey, and sit down to that. I should say a full bottle, this is a double celebration!"

I took it smiling, but I was stunned. Yes, there is many a truth spoken in jest. This is our mutuality, the tiredness of our marriage. Young love does not end in old love, it ends in satiety and boredom. But I have never expressed it so crudely to Ted. I write down here my wearinesses, disgusts, disillusionments, and disappointments. I have never spoken them to Ted, and I never shall. Undoubtedly, for either of us the death of the other would be a great relief, but if Ted died I *should* suffer a grief, hard as life has been with him. I should feel a desolation, though I should probably recover from it. Certainly I should never feel his death as an occasion for rejoicing. I have been going around all morning in a sort of a daze. There is nothing to say.

WEDNESDAY, FEBRUARY 9TH.

Fresh disquietness about Cuthie. Ted received a letter from the dean saying that Cuthie had not been attending classes very regularly this past month. Did we know? What was the reason?

We did not know. Cuth has been going to town every day, presumably to class, and he has been at home very little in the evenings. In fact, we scarcely ever see him. What is wrong with the boy now, I wonder. Is it that he finds he has mistaken his vocation, does not want to be a doctor after all, yet is afraid to say so? Perhaps it is that he cannot bear to live at home. Ted has just paid the coming year's tuition fees, and the boy ought to attend school.

THURSDAY, FEBRUARY 17TH.

On waking, my inner woman was saying, "Even the mere physical act of writing is happiness for you." Of course it is. Merely to transcribe a recipe, or a poem, or to make up the laundry list gives me a definite satisfaction.

I remembered how in very early childhood Mother taught me to write. First it was on a slate. I made pothooks and hangers, strokes, naughts, and crosses. Then I was taught to form the letters on a stave of three lines. Then I was promoted to all these exercises on paper, with a lead pencil, never ink, because, I think, Mother feared for her tablecloth. In those lessons I was happy. They are some of my happiest memories of Mother.

THURSDAY, FEBRUARY 24TH.

Two-thirty P.M. When Ted came in for dinner just now, he told me that the dean of Cuthie's medical school has said that Cuthie is not suited to a career as a physician. He said that even if Cuthie passed his exams he would never like the life of a physician. He is not suited to the part. We have been arguing and arguing with Cuthie to work, and to study properly, to return to college and to attend lectures faithfully, and to work hard. But all he would do was to keep saying he wanted to leave. Maybe Cuthie is right and it is only a case of a mistaken vocation. Let's hope it's that, merely a mistaken vocation.

TUESDAY, MARCH 1ST.

Today I've done a little smartening up. I had my hair done, a manicure and had my nails colored coral, and bought a lipstick. My first lipstick. I needed some gesture of getting away from the boneyard. Then it was off to the movies with Ted. Paul Muni playing Emile Zola. In the movies I can sit in the dark, watching idiotic dramas of the screen where every knot is untied, and every story has a satisfactory ending. I can stop thinking and my nerves are calmed.

MONDAY, MARCH 7TH.

Eleven-thirty A.M. I have sent Cuthie to the American Consulate, to find out how he can get into the States. I think he and Artie should both go back there.

Cuthie and his father are at a complete deadlock. Ted wants him to find a job in town and refuses to give him his signature for an application for the air force or fare for New York. Since Cuthie can't get into the air force without Ted's signature, he says he will work in the States, where he belongs. Last night, after hours and hours of talking, Cuthie said to me, when Ted finally went to bed, "If I had to live in the same house with Dad another year, I shouldn't be able to keep my hands off him." I shall do all I can to see that Cuthie goes to the States.

Ted's reason for declining to let Cuthie go to the States is that he would be thrown into a heathenish and pagan environment, he would fall into temptation, might lose his faith, earn damnation. The boys' influence would not be good for him. Yes, this is exactly how Ted talks, and it infuriates me. What is wrong with our boys, I'd like to know? All five of them are decently married and bringing up families like good citizens. They are good workers, good husbands, good fathers, but they have lapsed from the faith, they have frivolous friends and enjoy a good time. They would contaminate Cuthie, therefore he mustn't go near them. This just makes me sick. Where would Cuthie go but to his brothers, back to his native land?

Two-thirty P.M. At lunch Ted was angry because Cuthie had not told me when he would be back from town, and I didn't ask. He will come when he is ready. Ted's father, grandfather, and brother Bert all married at the age of eighteen, and at eighteen Ted himself went off to the Klondike. Does he suppose a male Thompson, turned nineteen, is going to punch a clock on the premises? Does he suppose a young man in town on a spring day isn't going to stroll around and enjoy the day a bit? Ted wants to keep tabs on him. Cuthie finds it intolerable. Any young man would.

Cuthie has not yet spoken to Ted about going to America. He had one conversation with old Bert, who advised him to wait until he heard from the boys. So we are waiting for American letters.

Meanwhile, Cuthie has taken a job as a fitter's mate, of all things. He goes into town on the workman's train and gets back here, filthy and grimed, in time for tea. This is better than sitting around at home in idleness.

Speaking to Ted of the approaching marriage of Dorothy and Bert, I said, "I suppose if I died, that you would respectfully mourn me for twelvemonths, and then take another wife?" Ted replied, "You underrate my intelligence, Lady. No, if you died I should be so relieved, so thankful! But I should be too mean to marry again. I should say, Well I'm free now, thank heaven, and I'll stay free! And do you know what? When I die and get to heaven, I shall look for your father, and when I meet him, as of course I shall, somewhere in heaven, I shall say, Hello Sir, so you're here! Well, you had the mother, and I had the daughter, so we *deserve* to be here!"

Here it is in plain speech, Ted's hatred of me. For what? For being his wife. For being his *old* wife. Well, one might, and one does, have these private thoughts, but one does not voice them. Above all, not to the offending party. When I was a young girl I thought there wasn't a happy marriage in the world and I still think it.

Eleven A.M. I have ordered from Boots the March issue of *Quarterly on Psychology*, called "Character and Personality." This issue contains an article on euphoria and depression. I am quite sure that from early childhood I have suffered acutely from the phenomena of euphoria and depression. Perhaps all human beings do, but I know that I do. So I want to see what the professors have to say about it. I expect they will say it is a madness. Probably I have never been a normally rational and sane being. But there is one thing: I think I am more in control now of my mind, and certainly of my feelings, than I used to be.

Evening. I have been seething with resentment these past two days, but am now cooling down. The cause is Ted, of course. He had a talk with Cuthie about his prospects, and then came into the parlor and talked *at* me. He re-

fuses to give the boy any money, refuses him permission to go to America, refuses him his birth certificate, and has made him promise not to ask his Uncle
Bert for any help or advice. He told me he knew he had said things to Cuthie
which would hurt but they "had to be said." Then I got a harangue about my
faults and failings. Ted is really impossible, but it is useless to talk to him. As
Eddie said, he is inhuman.

Cuthie will get to America some way or other and so will Artie. What
sense is there in being unfriendly to the boys? How blind he must be to get satisfaction out of that. Wouldn't any normal father prefer to help his boys, to
make ways as easy for them as he could? Of course, but not Ted.

THURSDAY, APRIL 14TH.

Eleven A.M. Last night the BBC broadcast the entire opera of Gounod's *Faust*.
As it went on I was stirred with deep emotion. In my life this opera is associ-
ated with the two men who most loved me and whom I most loved: my father,
and W. H. This was my first opera. Dad took me to hear the old Carl Rosa
Company, in the old Hammersmith Lyric. Perhaps I was fourteen; at any rate it
was long before I left school. When I was twenty, W. H. wrote, "You make me
think of music, and most especially the song in *Faust* which begins with the
phrase, 'Oh tender moon! Oh starry heavens!' Those bars particularly I associ-
ate with you. It is as you come; beautiful!" This an old love letter destroyed a
lifetime ago, but still remembered.

It was absurd, really. There I lay on the sofa, a fat, spectacled old woman
knitting a sock: and over in his arm chair was my old husband, sucking and
puffing on his pipe, yet inside, *inside* I was the beautiful and beloved young
virgin, thrilling with power and glory.

SATURDAY, MAY 7TH.

Joan and George came in with Artie just in time for midday dinner.
Afterwards, Ted and the boys took George to Arden Cottage for bridge. Joan
and I had a good, cozy fireside chat. I told her about Cuthie and Artie, and
their imminent departure for America.

*During the past month Ted eased his position and was no longer opposing
the idea of Cuthie going to America. With Ted's opposition out of the way,
Artie decided to join Cuthie.*

SUNDAY, MAY 8TH.

Suddenly I have made up my mind to go to America myself. The tension between Ted and myself is unendurable. When the twins go, I must go also. I
look at the future and I cannot face it. I cannot live on here alone with Ted. I
simply cannot do it.

MONDAY, MAY 9TH.

I have been to the American Consulate to inquire about a visa for permanent residence in the United States. I must present affidavits from my sons in New York regarding their financial stability. This means I cannot sail with the twins, but since I know I shall be able to follow on in a few weeks, I can bear up.

From the consulate I phoned Aileen and went to Primrose Hill for dinner with her and Roger. I told them the whole story of Cuthie, Artie, and finances. The upshot is, *they* are going to help me get away. As soon as I can get the affidavits required from the boys, Aileen and Roger will help me with the money side of the business. Isn't that great? I'm ready to sing.

MONDAY, MAY 16TH.

This morning I telephoned Father Bishop and asked for an interview, which he granted at once. I told him of my determination to go to America, and asked him for a recommendation letter, as required by the Consul. This he promised to give as soon as I have told Ted of my plans. He did not say one word to dissuade me. On the contrary, he thought that my being with the twins "would be very good for the boys." When I said that I should ask Ted for an allowance, but did not expect he would give me one, he said, "Oh, but I think he should!" Father Bishop was most helpful and kind.

SUNDAY, MAY 22ND.

Late tonight I told Ted I was going to America and not returning. I had not meant to tell him until after the twins had left but I was so angry, and one word led to another, suddenly I told him. He does not believe me. However, he'll find out.

FRIDAY, MAY 27TH.

The twins sailed this evening on the S.S. *American Farmer* for New York. Nobody went to see them off. I said good-bye to them here in the house. Cuthie was not here for lunch so I sent him to the office to say good-bye to his father. I don't know what Ted said to him there but when the boy came back to the house he was crying. I'm sorry, for this makes an even more unhappy parting. Presumably Ted gave him one last sweet lecture.

It feels to me like the end of the world.

FRIDAY, JUNE 3RD.

After a trip to town I came home and found two American letters waiting for me. One was from Johnnie, declining to give the af-fidavits I asked for. The other was from Harold, containing four affidavits, two from him, two from his boss. There was no personal word in Harold's envelope, but his immediate response to my requests, his acquiescence and acceptance of my ideas, filled me with gladness. Johnnie is all argument, talk, and reprisals, just like Ted. Harold's response is in generosity of heart and in love.

FRIDAY, JUNE 17TH.

Old Bert and Dorothy were married at Caxton Hall today. We did not go to view.

We received a card from Artie saying they got to Boston on the sixth, and one from Cuthie saying they reached New York on the eighth. No other news.

FRIDAY, JULY 1ST.

Ted left for Italy this evening.

Ted went to Italy several times and especially loved to visit the Vatican. Ted and Ruby often took separate vacations.

FRIDAY, JULY 15TH.

I returned from Plymouth today. The weather was cold and rainy all the time, but Gladys was dear.

I was agreeably surprised to see Ted waiting on the Paddington platform for me. He brought me a rosary. The beads are amethysts and it is strung in silver. The rosary was blessed by the pope when Ted had his audience.

Here is a thought I want to record about our mother. Gladys said, "I reconciled myself to Mother's impossibilities years ago. I realized that she was a person of very limited intelligence. Mother has character. Dad was a weakling but Dad had brains. Theirs was a particularly unfortunate marriage but it worked out well for us. We got our brains from Dad and our character from Mother."

This was a new idea to me, and I said so. Gladys said: "She had strength of character, the only one in her family who did have it. Just look at the Searles, a worthless, brainless lot, particularly the women. Uncle Will had brains, but he was soft, and look at his children! We might have turned out like the Searle girls, but we didn't. Mother aimed at goodness and rightness, and she lived up to her lights such as they were. We can see how wrong she was, and we can regret that she didn't do differently, but she *did* do her best. Ever since I realized what a very limited intelligence she has, I've been able to make excuses for her, and to endure her. And she did have a rough time with Dad."

I did not pursue this last idea. Gladys has a very limited intelligence about marriage, and to talk to her about sex would be to talk Greek. How could she guess, or if she could guess, how could she understand what a failure Mother must have been in the marriage bed? Gladys admires Mother's character because it is a positive one. What she fails to see is the curse of its undisciplined-ness. Yet she suffered under mother's aggressiveness and domination as much as the rest of us. Positiveness in itself is not a virtue, and in Mother it was, and is, an excessive vice. I am glad to be presented with this idea about Mother's intelligence. All my life I have been defending myself against her hateful character, I never recognized that actually she had no more brains than any of the rest of the Searle girls. Let's hope I can remember it now that Gladys has pointed it out, and excuse her sins to invincible ignorance, as Gladys has.

FRIDAY, AUGUST 5TH.

I have written to all the boys about my unrelinquished plan for coming to the States. My mind is made up as far as intention goes. If Aileen is still willing to help me about money, I will ask for the visa on just one set of affidavits. If the consul refuses the visa, I am done. I can't move. If he will give it, I am going to America. I am.

MONDAY, AUGUST 8TH.

Aileen's letter arrived today with this news. "You can have the fifty pounds for passage whenever you want it, but the other two hundred pounds is not so easy to transfer, and we naturally don't want to do it unless and until you are sure you need it. I am not sure from your letter what you propose to do, but I take it you will be seeing the consul about getting a visa with one set of affidavits, and will then let us know. You can tell him it will be alright about the money."

This is useless. You can tell the consul anything. What he wants is proof, in the case of money, a bank book. So that's out. Then Aileen goes on for two pages with advice. Again, useless. I did not ask her for advice. She concludes, "I'm afraid you will not find this letter very cheering, but go and see the consul and see how he feels about the mother of seven upstanding American citizens. In the meantime, go on being tough and remember that I love you. Aileen."

TUESDAY, AUGUST 9TH.

We've had a great shock this morning in letters from the twins. Artie has decided to join the marines and wrote asking for a note of parental consent from each of us. Cuthie wrote that he was considering joining the army and that he and Artie were going to New York to see about it.

Ted replied to Artie immediately. Presumably he gave his consent, because he said since Artie no longer lived at home, he thought he should leave the boy free to do whatever he liked.

I have written to them both. I refused to give Artie my consent for the marines, and I implored Cuthie *not* to join the army. I told both of them to return to England if they were disappointed with America, as they seem to be. I promised to find the money for their passages.

They have not yet been in the States two months. To join the army is always a last resource, a confession of failure. What stuck out in their letters was a wish to get away from 523 Knickerbocker and "not go on eating Johnnie's food." I suppose Johnnie or Ruth has been making them feel uncomfortable. If Johnnie is telling them that he can't afford to keep them anymore, that is preposterous. Johnnie has a salary of eighty dollars per week and he lives in *our* house, rent free. He has never paid a cent of interest on the mortgage and has never even kept the taxes up to date.

I wrote to the twins to this effect to reassure them that Johnnie could quite well afford to give them hospitality, and for an indefinite period. If Johnnie has made them feel they are a burden upon him, I'm through with Johnnie.

So what now? All I know is, I'm glad I haven't had a second interview with the consul. God help the Thompson family, especially my poor twins!

FRIDAY, AUGUST 19TH.

We've had a letter from Artie saying he had changed his mind about joining the marines. Everybody he had spoken to about it was against such a procedure, and said the marines have a very bad name. Were we relieved!

MONDAY, AUGUST 22ND.

Seven-thirty P.M. I am feeling fed up. I really think Ted is getting potty. Today when Ted came home early for dinner, he went upstairs, undressed, and came down barefoot and with nothing on but his bathrobe. He went out into the garden, singing la-la-la. Maybe he imagined he was Saint Francis with the birds. When he came into the house for dinner, he neither bathed nor dressed. He sat down to table exactly as he was, took out his false teeth, as per usual, and began to eat his dinner. His bathrobe fell open and I could see his naked belly. I was disgusted. This is my husband, this Beau Brummell. Outside he is so polished and courteous, inside he is crude and gross. I think he's cracked.

SATURDAY, AUGUST 27TH.

Artie has written that he wants to return to England, and has asked his father if he can come back to us here. I was suffused with happiness, but Ted's response was to think up obstacles: the money, the passport, the citizenship, and the lack of job. The effect was to whip me into anger and hatred. What kind of father is this man? Artie is unhappy and he turns his face home to his parents. Ted promptly thinks up all the reasons and difficulties in the way.

Then he rounded on me. I sent the boy away. I did him out of a good job. I am the cause of his wasting money on double passages. I interposed: "As usual, the most important aspect of the affair to you is the money involved.

What's money?" Then I got a tirade about my extravagance, my complete foolishness about figures, and ending with his usual threat of late, that soon we'll be starving, and how will I like that?

This has no effect upon me except to anger me. A man who owns a score of houses doesn't starve. All I see is that Ted doesn't wish Artie back and that he doesn't care for his grown children. They are some kind of check to his liberty, some kind of hindrance to his personality.

I will not be destroyed by this man. Sometime, somehow, somewhere I will yet have myself for myself, my life for my own. Patience, Ruby Alice, patience.

SUNDAY, SEPTEMBER 18TH.

Everyone is very anxious about the news. Mr. Chamberlain flew to Germany this week to have a personal talk with Hitler. Today, the French diplomats are at Downing Street for conferences. There are cabinet meetings and cabinet meetings. All Europe is on the verge of war. Terrible.

I wrote to Artie imploring him to stay where he is.

TUESDAY, SEPTEMBER 27TH.

Tonight Mr. Shaw from next door called in. He was seeking advice about what to do about his house. War preparations are going ahead. People are getting fitted with gas masks, trenches are being dug, and so on. Mrs. Shaw is in a panic and wants to take their child and go to Wales. Shaw doesn't want to give up the house, where all his valuable photography apparatus is installed. Ted was able to calm his fears and infuse into him some of his own optimism, but after awhile Ted began talking about religion. Shaw is a Jew and today is the Jewish New Year. So Ted began questioning and cross-questioning Shaw about the rites and beliefs of Judaism. I sat by and said nothing, but when Ted carries on like this I'd like to choke him. How dare he pry into Shaw's religion!

WEDNESDAY, SEPTEMBER 28TH.

Mr. Chamberlain has given Parliament an account of his recent visits to Herr Hitler. Hitler has agreed to wait twenty-four hours before marching into Czechoslovakia and to meet again with Chamberlain. Mussolini and Deladier will also be present. Chamberlain is to fly to Munich tomorrow.

The news fills the world with a sense of respite. The whole world is on the edge of a volcano. At any moment humanity and civilization may be engulfed into annihilation. Having lived through 1914–1918, who could dream that once again we would let statesmen plunge the nations into the abyss? Yet it looks as if war is imminent.

FRIDAY, SEPTEMBER 30TH.

The Munich Wireless Service announced this morning that the Fuhrer, the Duce, the British prime minister, and the French prime minister signed an agreement as to the methods to be adopted in the transfer of the Sudeten Territory.

So, war is averted. Thank God.

WEDNESDAY, OCTOBER 5TH.

I want to start writing. I want to put down for my children the story of my life; my life as I see it and interpret it. The desire is urging me more and more imperatively. When life on this island is becoming daily more dangerous and more precarious, I feel I must write *now*, whilst I know I still have time in the land of the living.

Not that it would matter if my children never knew the truth of my life. At the back of everything I suppose is my deep desire to state the truth of myself. I await the recognition of that female descendant of myself who will be the most like me: a repetition of myself. This is a great egotism, of course, and I know it. But there it is. Fifty or sixty years hence some other woman, some creature of my blood, may be able to find in my old writings the explanations for her own cursed self. All I can manage are these sporadic diaries. My days are frittered away and I with them. W. E. Henley wrote, "I am the master of my fate," but Henley was a man. Mary Colum says, "The total experiences of the most ordinary man, woman, or child has never yet been expressed in literature." Well, that's what I'm after, the total experience of the most ordinary.